Lecture Notes in Computer Science   8254

Commenced Publication in 1973
Founding and Former Series Editors:
Gerhard Goos, Juris Hartmanis, and Jan van Leeuwen

Hüsnü Yenigün   Cemal Yilmaz
Andreas Ulrich (Eds.)

Testing Software and Systems

25th IFIP WG 6.1 International Conference, ICTSS 2013
Istanbul, Turkey, November 13-15, 2013
Proceedings

 Springer

Volume Editors

Hüsnü Yenigün
Sabanci University, Faculty of Engineering and Natural Sciences
Orhanli Tuzla, 34956 Istanbul,Turkey
E-mail: yenigun@sabanciuniv.edu

Cemal Yilmaz
Sabanci University, Faculty of Engineering and Natural Sciences
Orhanli Tuzla, 34956 Istanbul,Turkey
E-mail: cyilmaz@sabanciuniv.edu

Andreas Ulrich
Siemens AG, Corporate Technology, CT RTC SAD SDT-DE
Otto-Hahn-Ring 6, 81739 Munich, Germany
E-mail: andreas.ulrich@siemens.com

ISSN 0302-9743   e-ISSN 1611-3349
ISBN 978-3-642-41706-1   e-ISBN 978-3-642-41707-8
DOI 10.1007/978-3-642-41707-8
Springer Heidelberg New York Dordrecht London

Library of Congress Control Number: 2013951161

CR Subject Classification (1998): D.2.4-5, D.2.9, D.2.11, C.2.2, C.2.4, D.3.2, C.3, F.3.1, K.6.3-4

LNCS Sublibrary: SL 2 – Programming and Software Engineering

Typesetting: Camera-ready by author, data conversion by Scientific Publishing Services, Chennai, India

Printed on acid-free paper

Springer is part of Springer Science+Business Media (www.springer.com)

Preface

Testing is the most important quality assurance technique for the validation of software and systems as well as their models. Yet, testing remains challenging in the underlying theory, methods, and tools in industrial use and in its systematic combined application with other validation and verification techniques. Therefore, researchers and practitioners need a focused forum to discuss new theories and directions for testing, to share successful industrial testing applications, and to put forward new challenges of testing to scientists and engineers.

The IFIP International Conference on Testing Software and Systems (ICTSS) is a series of international conferences addressing the conceptual, theoretic, and practical problems of testing software systems, including communication protocols, services, distributed platforms, middleware, embedded and cyber-physical systems, and security infrastructures. ICTSS was founded and achieved to be a persistent and dedicated venue for researchers, developers, testers, and users from industry to review, discuss, and learn about new approaches, concepts, theories, methodologies, tools, and experiences in the field of testing of software and systems.

The previous instances of ICTSS were held in Aalborg, Denmark (2012), in Paris, France (2011), and in Natal, Brazil (2010). But the ICTSS conference series has a much longer history. ICTSS is the successor of TestCom (the IFIP International Conference on Testing of Communicating Systems, 2000–2009) and FATES (the International Workshop on Formal Approaches to Testing of Software, 2001–2009). TestCom emerged from the previous International Workshop on Testing of Communicating Systems (IWTCS, 1997–1999), which in turn was the successor of the International Workshop on Protocol Test Systems (IWPTS, 1988–1996).

It is our pleasure and honor to present the proceedings of the 25th IFIP International Conference on Testing Software and Systems (ICTSS 2013), held in Istanbul, Turkey, during November 13–15, 2013. Marking a cornerstone in the history of ICTSS series, this book contains the refereed proceedings of the 25th instance of the ICTSS series. We received 68 submissions including 11 short paper submissions. Each submission was thoroughly reviewed by at least three Program Committee members or sub-reviewers. Based on the subsequent discussions, the Program Committee selected 17 full paper and three short paper contributions for presentation and publication. The accepted papers were revised based on the comments made by the reviewers. These revised papers are presented in this volume.

The conference program also included three invited talks. Alexandre Petrenko (CRIM, Canada) titled his talk "Some Observations on Progress in Model-Based Testing." Applying formal methods to testing, he discussed the advancements in model-based testing during the course of the last 25 years by highlighting a number of research problems and challenges that cover a variety of models, non-determinism, fault models, and their applications.

In her talk "From Active Testing to Monitoring Techniques – Application to Test Secure Interoperability" Ana Rosa Cavalli from Télécom SudParis, France, motivated the use of passive testing techniques that are based on the observation of the exchange of messages (input and output events) of the system under test during runtime. In the last few years important research activities have taken place dealing with monitoring techniques based on passive testing. Recent advances in these techniques also allow their application to test the secure interoperability of information systems. She presented the evolution of monitoring techniques and discussed their advantages and limitations.

Last but not least, Jens Herrman (Daimler AG, Germany) presented technical outcomes and experiences from the "ARTEMIS Project MBAT on Combining Model-Based Testing and Static Analysis to Improve Quality and Reduce Efforts." MBAT is a strongly industrial-oriented 3-year ARTEMIS R&D project comprising 39 partners from eight European countries, which started in 2011. The project will provide European industry from the transportation domain (automotive, aerospace, rail) with leading-edge technology to develop high-quality and safe embedded systems at reduced costs. It focuses on the combined application of different validation and verification techniques to gain advantages in the system development process.

Furthermore, the program of ICTSS 2013 contained the tutorial titled "Survey of Bug Localization Approaches using Dynamic Analysis" by Jason Lee (Dolby Laboratories, Australia). In this tutorial, a review of the literature for software bug localization using dynamic analysis was given. This was followed by presenting the main approaches that are known to be effective in bug localization, such as test coverage, statistical methods, program states, and machine learning with test coverage. Finally, current trends and directions for bug localization using dynamic analysis were given.

In addition, a doctoral workshop was organized to provide a forum for PhD students to present preliminary results of their thesis work and to receive constructive feedback from experts in the field as well as from peers. This workshop also presented an opportunity for researchers to get an overview of the latest research topics in the field.

Moreover, two workshops were co-located with ICTSS 2013. The Workshop on Future Internet Testing (FITTEST) was organized by Kiran Lakhotia (CREST, University College London, UK) and Tanja E.J. Vos (Universidad Politecnica de Valencia, Spain). The Workshop on Risk Assessment and Risk-Driven Testing (RISK) was organized by Thomas Bauer (Fraunhofer IESE, Germany), Jürgen Großmann (Fraunhofer FOKUS, Germany), Fredrik Seehusen (SINTEF ICT, Norway), Ketil Stølen (SINTEF ICT, University of Oslo, Norway), and Marc-Florian Wendland (Fraunhofer FOKUS, Germany).

We would like to thank all authors who submitted their work to ICTSS 2013. We also wish to thank the distinguished invited speakers for accepting our invitation. We are grateful to the members of the Program Committee and the additional reviewers for their hard work in the review process that made this conference possible. We appreciate their competent handling of the submissions during the summer period. The Chair Robert M. Hierons and the members of the ICTSS Steering Committee were always ready whenever we needed them. We are indebted for their guidance and help. We got special support from Rui Abreu as the PhD Workshop Chair, Vahid Garousi as the Workshops Chair, and César Viho as the Tutorials Chair, the efforts of whom are greatly appreciated. We would also like to thank Hasan Ural for encouraging us and guiding us in submitting a proposal to organize ICTSS 2013 in Istanbul. We express our gratitude to the organizers of FITTEST and RISK workshops for complementing the ICTSS 2013 program with more focused topics.

Our special thanks go to our friends and colleagues at Sabanci University, especially Gülşen Demiröz, Uraz Cengiz Türker, Canan Güniçen, Uğur Koç, Veli Akçakaya, Sezen Sefayi, Selma Arısüt, and Banu Ayşe Kerse for helping us with the local organization of the conference. We thank the providers of the EasyChair conference management system, which has been of great value, and the Springer LNCS team for their support.

Finally, we gratefully acknowledge the financial support we received from IFIP and Sabanci University. In addition, Formal Methods Europe has kindly provided financial support of Alexandre Petrenko's invited talk.

November 2013

Hüsnü Yenigün
Cemal Yilmaz
Andreas Ulrich

Organization

ICTSS 2013 was organized by Sabanci University in cooperation with the International Federation for Information Processing (IFIP).

Steering Committee

Rob Hierons	University of Brunel, UK (Chair)
Alexandre Petrenko	CRIM, Canada
Ana R. Cavalli	Telecom SudParis, France
Brian Nielsen	Aalborg University, Denmark
Burkhart Wolff	Université Paris-Sud, France
Carsten Weise	IVU Traffic Technologies, Germany
Fatiha Zaidi	Université Paris-Sud, France
Andreas Ulrich	Siemens AG, Germany

Conference Chairs

General Chairs

Hüsnü Yenigün	Sabanci University, Turkey
Cemal Yilmaz	Sabanci University, Turkey
Andreas Ulrich	Siemens AG, Germany

Workshops Chair

Vahid Garousi	Middle East Technical University, Turkey and University of Calgary, Canada

PhD Workshop Chair

Rui Abreu	University of Porto, Portugal

Tutorial Chair

César Viho	IRISA Rennes, France

Program Committee

Rui Abreu	University of Porto, Portugal
Bernhard K. Aichernig	TU Graz, Austria
Fevzi Belli	University of Paderborn, Germany
Ana Cavalli	Telecom SudParis, France

Byoungju Choi	Ewha Womans University, Korea
John Derrick	University of Sheffield, UK
Angelo Gargantini	University of Bergamo, Italy
Vahid Garousi	Middle East Technical University, Turkey and University of Calgary, Canada
Jens Grabowski	Georg-August-Universität Göttingen, Germany
Roland Groz	Grenoble INP - LIG, France
Toru Hasegawa	Osaka University, Japan
Klaus Havelund	NASA Jet Propulsion Laboratory, USA
Robert M. Hierons	Brunel University, UK
Teruo Higashino	Osaka University, Japan
Guy-Vincent Jourdan	University of Ottawa, Canada
Moez Krichen	University of Sfax, Tunisia
Pascale Le Gall	Ecole Centrale Paris, France
Hareton Leung	Hong Kong Polytechnic University, SAR China
Keqin Li	SAP Product Security Research, France
Stephane Maag	Telecom SudParis, France
Karl Meinke	KTH Royal Institute of Technology, Sweden
Mercedes Merayo	Universidad Complutense de Madrid, Spain
Zoltán Micskei	Budapest University of Technology and Economics, Hungary
P.V.R. Murthy	Siemens, India
Brian Nielsen	Aalborg University, Denmark
Manuel Núñez	Universidad Complutense de Madrid, Spain
Jan Peleska	Universität Bremen, Germany
Alexandre Petrenko	CRIM, Canada
Andrea Polini	University of Camerino, Italy
Ina Schieferdecker	FU Berlin/Fraunhofer FOKUS, Germany
Holger Schlingloff	Fraunhofer FOKUS/Humboldt University, Germany
Martin Schäf	United Nations University, Macao
Adenilso Simão	University of Sao Paulo, Brazil
Jan Tretmans	TNO - Embedded Systems Innovation, The Netherlands
Andreas Ulrich	Siemens AG, Germany
Jüri Vain	Tallinn University of Technology, Estonia
Margus Veanes	Microsoft Research, USA
César Viho	IRISA Rennes, France
Carsten Weise	IVU Traffic Technologies AG, Germany
Stephan Weißleder	Fraunhofer FOKUS, Germany
Burkhart Wolff	Université Paris-Sud, France
Hüsnü Yenigün	Sabanci University, Turkey
Nina Yevtushenko	Tomsk State University, Russia
Cemal Yilmaz	Sabanci University, Turkey
Fatiha Zaïdi	Université Paris-Sud, France

Additional Reviewers

Paolo Arcaini
Stephan Arlt
Cecile Braunstein
Jan Calta
José Campos
Ming Chai
Xiaoping Che
André Takeshi Endo
Voisin Frédérique
Christophe Gaston
Elena Gorbachuk
Maxim Gromov

Patrick Harms
Steffen Herbold
Joachim Hänsel
Afef Jmal Maâlej
Hartmut Koenig
Natalia Kushik
Hartmut Lackner
Mariam Lahami
Luis Llana
Delphine Longuet
Philip Makedonski
Aouadi Mohamed

Anderson Morais
Pramila Mouttappa
Petur Olsen
Sanjay Rawat
Thomas Rings
Uwe Schulze
Fabian Sudau
Jaroslav Svacina
Ramsay Taylor
Khalifa Toumi
Pierre van de Laar
Michele Volpato

Sponsoring Institutions

International Federation for Information Processing (IFIP), Laxenburg, Austria
Formal Methods Europe (FME), Uppsala, Sweden
Sabanci University, Istanbul, Turkey

Table of Contents

Model-Based Testing

Using Logic Coverage to Improve Testing Function Block Diagrams 1
  Eduard Paul Enoiu, Daniel Sundmark, and Paul Pettersson

Automatic Grammar-Based Test Generation 17
  Hai-Feng Guo and Zongyan Qiu

Adaptive Homing and Distinguishing Experiments for Nondeterministic
Finite State Machines 33
  Natalia Kushik, Khaled El-Fakih, and Nina Yevtushenko

Exhaustive Model-Based Equivalence Class Testing.................. 49
  Wen-ling Huang and Jan Peleska

Testing Timed and Concurrent Systems

Remote Testing of Timed Specifications........................... 65
  *Alexandre David, Kim G. Larsen, Marius Mikučionis,
  Omer L. Nguena Timo, and Antoine Rollet*

An Implementation Relation and Test Framework for Timed
Distributed Systems 82
  Christophe Gaston, Robert M. Hierons, and Pascale Le Gall

Unfolding-Based Test Selection for Concurrent Conformance 98
  Hernán Ponce de León, Stefan Haar, and Delphine Longuet

Test Suite Selection and Effort Estimation

Predicting the Size of Test Suites from Use Cases: An Empirical
Exploration 114
  Mourad Badri, Linda Badri, and William Flageol

Chaining Test Cases for Reactive System Testing 133
  Peter Schrammel, Tom Melham, and Daniel Kroening

Variations over Test Suite Reduction 149
  *Dennis Güttinger, Vitaly Kozyura, Dominik Kremer, and
  Sebastian Wieczorek*

Tools and Languages

Case Studies in Learning-Based Testing 164
Lei Feng, Simon Lundmark, Karl Meinke, Fei Niu,
Muddassar A. Sindhu, and Peter Y.H. Wong

Techniques and Toolset for Conformance Testing against UML Sequence
Diagrams 180
João Pascoal Faria, Ana C.R. Paiva, and Mário Ventura de Castro

Parallel SMT-Constrained Symbolic Execution for Eclipse
CDT/Codan 196
Andreas Ibing

Challenges of Testing Periodic Messages in Avionics Systems Using
TTCN-3 207
Bernard Stepien and Liam Peyton

Debugging

Guided Algebraic Specification Mining for Failure Simplification 223
Alexander Elyasov, I.S. Wishnu B. Prasetya, and Jurriaan Hage

Spectrum-Based Fault Localization for Diagnosing Concurrency
Faults 239
Feyzullah Koca, Hasan Sözer, and Rui Abreu

A Dynamic Approach to Locating Memory Leaks 255
Kostyantyn Vorobyov, Padmanabhan Krishnan, and Phil Stocks

Short Contributions

Towards a GUI Test Model Using State Charts and Programming
Code 271
Daniel Mauser, Alexander Klaus, and Konstantin Holl

A Tool for Supporting Developers in Analyzing the Security
of Web-Based Security Protocols 277
Giancarlo Pellegrino, Luca Compagna, and Thomas Morreggia

Finding Errors in Python Programs Using Dynamic Symbolic
Execution 283
Samir Sapra, Marius Minea, Sagar Chaki, Arie Gurfinkel, and
Edmund M. Clarke

Author Index 291

Using Logic Coverage
to Improve Testing Function Block Diagrams

Eduard Paul Enoiu, Daniel Sundmark, and Paul Pettersson

Mälardalen Real-Time Research Centre (MRTC)
Mälardalen University Västerås, Sweden
{eduard.paul.enoiu,daniel.sundmark,paul.pettersson}@mdh.se

Abstract. In model-driven development, testers are often focusing on functional model-level testing, enabling verification of design models against their specifications. In addition, in safety-critical software development, testers are required to show that tests cover the structure of the implementation. Testing cost and time savings could be achieved if the process of deriving test cases for logic coverage is automated and provided test cases are ready to be executed. The logic coverage artifacts, i.e., predicates and clauses, are required for different logic coverage, e.g., MC/DC. One way of dealing with test case generation for ensuring logic coverage is to approach it as a model-checking problem, such that model-checking tools automatically create test cases. We show how logic coverage criteria can be formalized and used by a model-checker to provide test cases for ensuring coverage on safety-critical software described in the Function Block Diagram programming language. Based on our experiments, this approach, supported by a tool chain, is an applicable and useful way of generating test cases for covering Function Block Diagrams.

Keywords: logic coverage, function block diagram, timed automata, model-driven engineering, structural testing.

1 Introduction

Within the last decade model-checking has turned out to be a useful technique for generation of test cases from finite-state models [12]. However, the main problem in using model-checking for testing industrial software systems is the potential combinatorial explosion of the state space and its limited application to models used in practice. Safety-critical and real-time software systems implemented in Programmable Logic Controllers (PLCs) are used in many real-world industrial application domains. One of the programming languages defined by the *International Electrotechnical Commission* (IEC) for PLCs is the *Function Block Diagram* (FBD). Programs developed in FBD are transformed into program code, which is compiled into machine code automatically by using specific engineering tools provided by PLC vendors. The motivation for using FBD as an implementation model comes from the fact that this language is the standard in many industrial software systems, such as rail transport control.

In this paper, our goal is to help testers automatically develop test cases for safety-critical software systems modeled in FBD that require a certain level of certification.

H. Yenigün, C. Yilmaz, and A. Ulrich (Eds.): ICTSS 2013, LNCS 8254, pp. 1–16, 2013.

One example of certification includes logic coverage which needs to be demonstrated on the developed programs. There has been little research on using logic coverage criteria for FBD programs in an industrial setting. One way is that logic coverage is analyzed at the code level [9] while tests are designed at the FBD program level, so time-consuming iterations between levels are required. Even if at the code level, logic coverage is used, it would be difficult to standardize the code generation scheme for different PLC tool vendors in order to map directly the criteria to the original FBD program. Hence, in this model-driven environment it is advantageous to move as much testing activity from code level to FBD program level as possible.

As the first contribution of this paper, we present a framework suitable for transforming FBD programs to a formal representation of both its functional and timing behavior. For this, we implement an automatic model–to–model transformation to timed automata, a well known model introduced by Alur and Dill [2]. The choice of timed automata as the target language is motivated primarily by its formal semantics and tool support for simulation and model-checking. Our goal is not to solve all testing issues (e.g., robustness, schedulability, etc.), but to allow the usage of a framework for formal reasoning about logic coverage on FBD programs. The transformation accurately reflects the data-flow characteristics of the FBD language by constructing a complete behavioral model which assumes a *read-execute-write* program semantics. The translation method consists of four separate steps. The first three steps involve mapping all the interface elements and the existing timing annotations. The latter step produces a formal behavior for every standard component in the FBD program. These steps are independent of timed automata thus are generic in the sense that they could also be used when translating an FBD program to another target language.

As the second contribution, we develop a test case generation technique based on model-checking, tailored for logic coverage of FBD programs. There have been a number of testing techniques used for defining logic coverage using model-checkers, e.g., [7,19,20]. However, these techniques are not directly applicable to FBD programs and semantics. We define logic coverage for FBD programs based on the transformed timed automata model. This copes with both functional and timing behavior of an FBD program. This formal definition is necessary for the approach to be applicable to model-checking. We present how a model-checker can be used to generate test cases for covering an FBD program. Based on our experiments, this method is — for the real world models provided by Bombardier Transportation AB — a useful way of generating test cases for logic coverage both in terms of automation and robustness to changes in the FBD programs as monitored by the model-checker.

The paper is organized as follows. Section 2 briefly overviews PLC software, the IEC 61131-3 standard, timed automata and logic coverage. Section 3 describes our overall testing methodology roadmap. Section 4 introduces the modeling approach for FBD programs and Section 5 shows the transformation scheme into timed automata. Section 6 and Section 7 presents the test case generation method required for logic coverage criteria. Next, we apply our method on a Train Startup Mode example in Section 8. In Section 9 we compare to related work, before concluding in Section 10.

2   Preliminaries

This paper describes how to generate test cases that cover the logical structure of FBD programs, by transforming them to networks of timed automata. In this section, we provide some background details on FBD programs, timed automata and logical coverage.

2.1   FBD Programs and Timer Components

PLCs are widely used in control software from nuclear plants to train systems. A PLC is an integrated embedded system that contains a processor, a memory, and a communication bus. Programs execute in a loop, in which the computation follows the *"read-execute-write"* semantics. In this way a PLC reads all inputs, executes the computation without interruption, and then writes to its output. FBD, a PLC programming language standardized by IEC 61131-3, is very popular in the industrial practice because of its graphical notations and its data flow nature [18]. Components in an FBD program are the base for a structured and hierarchical application. They are supplied by the manufacturer, defined by the user, or predefined in a library. An application generator is utilized to automatically transform each component to a C compliant program with its own thread of execution.

The type of systems we are studying contain a particular type of components named *PLC timers*. These timers are output instructions that provide the same functions as timing relays and are used to activate or deactivate a device after a preset interval of time. There are two different timer components (i) On-delay Timer (TON) and (ii) Off-delay Timer (TOF). Basically, a timer counts time-based intervals when the input instruction is true or false. In practice many other time configurations can be derived from this basic timers. In order to study how to generate test cases using a model checker for these types of FBD programs we use a formal representation that can cope with timers and timing information.

2.2   Networks of Timed Automata

A timed automaton is a standard finite-state automaton extended with a finite collection of real-valued clocks. The model was introduced by Alur and Dill [2] and has gained in popularity as a suitable model for real-time systems. We give here a brief summary for readers unfamiliar with timed automata theory.

Let C be a finite set of real-valued clocks and $B(C)$ the set of clock constraints, which are finite conjunctions of atomic guards of the form $x \bowtie n$, where $x \in C$, n is a natural number, and $\bowtie \in \{<, \leq, =, \geq, >\}$.

A *timed automaton* (A) over actions $\mathscr{A}$, atomic propositions P and clocks C is a tuple $\langle N, l_0, E, I, V \rangle$ where N is a finite set of control locations, l_0 is the initial location, $E \subseteq N \times B(C) \times \mathscr{A} \times R^1 \times N$ is the set of edges. In the case of and edge $\langle l, g, a, r, l' \rangle \in E$, we write $l \xrightarrow{g,a,r} l'$ where the label g is a guard of the edge, r is the data- or clock reset assignments of the edge, and a is the action of the edge. $I : N \to B(C)$ is a function

---

[1] R denotes the reset set i.e., assignments to manipulate clock- and data variables.

which for each control location assigns an invariant condition and $V : N \rightarrow 2^P$ is a function which for each control location gives a set of atomic propositions true in the location.

The semantics of A is defined in terms of a state transition system, where the state of A is defined as a pair (l, u), where l is a location and $u \in \mathbb{R}^C$ is a clock assignment in C. A state of A depends on its current location and on the current values of its clocks.

We denote by $T(A)$ all traces σ of A starting from the initial state (l_0, u_0) as a sequence of alternating transitions $\sigma = (l_0, u_0) \xrightarrow{a_1} (l_1, u_1) \xrightarrow{a_2} ... \xrightarrow{a_n} (l_n, u_n)$.

A network of timed automata $B_0 \parallel ... \parallel B_{n-1}$ is a parallel composition of n timed automata over C, $\mathscr{A}$ and synchronization functions (i.e., $a!$ is correlative with $a?$). We refer the reader to [1] for more information on the theory of timed automata.

We consider in this paper model-checking algorithms that perform reachability analysis to check for properties of the form $\exists \Diamond \beta$, with respect to a property β of the locations and the values of the clock. $\exists$ is the existential quantifier, and $\Diamond$ is the temporal operator. A reachability property states that there is a path in which β in A is reached. This type of property serves as a basis for formulating various coverage criteria and for deriving properties that could be used by a model-checker to produce test sequences for the timed automaton A.

2.3 Logic-Based Coverage Criteria

In this section we briefly describe existing logic-based coverage criteria. In the literature, there are many similar criteria defined, but with different terminology [4]. Also, some definitions of coverage criteria (e.g., MC/DC) have some ambiguities. In order to eliminate the ambiguities and conflicting terminologies, Ammann et al. [5] abstracted logic criteria with a precise definition and formal representation. A *predicate* is an expression that evaluates to a Boolean value. It consists of one or more clauses. A *clause* is a predicate that does not contain any logical operators and can be a Boolean variable, non-Boolean variables used for comparison, or a call to a Boolean function.

Clauses and predicates are used to introduce a variety of coverage criteria. This paper presents three different test criteria, each of which requires a different amount of test cases: (1) *Predicate Coverage (PC)*, (2) *Clause Coverage (CC)*, and (3) *Correlated Active Clause Coverage (CACC)*. These are defined in the next sections in terms of the FBD program. We note that modified condition/decision coverage (MC/DC) is equivalent to CACC and relies on its original definition [5].

3 Testing Methodology and Proposed Solutions

In this section, we describe our approach to automate test-case generation for FBD programs. Logic coverage criteria are used to define what test cases are needed and we use a model-checker to generate test traces. In addition, the formal framework presented in this paper is tailored for FBD programs, and is composed of the following steps, mirrored in Figure 1:

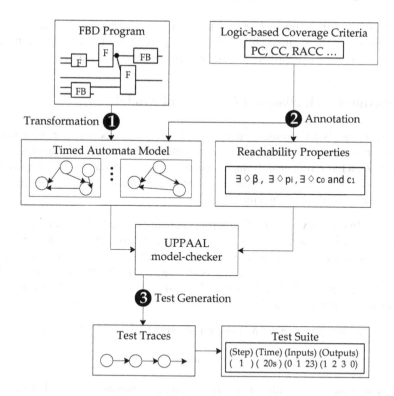

Fig. 1. Testing Methodology Roadmap

1. *Model Transformation.* To test an FBD program we map it to a finite state system suitable for model checking. In order to cope with timing constraints we have chosen to map FBD programs to timed automata.
2. *Logic Coverage Annotation.* We annotate the transformed model such that one can formulate a condition describing a single test case. This is a property expressible as a reachability property used in most model checkers.
3. *Test Case Generation.* We now use the model-checker to generate test traces. To provide a good level of practicality to our work we use a specific model-checker called UPPAAL which is using timed automata as the input modeling language[2]. The verification language supports reachability properties. In order to generate test cases for logic coverage of FBD programs using UPPAAL, we make use of UPPAAL's ability to generate test traces witnessing a submitted reachability property [13]. Currently UPPAAL supports three options for *diagnostic trace generation*: some trace leading to a goal state, the shortest trace with the minimum number of transitions, and fastest trace with the shortest time delay.

While UPPAAL is a viable tool for model checking, it is not tailored to test case generation in practice. We demonstrate how to work around this by automatically generating traces for logic coverage of FBD programs described in timed automata and

---

[2] The UPPAAL tool is available at www.uppaal.org

how we transform these traces to actual test cases. We discuss these steps in further detail in the following sections. First we start by introducing the FBD programs as a finite syntactical representation to describe its component model nature.

4   Function Block Diagram Component Model

An FBD program is a component model which obeys the read-execute-write semantics with a mechanism for monitoring the internal components to determine when the implementation has terminated. Components can be categorized into functions (FUNC) and function blocks (FB). A FUNC does not have any internal state and its output is determined only by the current inputs.

Example 1. An example of an FBD program depicting a Loadshed Contactor Control is shown in Figure 2. Basically the components are equivalent to predicates and instrumentation points shown in a circuit diagram fashion. The system consists of basic functions (e.g., AND, OR) and function blocks (e.g., FAULTEN, RS). In Figure 2, AND is a FUNC. In contrast, FAULTEN is an FB because it maintains an internal state and produces outputs based on this state and inputs.

Assume an FBD program defined as the following tuple:

$$FBDProgram \triangleq \langle Name, FE, V, P, Con \rangle,$$

where *Name* is the program identifier, FE is the set of components defined as the union of FUNC and FB instances, V is the variable set, defined as the union of input (VI) and output (VO) variables, P is the parameter set, defined as the parameters used internally by the program, and *Con* is the set of connectors between all components (e.g., FB and FUNC).

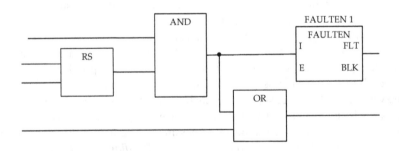

Fig. 2. An FBD program showing the graphical nature of the language

A component in FE has an interface, consisting of a name identifier, input and output ports, and a list of parameters. The interface is used to access the component behavior. When the component is activated the behavior is started using the values read on the input ports. When the behavior ends, i.e., when the component implementation terminates its execution, the output ports are updated. The behavior of a component is typically implemented by a code fragment that updates local variables. We define a component as a tuple $\langle Name, Port, B \rangle$, where $Name$ is the name identifier, Port is the set ports, defined as the union of input (IP), output ports (OP), and a list of parameters, whereas B is the behavior description of a component.

Recall that in order to express timing constraints within one component, standard PLC timers are used. The timers in a PLC are operated by an internally generated clock that originates in the processor module. Consider the following PLC timer TON defined as a tuple $TON = \langle TON1, (IN, PT, ET, Q), B_t \rangle$, where $TON1$ is the name identifier, IN, PT, ET, and Q are the set of ports and parameters in Port, and B_t is the behavior description. This timer component is an attempt to specify its interface and behavior. From a semantic point of view, FBD programs are a special case of deterministic reactive systems. We use more informative notations to denote the actual behavior. In the following section we present several such notations to describe how FBD programs can be handled by the UPPAAL model checker.

5   Transforming Function Block Diagrams into Timed Automata

In this section, we introduce the rules that describe the way we transform FBD programs into a network of timed automata, being one step away from test suite generation with the UPPAAL tool. Note that the current transformation rules cover one-level hierarchy only. The transformation maps to timed automata all the interface elements FE, V, P, and Con alongside the existing timing annotations within the FBD program. These timing annotations are based on the specifications used from structure and behavioral elements as defined in the FBD language. The transformation process starts by creating a timed automaton for the program description. We place templates of components and list the composed timed automata network representing the FBD program as $FE_1 \parallel ... \parallel FE_n$.

We consider the target model as a network of timed automata named Timed Automata Component Model (TACM) and defined as a tuple as follows:

$$TACM \triangleq \langle Comp, P_{in}, P_{out}, Connections, B_{TACM} \rangle,$$

where $Comp$ is the set of components that TACM contains, P_{in} and P_{out} are the input and output dataflow ports, respectively, and B_{TACM} is the $TACM$'s behavior. If $Comp = \emptyset$ and $Connections = \emptyset$, then $TACM$ is a primitive component.

The mapping between an $FBDProgram$ and $TACM$ is a function $\pi : FBDProgram \rightarrow TACM$, which maps each component to a $TACM$ primitive component, input variables VI to the $TACM$'s component dataflow input ports, output variables VO to the $TACM$'s component dataflow output ports, connectors to the $TACM$'s component connections, and the behavioral specification of a component to B_{TACM}. The execution of a component is modeled as a timed automaton. The following rules establish in more details B_{TACM} with regard to the mapping of an $FBDProgram$ to $TACM$.

An FBD program is executed in a loop and the computation follows the run-to completion semantics. The timed automaton of the FBD program contains a clock variable for modeling a delay between the cycles. A cycle starts when the automaton enters

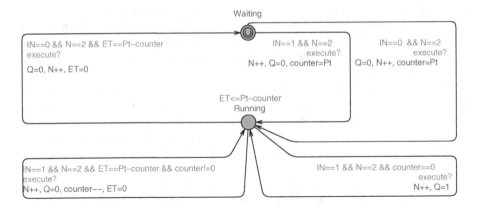

Fig. 3. Timed Automaton of a TON component

the `ReadInputs` node and ends in `UpdateScanTime` node. For a composition $TACM$ the execute operation of each component is extended according to connections and P_{in} and P_{out} variables. A composition is a set of interconnected components closed under a specific execution order. The execution order is automatically defined according to the general rules included in the IEC standard. We use the notion of precedence to describe such dependencies on the convention of reading such FBD programs in a top-to-bottom, left-to-right fashion. For each component we assign a precedence priority to the corresponding timed automaton. A counter is created in this step to represent the execution priority of a component. In this way we ensure that components are executed one by one. After the last component is evaluated, the counter is reset to repeat the scan cycle.

For standard components we assign a timed automaton B_{TACM} with its own logical execution and no internal concurrency. A component is initially *Waiting*, and after performing the read action it starts executing until its internal computation is done. Reconsider the PLC timer TON as described in Section 4. A rather straightforward model of the TON component is shown as a timed automaton in Figure 3. The composition interacts with the TON component via `execute?` action. TON is modeled by a standard time on timer that sets the output Q to true if IN variable is true at least as long as the time PT. In this way, we comply with the standard specification of a PLC timer and the structural definition of the program. The timed automaton encapsulates the internal behavior with both functional and timing properties. This means that when we create a TON model we use a separate instantiation of the behavioral model. Also, every instance of TON needs to contain all the variables listed in the interface description and for this reason it is necessary to give each instance of the TON behavioral model a unique identifier.

6   Test Case Generation Using the UPPAAL Model-Checker

As a result of the transformation described in Section 5, we consider that the FBD program is given as a closed network of timed automata as shown in Figure 4. This model

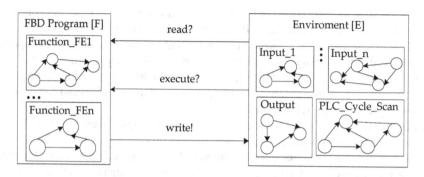

Fig. 4. Test TA Network for a FBD Program

contains two sub-networks, one modeling the FBD `Program` and the other one modeling its `Environment`. In addition, we consider a completely unconstrained environment that allows all possible interactions between the timed automata network elements. In this way the cycle scan is used to control the FBD program via `read?`, `execute?`, and `write!` actions.

Let us assume the generic timed automata network of an FBD program together with its PLC cycle scan and environment shown in Figure 4. A trace produced by the model checker for a given reachability property defines the set of actions executed on the FBD program. An example of a diagnostic trace has the following form:

$$(F_0, E_0) \xrightarrow{a_1} (F_1, E_1) \xrightarrow{a_2} ... \xrightarrow{a_n} (F_n, E_n),$$

where (F_k, E_k) are states of the FBD program and PLC cycle scan with environment constraints, respectively, and a_k are either internal synchronization actions, time-delays or `read?`, `execute?`, and `write!` global synchronizations. For FBD programs the sequence represents only the global synchronizations shown in Figure 4. Test cases are obtained by extracting from the diagnostic trace the observable actions `read?`, `execute?`, and `write!`. Obviously a single test case cannot be obtained for every test purpose or criterion. By using a program scan cycle we allow the test suite to be implemented as one or more test sequences separated by resets. To introduce resets in the model, we annotate the PLC cycle scan with a reset transition leading to the initial `ReadInputs` location. On this transition all variables and parameters (excluding encoded internal variables) are reset to their default value. This reset is hardcoded into the PLC scan cycle for any modeled FBD program in UPPAAL, being an atomic communication between all timed automata.

7   Logic Coverage Criteria for Function Block Diagrams

As mentioned earlier, the basic approach to generating test cases for logic coverage using model-checking is to define a test case as a finite execution trace. If one can characterize this execution trace as a temporal logic property to be used, model-checking techniques can be used to produce a test trace for the property. It has also been observed that criteria such as logic coverage that have constraints involving more than one test trace cannot be handled in this way. Based on *TACM* description, we propose here to use the logic coverage to annotate the original model and the temporal logic property to be checked with auxiliary data variables and transitions in such way that a set of test traces in the *TACM* can be used as a test suite in the annotated model. The temporal logic property is described in terms of adding these auxiliary variables and can be used to produce the necessary set of test cases.

In this section we describe what is needed to achieve logic coverage for FBD programs. We envision our logic coverage measurement process where model checking is used to perform more systematic testing. Informally, our approach is based on the idea that to get logic coverage of a specific program it would be enough to (*i*) find a test trace from the initial state to the end of the FBD program, (*ii*) annotate the clauses and predicates in the FBD program, (*iii*) formulate a reachability property for logic coverage. In addition, the values of the clauses and predicates are remembered in every program execution with the outcome of the trace being different. To apply the criteria, necessary properties for the integration of logic coverage need to be fulfilled.

Program Reset: The FBD program is assumed to have an implicit control loop, so the reset can occur in the program without modifying in any way the transformed timed automata. We consider that *TACM* has a special reset transition that restores the program to its initial state and the program cycle enters the `ReadInputs` node. Clearly, multiple execution traces of the FBD program are mapped to a single execution trace containing sub-traces separated by resets. An example of a single execution trace for an FBD program has the following form:

$$(F_0, E_0) \xrightarrow{read} (F_1, E_1) \xrightarrow{execute} (F_2, E_2) \xrightarrow{write}$$

$$(F_3, E_3) \xrightarrow{read} (F_4, E_4) \xrightarrow{execute} (F_5, E_5) \xrightarrow{write} .$$

The test trace [3] indicates that the checked reachability property is satisfied. This particular trace contains two-sub traces, each finishing with the `write` actions.

Component Annotation: Predicates in an FBD program are components that can be evaluated to a boolean value, i.e., true or false. Predicates can be identified from the instrumentation points in the FBD program. Let P be a set of predicates in an FBD program and C be the set of clauses in P. For each predicate $p \in P$, let C_p be the set of clauses in p. C is the union of the clauses in each predicate in P. The following coverage criteria are defined as follows:

- *PC*: For each p corresponding to a component in the FBD program, a test suite contains two requirements: p evaluates to true, and p evaluates to false.
- *CC*: For each c corresponding to a component in the FBD program, a test suite contains two requirements: c evaluates to true, and c evaluates to false.

---

[3] The states are shown in this trace where (F_k, E_k) are states of the FBD program and PLC cycle scan with environment constraints, respectively, and the global actions are `read`, `execute`, and `write`.

– *CACC*: For each $p \in P$ and each clause $c_i \in C_p$, a test suite contains two requirements: c_i evaluates to true and false so that it solely determines p.

For PC a solution is to analyze every predicate in the FBD program. PC indicates that each component in the FBD program has taken every outcome at least once. This mechanism is implemented by specifying a set of predicate parameters. We annotate every B_{TACM} with an auxiliary boolean variable v_i for each predicate p to be covered. For every edge in a component with destination $waiting : l \xrightarrow{g,a,r} waiting$, v_i is added to r assignment. In addition, for CC the annotation of clauses c_i is done based on the evaluated components. A test trace achieves full CC when it causes each input and parameters of all components to be true at least once during model checking. Similarly for CACC we store the values of p and c_i : and pass the information as a pair (p, c_i). We refer to these value combinations which are needed for logic coverage criteria as test goals.

Reachability Property Annotation: For using the test generation capability of a model-checker, the test property must be formulated as a reachability property and checked by the timed automata. Hessel et al. [14] already proposed a way to apply coverage criteria to specifications described in timed automata. In addition, we propose the usage of logic coverage directly on implementation models. The reachability property for full PC will require that for all p to be exercised:

$$\exists \, \Diamond \, (v_0 == 1 \text{ and } v_1 == 1 \, \ldots \, \text{and } v_k == 1).$$

For generating test traces for CC we check whether the auxiliary variables are covered for each c_i in the program similarly to the reachability property for full PC. In addition, to achieve CACC for a component in the FBD program, we would need to define a reachability property that leads to a goal set satisfying CACC for every c_i in p. What remains is to calculate the total desired set of combinations for each component in an FBD program.

8 Example: Train Startup Mode

In the previous section we presented a technique to compute logic coverage for FBD programs. In the following we show empirically that the performance of our technique is sufficient for practically relevant examples. We have applied our method on a real world example provided by *Bombardier Transportation AB*. We present here how our method is applied to test a part of the MITRAC *Train Control and Management System* (TCMS) provided within the ATAC research project. TCMS is a distributed system, built on open standard *IP-technology* that allows easy integration of control and communication functions for high speed trains. We are concerned with both the transformation of FBD programs to timed automata models and the time and memory used to generate test cases. The tools used for developing these programs are based on the *MULTIPROG* software. The FBD program is transformed using the MOS tool [4] [10].

---

[4] MOS is a tool for model-based and search-based testing of safety-critical systems implemented in FBD language, developed at Mälardalen University since 2012.

8.1   Experiments

The experiments reported here are based on an example program, part of TCMS. We use an FBD program of a train Startup Mode System (TSM) and generate test cases for logic coverage. In the process, we describe the FBD program, the program to timed automata model transformation and the annotations made to the model.

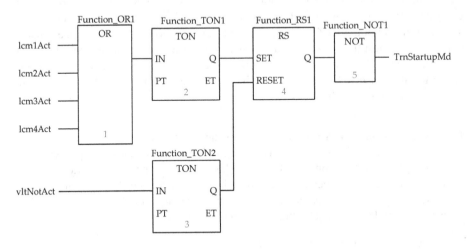

Fig. 5. Simplified Train Startup Mode modeled as an FBD program

The train is built up using motorized cars and intermediate trailer cars with pantographs. These cars are combined to create a fixed 8-cars train set, each with its own complete system for control and propulsion. The task of the train operating in the startup mode is imposed by the controller FBD program depicted in Figure 5. When the first Line Converter Module (LCM) is active, the propulsion unit becomes active, i.e. any of the four inputs becomes true. When activating the propulsion system, the program waits an additional five seconds and then sets the output to false, which means that the train is not in the startup mode anymore. If the NotAct is true for at least five seconds, the element is reset and the output is set true as in the startup mode.

To validate our approach for generating test cases for logic coverage, we implemented our method in our previously developed MOS tool for analyzing and executing FBD programs. The TSM system is transformed automatically in the fully formal and executable timed automata used by UPPAAL. The TSM system is modeled as a parallel composition of several processes. Several boolean and integer variables are used for recording information: read!, execute! and write! synchronization channels are used to model the execution of the FBD program, et is used to keep track of the elapsed time in timer components, lcm1act, lcm2act, lcm3act, lcm4act for recording the input variables generated by the LCM input automaton, notact for representing the line voltage activation, TrnStartupMd for recording the startup mode of the train, p_i and c_i for recording each covered item, and pt for recording the delay from the first LCM starts to communicate. The TSM program has been transformed and checked by

UPPAAL model checker for generation of test suites for logic coverage by reachability analysis.

Table 1 shows the generation time (in seconds) for test suites generated from different logic coverage criteria of the TSM example, and the length (number of program cycles) of the generated test suite. We notice that for CACC test cases result in longer traces than for PC and CC. The generation time for CACC is slightly higher than the number for PC and CC. However, the number of program cycles is twice as high because CACC is combining already generated test suites for PC and CC.

Table 1. Generation time and test suite length for various coverage criteria

Coverage Criterion	Generation Time (seconds)	Test Suite Length (program cycles)
PC	18,04	14
CC	18,21	14
CACC	22,86	25

8.2   Logic Coverage and Timing Components

One of the objectives for this experiment is to assess the applicability and scalability of using logic coverage for testing FBD programs with various sizes and complexities. An expected characteristic of the FBD program is its associated timing behavior. For the TSM model, the TON automaton appears to be significantly affecting the generation time. Therefore, we focus the discussion on timer components (e.g., TON, TOF, etc.) because these cases lead to a bigger search space. We modify the program by increasing or decreasing the number of TON components in the TSM model. We observed that an FBD program consisting of ten or more TON components are difficult to cover. This is not surprising as the timing components are varying the timing of the entire model and therefore the number of predicates and clauses in the program. The programming of two or more timers components together in the same FBD program is called *cascading*. From our experiments with timer components in TCMS (over 300 FBD programs), the number of TON and TOF components is always lower than five. Nevertheless we were interested to show that —for the studied program— our method of generating test cases for covering FBD programs is applicable and scalable.

The results, listed in Table 2, show that the memory usage increase essentially linearly with the number of timing elements. If we compare test suite length with the generation time, it can be seen that is much cheaper to compute FBD programs for FBDs with less than ten timer components than computing for fifty timer components. We can try to explain this behavior in the sense that timer components pose restrictions on the solution because it contains more possible behaviors. Thus, searching through more timer components takes longer. We note that the use of timer elements restricts the handling of larger systems, with an increased cost of generation time and used memory.

Table 2. Results of obtaining PC of the TSM example with increasing timer elements

Timers	Generation Time (seconds)	Test Suite Length (program cycles)	Memory Usage (MB)
0	0,62	4	15
1	1,54	5	27
2	3,29	7	61
5	6,38	14	122
10	6,79	18	200
50	31	36	520

9 Related Work

Previous contributions in testing of FBD programs range from a simulation-based approach [21] to verification of the actual FBD program code [6,16]. The technique in [6] is based on Petri Nets models. In comparison to our work, they are not coping with the internal structure of the PLC logical and timing aspects. It is our opinion that testing FBD programs can be complemented by using a model-checker as presented in this paper. Similar to this work, Rayadurgam and Heimdahl [20] have defined a complete formal framework that can be used for coverage based test-case generation using a model checker. For a detailed overview of testing with model checkers we refer the reader to Fraser et al. [12].

A model checker has been used to find test cases to various criteria and from programs in a variety of formal languages [7,15]. In addition, Black et al. [3] discuss the problems encountered in using a model-checker for test case generation for full-predicate coverage and explain why logic coverage criteria is not directly applicable for model-checking. Rayadurgam et al. [19] present an alternative method that modifies instead the system model and are obtaining MC/DC adequate test cases using a model-checking approach. Similarly to our work, the system model is annotated and the properties to be checked are expressible as a single test sequence. However, this technique is not coping with the timing behavior of an FBD program as we do and only MC/DC criteria is investigated. We provide an approach to generate test cases for different logic criteria (e.g., PC, CC, and CACC) that are directly applicable to FBD programs.

The idea of using model-checkers for verifying and testing FBD programs is not new [22,8]. These two approaches use the UPPAAL model checker and UPPAAL TRON for verification of FBD programs, however they translate their model for functional verification. Soliman et al. [22] provide an automatic transformation to timed automata and their verification methodology is used to check the model against safety requirements. In contrast to the online model-based testing approach used in [8] we generate test suites for offline execution.

Related to this work but outside the PLC testing community, the most notable efforts have been focusing on test coverage for data flow languages. For example, for the Lustre language there are contributions [17] describing an activation condition concept that can be used when data flows from an input edge to an output edge. While this approach studied the effect of structural coverage criteria on the overall program, we study the ability to generate test cases and its effect on the test artifacts, i.e., predicates and clauses, tailored for FBD programs.

To our knowledge, not much theoretical and experimental data is available regarding the usage of logical coverage for Function Block Diagrams. In our previous work [11] we have defined a model-based test generation method tailored for Function Block Diagram programs and demonstrated how to use the UPPAAL tool for model checking the implementation in order to ensure compliance to quality requirements including unit testing. As a consequence of these results we have developed our own tool chain called MOS [10] to support both a model and search-based testing approach which can include specific coverage measurements. The criteria in this paper is based on our previous work and is an attempt to automatically compute logic coverage using a model checker for Function Block Diagrams.

10   Conclusion

In this paper we have shown how test case generation for ensuring logic coverage on Function Block Diagrams can be solved as a model-checking problem, such that model-checking tools are automatically creating traces which can be transformed to test cases. We show how logic coverage criteria can be formalized and used by a model-checker to provide test cases. The results show that model checking scales well for handing logic coverage and we suggest a general approach for handling tests to cover the structure of the implementation model. The method is supported by a tool chain that can be used to produce relevant test cases. We are currently investigating this approach on a larger case study. In addition, we want to extend the evaluation to measure both efficiency and effectiveness of our approach.

Acknowledgments. The authors would like to thank Elaine Weyuker and Thomas Ostrand for their valuable comments on this work. This research was supported by VINNOVA, the Swedish Governmental Agency for Innovation Systems within the ATAC project.

References

1. Alur, R.: Timed Automata. In: Halbwachs, N., Peled, D.A. (eds.) CAV 1999. LNCS, vol. 1633, pp. 8–22. Springer, Heidelberg (1999)
2. Alur, R., Dill, D.: Automata for Modeling Real-time Systems. In: Automata, Languages and Programming, pp. 322–335 (1990)
3. Ammann, P., Black, P.E., Ding, W.: Model Checkers in Software Testing. In: NIST-IR 6777, National Institute of Standards and Technology Report (2002)
4. Ammann, P., Offutt, J.: Introduction to Software Testing. Cambridge University Press
5. Ammann, P., Offutt, J., Huang, H.: Coverage Criteria for Logical Expressions. In: 14th International Symposium on Software Reliability Engineering, pp. 99–107. IEEE (2003)
6. Baresi, L., Mauri, M., Monti, A., Pezze, M.: PLCTools: Design, Formal Validation, and Code Generation for Programmable Controllers. In: IEEE International Conference on Systems, Man, and Cybernetics, vol. 4, pp. 2437–2442. IEEE (2000)

7. Black, P.: Modeling and Marshaling: Making Tests from Model Checker Counter-examples. In: Proceedings of the 19th Digital Avionics Systems Conference, vol. 1, pp. 1B3–1. IEEE (2000)

8. da Silva, L.D., de Assis Barbosa, L.P., Gorgônio, K., Perkusich, A., Lima, A.M.N.: On the Automatic Generation of Timed Automata Models from Function Block Diagrams for Safety Instrumented Systems. In: 34th Annual Conference of IEEE Industrial Electronics, pp. 291–296. IEEE (2008)

9. Doganay, K., Bohlin, M., Sellin, O.: Search Based Testing of Embedded Systems Implemented in IEC 61131-3: An Industrial Case Study. In: International Conference on Software Testing, Verification and Validation Workshops. IEEE (March 2013)

10. Enoiu, E.P., Doganay, K., Bohlin, M., Sundmark, D., Pettersson, P.: MOS: An Integrated Model-based and Search-based Testing Tool for Function Block Diagrams. In: International Conference on Software Engineering Workshops. IEEE (May 2013)

11. Enoiu, E.P., Sundmark, D., Pettersson, P.: Model-based Test Suite Generation for Function Block Diagrams using the UPPAAL Model Checker. In: International Conference on Software Testing, Verification and Validation Workshops. IEEE (April 2013)

12. Fraser, G., Wotawa, F., Ammann, P.E.: Testing with Model Checkers: a Survey. Journal on Software Testing, Verification and Reliability 19, 215–261 (2009)

13. Hessel, A., Larsen, K.G., Mikucionis, M., Nielsen, B., Pettersson, P., Skou, A.: Testing Real-time Systems using UPPAAL. In: Hierons, R.M., Bowen, J.P., Harman, M. (eds.) FORTEST. LNCS, vol. 4949, pp. 77–117. Springer, Heidelberg (2008)

14. Hessel, A., Larsen, K.G., Nielsen, B., Pettersson, P., Skou, A.: Time-Optimal Real-Time Test Case Generation Using UPPAAL. In: Petrenko, A., Ulrich, A. (eds.) FATES 2003. LNCS, vol. 2931, pp. 114–130. Springer, Heidelberg (2004)

15. Hong, H.S., Lee, I., Sokolsky, O., Ural, H.: A Temporal Logic-Based Theory of Test Coverage and Generation. In: Katoen, J.-P., Stevens, P. (eds.) TACAS 2002. LNCS, vol. 2280, pp. 327–341. Springer, Heidelberg (2002)

16. Jee, E., Kim, S., Cha, S., Lee, I.: Automated Test Coverage Measurement for Reactor Protection System Software Implemented in Function Block Diagram. In: Schoitsch, E. (ed.) SAFECOMP 2010. LNCS, vol. 6351, pp. 223–236. Springer, Heidelberg (2010)

17. Lakehal, A., Parissis, I.: Lustructu: A Tool for the Automatic Coverage Assessment of Lustre Programs. In: International Symposium on Software Reliability Engineering, p. 10. IEEE (2005)

18. Öhman, M., Johansson, S., Årzén, K.E.: Implementation Aspects of the PLC standard IEC 1131-3. Journal on Control Engineering Practice 6, 547–555 (1998)

19. Rayadurgam, S., Heimdahl, M.P.E.: Generating MC/DC Adequate Test Sequences Through Model Checking. In: NASA Goddard Software Engineering Workshop Proceedings, pp. 91–96. IEEE (2003)

20. Rayadurgam, S., Heimdahl, M.P.E.: Coverage Based Test-Case Generation using Model Checkers. In: International Conference and Workshop on the Engineering of Computer Based Systems, pp. 83–91. IEEE (2001)

21. Richter, S., Wittig, J.U.: Verification and Validation Process for Safety IC Systems. Nuclear Plant Journal 21, 36 (2003)

22. Soliman, D., Thramboulidis, K., Frey, G.: Function Block Diagram to UPPAAL Timed Automata Transformation Based on Formal Models. Information Control Problems in Manufacturing 14(1), 1653–1659 (2012)

Automatic Grammar-Based Test Generation

Hai-Feng Guo[1] and Zongyan Qiu[2]

[1] Department of Computer Science, University of Nebraska at Omaha, USA
haifengguo@unomaha.edu
[2] Department of Informatics, Peking University, Beijing 100871, P.R. China
qzy@math.pku.edu.cn

Abstract. In this paper, we present an automatic grammar-based test generation approach which takes a symbolic grammar as input, requires zero control input from users, and produces well-distributed test cases. Our approach utilizes a novel dynamic stochastic model where each variable is associated with a tuple of probability distributions, which are dynamically adjusted along the derivation. The adjustment is based on a tabling strategy to keep track of the recursion of each grammar variable. We further present a test generation coverage tree illustrating the distribution of generated test cases and their detailed derivations, more importantly, it provides various implicit balance control mechanisms. We implemented this approach in a Java-based system, named *Gena*. Experimental results demonstrate the effectiveness of our test generation approach and show the balanced distribution of generated test cases over grammatical structures.

1 Introduction

Grammar-based test generation is especially useful on testing applications which require structured data as inputs, such as data conversion tools and compilers [7,3], and those which response to well-ordered external events, such as reactive systems [18], VLSI circuit simulator [14], and software product line [1]. One common setting of these applications is using a context-free grammar (CFG) to describe the input structures for the systems. However, even though grammar-based test generation has been introduced since early 1970s [5] and has played important roles in software development and testing [9,3], it is well known that without extra control mechanisms, naive grammar-based test generation has never become practical due to the facts that exhaustive test production is often explosive and its testing coverage is often quite unbalanced.

Prior work on grammar-based test generation mainly fall into the following two approaches: *stochastic* or *annotating*. The stochastic approach [13,15,19] randomly select production rules for derivation based on their pre-assigned probabilities. Practically, a test case may easily blow out – becoming infinitely long – even if it is suggested that the probabilities of non-recursive production rules should be much higher than those of recursive rules [13] to avoid an infinite recursion [15]. Hence, other constraints (e.g., length control), heuristics, or hints are often required to make sure the termination of generating test cases. The *lava* tool [19] takes a production grammar as well as a seed, which consists of a high-level description that guides the production process, to generate effective test suites for Java virtual machine.

H. Yenigün, C. Yilmaz, and A. Ulrich (Eds.): ICTSS 2013, LNCS 8254, pp. 17–32, 2013.

The annotation approaches [10,11,7] become much popular recently. *Geno* [11], a C#-based test data generator, takes a hybrid between EBNF and algebraic signatures, where combinatorial control parameters are specified, to approximately achieve expected full combinatorial coverage. *YouGen* [7] supports many extra-grammatical annotations which guide effective test generation, and uses a generalized tag form of pairwise testing [20]. However, embedding tags into a grammar to control its production is not only a burden on users, but may be still difficult to get expected test cases.

In this paper, we present an automatic grammar-based test generation approach which takes a symbolic CFG [12] as an input, requires zero annotation, and produces well-distributed test cases for testing. Symbolic terminals are adopted to hide the complexity of different terminal inputs which share syntactic as well as expected testing behavior similarities. Our approach utilizes a novel dynamic stochastic model where each variable is associated with a tuple of probability distributions, which are dynamically adjusted along with the derivation. The more a production rule has contributed to self-loops while generating a test case, the *significantly* less probability the same rule will be applied in the future. To achieve the dynamic adjustment, we use a tabling strategy [4] to keep track of re-occurrences of grammar variables. The tuple associated with a grammar variable records the degrees of recursion caused by each of its rules. These tuples eventually determine the probability distribution of selecting a next rule for further derivation. We further use a test generation coverage tree, where each path from the root to a leaf node corresponds to a generated test case. Not only does the tree show the distribution of test cases and how each of them has been generated, but it also contains implicit balance control mechanism based on local probability distribution on each node.

We implemented the proposed test generation algorithm in a Java-based tool *Gena*, which takes a symbolic grammar and a number, the total number of test cases to request, as inputs, and automatically produces a set of test cases with test requirements and a test generation coverage tree. Experimental results demonstrate the effectiveness of our test generation approach, and indicate the balanced distribution of generated test cases over grammatical structures.

The rest of the paper is organized as follows. Section 2 introduces the grammar-based test generation. Section 3 presents our dynamic stochastic approach as well as a tabling strategy to keep track of recursion. Section 3.2 illustrate how a dynamically growing test generation coverage tree maintains its local probability tuples on each node to balance test generation distribution, followed by detailed algorithms and termination properties. Section 4 and Section 5 present a Java-based implementation and our experimental results, respectively. Conclusions and discussions are given in Section 6.

2   Grammar-Based Test Generation

A CFG is represented as a four-tuple $G = (V, T, S, P)$, where V is a set of variables (or non-terminals), T is a set of terminals, S is the start variable, and P is a set of production rules in the form of $A ::= x$, where $A \in V$ and $x \in (V \cup T)^*$. Given a CFG G, automatic test generation is typically done by simulating the leftmost derivation from its start variable S.

2.1 Symbolic Terminal

We first introduce a notation of symbolic terminals [12], which are adopted to hide the complexity of different terminal inputs which share syntactic similarities as well as similar expected testing behaviors. A symbolic terminal, highlighted by a pair of square brackets, is an abstract notation for a finite domain, which is represented as an ordered sequence of individual atoms or a bound form $Lower..Upper$, where $Lower$ is smaller than or equal to $Upper$ in their lexicographic order. We treat a symbolic terminal as a regular terminal except that it returns a random element within the defined domain whenever a symbolic terminal is seen during derivation.

Example 1. Consider the following CFG:

$$E ::= [N] \mid E + E \mid E - E \qquad\qquad [N] ::= 1..100$$

where $[N]$ is a symbolic terminal. An example of test generation based on leftmost derivation would be as follows:

$$E \Rightarrow E + E \Rightarrow E - E + E \Rightarrow [N] - E + E \Rightarrow [N] - [N] + E \Rightarrow [N] - [N] + [N].$$

2.2 A Penalty Maze

In fact, generating a terminal string acts like getting out a penalty maze, which is not only a confusing intricate network of passages, but also a network with many self-loops; and those self-loop passages, once taken, would *magically* make the maze bigger and harder to find an exit.

Consider Example 1 again, where the variable E has two double-recursive rules. As shown in Table 1, the start variable E is similar to the beginning of a maze; the leftmost derivation, like navigating a penalty maze, is actually a procedure finding each variable in the current derived string a terminal, like a segmented exit in a penalty maze. The more variables in a current derived string, the more challenges – each variable needs to become terminal – for a leftmost derivation to generate a terminal string.

Derived String	Probability of becoming terminal
E	$1/3$
$\Rightarrow E + E$	$1/3 * 1/3 = 1/9$
$\Rightarrow E - E + E$	$1/3 * 1/3 * 1/3 = 1/27$
$\cdots$	$\cdots$

Fig. 1. A penalty maze

Figure 1 shows how fast the probability, for a derived string to become terminal instantly, could drop as a leftmost derivation moves on. Each occurrence of E has a probability, $1/3$, to become a terminal instantly since E has only one terminal rule out of three rules. However, as the derivation moves on, the number of E's expands much faster than they become terminal. It is in nearly two-third probability that a naive grammar-based test generation will blow out generating a single terminal string of E due to non-termination.

Example 2. Consider a grammar for a subset of arithmetic expressions as follows:

$$E ::= F \mid E + F \mid E - F \qquad F ::= T \mid F * T \mid F / T$$
$$T ::= [N] \mid (E) \qquad\qquad [N] ::= 1..1000$$

The grammar has only one terminal exit, $E \Rightarrow F \Rightarrow T \Rightarrow [N]$, but the rest are full of recursive rules. Moreover, direct recursions (e.g, $E \Rightarrow E + F$) are even entangled with indirect one (e.g., $E \Rightarrow T \Rightarrow (E)$), which makes static analysis difficult. For example, without runtime information, it is difficult to tell whether the production rule $E ::= F$ is going to be recursive or not due to the possibility of indirect recursion.

It is a common phenomenon getting into infinite recursion during grammar-based test generation due to the recursive natures of a CFG. Hence, it is really challenge getting out of a penalty maze, so is generating a terminal string.

3   A Dynamic Stochastic Approach

The essential problem in grammar-based test generation is how to generate a terminal string without getting lost in a "penalty maze". Our approach utilizes a novel dynamic stochastic model where each variable is associated with a tuple of probability distributions, which are dynamically adjusted along the derivation. When a variable is encountered during left-most derivation, it applies one of its defined production rules stochastically, based on the tuple of probability distribution among those rules. Then the key problem is how to dynamically adjust the probability distribution so that a test generator is able to avoid keeping getting into loops with potential explosive "penalties". The general principles, for a dynamic stochastic model to satisfy, are:

- initially, the probability distribution allows a variable to have an equal chance to apply different defined production rule;
- as a derivation moves on, since the probability of generating a terminal string could become low in a dramatic speed (see the example in Figure 1), it has to be effectively fast pushing derivations to applying non-recursive rules;
- the generated terminal tests are evenly distributed over the grammatical structures of the given CFG; in other words, every terminal test may have a good chance to be generated as long as the total requested number of test cases is sufficiently big.

3.1   A Tabling Strategy

We present a tabling strategy to detect derivation loops and eventually achieve dynamic probability distribution. Tabling has been extensively used in logic programming [21,4], where it successfully resolves lots of termination issues by detecting re-occurrences of recursively defined predicates at runtime in an automatic way.

In grammar-based test generation, we introduce a global data structure **table**, where each grammar variable has a tuple entry, initially all 1's, recording the degrees of recursion caused by each of its defined production rules at runtime, and the size of a tuple is determined by the number of its defined production rules.

Definition 1. *Given a CFG $G = (V, T, S, P)$, where E is a variable in V and $\mathcal{R}$ is a production rule of E, we say that $\mathcal{R}$ **causes a recursion** of E, if there exists a leftmost derivation of E in a form of*

$$E \xRightarrow{\mathcal{R}} \omega \xRightarrow{*} \alpha E \beta,$$

where $\overset{\mathcal{R}}{\Longrightarrow}$ *is a single derivation applying the rule* R, $\omega \in (V \cup T)^*$, $\alpha \in T^*$, $\beta \in$ $(V \cup T)^*$, *and there is no other leftmost occurrence of a variable* E *during* $\omega \overset{*}{\Longrightarrow} \alpha E \beta$.

Such a caused recursion is dynamically detected by maintaining a derivation stack that tracks whether a variable leads to a self-loop during its leftmost derivation. Once a recursion of E, caused by a defined rule $\mathcal{R}$, is detected, the degree tuple of E will be adjusted by *doubling* the degree of recursion associated with the contributing grammar rule $\mathcal{R}$. We say such an adjustment a **double strategy**.

The main purpose of maintaining a table of degree tuples is determining a dynamic probability distribution for selecting a next production rule. Given a degree tuple $(d_1, d_2, \cdots, d_n)$, where $n \geq 1$ is the number of rules for a variable, its corresponding probability distribution $(p_1, p_2, \cdots, p_n)$ is determined as follows:

$$p_i = \frac{w_i}{T}, \text{ where } w_i = \frac{d_1}{d_i} \text{ and } T = \sum_{i=1}^{n} w_i.$$

vars	deg. tuple	probabilities
E	(1, 1, 1)	(.33, .33, .33)
F	(1, 1, 1)	(.33, .33, .33)
T	(1, 1)	(.5, .5)

Fig. 2. Initial degree/prob

We introduce a probability weight w_i, which is a ratio showing the relative degrees of the first rule over the i-th production rule. Hence, the probability weight w_1 is always 1, while other weight w_i, $i > 1$, may drop below 1 if the i-th rule causes more recursions than the first rule does; otherwise, $w_i \geq 1$. Thus, the initial table for the grammar in Example 2 is given in Figure 2.

Dynamic probability distribution is shown in Figure 3 as the double strategy pushes the derivation to choose the exit rule of E at runtime. Note that when the leftmost variable T is derived to (E), the *tabling strategy* will detect this indirect recursion caused by the rule $E ::= F$, and then apply the double strategy to adjust its degree of recursion from 1 to 2; at this point,

derivation	tuple of E	probabilities
E	(1, 1, 1)	(.33, .33, .33)
$\Rightarrow E + F$	(1, 2, 1)	(.4, .2, .4)
$\Rightarrow E - F + F$	(1, 2, 2)	(.5, .25, .25)
$\Rightarrow E + F - F + F$	(1, 4, 2)	(.57, .14, .29)
$\Rightarrow T + F - F + F$	(1, 4, 2)	(.57, .14, .29)
$\Rightarrow (E) + F - F + F$	(2, 4, 2)	(.4, .2, .4)
$\Rightarrow (E + F) + F - F + F$	(2, 8, 2)	(.44, .11, .44)
$\cdots$	$\cdots$	$\cdots$

Fig. 3. Dynamic Probability Distribution

the degree tuple of T remains $(1, 1)$. However, as the derivation continues, only when another T is seen as a leftmost variable, the degree of tuple of T will then be updated to $(1, 2)$ due to its indirect recursion, leaning the derivation of T toward its exit rule.

The more a production rule has contributed to self-loops while generating a test case, the *significantly* less probability the same rule will be selected in the future due to the double strategy. Note that our tabling strategy detects a self-loop by actually seeing a same variable during its own derivation, instead of by selecting a potential recursive rule; therefore, a non-recursive rule, no matter how many times it has been applied, its corresponding degree of recursion will not be doubled. Our tabling strategy, incorporated with the double adjusting strategy, provides an effective approach to solving the "penalty maze" challenges.

3.2   A Coverage Tree

Our approach ensures that the test case generator will generate a terminal string. Once a terminal string has been successfully generated, all the degree tuples in the global table will be reset to 1's for next test case generation. The next problem is that how to generate test cases in a balanced coverage distribution on given CFG structures.

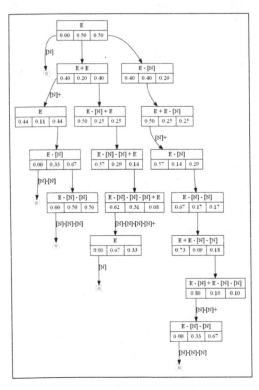

Fig. 4. A Coverage Tree on Example 1

We present a test generation coverage tree, a *coverage tree* in short, to show the distribution of generated test cases and how each of them are generated. Figure 4 shows a coverage tree, generating five different test cases based on the CFG in Example 1. Each node in a coverage tree contains an intermediate derived string, starting from a leftmost variable, and a *local probability tuple* for the leftmost variable. Each label along the transition from a parent node to a child node, if any, shows a leftmost terminal substring derived from the parent node, where the rest derived substring, beginning with a leftmost variable, is shown in the child node. Thus, each path from the root to a leaf node corresponds to a complete leftmost derivation generating a test case, where each transition corresponds to a derivation step, and a leaf node, represented by a little gray box, denotes the completion of a leftmost derivation. A coverage tree always starts with a root node containing the start variable of a CFG.

Not only does a coverage tree show the distribution of generated test cases and each detailed derivation step, but it also contains implicit balance control mechanism based on the local probability tuple on each tree node. Consider the coverage tree in Figure 4. When a new node is created with an intermediate string whose leftmost variable is E, its local probability tuple is calculated based on the *current* degree tuple of E stored in the global table. For example, when the root node E in Figure 4 was initially created, its local probability tuple is $(0.33, 0.33, 0.33)$, which tells that at this point, each of the three possible derivation branches has equal probability. The test generator will take one branch stochastically based on the local probability, to continue a test generation.

Once a derivation branch has been fully explored for test generation, its local probability tuple will be adjusted dynamically for future test generation. See the present status of the root node E in Figure 4, its local probability tuple has been updated to

$(0.00, 0.50, 0, 50)$; that is because the first branch, corresponding to the rule $E ::= [N]$, has been fully explored. Therefore, the probability of the first branch will be set to 0, and the remaining probabilities on the same node will be adjusting accordingly.

In Figure 4, even though there is only a single variable E, and all the local probability tuples are used to direct the derivation of E's, probability tuples in different nodes are quite different. That is mainly because each local probability tuple is like a snapshot of the degree tuple of E in the global table when the hosting node is created, while the degree tuple dynamically changes during a test generation.

Example 3. Consider the coverage tree with 10 generated test cases in Figure 5, given the following symbolic grammar:

$$ E ::= [N] \mid F - F \mid E + F \qquad F ::= [N] * [N] \mid [N] \qquad [N] ::= 1 .. 100 $$

Example 3 gives a better idea how complete branches will shift probabilities to incomplete branches, thus pushing future test generation to other unexplored parts. As a result, our test generation algorithm, based on a dynamic stochastic approach as well as a test generation coverage tree for implicit balance control, guarantees that every generated test case is *structurally different* as long as the given grammar is unambiguous. The coverage tree expands as more test cases are generated.

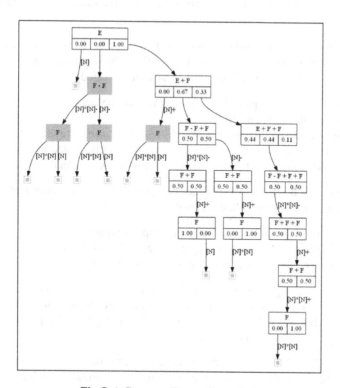

Fig. 5. A Coverage Tree on Example 3

Note that the starting position of each transition tells which production rule to apply. If a transition starts from a second probability number, it is implied applying the second corresponding production rule for derivation. We use a gray box to denote a *complete node*, all of whose branches have been completely explored.

3.3   Algorithms

This subsection presents a complete algorithm for our dynamic stochastic model, including the tabling strategy and a coverage tree construction. To support the tabling strategy, we use a **derivation stack**, which dynamically maintains an ancestor relation among the grammar variables to detect self-loops during derivation. Next, we outline the basic supported functionalities for a derivation stack, a global table supporting the tabling strategy, and a coverage tree node, respectively.

Definition 2. *Following the same convention as Definition 1, let E_1 and E_2 be two different occurrences of a variable E, we say E_1 is an* **ancestor** *of E_2 if there exists a leftmost derivation as follows:*

$$E_1 \stackrel{\mathcal{R}_i}{\Longrightarrow} \omega \stackrel{*}{\Longrightarrow} \alpha E_2 \beta,$$

where $\mathcal{R}_i$, the i-th production rule of E, is the cause of recursion. If there is no other leftmost occurrence of a variable E during $\omega \stackrel{*}{\Longrightarrow} \alpha E_2 \beta$, we say E_1 is **the least ancestor** *of E_2.*

The derivation stack contains entries in a form of pair, (E, i), which corresponds to a derivation step of a variable E by applying its i-th production rule. Note that the index i begins from 1. Following methods for the stack are provided:

- *void push(E, i)*: push a pair (E, i) into the derivation stack;
- *void pop()*: pop out a pair (E, i);
- *int leastAncestor(E)*: given a variable E, *leastAncestor(E)* returns an integer i; if $i \geq 1$, it means that there exists a pair entry (E, i) in the stack, that is, a self-loop detected; otherwise, $i = 0$, which tells no occurrences of E in the current stack.

The global table is used for storing and retrieving the dynamic degree tuples for each variable, which supports the following methods:

- *void reset()*: set for each variable a degree tuple with all 1's.
- *Degree-Tuple get(E)*: return the degree tuple of E in the table;
- *void doubleDegree(E, i)*: double the ith-degree entry of E.

A coverage tree is gradually constructed during a test generation, and further expanded as more test cases are generated. A coverage tree node, containing a derived substring, which always starts with a variable if non-empty, and a probability tuple. The tree supports the following methods:

- *Node newChild(i, str)*: create the i-th child node, set *str* as the child's derived substring, and return the child node; if *str* is an empty string, the child node will be automatically a compete node.

- *Node childAt(i)*: return the i-th child node if already exists; otherwise, *null* is returned.
- *void setProbFromDTuple(t)*: transform a degree tuple t into a probability tuple, and then set the probability tuple into the node;
- *void setZeroProbability(i)*: set the i-th probability 0, and adjust the rest of probabilities accordingly to make sure that the sum of all probabilities equals to 1, except that all probabilities have been set 0, that is, the node has been fully explored.
- *bool isComplete( )*: check whether the node has been fully explored or has an empty derived substring.
- *int chooseByProbability( )*: return a random index of production rule based on the probability distribution in the node.

Algorithm 1. Generating A Test Case

1: **Global:** symbolic grammar $G = (V, T, S, P)$, table TABLE , and derivation stack DS
2: **Input:** a dummy node $root$ for the coverage tree
3: **Output:** a test case
4: **function** TESTGENERATION($root$)
5:     DS ← an empty stack   ▷ initialize the derivation stack
6:     TABLE.$reset()$ ▷ initialize the global TABLE
7:     **return** DERIVATION($root$, 1, "S", "")
8: **end function**

Algorithm 1 shows a main procedure, TESTGENERATION, on how to generate a new test case, given a dummy root node for a coverage tree. We give a dummy root node outside the test case generation procedure, so that it can use a same coverage tree for generating as many test cases as users expect. The procedure starts with creating an empty derivation stack and initializing the global TABLE for simulating a new leftmost derivation, which is implemented in a recursive function, named DERIVATION.

Algorithm 2 shows how a leftmost derivation has been implemented by applying a dynamic stochastic model. Assuming that a string, *str*, has been derived from a parent node, *pNode*, in the coverage tree by applying i-th production rule of the leftmost variable in *pNode*, the function DERIVATION takes the four-tuple as an input, prepares to create a child node holding *str*, and then continue the derivation from the child node recursively until *str* is empty (lines 5-7).

If the derived string, *str*, starts with a variable E (line 8), we first checks whether there exists a least ancestor of E in the derivation stack; if that is the case (lines 10-12), we apply the *double strategy* to increase its associated degree of recursion. Secondly, we create the i-th child node *cNode*, if not existing yet, to hold *str* and a corresponding probability tuple based on its latest degree tuple of E (line 13-17). We then choose a production rule (e.g., a j-th rule $E ::= \alpha$) of E randomly based on the local probability distribution of *cNode*, and push a pair (E, j) into the derivation stack for future self-loop detection (line 18-19). To find out when the substring α will become completely terminal, we insert a special symbol $\updownarrow$ as an indicator right after the substring α in the derived string (lines 20-22). The pair (E, j) will be popped only after the derived substring α has become completely terminal (lines 29-31), that is, when the indicator " $\updownarrow$ " becomes the leftmost symbol of *str* (line 29). After a recursive call, in line 22,

---

Algorithm 2. DERIVATION: Core Algorithm

1: **Global:** symbolic grammar $G = (V, T, S, P)$; table TABLE, and derivation stack DS
2: **Input:** a coverage tree parent node, *pNode*; the index of a next rule to apply, i; a derived
   substring, *str*; and a label on the transition from the parent node to a child node, *label*
3: **Output:** a partial or complete test case
4: **function** DERIVATION(*pNode*, i, *str*, *label*)
5:     **if** (*str* is an empty string) **then**   ▷ end of a derivation
6:         $pNode.newChild(i, \text{""})$ ▷ a complete node
7:         **return** *label*
8:     **else if** (*str* is in form of $E\beta$) **then**   ▷ $E \in V, \beta \in (V \cup T)^*$
9:         int $k \leftarrow$ DS.*leastAncestor*(E)
10:        **if** ($k \geq 1$) **then**   ▷ self-loop detected
11:            TABLE.*doubleDegree*(E, k)   ▷ Double Strategy
12:        **end if**
13:        Node $cNode \leftarrow pNode.childAt(i)$
14:        **if** (*cNode* is *null*) **then**   ▷ expanding the tree
15:            $cNode \leftarrow pNode.newChild(i, E\beta)$
16:            $cNode.setProbFromDTuple(\text{TABLE}.get(E))$
17:        **end if**
18:        int $j \leftarrow cNode.chooseByProbability()$
19:        DS.*push*(E, j)   ▷ critical to track self-loop
20:        **Let** $E ::= \alpha$ be the j-th production rule of E
21:        $str \leftarrow \alpha + \text{"}\updownarrow\text{"} + \beta$ ▷ special symbol $\updownarrow$ is an indicator to pop (E, j)
22:        String $rLabel \leftarrow$ DERIVATION(*cNode*, j, *str*, "")
23:        **if** (*cNode*.*isComplete*()) **then**
24:            $pNode.setZeroProbability(j)$
25:        **end if**
26:        **return** *label* + *rLabel*   ▷ + is concatenation
27:     **else if** (*str* is in form of $a\beta$) **then**   ▷ $a \in T, \beta \in (V \cup T)^*$
28:        **return** DERIVATION(*pNode*, i, β, *label* + "a")
29:     **else if** (*str* is in form of "$\updownarrow$"β) **then**   ▷ $\beta \in (V \cup T)^*$, *str* leads with $\updownarrow$
30:        DS.*pop*()   ▷ paired with push operations
31:        **return** DERIVATION(*pNode*, i, β, *label*)
32:     **end if**
33: **end function**

---

processing further derivation from *cNode*, lines 23-25 check whether a child node has been completely explored, if so, the information will be propagated to its parent node by adjusting its local probability distribution. A generated test case is the concatenation of all labels from the dummy root node to a leaf node where *str* becomes empty.

3.4   Termination

Our dynamic stochastic approach *almost surely* [8] guarantees the termination of a single test case generation, as long as a *proper* symbolic CFG is given, where a symbolic CFG is said to be *proper*, if it has

- no inaccessible variables: $\forall E \in V, \exists \alpha, \beta \in (V \cup \Sigma)^* : S \overset{*}{\Rightarrow} \alpha E \beta$;
- no unproductive variables: $\forall E \in V, \exists \omega \in \Sigma^* : E \overset{*}{\Rightarrow} \omega$.

Let E be a variable in a given symbolic CFG, R be a recursive rule of E, and n be the number of times that R has been applied to cause its own recursions. Assuming that E has only two rules, R and a non-recursive one, we have $(1, 1)$ as the initial degree tuple of E; and $(2^n, 1)$ will be degree of tuple after n applications of R. Thus, the probability of choosing R in the next derivation of E, $P(R, n) = \frac{1}{2^n} / (1 + \frac{1}{2^n})$, and we have

$$\lim_{n \to \infty} P(R, n) = \lim_{n \to \infty} \frac{\frac{1}{2^n}}{1 + \frac{1}{2^n}} = \lim_{n \to \infty} \frac{1}{2^n} = 0$$

If a variable E contains more than two production rules, the probability drops even faster. On the other hand, the probability that a derivation will take terminal exits approximates to 1 infinitely as the derivation gets deeper and deeper. One say that an event happens **almost surely** if happens with probability one in probability theory [8].

4   Gena – A Java Implementation

In this section, we present *Gena*, a Java-based implementation of an automatic grammar-based test generator. Its system overview is illustrated in Figure 6.

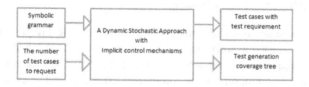

Fig. 6. Gena – a system overview

Gena, requiring zero annotation from users, takes inputs a symbolic grammar and how many test cases to request, and produces well-distributed test cases as well as a coverage tree showing the distribution of test cases along with their detailed leftmost derivation. Our test generator utilizes a novel dynamic stochastic model and local control mechanisms to maintain balanced distribution of test cases; and the distribution is demonstrated in a coverage tree.

Note that the graphical representation of a coverage tree, as seen in Figure 4 and Figure 5, is automatically produced by *Gena* along with the test generation.

4.1   Implicit Control Mechanisms

Even though *Gena* requires zero control from users, it implicitly enables various useful control mechanisms through the implementation of tabling, double strategy, and coverage tree maintenance, while in Geno [11], those control mechanisms are defined by users. We introduce some typical control mechanisms as follows:

Depth Control: Due to our double strategy, Gena always puts high penalty on the rules causing recursion, which brings about a low probability distribution to the recursive rules. As a result, when generating multiple test cases, Gena tends to generate test cases in an order, not strictly, from short to long ones; and in terms of the coverage tree, it will be explored from shallow towards deep as more test generations are requested.

Recursion Control: Our tabling strategy, utilizing a derivation stack, detects causes of recursion, and then applies the double strategy to put exponentially increased penalty on the recursive rules. Based on probability theory, it will almost surely push derivation to stay away from those recursive rules eventually.

Balance Control: Incorporated with the double strategy for recursion control and complete nodes detection for local probability adjustment, Gena does not only avoid non-terminating recursion, but also work along the derivation in an evenly distributed way. It is extremely important that if a grammar has multiple recursive rules, each recursive rule under a same variable is explored with similar probabilities. Also, due to complete nodes detection, Gena guarantees that every generated test case is **structurally different** in terms of grammar structures, as long as the grammar is unambiguous.

Construction Control: With such a coverage tree, it is easy to extend Gena with customized constraint controls. For example, users could specify the lengths of expected test cases, or specify the quantitative data constraints; both specifications can be easily supported by incorporating constraints as part of coverage nodes, so that the test generator will only explore those tree parts where constraints are satisfied.

4.2   Structural Test Case Requirements

A test case generated automatically often comes with a set of test requirements, so that when the test case is used in software testing, we know what features of a system have been tested. Test requirements are also critical to the areas of test cases minimization, selection and prioritization, serving as comparison criteria [22]. For example, in automated model-based test case generation where test cases are typically generated based on a data flow model, definition-use pairs of variables [6] in a program are popularly identified as test requirements serving as effective reduction criteria.

Gena generates a test case as well as an associated set of structured test requirements. It breaks each complete derivation path, from the root node to a leaf one in a coverage tree, into small basic components which represent structural patterns of the generated test case. For example, consider the Figure 4. The rightmost path in the coverage tree corresponds to a generated expression:

$$[N] + [N] - [N] + [N] - [N] - [N],$$

where each $[N]$ is automatically substituted with a random integer from its domain during the generation. Its associated set of test requirements, produced by *Gena*, is $\{E3E2E1, E3E2E3E1, E1\}$. Each test requirement is actually a structural input pattern which consists of a sequence of production rule indices, denoting a leftmost derivation sub-sequence starting from a leftmost variable E until a terminal symbol is seen at the leftmost while deriving E.

For example, $E3E2E1$ represents a segment of derivations starting from the root, where the leftmost system is the variable E. The derivation moves on by first applying the third production rule of E, followed by applying a second rule of E and a first rule of E in order, until the leftmost symbol in the derived string becomes a terminal

Table 1. Among 1000 generated expressions

Operators	Total Frequencies
+	2149
−	2162
*	4452
/	4472
()	1823
$[N]$: a random integer	14235

Table 2. Among 2000 generated program code

Keywords	Total Frequencies
:=	3353
print	3554
if-then	2116
if-then-else	1693
while	2099
repeat	1829

$[N]$ (shown in a label "$[N]$+"). The other two terms $E3E2E3E1$ and $E1$ are similar, representing the segments of derivations following that of $E3E2E1$. Figure 7, using a standard derivation tree for the generated expression, shows that each requirement actually corresponds to a lefty tree showing nested structural information.

We believe that each test case may contain some structural patterns which could be possibly linked to potential failures of software under test. These structural test requirements could serve as testing coverage measurement criteria for test case minimization, selection and prioritization, especially in data-intensive or data-critical applications.

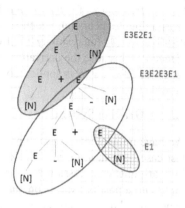

Fig. 7. Lefty Subtrees

5 Experimental Results

We have carried out some experiments to measure how balanced the test cases generated by *Gena* over grammar structures, and tried some related applications.

5.1 Balance Results

Table 1 shows a statistic report among the first 1000 generated arithmetic expressions by *Gena*, given a symbolic grammar in Example 2. By comparing the total frequencies among operators, we measure how balanced in overall among test case generation. (1) The total frequencies of the operators + and − are close, which indicates the balanced distribution between two recursive rules under the same variable E; similar reasons apply on the frequency observation between * and /. (2) The total frequency of +, an operator at the production rule of E, is about half lower than the total frequency of *, an operator at the level of F. This observation makes sense because every single + and − involved in the derivation introduces an extra F variable into a derived string, and every F may possibly derive multiple * or / operators. Similar reasons for the observation that the frequency sum of () and $[N]$ is almost double than the sum of * and /. (3) The total frequency of () is much lower than $[N]$ due to the reasons that the indirect recursion caused by $T ::= (E)$; and the majority of T derivation takes the terminal rule $T ::= [N]$ due to unbalanced probability distribution caused by our double strategy.

We further tested *Gena* on a symbolic grammar for a *pascal*-like program code. The grammar, containing 34 production rules and 13 variables, is partially shown below:

$$P ::= K. \qquad K ::= \text{begin } C \text{ end} \qquad C ::= S; C \mid S$$
$$S ::= I := E \mid \text{if } (B) \text{ then } S \mid \text{if } (B) \text{ then } S \text{ else } S \mid$$
$$K \mid \text{while } (B) \text{ do } S \mid \text{repeat } C \text{ until } (B) \mid \text{print } E$$
$$\cdots$$

Table 2 shows a statistic report among the first 2000 generated programs by *Gena*. Here we compare the total frequencies of keywords to measure how balanced in overall among generated cases in a more complicated grammar setting, where all those listed keywords are distributed in the production rules of S. (1) The observation, that the frequencies of keywords $:=$ and *print* are similar, justifies the even probability distribution among terminal rules if multiple ones exist. (2) The frequencies of *if-then* and *while* are less than that of *print* because a single recursion of S is involved in both statements. (3) The frequency of *if-then-else* is lower than that of *if-then* because *if-then-else* contains a double recursion, which results in double penalties in the dynamic probability distribution. (4) Interestingly, the frequency of *repeat* is between those of *if-then* and *if-then-else* because the derivation of C in the *repeat* statement may result in a single recursion (if $C ::= S$ is applied), or a double recursion (if $C ::= S; C$ is applied).

5.2 A Grading System

We have implemented an automatic grading system for Java programs, based on our test case generator, *Gena*. Consider a Java programming assignment which takes an infix arithmetic expression as an input string, performs stack operations to convert the input into a postfix expression, and finally returns a number by calculating the postfix expression. We use a correct program to calculate the expected results for each generated expression, and compare the result with the one returned from each submission.

Table 3 shows grading results on 14 Java program submissions, by running 1000 different arithmetic expressions generated by *Gena*. The second column shows the ratios

Table 3. Grading Results

	ratio	failure-inducing patterns	Possible Causes
1	14%	{-+, //, /*, --, */}	right-associativity
2	78%	{()}	parenthesis not properly handled
3	100%	{}	
4	2%	{+, -, /, *, ()}	not working at all
5	9%	{*/, /-, *-, *+, /*, //, /+, -+, --}	right-associativity; operator precedence ignorance
6	6%	{*/, /-, *-, *+, /*, //, /+, +/, --, -/}	right-associativity; operator precedence ignorance
7	53%	{*/}	$[N] * [N]/[N]$
8	100%	{}	
9	68%	{-*-, -*+, -/-, -/+}	partial operator precedence ignorance
10	100%	{}	
11	14%	{*/, //, -+, --, /*}	right-associativity
12	54%	{/-, *-, *+, /+}	operator precedence ignorance
13	4%	{/, *, -, +}	operators not supported
14	10%	{*/, /*, //, -+, (), --}	right-associativity and parenthesis problem

of correctness for each submission. For example, the first submission performs correctly on 14% of the 1000 test cases. The third column demonstrates common failure-inducing patterns for each submission; and the last column gives typical causes on processing arithmetic expressions.

The *Gena*-based grading system frees users from constructing test cases manually and worrying about their coverage. The grading system is able to find out significant number of failing test cases on those Java programs, which lays important foundation for further program fault localization. The failure-inducing patterns, extracted from those test requirements associated with failing test cases, contain clear clues for understanding root causes of software testing failure. Due to space limitation, we will have to leave details of our *Gena*-based fault localization in our future work.

6   Conclusions

We presented an automatic grammar-based test generation algorithm requiring zero control inputs. Our algorithm utilizes a novel dynamic stochastic model where each grammar variable is associated with a probability tuple, which is dynamically adjusted via a tabling strategy. Our dynamic stochastic approach almost surely guarantees the termination of test case generation, as long as a *proper* CFG is given. We further presented a test generation coverage tree which does not only illustrate how each test case is generated and their distribution, more importantly, it provides various implicit control mechanisms for maintaining balanced coverage. Our grammar-based test generation guarantees that every generated test case is *structurally different*.

We have presented, *Gena*, a Java-based system based on our grammar-based test generation algorithm. *Gena*, requiring zero annotation from users, takes input a symbolic grammar and how many test cases to request, and produces well-distributed test cases as well as a graphical test case coverage tree showing the distribution of test cases along with their respective derivations. Experimental results justify the effectiveness of our test generation approach and show the balanced distribution of test cases.

Grammar-based test generation can be thought of a branch of model-based test generation since a grammar actually describes the input data model. Model-based testing [2,16,17] has been extensively researched and become increasingly popular in practical software testing. Model-based test generation typically derives test cases from a given system model (e.g. UML chart, or a control flow graph), representing the desired system behaviors. The major issues involved in grammar-based test generations, such as depth control, recursion control, and balance control, etc., occur as well in model-based test generation when dealing with a complicated control flow graph with loops and branches structures. Hence, our test generation algorithm based on a dynamic stochastic model can also be valuable in implementing other model-based test generations.

References

1. Bagheri, E., Ensan, F., Gasevic, D.: Grammar-based test generation for software product line feature models. In: Proceedings of the 2012 Conference of the Centre for Advanced Studies on Collaborative Research (CASCON 2012). IBM (2012)

2. Belli, F., Endo, A.T., Linschulte, M., da Silva Simo, A.: Model-based testing of web service compositions. In: IEEE 6th International Symposium on Service Oriented System Engineering, pp. 181–192 (2011)

3. Godefroid, P., Kiezun, A., Levin, M.Y.: Grammar-based whitebox fuzzing. ACM Sigplan Notices 43(6), 206–215 (2008)

4. Guo, H.F., Gupta, G.: Simplifying dynamic programming via mode-directed tabling. Software Practice & Experience 38(1), 75–94 (2008)

5. Hanford, K.: Automatic generation of test cases. IBM Systems Journal 9(4), 242–257 (1970)

6. Harrold, M.J., Koltit, P.C.: A compiler-based data flow testing system. In: Pacific Northwest Quality Assurance, pp. 311–323 (1992)

7. Hoffman, D.M., Ly-Gagnon, D., Strooper, P., Wang, H.Y.: Grammar-based test generation with yougen. Software Practice and Experience 41(4), 427–447 (2011)

8. Jacod, J., Protter, P.: Probability Essentials, p. 37. Springer (2003)

9. Kosindrdecha, N., Daengdej, J.: A test case generation process and technique. Journal of Software Engineering 4(4), 265–287 (2010)

10. Lämmel, R.: Grammar testing. In: Hussmann, H. (ed.) FASE 2001. LNCS, vol. 2029, pp. 201–216. Springer, Heidelberg (2001)

11. Lämmel, R., Schulte, W.: Controllable combinatorial coverage in grammar-based testing. In: Uyar, M.Ü., Duale, A.Y., Fecko, M.A. (eds.) TestCom 2006. LNCS, vol. 3964, pp. 19–38. Springer, Heidelberg (2006)

12. Majumdar, R., Xu, R.G.: Directed test generation using symbolic grammars. In: Proceedings of the 22nd IEEE/ACM International Conference on Automated Software Engineering, pp. 134–143. ACM (2007)

13. Maurer, P.M.: Generating test data with enhanced context-free grammars. IEEE Software 7(4), 50–55 (1990)

14. Maurer, P.M.: The design and implementation of a grammar-based data generator. Softw. Practice and Experience 22(3), 223–244 (1992)

15. McKeeman, W.: Differential testing for software. Digital Technical Journal of Digital Equipment Corporation 10(1), 100–107 (1998)

16. Offutt, J., Liu, S., Abdurazik, A., Ammann, P.: Generating test data from state based specifications. The Journal of Software Testing, Verification and Reliability 13, 25–53 (2003)

17. Pretschner, A., Prenninger, W., Wagner, S., Kühnel, C., Baumgartner, M., Sostawa, B., Zölch, R., Stauner, T.: One evaluation of model-based testing and its automation. In: Proceedings of the 27th International Conference on Software Engineering, pp. 392–401. ACM (2005)

18. Raymond, P., Nicollin, X., Halbwachs, N., Weber, D.: Automatic testing of reactive systems. In: 32nd IEEE Real-Time Systems Symposium, pp. 200–209. IEEE Computer Society (1998)

19. Sirer, E.G., Bershad, B.N.: Using production grammars in software testing. In: Proceedings of the 2nd Conference on Domain-Specific Languages, pp. 1–13. ACM (1999)

20. Tai, K.C., Lei, Y.: A test generation strategy for pairwise testing. IEEE Transactions on Software Engineering 28(1), 109–111 (2002)

21. Warren, D.S.: Memoing for logic programs. Communications of the ACM 35(3), 93–111 (1992)

22. Yoo, S., Harman, M.: Regression testing minimization, selection and prioritization: a survey. Software Testing, Verification and Reliability 22(2), 67–120 (2012)

Adaptive Homing and Distinguishing Experiments for Nondeterministic Finite State Machines

Natalia Kushik[1,2], Khaled El-Fakih[3], and Nina Yevtushenko[1]

[1] Tomsk State University, Tomsk, Russia
ngkushik@gmail.com, ninayevtushenko@yahoo.com
[2] Telecom SudParis, Evry, France
[3] American University of Sharjah, Sharjah, UAE
kelfakih@aus.edu

Abstract. Adaptive experiments are well defined in the context of finite state machine (FSM) based analysis, in particular, in FSM based testing where homing and distinguishing experiments with FSMs are used in test derivation. In this paper, we define and propose algorithms for deriving adaptive homing and distinguishing experiments for non-initialized nondeterministic finite state machines (NFSM). For NFSMs, the construction of adaptive experiments is rather complex as the partition over produced outputs does not define a partition over the set of states but rather a collection of intersecting subsets, and thus, the refinement of such subsets is more difficult than the refinement of a partition. Given a complete non-initialized observable NFSM, we establish necessary and sufficient conditions for having adaptive homing and distinguishing experiments and evaluate the upper bound on the height of these experiments. Simple application examples demonstrating a proposed approach are provided.

Keywords: Nondeterministic finite state machine, conformance testing, adaptive homing and distinguishing experiments.

1   Introduction

Many methods are known for the development of experiments and conformance tests based on the specification given in the form of a finite state machine (FSM) [see, for example, 1-7]. In FSM-based testing, given a machine or an implementation under test (IUT) about which we lack some information, experiments are performed with the machine to deduce some lacked information. An experiment consists of applying input sequences to the machine, observing corresponding output responses and drawing the conclusion about the machine under test. An experiment is *preset* if input sequences are known before starting the experiment and an experiment is *adaptive* if at each step of the experiment the next input is selected based on previously observed outputs [3][8]. Well-known types of experiments include distinguishing and homing experiments which are used when deriving FSM based tests with the guaranteed fault coverage and those experiments are elaborated for different types of FSMs. An FSM is *initialized* if it has one initial state, otherwise, *weakly-initialized* or *non-initialized*.

H. Yenigün, C. Yilmaz, and A. Ulrich (Eds.): ICTSS 2013, LNCS 8254, pp. 33–48, 2013.

An FSM is *observable* if at each state the machine has at most one transition under a given input/output pair. Given an FSM, assuming that the initial state is unknown, a *distinguishing experiment* determines the initial state of the FSM, i.e., a state of the FSM before the experiment and such an experiment is widely used when checking the correspondence between transitions of an IUT and those of the specification FSM. A *homing experiment* identifies the final state reached at the end of the experiment and it is used when deriving a checking sequence for non-initialized FSMs [9,10].

Ongoing research on preset and adaptive homing experiments for deterministic FSMs started since the seminal paper on "gedanken experiments" by Moore [8]. For information and surveys on FSM-based experiments and some related algorithms, a reader may refer to [4, 5, 11]; in particular, in [3, 5] a reader can find methods for deriving preset and adaptive distinguishing experiments for deterministic FSMs with corresponding evaluation of the length of these experiments. Preset homing experiments are considered in [3, 4, 12, 13]. Derivation of minimal length preset homing sequences can be done using the homing tree method introduced by Gill [3] and reported in details in Kohavi [4]. Any deterministic complete reduced FSM with n states has been shown to have a homing sequence of length up to $n(n - 1)/2$ and Hibbard [14] showed that deterministic machines require adaptive homing sequences with length of the same order. There is also some work devoted to the derivation of a synchronizing sequence that takes the FSM from any initial state to the same state independent of produced output sequences. As in this case, outputs are not important, most researchers derive such sequences for corresponding automata where only input actions are considered. A related detailed survey is given by Sandberg in [15]. Parallel algorithms for related problems are surveyed by Ravikumar [see, for example, 16].

In this paper, we consider homing and distinguishing experiments with nondeterministic FSMs, as nowadays, analysis and testing of nondeterministic systems are capturing a lot of attention. Preset distinguishing and homing experiments for nondeterministic FSMs are considered in [17, 18]. In particular, Spitsyna et al. [17] presented the method for deriving a sequence that separates two initialized nondeterministic FSMs. An input sequence is a *separating sequence* of two FSMs if the sets of output sequences produced by the NFSMs to the input sequence do not intersect [19]. Kushik et al. [18] showed that differently from deterministic FSMs a homing sequence does not necessarily exist for a complete reduced nondeterministic FSM and proposed an algorithm for deriving a preset homing sequence for a given nondeterministic FSM when such a sequence exists. A tight lower bound on a shortest preset homing sequence is shown to be of the order 2^{n^2} where n is the number of states of the nondeterministic FSM. Moreover, it has been shown [20] that there exists a special class of FSMs with n states and $(n - 1)$ inputs, for which a shortest homing sequence has the length $2^{n-1} - 1$. i.e., its length is exponential not only with respect to the number of FSM states but also the number of FSM transitions. Zhang and Cheung studied related problems when deriving transfer and distinguishing trees for observable nondeterministic FSMs with probabilistic and weighted transitions [21].

Adaptive experiments with nondeterministic FSMs are considered in [22-25]. In [23], Petrenko and Yevtushenko introduced the notion of a test case for describing an adaptive experiment as an initialized observable FSM with an acyclic transition diagram such that at each non-deadlock state only one input is defined with all possible outputs. A representation of a test case using the same formal model is widely used for transition systems such as LTS, input/output automata etc. [see, for example 26]. Such definition of a test case allows defining distinguishing/checking/homing test cases based on the properties of the intersection of a transition system under experiment and a given test case. In [22-25] it is shown how a distinguishing test case can be derived for two states of NFSMs when such a distinguishing test case exists. In particular, Alur et al. [22] show that the length of a shortest adaptive distinguishing test case that distinguishes two states of an observable nondeterministic FSMs with n states is at most $n(n - 1)/2$. Petrenko and Yevtushenko [25] consider a set of adaptive test cases which have three parts: a preamble for reaching an appropriate state, a traversal input/output sequence and a state identifier. In this case, the length of an identifier can be optimized when distinguishing not two but several states with the same distinguishing test case. In addition, a checking sequence derived for a non-initialized FSM [9, 10] also can be adaptive but in this case, an adaptive homing experiment should be performed before applying such a sequence. Gromov et al. [27] and El-Fakih et al. [28] presented adaptive experiments for two timed nondeterministic observable FSMs.

In this paper, we consider adaptive homing and distinguishing experiments for non-initialized nondeterministic finite state machines. Similar to many other papers described above, an adaptive experiment is represented by a test case that is an initialized observable FSM with the acyclic flow diagram where only one input is defined at each intermediate state. Lee and Yannakakis [5] proposed an approach for deriving an adaptive distinguishing sequence of a deterministic FSM that is based on refining a partition of the set of states based on different outputs. In this paper, we deal with nondeterministic FSMs and unlike [5], the output partition defines not a partition of the set of states but rather a set system, which is a collection of intersecting subsets, for which it is difficult to define a corresponding refinement. For this reason, in this paper, necessary and sufficient conditions for having adaptive homing/distinguishing test cases are established based on extending the notion of k-r-distinguishability of two states [29] to subsets of states and an algorithm for deriving a homing/distinguishing adaptive test case with minimal length is proposed. The upper bound on the length of homing/distinguishing experiments is determined and an example illustrating that the upper bound seems to be tight for the length of distinguishing test cases is presented.

This paper is organized as follows. Section 2 includes preliminaries. Homing and distinguishing test cases with related properties are introduced in Section 3. Section 4 contains an approach for deriving a homing/distinguishing test case with corresponding statements about the complexity. Section 5 concludes the paper.

2   Preliminaries

In this paper, we consider experiments with weakly initialized Finite State Machines. A *weakly initialized Finite State Machine* (FSM) S is a 5-tuple (S, I, O, h_S, S'), where S is a finite set of states with the set $S' \subseteq S$ of initial states; I and O are finite nonempty disjoint sets of inputs and outputs, respectively; $h_S \subseteq S \times I \times O \times S$ is a *transition relation*, where a 4-tuple $(s, i, o, s') \in h_S$ is a *transition*. If $|S'| = 1$ then the FSM S is an *initialized* FSM. An input $i \in I$ is a *defined* input at state s of S if there exists a transition $(s, i, o, s') \in h_S$ for some $s' \in S$ and $o \in O$.

An FSM $S = (S, I, O, h_S, S')$ is *complete* if for each pair $(s, i) \in S \times I$ there exists $(o, s') \in O \times S$ such that $(s, i, o, s') \in h_S$. FSM S is *nondeterministic* if for some pair $(s, i) \in S \times I$, there exist at least two transitions $(s, i, o_1, s_1), (s, i, o_2, s_2) \in h_S$, such that $o_1 \neq o_2$ or $s_1 \neq s_2$. FSM S is *observable* if for each two transitions (s, i, o, s_1), $(s, i, o, s_2) \in h_S$ it holds that $s_1 = s_2$. FSM S is *single-input* if at each state there is at most one defined input at the state, i.e., for each two transitions $(s, i_1, o_1, s_1), (s, i_2, o_2, s_2) \in h_S$ it holds that $i_1 = i_2$, and FSM S is *output-complete* if for each pair $(s, i) \in S \times I$ such that the input i is defined at state s, there exists a transition from s with i for every output in O [21, 25].

A *trace* of S at state s is a sequence of input/output pairs of sequential transitions starting from state s. Let $Tr(S/s)$ denote the set of all traces of S at state s including the empty trace and let $Tr(S/S')$ denote the union of $Tr(S/s)$ over all states $s \in S'$. As usual, for state s and a sequence $\gamma \in (IO)^*$ of input-output pairs, $next\_state_S(s, \gamma)$ denotes the set of all states that are reached from s by γ. If γ is not a trace at state s then the set $next\_state_S(s, \gamma)$ is empty; otherwise, each state of the set $next\_state_S(s, \gamma)$ is a γ-*successor* of state s. For an observable FSM S, $|next\_state_S(s, \gamma)| \leq 1$ for any string $\gamma \in (IO)^*$. Given a nonempty subset S' of states of the FSM S and $\gamma \in (IO)^*$, the set $next\_state_S(S', \gamma)$ is the union of the sets $next\_state_S(s, \gamma)$ over all $s \in S'$ and this set is a γ-*successor* of the set S'. An FSM S is *acyclic* if the set $Tr(S/S')$ is finite, i.e., the FSM transition diagram has no cycles.

To characterize the common behavior of two weakly initialized machines, we extend the operation of the intersection of initialized FSMs as follows. Given two complete FSMs S and P with the sets S' and P' of initial states, the *intersection* S $\cap$ P is the connected FSM Q such that states of Q are pairs (b, c) of sets of states of FSMs S and P, the initial state of Q is (S', P'), and h_Q is the smallest set derived using the following rule: Given state (b, c), $b \subseteq S$ and $c \subseteq P$, and an input/output pair i/o, the FSM Q has a transition $((b, c), i, o, (b', c'))$ if there exist states $s \in b$ and $p \in c$ with an outgoing transition labeled by the pair i/o, and b' and c' are i/o–successors of subsets b and c. By definition, the FSM S $\cap$ P is observable even for non-observable FSMs S and P.

As an example of the FSM intersection, consider FSMs P (Fig. 1) and S (Fig. 2). FSM P is an initialized FSM while S has three initial states marked in bold. The intersection S $\cap$ P is shown in Fig. 3. As usual, the intersection of two weakly initialized FSMs describes the common behavior of component FSMs, and in addition, it also provides some information about the structure of their transition sets. For example, a state of the intersection provides information about which states of the corresponding machines are reachable from the initial states under a corresponding trace. In fact, the following proposition holds.

Proposition 1. Given FSMs S and P with the sets S' and P' of initial states and state (b, c) of the intersection S $\cap$ P that is reachable from the initial state under a trace γ, the set b is the γ-successor of the set S' while the set c is the γ-successor of the set P'.

As in this paper we consider adaptive experiments with nondeterministic FSMs, in order to identify a state of a weakly initialized FSM before or after the experiment, a finite input sequence is applied to an FSM under experiment where the next input (except of the first one) of the sequence is determined based on the output of the FSM produced to the previous input. Formally, such an experiment can be described using a single-input output-complete FSM with an acyclic transition graph and similar to [23, 25] we refer to such an FSM as a *test case*.

Given an input alphabet I and an output alphabet O, a *test case TC(I, O)* is an initially connected single-input output-complete observable initialized FSM $P = (P, I, O, h_P, p_0)$ with acyclic transition graph. By definition, if $|I| > 1$ then a test case is a partial FSM.

A test case P over alphabets $I = \{a, b\}$ and $O = \{0, 1\}$ is shown in Fig. 1.

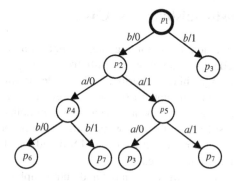

Fig. 1. A test case P over alphabets $I = \{a, b\}$ and $O = \{0, 1\}$

A test case $TC(I, O)$ over alphabets I and O defines an adaptive experiment with any FSM S over the same alphabets. As an example, consider the test case P in Fig. 1. An adaptive experiment with an FSM S over alphabets $I = \{a, b\}$ and $O = \{0, 1\}$ is conducted using P as follows. At the first step the input b is applied to S as this input is the only input defined at the initial state of P. If the output of the FSM S to this input is 1, then the experiment is over, since we reach the deadlock state p_3 of P. If the FSM S produces the output 0 to input b then the experiment is not over, since the test case P enters the intermediate state p_2 where the single input a is defined. As this input does not take the test case to a deadlock state, the next input which is also a is applied. If the output to a is 0 then the next input is b; otherwise, the next input is a. For this example, the length of a longest trace of the test case is three, i.e., at most three inputs are applied during this adaptive experiment.

In general, given a test case P, the *length* of the test case P is determined as the length of the longest trace from the initial state to a deadlock state of P and it specifies the length of the longest input sequence that can be applied to an FSM S during the experiment that is also often called the *height* of the adaptive experiment. As usual, for testing, one is interested in deriving a test case (experiment) with minimal length (height).

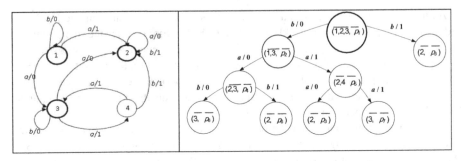

Fig. 2. FSM S with three initial states

Fig. 3. The intersection **S** ∩ **P**

3   Homing and Distinguishing Test Cases

In this section, we define the notions of homing and distinguishing test cases that can be used in the context of adaptive testing of non-initialized nondeterministic observable FSMs. A homing (distinguishing) experiment allows determining the unknown current (initial) state of the machine under experiment. Hereafter, if not stated otherwise, we consider an FSM under experiment to be a weakly initialized complete nondeterministic observable FSM and in the following sections we propose a method for deriving homing and distinguishing test cases for an FSM and we also determine the upper bound on minimal length of a test case.

Given a complete observable FSM S over input and output alphabets I and O, let S' be the set of initial states of FSM S. A test case P is a *homing* test case for FSM S if for each deadlock state (b, c) of the intersection S ∩ P, the set b is a singleton.

A test case P is a *distinguishing test case* for FSM $S = (S, I, O, h_S, S')$ if **(1)** for each deadlock state (b, c) of the intersection S ∩ P subset b is a singleton, and **(2)** for each transition $((b, c), i, o, (b', c'))$ of the intersection S ∩ P the subset b does not have two different states which have the same i/o–successor, i.e.,

$$\forall s_1, s_2 \in b\,((s_1, i, o, s') \in h_S\ \&\ (s_2, i, o, s') \in h_S \Rightarrow s_1 = s_2).$$

If there exists a homing (distinguishing) test case for the FSM then the set is S' is a *homing (distinguishing)* set and the test case P is a *homing (distinguishing) test case* for the set S' or the test case P *homes (distinguishes)* states of the set S'.

According to the above definitions, the following statement holds.

Proposition 2. Given a weakly initialized observable FSM S, each distinguishing test case for S is also a homing test case. However, the converse is not necessarily true.

Example. As an example of homing and distinguishing test cases, consider a weakly initialized FSM S in Fig. 2 and the test case P in Fig. 1. By direct inspection, one can assure that each deadlock state of the intersection S ∩ P (Fig. 3) is labeled by a pair of singletons and each two different states of any subset b such that (b, c) labels an intermediate state of the intersection do not have the same i/o-successor. Thus, the set $\{1, 2, 3\}$ is not only a homing but also a distinguishing set and the test case in Fig. 1 is a homing test case and a distinguishing test case for FSM S. For example, if the output 1 is produced to the input b at the initial state of the FSM S then the FSM reaches state 2 after experiment and we certainly know that the initial state before the experiment was 2. However, we later show that the FSM S has a shorter homing test case.

A homing (distinguishing) test case is used for representing a homing (distinguishing) adaptive experiment with a nondeterministic FSM. An adaptive homing (distinguishing) experiment has two steps. At the first step a finite input sequence is applied to an FSM under experiment where the next input (except of the first one) significantly depends on the output of the FSM produced to the previous input. At the next step, after observing a produced output sequence, the conclusion is drawn about a state of the FSM after (before) the experiment and such a state has to be unique for the homing (distinguishing) experiment. If all the traces of a test case have the same input projection, then the test case defines a preset input sequence and a corresponding adaptive experiment becomes a preset experiment. In the same way, when having a homing or separating sequence for a given FSM a corresponding test case can be derived by augmenting this sequence with all possible output sequences.

Propositions 3 and 3′ state necessary and sufficient conditions for a test case to be a homing and/or a distinguishing test case. As the proofs are almost the same, we only prove Proposition 3.

Proposition 3. Given a weakly initialized observable FSM S $= (S, I, O, h_S, S')$, a test case P is a homing test case for S if and only if every trace of P from the initial state to a deadlock state that is a trace at two different initial states of the set S' takes the FSM S from these initial states to the same state.

Proof. $\Rightarrow$ Let P be a homing test case for FSM S $= (S, I, O, h_S, S')$. Suppose that $\exists\, s_1$, $s_2 \in S'\ \exists\, \alpha \in I^*\ \exists\, \beta \in O^*\ (\beta \in out(s_1, \alpha) \cap out(s_2, \alpha))$ and the trace α/β takes the FSM P from the initial to a deadlock state (b, c). The deadlock state (b, c) of the intersection S $\cap$ P contains α/β-successors of states s_1, s_2 (Proposition 1), i.e., α/β-successors of these states coincide.

$\Leftarrow$ Consider a trace α/β that takes the FSM P from the initial state to a deadlock state p. Let s_1, $s_2 \in S'$ be initial states where the trace α/β can be executed and state s' is an α/β-successor of states s_1 and s_2 (since FSM S is observable). By the intersection construction, the FSM S $\cap$ P has a deadlock state $(\overline{s'}, \overline{p})$ where both items are singletons. $\qquad\square$

Proposition 3′. Given a weakly initialized observable FSM S $= (S, I, O, h_S, S')$, a test case P is a distinguishing test case for FSM S if and only if every trace from the initial state to a deadlock state of P is a trace at only one initial state of the set S'.

According to the above Propositions 3 and 3′, given a weakly initialized FSM S there exists an adaptive homing (distinguishing) experiment for the FSM S if and only if the FSM S has a homing (distinguishing) test case.

Here we note that the above propositions establish one-to-one correspondence between homing/distinguishing test cases and adaptive homing/distinguishing experiments only for observable FSMs; for non-observable FSMs, the definition of a distinguishing test case that corresponds to an adaptive distinguishing experiment should be modified. If a given FSM S is observable then according to the following proposition there is a simple way to check whether there exists a corresponding homing experiment.

Proposition 4. Given a weakly initialized observable FSM S with the set S' of initial states, there exists a homing test case for the set S' of S if each subset $\{s_i, s_j\}$ of two states of S is a homing set.

Proof. We prove this proposition by construction. Let for each two different states s_i and s_j, $s_i \neq s_j$, of S there exist a homing test case $P_{i,j}$. Without loss of generality we assume that $S' = \{s_1, .., s_m\}$. Consider a homing test case $P_{1,2}$ for the set $\{s_1, s_2\}$ and derive a test case $P_{1,2,3}$ by adding the state s_3 into the set labeling the initial state of $P_{1,2}$ and obtain $P_{1,2,3}$ that includes all the transitions of $P_{1,2}$. Subsets of states that label deadlock states of S $\cap$ $P_{1,2,3}$ are not necessarily singletons but they contain at most two states, since FSM is observable. Each pair of different states of S is homing, thus, for each deadlock state $(\overline{s_i, s_j}, \overline{p})$ of S $\cap$ $P_{1,2,3}$ we concatenate the initial test case $P_{1,2,3}$ with the corresponding test case $P_{i,j}$. Proceeding in the same way we derive test case $P_{1,2,...,m}$. By construction, the derived test case is homing for the FSM S. □

Corollary. Given a weakly initialized observable FSM S with the set S of initial states, there exists a homing test case for FSM S if and only if there exists a homing test case for each two different states s_i and s_j of S.

Proposition 4'. Given a nondeterministic observable FSM $S = (S, I, O, h_S, S)$, if for each two different states s_i and s_j of S there exists a homing test case, then there exists a homing test case for FSM S with length $O(n^3)$.

Proof. Each pair of states of an observable FSM can be homed by a sequence of inputs of length at most C_n^2 that covers in the worst case all pairs of different FSM states. The number of states to be appended at each step of the procedure used in the proof of Proposition 4 equals $(n - 1)$. Thus, the maximal length of the trace in the test case $P_{1,2,...,n}$ has length at most of the order n^3. □

In other words, if each pair of states of an observable FSM S with n states can be adaptively homed then there exists a homing test case for the set S of FSM states and the length of this test case is of the order n^3. The proof of Proposition 4 proposes a procedure for deriving such a homing test case when the conditions of the proposition hold.

Example. As an example of applying the construction stated in Proposition 4, consider the FSM S with the set of initial states $S' = \{1, 2, 3\}$ in Fig. 4 below. FSM S is complete and observable. We derive a homing test case for this FSM by deriving a test case $P_{i,j}$ for each pair (i, j), $i \neq j$, of the FSM states and then derive a test case for the set S'. The set of transitions of P_{12} equals $\{(\overline{1,2}, i_1, o_1, \overline{1}), (\overline{1,2}, i_1, o_2, \overline{2})\}$; the set of transitions of P_{13} equals $\{(\overline{1,3}, i_3, o_1, \overline{1}), (\overline{1,3}, i_3, o_2, \overline{3})\}$; and the set of P_{23} transitions equals $\{(\overline{2,3}, i_2, o_1, \overline{2}), (\overline{2,3}, i_2, o_2, \overline{3})\}$. We add state 3 to the pair $\overline{1,2}$, include transitions of P_{12} into P_{123} and concatenate the obtained test case with appropriate test cases for subsets of two states. More precisely, this is done as follows. First, we consider input i_1 at state 3 for which a single output o_1 can be obtained, thus, the corresponding transitions at state $\overline{1,2,3}$ of P_{123} are $\{(\overline{1,2,3}, i_1, o_1, \overline{1,2}), (\overline{1,2,3}, i_1,$ $o_2, \overline{2})\}$. At state $\overline{1,2}$, we append corresponding transitions from the test case P_{12} and obtain the set of transitions for P_{123}: $\{(\overline{1,2,3}, i_1, o_1, \overline{1,2}), (\overline{1,2,3}, i_1, o_2, \overline{2}), (\overline{1,2}, i_1, o_1,$ $\overline{1}), (\overline{1,2}, i_1, o_2, \overline{2})\}$. The length of such adaptive homing test case equals two. However, if we selected an input i_3 when deriving the set of transitions of P_{12} a corresponding adaptive homing test case for the set $S' = \{1, 2, 3\}$ would have length 1.

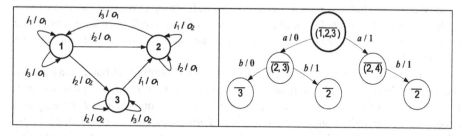

Fig. 4. FSM S   **Fig. 5.** Homing test case P for the FSM in Fig. 2

Thus, we observe that when deriving an adaptive test case using the above procedure the length of a returned test case significantly depends on the enumeration of states of the set S' as well as on selected inputs at each step and therefore, does not guarantee the derivation of a homing test case of minimal length. Moreover, such a procedure does not guarantee the homing test derivation when there exists a pair of two different states of the FSM that is not homing. In the following we propose an algorithm that returns a homing test case with minimal length for a given FSM.

We also note that a proposition similar to Proposition 4 does not hold for a distinguishing test case. That is, given an observable FSM where each pair of two different states has a distinguishing test case, there is no guarantee that there exists a distinguishing test case for FSM S.

In order to derive a homing/distinguishing test case with minimal length, we introduce the notion of k-homing/k-distinguishing sets not only for pairs but for arbitrary subsets of states.

A subset g of states of an observable FSM S is 0-*homing* if g is a singleton. Let all $(k-1)$-homing sets, $k > 0$, be already defined. The subset g is a k-*homing set* if **(1)** g is a $(k-1)$-*homing*, or **(2)** there exists an input $i \in I$, such that for each $o \in O$, the set of i/o-successors of states of g is either empty or is a $(k-1)$-homing set.

In order to define a distinguishing test case for an observable FSM, the previous definition can be used, where the notion of k-homing is replaced by k-distinguishing and a subset g of an FSM S $= (S, I, O, h_S, S')$ is called a k-distinguishing set if **(1)** applies, i.e., g is a $(k-1)$-distinguishing set, and for **(2)** as previously, there exists an input $i \in I$, such that for each $o \in O$, the set of i/o-successors of states of g is either empty or is a $(k-1)$-distinguishing set, and in addition, the i/o-successors of two different states of g do not coincide.

Proposition 5. Given a weakly initialized observable complete FSM S with the set S' of the initial states, the set S' is k-homing/k-distinguishing, $k > 0$, if and only if there exists a homing/distinguishing adaptive experiment of height k for the weakly initialized FSM $S = (S, I, O, h_S, S')$. If S' is k-homing/k-distinguishing, $k > 0$, but is not $(k-1)$-homing/$(k-1)$-distinguishing then k is the minimal height of a corresponding adaptive experiment.

Proof. We provide the proof of the Proposition for the case of a homing experiment as for the distinguishing test case the proof is almost the same.

$\Rightarrow$ We use the induction on k. Let $k = 1$. By definition, there exists an input $i \in I$, such that for each $o \in O$, the set of i/o-successors of states of S' is either empty or is a 0-homing set (a singleton), i.e., there exists an adaptive experiment of length 1 for the $S = (S, I, O, h_S, S')$.

Let the statement hold for all $k \leq K$ and S' is not a K-homing set but S' is a $(K + 1)$-homing set. In this case, by definition, there exists an input $i \in I$, such that for each $o \in O$, the set of i/o-successors of states of S' is either empty or is a K-homing and according to the induction assumption, each if i/o-successors can be homed by an adaptive experiment of length at most K. Thus, S' can be homed by an adaptive experiment of length at most $(K + 1)$.

$\Leftarrow$ Suppose there exists a test case P of a height $k > 1$. By definition, the states of P that have transitions to deadlock states are 1-homing. Thus, the states of P that are connected to these states are 2-homing, etc. The states of P that are connected to the deadlock states via a sequence of length k are k-homing.   □

Based on Propositions 3, 3' and 5, the following proposition holds.

Proposition 6. Given a set S', $|S'| > 1$, of states of an observable FSM S, the set S' is homing/distinguishing if and only if S' is k-homing/k-distinguishing for some $k > 0$.

4   Deriving Homing and Distinguishing Test Cases

Based on the notion of k-homing sets, Procedure 1 given below can be used for deriving a homing/distinguishing test case for a homing/distinguishing set S' of states of a given observable FSM S. If the set S' is not homing/distinguishing then the states of the set S' cannot be homed/distinguished by an adaptive experiment. The main idea of the procedure below is to iteratively derive subsets of states that are homed/distinguished by adaptive applying an input sequence of the length $j \in \{1, 2, ..., k\}$. The set of corresponding subsets we hereafter denote as Q_j. If for some j the Q_j is empty and the subset $S' \notin \bigcup_{k=1}^{j-1} Q_j$ then a fixed point is reached and a homing experiment for the FSM S does not exist. The states of a test case under construction are labeled by subsets of S states. We describe a procedure for a homing test case, since for a distinguishing test case the procedure is almost the same.

Procedure 1: **Deriving a homing test case for a subset S' of states of an FSM S**

Input: Complete observable nondeterministic weakly initialized FSM $S = (S, I, O, h_S, S')$, $|S'| > 1$

Output: A homing test case P with minimal length for the subset S' of FSM S or a message "there is no adaptive homing experiment for the subset S'"

Step-1: $j := 0$

Derive the set Q_j of all singletons $\{s\}$ of the set S of FSM S

Step-2: Derive the set Q_{j+1} that contains each $(j+1)$-homing set of states of the FSM S that is not j-homing as follows:

> **For** each subset A of states of FSM S that is not in the set $\bigcup_{k=1}^{j} Q_k$
>
> If there exists an input $i \in I$, such that for each $o \in O$, the i/o-successor of A is either empty or is an item of the set $\bigcup_{k=1}^{j} Q_k$ then
>
> > Include the set A into Q_{j+1},
> > Derive a set Tr_A that contains each 4-tuple (A, i, o, A') where A' is a non-empty i/o-successor of the set A;
>
> **End For**

If the set of subsets Q_{j+1} is empty then **Return** the message "there is no adaptive homing experiment for the subset S'".

If Q_{j+1} does not contain the set S' as an item then

> $j := j + 1$ and **Go-to Step-2**;

Step-3: Derive a homing test case P with the set P of states as follows:

> States of P are subsets of states of the FSM S and the initial state of P is the set S'; i.e., include S' into P;
> Mark the initial state of P labeled with the set S' as a "*non-visited*" state in P;
> **While** there is a '*non-visited*' state A in P
> > **For** each 4-tuple (A, i, o, A') in Tr_A
> > > Add to the test case P as an outgoing transition of the state A the transition (A, i, o, A');
> > > If $A' \notin P$
> > > > Then add A' to P and if A' is not a singleton, mark the added state with A' as a '*non-visited*' state.
> >
> > **EndFor**
>
> **EndWhile**

If P is not output-complete then

> **For** each intermediate state p of P where a single input i is defined
> > If there is no transition (p, i, o, p') for some $o \in O$ then
> > add a transition (p, i, o, p') where p' is any state of P;
>
> **EndFor**

Return P.

END Procedure 1.   □

Theorem 1. FSM P returned by Procedure 1 is a homing test case with minimal length for observable FSM S if and only if the set S' is a homing set.

Proof. $\Leftarrow$ The set S' is homing if this set is k-homing for some k. For this reason, when deriving at Step 2 $(j + 1)$-homing sets an input $i \in I$ with the desired features always exists. By construction, FSM P returned by Procedure 1 is acyclic and at each intermediate state only one input is defined with all possible outputs, i.e., P is a test case. At Step 3, each trace $\alpha/\beta \in Tr_S(s)$, $s \in S'$, that takes P to a deadlock state $\overline{s_k}$, takes FSM S from any state of the set S' where this trace can be executed to state s_k of S. Thus, the test case P is a homing test case for FSM S.

$\Rightarrow$ Let FSM P returned by Procedure 1 be a test case for FSM S of the height l. By definition, in this case the set S' is a l-homing set, i.e. S' is a homing set.

According to Procedure 1, if S' is an l-homing but it is not $(l-1)$-homing, then the procedure returns a test case (Step-3) of length l (the set Q_l, Step-2) that is a test case of minimal length (Proposition 5). $\qquad\Box$

Example. Consider the FSM S in Fig. 2. At Step-1, $Q_0 = \{\{1\}, \{2\}, \{3\}, \{4\}\}$. Then, at Step-2, the set $Q_1 = \{\{1, 4\}, \{2, 3\}, \{3, 4\}, \{2, 4\}, \{2, 3, 4\}\}$ as by direct inspection, one can assure that the sets $\{1, 4\}$, $\{2, 3\}$, $\{3, 4\}$, $\{2, 4\}$ and $\{2, 3, 4\}$ are 1-homing with the corresponding sets of transitions $Tr_{\{1,4\}} = \{(\overline{1,4}, b, 0, \overline{1}), (\overline{1,4},$ $b, 1, \overline{2})\}$, $Tr_{\{2,3\}} = \{(\overline{2,3}, b, 1, \overline{2}), (\overline{2,3}, b, 0, \overline{3})\}$, $Tr_{\{3,4\}} = \{(\overline{3,4}, b, 1, \overline{2}), (\overline{3,4},$ $b, 0, \overline{3})\}$, $Tr_{\{2,4\}} = \{(\overline{2,4}, b, 1, \overline{2})\}$ and $Tr_{\{2,3,4\}} = \{(\overline{2,3,4}, b, 1, \overline{2}), (\overline{2,3,4}, b, 0,$ $\overline{3})\}$. As the set Q_1 does not contain the set $S'=\{1,2,3\}$ of the FSM S, we go back to Step-2, and then observe that the subset $\{1, 2, 3\}$ is 2-homing with the corresponding set of transitions $Tr_{\{1,2,3\}} = \{(\overline{1,2,3}, a, 1, \overline{2,4}), (\overline{1,2,3}, a, 0, \overline{2,3})\}$. The corresponding homing test case derived by Procedure 1 for the FSM S is presented in Fig. 5. Therefore, the distinguishing test case in Fig. 1 is not a shortest homing test case for the FSM S, as there exists a homing test case for S of length 2. A distinguishing test case returned by Procedure 1 for the FSM S is a test case in Fig. 1.

We now add some comments how Procedure-1 can be optimized. Step-2 of Procedure 1 can be performed by an exhaustive search of all subsets and of all possible inputs with all possible output responses. To optimize this search at each step the subsets with minimal cardinality can be checked first. The reason is that if a subset A is not j-homing, thus each superset of A is not j-homing too. Therefore, when checking all subsets of S states that are not in the set $\bigcup_{k=1}^{j} Q_k$ an optimal solution can be to start with pairs of states, then turn to triples, 4-tuples, etc.

For the same reason, at Step-2 only maximal subsets A can be included into the set Q_{j+1}, i.e., if A contains a subset $B \subset A$ that is $(j + 1)$-homing then B is not included into the set Q_{j+1}. In this case, given a 4-tuple (A, i, o, B) where B is an i/o successor of A, the set B not necessary is in the set $\bigcup\limits_{k=1}^{j} Q_k$; for this reason, we add to the set Tr_A a

transition (A, i, o, A') where $A' \in \bigcup\limits_{k=1}^{j} Q_k$ and $B \subset A'$.

The lower bound on the height of a shortest adaptive homing/distinguishing experiment significantly depends on the number of initial states of the observable FSM under experiment.

Theorem 2. Given a complete observable FSM S with n states and m initial states, the

lower bound on the length of a shortest homing/distinguishing test case is $\sum\limits_{i=2}^{m} C_n^i$.

Proof. If an FSM S is observable, then the corresponding lower bound on the length of adaptive experiment is proven for homing experiments in [18]. Since the length of adaptive distinguishing experiment is bounded by the same number of different subsets of states with cardinality $(m - 1)$, $(m - 2)$, ..., 2, thus, the lower bound is

exactly $\sum\limits_{i=2}^{m} C_n^i$.   □

Additional research is needed in order to check whether the bound $2^n - n - 1$ is tight for distinguishing test cases and for homing test cases for machines that have non-homing pairs of states. For distinguishing test cases, the upper bound seems to be exponential. Below we show that there exists an observable FSM with four states, all of which are initial states, such that the longest trace in the distinguishing test case traverses all subsets with at least two states, i.e., its length equals $11 = 2^4 - 4 - 1$.

Consider an FSM S with the flow table in Table 1 and with the set $\{1, 2, 3, 4\}$ of initial states. The FSM S has 11 inputs and four outputs. The inputs are defined x_{123}, x_{124}, x_{134}, ..., x_{12} to demonstrate which subset is traversed when applying this input. An input x_{123} defines x_{123}/0-successor of the subset $\{1, 2, 3, 4\}$ in the distinguishing test case, this successor coincides with the index of the input, i.e. it is the set $\{1, 2, 3\}$.

Table 1. Flow Table of the FSM S

$x\backslash s$	1	2	3	4
x_{123}	1/0, 2, 3	2/0, 2, 4	3/0, 3, 4	4/2, 3, 4
x_{124}	1/0, 1	2/0, 1	4/0	3/0; 4/1
x_{134}	1/0, 1	3/0	2/0; 3/1	4/0, 1
x_{234}	2/0; ½	1/0; 2/1	3/0, 2	4/0, 1
x_{34}	1/1, 2, 4; 2/5	3/2; 2/4, 5	3/0, 1, 4	4/0, 1, 5; 2/2
x_{24}	1/0, 1, 2	3/0; 2/1	2/0; 3/2	4/0; 3/1
x_{14}	2/0; 1/1	1/0	3/0, 1	4/0, 1
x_{13}	1/0, 1	2/0, 1, 2	4/1; 3/0	3/0, 1; 4/2
x_{23}	2/0, 3; 1/1	1/0; 2/1, 2	3/0, 2 3	3/1; 4/2, 3; 1/0
x_{12}	3/0; 1/1	2/0, 1	1/0; 3/2	4/0, 1, 2
x_{sep}	1/0, 2	2/1, 3	2/1; ½	1/0; 2/1

The two last state subsets that are traversed by a longest trace in the distinguishing test case are $\{2, 3\}$ and $\{1, 2\}$. The set $\{1, 2\}$ is an $x_{12}/0$-successor of the subset $\{2, 3\}$ in the test case. The last input x_{sep} separates states 1 and 2 of the FSM S and takes the test case to different 0-distinguishing sets. We further illustrate how this distinguishing test case can be derived for the FSM S using a Procedure similar to Procedure 1.

We first derive all 0-distinguishing sets that are singletons $\{1\}$, $\{2\}$, $\{3\}$, $\{4\}$. according to the Procedure similar to Procedure 1, we then derive a set Q_1, and one can assure that there is a single 1-distinguishing set for the FSM S. This is the set $\{1, 2\}$ that is included into the set Q_1. The set Q_2 contains a single set $\{2, 3\}$, the set $\{1, 3\}$ is a single 3-distinguishing set that is included into the set Q_3, etc. Thus, one can iteratively derive all Q_1, Q_2, Q_3, ..., sets, till reaching the set Q_{11} that contains the set $\{1, 2, 3, 4\}$ of initial states. A shortest distinguishing experiment traverses all non-empty subsets of the set $\{1, 2, 3, 4\}$ and thus, has the length 11. The longest trace of the experiment covers the chain of sets $\{1, 2, 3, 4\}$, $\{1, 2, 3\}$, $\{1, 2, 4\}$, $\{1, 3, 4\}$, $\{2, 3, 4\}$, $\{3, 4\}$, $\{2, 4\}$, $\{1, 4\}$, $\{1, 3\}$, $\{2, 3\}$, and $\{1, 2\}$, respectively. All other traces do not allow to uniquely determine a state of the FSM before the experiment and thus, since a sequence of all subsets of some set is traversed by a trace of a test case of minimal length it seems that the exponential upper bound can be reached for adaptive experiments with observable nondeterministic FSMs.

5   Conclusion

Given a non-initialized complete nondeterministic observable FSM, a method for deriving adaptive homing/distinguishing experiments is proposed. Adaptive experiments are represented as special nondeterministic observable machines, called test cases, and necessary and sufficient conditions for having adaptive homing/distinguishing test cases with minimal length for observable nondeterministic FSMs are presented. The lower bound on the length of shortest homing/distinguishing test cases is evaluated. Possible extensions to the proposed work include extending the proposed method for non-observable FSMs and adapting the work to partial nondeterministic FSMs by extending related work in [23] and to timed nondeterministic FSMs based on the work presented in [28]. Also it would be interesting to determine the tight lower bound on the length of shortest homing/distinguishing test cases.

References

1. Bochmann, G.V., Petrenko, A.: Protocol testing: review of methods and relevance for software testing. In: Proc. of International Symposium on Software Testing and Analysis, Seattle, pp. 109–123 (1994)
2. Dorofeeva, R., El-Fakih, K., Maag, S., Cavalli, A.R., Yevtushenko, N.: FSM-based conformance testing methods: a survey annotated with experimental evaluation. Information and Software Technology 52, 1286–1297 (2010)
3. Gill, A.: State-identification experiments in finite automata. Information and Control, 132–154 (1961)

4. Kohavi, Z.: Switching and Finite Automata Theory. McGraw-Hill, New York (1978)
5. Lee, D., Yannakakis, M.: Testing finite-state machines: state identification and verification. IEEE Trans. on Computers 43(3), 306–320 (1994)
6. Lee, D., Yannakakis, M.: Principles and methods of testing finite state machines-a survey. Proceedings of the IEEE 84(8), 1090–1123 (1996)
7. Simao, A., Petrenko, A., Maldonado, J.C.: Comparing finite state machine test. IET Software 3(2), 91–105 (2009)
8. Moore, E.F.: Gedanken-experiments on sequential machines. In: Automata Studies (Annals of Mathematical Studies no.1), pp. 129–153. Princeton University Press (1956)
9. Hennie, F.C.: Fault detecting experiments for sequential circuits. In: Proc. of 5th Annual Symposium on Switching Circuit Theory and Logical Design, pp. 95–110. Princeton (1964)
10. Petrenko, A., Simao, A., Yevtushenko, N.: Generating Checking Sequences for Nondeterministic Finite State Machines. In: Proc. of ICST 2012, pp. 310–319 (2012)
11. Mathur, A.: Foundations of Software Testing. Addison Wesley (2008)
12. Agibalov, G., Oranov, A.: Lectures on Automata Theory. Tomsk State University Publishers (1984) (in Russian)
13. Ginsburg, S.: On the length of the smallest uniform experiment which distinguishes the terminal states of a machine. Journal of the ACM 5(3), 266–280 (1958)
14. Hibbard, T.N.: Lest upper bounds on minimal terminal state experiments of two classes of sequential machines. Journal of the ACM 8(4), 601–612 (1961)
15. Sandberg, S.: Homing and Synchronization Sequences. In: Broy, M., Jonsson, B., Katoen, J.-P., Leucker, M., Pretschner, A. (eds.) Model-Based Testing of Reactive Systems. LNCS, vol. 3472, pp. 5–33. Springer, Heidelberg (2005)
16. Ravikumar, B.: Parallel algorithms for finite automata problems. In: Rolim, J.D.P. (ed.) IPPS-WS 1998 and SPDP-WS 1998. LNCS, vol. 1388, p. 373. Springer, Heidelberg (1998)
17. Spitsyna, N., El-Fakih, K., Yevtushenko, N.: Studying the separability relation between finite state machines. Software Testing, Verification and Reliability 17(4), 227–241 (2007)
18. Kushik, N., El-Fakih, K., Yevtushenko, N.: Preset and Adaptive Homing Experiments for Nondeterministic Finite State Machines. In: Bouchou-Markhoff, B., Caron, P., Champarnaud, J.-M., Maurel, D. (eds.) CIAA 2011. LNCS, vol. 6807, pp. 215–224. Springer, Heidelberg (2011)
19. Starke, P.: Abstract Automata. American Elsevier (1972)
20. Kushik, N., Yevtushenko, N.: On the Length of Homing Sequences for Nondeterministic Finite State Machines. In: Konstantinidis, S. (ed.) CIAA 2013. LNCS, vol. 7982, pp. 220–231. Springer, Heidelberg (2013)
21. Zhang, F., Cheung, T.: Optimal Transfer Trees and Distinguishing Trees for Testing Observable Nondeterministic Finite-State Machines. IEEE Transactions on Software Engineering 19(1), 1–14 (2003)
22. Alur, R., Courcoubetis, C., Yannakakis, M.: Distinguishing tests for nondeterministic and probabilistic machines. In: Proc. of the 27th ACM Symposium on Theory of Computing, pp. 363–372 (1995)
23. Petrenko, A., Yevtushenko, N.: Conformance Tests as Checking Experiments for Partial Nondeterministic FSM. In: Grieskamp, W., Weise, C. (eds.) FATES 2005. LNCS, vol. 3997, pp. 118–133. Springer, Heidelberg (2006)
24. Gromov, M.L., Evtushenko, N.V., Kolomeets, A.V.: On the Synthesis of Adaptive Tests for Nondeterministic Finite State Machines. Progr. and Comp. Software 34(6), 322–329 (2008)

25. Petrenko, A., Yevtushenko, N.: Adaptive Testing of Deterministic Implementations Specified by Nondeterministic FSMs. In: Wolff, B., Zaïdi, F. (eds.) ICTSS 2011. LNCS, vol. 7019, pp. 162–178. Springer, Heidelberg (2011)
26. Tretmans, J.: Model-Based Testing with Labelled Transition Systems: There is nothing More Practical than a Good Theory. Slides from the lecture at TAROT Summer School (2010), http://tarot2010.ist.tugraz.at/
27. Gromov, M., El-Fakih, K., Shabaldina, N., Yevtushenko, N.: Distinguing nondeterministic timed finite state machines. In: Lee, D., Lopes, A., Poetzsch-Heffter, A. (eds.) FMOODS/FORTE 2009. LNCS, vol. 5522, pp. 137–151. Springer, Heidelberg (2009)
28. El-Fakih, K., Gromov, M., Shabaldina, N., Yevtushenko, N.: Distinguishing experiments for timed nondeterministic finite state machines. Acta Cybernetica (to appear)
29. Petrenko, A., Yevtushenko, N., Bochmann, G.V.: Testing Deterministic Implementations from their Nondeterministic Specifications. In: Proc. of the IFIP Ninth International Workshop on Testing of Communicating Systems, pp. 125–140 (1996)

Exhaustive Model-Based Equivalence Class Testing

Wen-ling Huang and Jan Peleska*

Department of Mathematics and Computer Science
University of Bremen, Germany
{huang, jp}@informatik.uni-bremen.de
http://informatik.uni-bremen.de/agbs

Abstract. In this article we present a formal justification of model-based equivalence partition testing applied to black box tests of reactive systems with large input data types (floating point types or large integer ranges) and small internal and output data ranges. Systems of this variant typically perform control tasks, where a small number of control commands is issued, depending on analogue or discretised input data (e.g., sensors) and internal control states. We prove that a finite collection of input traces whose elements have been selected from a specific set of input equivalence classes suffices to prove a conformance relation between specification model and system under test. This proof holds under certain practically feasible fault hypotheses. The proof is performed on systems whose operational semantics may be encoded by means of Kripke Structures. It is shown how the semantics of SysML state machines can be represented in Kripke Structures, so that the theorem induces an equivalence class testing strategy for this formalism in a straightforward way. To our best knowledge, this is the first formal justification of the well-known equivalence class testing principle for systems with potentially infinite input data types.

Keywords: Model-based testing, Equivalence class partition testing, Kripke Structures, UML/SysML state machines.

1 Introduction

Motivation. Equivalence class testing is a well-known heuristic approach to testing software or systems whose state spaces, inputs and/or outputs have value ranges of a cardinality inhibiting exhaustive enumeration of all possible values within a test suite. The heuristic suggests to create *equivalence class partitions* structuring the input or output domain into disjoint subsets for which *"the behavior of a component or system is assumed to be the same, based on the specification"* [11, p. 228]. If this assumption is justified it suffices to test "just a few" values from each class, instead of exploring the behavior of the system under

---

* The authors' research is funded by the EU FP7 COMPASS project under grant agreement no.287829.

H. Yenigün, C. Yilmaz, and A. Ulrich (Eds.): ICTSS 2013, LNCS 8254, pp. 49–64, 2013.

test (SUT) for each possible value. In order to investigate that the SUT respects the boundaries between different equivalence class partitions *boundary values* are selected for each class, so that equivalence class and boundary value testing are typically applied in combination. As an alternative to deriving equivalence class partitions from the specification, the structure of the SUT or its model can be analyzed: classes are then defined as sets of data leading to the same execution paths [13, B.19].

For testing safety-critical systems the justification of the equivalence class partitions selected is a major challenge. It has to be reasoned why the behaviour of the SUT can really be expected to be equivalent for all values of a class, and why the number of representatives selected from each class for the test suite is adequate. While being quite explicit about the code coverage to be achieved when testing safety-critical systems, standards like [13,10,7] do not provide any well-defined acceptance conditions for equivalence class partitions to be sufficient.

Main Contributions. In this paper we present rules for generating input equivalence class partitions, whose justification is given by the fact that they lead to an *exhaustive* test suite: under certain hypotheses the generated classes and the test data selected from them *prove* conformance between a specification model and its implementation, if the latter passes all tests of this suite. The algorithm is applicable in a model-based testing context, provided that the behavioural semantics of the modelling formalism can be expressed using Kripke Structures. The equivalence class partitioning strategy is elaborated and proven to be exhaustive on Kripke Structures. As an example of a concrete formalism, we illustrate how the strategy applies to SysML state machine models [8]. To our best knowledge, this is the first formal justification of the well-known equivalence class testing principle for systems with potentially infinite input data types (see Section 6 for a discussion of related work).

Example 1. The following example describes a typical system of the class covered by our input equivalence class partition testing strategy. It will be used throughout the paper for illustrating the different concepts and results described in this paper. The example is taken – in simplified form, in order to comply with the space limitations of this publication – from the specification of the European Train Control System ETCS and describes the required behaviour of the *ceiling speed monitoring* which protects trains from overspeeding, as specified in [15, 3.13.10.3]. The interface is shown in Figure 1. The I/O variables have the following meaning.

Interface	Description
V_{est}	Current speed estimation [km/h]
V_{MRSP}	Applicable speed restriction [km/h] (MRSP = Most Restrictive Speed Profile)
W	Warning to train engine driver at driver machine interface (DMI) (1 = displayed, 0 = not displayed)
EB	Emergency brake (1 = active, 0 = inactive)

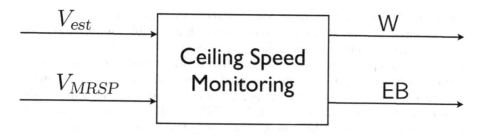

Fig. 1. Interface of the ETCS ceiling speed monitoring function (simplified)

The behaviour of the ceiling speed monitoring function is specified by the UML (or SysML) state machine shown in Figure 2. The function gives a warning to the train engine driver if the currently applicable speed limit V_{MRSP} is not observed, but the actual estimated speed V_{est} does not exceed the limit too far. If the upper threshold for the warning status is violated (this limit is specified by guard conditions g_{ebi_1} or g_{ebi_2}), the emergency brake is activated. After such an *emergency brake intervention* has occurred, the brakes are only released after the train has come to a standstill. While the specification model requires guard condition $g_{ebi_1} \vee g_{ebi_2}$, we assume for the purpose of this example that the implementation has an erroneous guard implementation $\overline{g}_{ebi_1} \vee g_{ebi_2}$. □

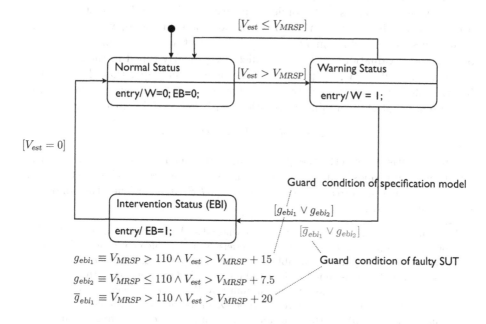

Fig. 2. State machine of the ETCS ceiling speed monitoring function

Overview. In Section 2 the basic concepts about *Reactive Kripke Structures* – a specialisation of general Kripke Structures which is suitable for application in a reactive systems context – are introduced. In Section 3 it is shown how input equivalence class partitionings for Reactive Kripke Structures are constructed. In Section 4, two test hypotheses are presented, whose validity allows us to prove that our equivalence class partitioning and test data selection principle leads to an exhaustive test suite (Theorem 1). While this theorem states that I/O equivalence can be established using a finite input alphabet only (though the input data types may be infinite), it does not state whether the number of input traces needed is finite. In Section 5 we therefore show by means of this theorem, that Reactive Kripke Structures associated with input equivalence partitionings can be abstracted to deterministic finite state machines. Then the well-known W-Method can be applied to establish a *finite* exhaustive test suite proving I/O equivalence between specification model and SUT. Section 6 discusses related work, and we conclude with a discussion of the results obtained and a conjecture about an extension of the main theorem's validity in Section 7.

2   Reactive Kripke Structures

2.1   Notation and Definitions

Let $K = (S, S_0, R, L, AP)$ be a Kripke Structure (KS) with state space S, initial states $S_0 \subseteq S$, transition relation $R \subseteq S \times S$ and labelling function $L : S \to \mathbb{P}(AP)$, where AP is a set of atomic propositions. We specialise on state spaces over variable valuations: let V be a set of variable symbols for variables $v \in V$ with values in some domain $D = \bigcup_{v \in V} D_v$. The state space S of K is the set of all variable valuations $s : V \to D$ which are properly typed in the sense that $s(v) \in D_v$ for all $v \in V$.[1] It is required throughout the paper that the labelling function shall be consistent with, and determined by these variable valuations, in the sense that AP contains propositions with free variable in V and[2]

$$\forall s \in S : L(s) = \{p \in AP \mid s(p)\}$$

Since s satisfies exactly the propositions contained in $L(s)$, it satisfies the negation of all propositions in the complement, that is, $\forall p \in AP - L(s) : \neg s(p)$.

K is called a *Reactive Kripke Structure (RKS)* if it satisfies the following additional properties.

---

[1] The state space is always total in the sense that all $s : V \to D$ are elements of S. This allows us to assume that specification models K and implementations K' operate on the same state space S, possibly with differing subsets of *reachable* states. The types D_v are always assumed to be maximal, like $\mathbb{R}$, `float` or `int` with a given bit width. Therefore we can assume that a faulty SUT may produce erroneous variable values $s'(v)$, but will never violate the type D_v of its interface variables v.

[2] We use notation $s(p)$ for the Boolean expression p, where every free variable $v \in var(p)$ has been replaced by its current value $s(v)$ in state s. For example, $s(x < y)$ is true if and only if $s(x) < s(y)$ holds. Observe that this can be alternatively written as $s \models p$, or $p[s(v)/v \mid v \in V]$.

1. V can be partitioned into disjoint sets $V = I \cup M \cup O$ called input variables, (internal) model variables, and output variables, respectively.[3]
2. The state space can be partitioned into states from where only input changing transitions are possible, and those from where only internal and output changing transitions are possible. The former states are called *quiescent*, the latter *transient*.

$$\exists S_Q, S_T \subseteq S : S = S_Q \cup S_T \wedge S_Q \cap S_T = \varnothing \wedge$$
$$\forall (s, s') \in R : s \in S_Q \Rightarrow s'|_{M \cup O} = s|_{M \cup O} \wedge$$
$$\forall (s, s') \in R : s \in S_T \Rightarrow s'|_I = s|_I$$

3. All initial states have the same internal and output variable valuations, and all possible inputs are allowed in initial states.[4]

$$\exists \bar{s} : M \cup O \to D : S_0 = \{\{x \mapsto c\} \oplus \bar{s} \mid c \in D_I\}$$

4. The input vector may change without any restrictions.

$$\forall s \in S_Q, s' \in S : s'_{M \cup O} = s|_{M \cup O} \Rightarrow (s, s') \in R$$

5. Transient states are always followed by quiescent ones. Internal and output state changes are deterministic in the sense that they only depend on the current state valuation.

$$\exists T : S_T \to S_Q : \forall s \in S_T, s' \in S : (s, s') \in R \Rightarrow s' = T(s)$$

Function T can be extended to the complete state space by defining $\forall s \in S_Q : T(s) = s$.
6. The transition relation is total on S.[5]

The rules above imply that the transition relation of an RKS can be written as $R = \{(s, s') \mid s \in S_Q \wedge s'|_{M \cup O} = s|_{M \cup O}\} \cup \{(s, T(s)) \mid s \in S_T\}$. While transient states always have quiescent ones as post-states (this is stated in rule 5), quiescent states may have both transient and quiescent ones as post-states.

Example 2. Consider the UML/SysML state machine described in Example 1. Its behavioural semantics can be described by an RKS $K = (S, S_0, R, L, AP)$ with variable symbols from $V = I \cup M \cup O$, $I = \{V_{est}, V_{MRSP}\}$, $M = \{\ell\}$, and $O = \{W, EB\}$. Sets I and O contain the interface variable symbols with domains $D_{V_{est}} = D_{V_{MRSP}} = [0, 350] \subseteq \mathbb{R}$ (maximum speed of ETCS trains under consideration is 350km/h). Symbol ℓ ("location") has values in $D_\ell = \{NS, WS, IS\}$ and its valuation signifies the current control state 'Normal Status', 'Warning Status', or 'Intervention Status', respectively. The output symbols have values

---

[3] Frequently we use input vectors c to the system, where c is an element of $D_I = D_{x_1} \times \cdots \times D_{x_{|I|}}$, and $x_1, \ldots, x_{|I|}$ are the input variables. Changing the valuation of all input variables of a state s_0 to $c = (c_1, \ldots, c_{|I|})$ is written as $s_1 = s_0 \oplus \{x \mapsto c\}$. State s_1 coincides with s_0 for all but the the the input variables, and $s_1(x_i) = c_i, i = 1, \ldots, |I|$.
[4] Observe that initial states may be quiescent or transient.
[5] Though not all states in S may be reachable from S_0.

in $D_W = D_{EB} = \mathbb{B} = \{0,1\}$. The state space S contains all valuations of these symbols, $S = V \to D$, with $D = [0,350] \cup D_\ell$. Setting $D_I = [0,350] \times [0,350]$, the initial states are elements of $S_0 = \{s_0 \in S \mid \exists(c_0,c_1) \in D_I : s_0 = \{V_{est} \mapsto c_0, V_{MRSP} \mapsto c_1, \ell \mapsto \mathsf{NS}, \mathsf{W} \mapsto 0, \mathsf{EB} \mapsto 0\}\}$. Fixing the variable order to vector $(V_{est}, V_{MRSP}, \ell, \mathsf{W}, \mathsf{EB})$, we will from now on describe states s by their value vector $(s(V_{est}), s(V_{MRSP}), s(\ell), s(\mathsf{W}), s(\mathsf{EB}))$, so that an initial state s_0 is written as $(c_0, c_1, \mathsf{NS}, 0, 0)$. The transition relation R is specified by the predicate (see [3] about how to express transition relations as first order predicates)

$$R((V_{est}, V_{MRSP}, \ell, \mathsf{W}, \mathsf{EB}), (V'_{est}, V'_{MRSP}, \ell', \mathsf{W}', \mathsf{EB}')) \equiv$$
$$\bigvee_{i=0}^{7} \varphi_i((V_{est}, V_{MRSP}, \ell, \mathsf{W}, \mathsf{EB}), (V'_{est}, V'_{MRSP}, \ell', \mathsf{W}', \mathsf{EB}'))$$
$$\varphi_0 \equiv (\ell = \mathsf{NS} \wedge V_{est} \leq V_{MRSP} \wedge \ell' = \mathsf{NS} \wedge \mathsf{W}' = \mathsf{W} \wedge \mathsf{EB}' = \mathsf{EB})$$
$$\varphi_1 \equiv (\ell = \mathsf{NS} \wedge V_{est} > V_{MRSP} \wedge \ell' = \mathsf{WS} \wedge \mathsf{W}' = 1 \wedge \mathsf{EB}' = \mathsf{EB} \wedge V'_{est} = V_{est} \wedge V'_{MRSP} = V_{MRSP})$$
$$\varphi_2 \equiv (\ell = \mathsf{NS} \wedge (g_{ebi_1} \vee g_{ebi_2}) \wedge \ell' = \mathsf{IS} \wedge \mathsf{W}' = 1 \wedge \mathsf{EB}' = 1 \wedge V'_{est} = V_{est} \wedge V'_{MRSP} = V_{MRSP})$$
$$\varphi_3 \equiv (\ell = \mathsf{WS} \wedge V_{est} > V_{MRSP} \wedge \neg(g_{ebi_1} \vee g_{ebi_2}) \wedge \ell' = \mathsf{WS} \wedge \mathsf{W}' = 1 \wedge \mathsf{EB}' = \mathsf{EB})$$
$$\varphi_4 \equiv (\ell = \mathsf{WS} \wedge V_{est} \leq V_{MRSP} \wedge \ell' = \mathsf{NS} \wedge \mathsf{W}' = 0 \wedge \mathsf{EB}' = 0 \wedge V'_{est} = V_{est} \wedge V'_{MRSP} = V_{MRSP})$$
$$\varphi_5 \equiv (\ell = \mathsf{WS} \wedge (g_{ebi_1} \vee g_{ebi_2}) \wedge \ell' = \mathsf{IS} \wedge \mathsf{W}' = \mathsf{W} \wedge \mathsf{EB}' = 1 \wedge V'_{est} = V_{est} \wedge V'_{MRSP} = V_{MRSP})$$
$$\varphi_6 \equiv (\ell = \mathsf{IS} \wedge V_{est} > 0 \wedge \ell' = \mathsf{IS} \wedge \mathsf{W}' = \mathsf{W} \wedge \mathsf{EB}' = 1)$$
$$\varphi_7 \equiv (\ell = \mathsf{IS} \wedge V_{est} = 0 \wedge \ell' = \mathsf{NS} \wedge \mathsf{W}' = 0 \wedge \mathsf{EB}' = 0 \wedge V'_{est} = V_{est} \wedge V'_{MRSP} = V_{MRSP})$$

The quiescent states are characterised by the pre-conditions ("unprimed conjuncts") in $\varphi_0, \varphi_3, \varphi_6$, the transient states by the pre-conditions in $\varphi_1, \varphi_2, \varphi_4, \varphi_5, \varphi_7$. Observe that in order to enforce the RKS rule 5 (transient states are followed by quiescent states), φ_2 specifies the direct transitions from control state NS to IS. Initial state $s_0 = (0, 90, \mathsf{NS}, 0, 0)$, for example, is quiescent; this follows from φ_0. In contrast to this, $s_1 = (95, 90, \mathsf{NS}, 0, 0) \in S_0$ is transient (φ_1 applies). The latter initial state applies in a situation where the ceiling speed monitoring controller is re-booted while the train is driving ($V_{est} = 95$), and the state is immediately left, since V_{est} exceeds the allowed speed V_{MRSP}. The atomic propositions AP and the labelling function L will be discussed in the examples below.

$\square$

2.2 Quiescent Reduction

The notion of transient states in RKSs is semantically redundant. They only help to facilitate the mapping of concrete modelling formalisms (such finite state machines or UML/SysML state machines) into RKSs. The redundancy of transient states is captured in the following definition.

Definition 1. *Given a Reactive Kripke Structure* $K = (S, S_0, R, L)$ *the Kripke structure* $Q(K)$ *defined by*

$$Q(K) = (Q(S), Q(S_0), Q(R), Q(L)), \quad Q(S) = S_Q$$
$$Q(L) = L|_{S_Q} : S_Q \to \mathbb{P}(AP), \quad Q(S_0) = \{T(s_0) \mid s_0 \in S_0\}$$
$$Q(R) = \{(s, s') \mid s, s' \in S_Q \wedge (R(s, s') \vee (\exists s'' \in S_T : R(s, s'') \wedge s' = T(s'')))\}$$

is called the quiescent reduction *of* K. $\square$

The state space of $Q(K)$ consists of quiescent K-states only, and its labelling function is the restriction of L to quiescent states. The initial states of $Q(K)$

consist of the union of the quiescent initial K-states and the quiescent post-states of transient initial K-states (recall that T maps quiescent states to themselves and transient states to their quiescent post-states). The transition relation $Q(R)$ relates quiescent states already related in K, and those pairs of quiescent states that are related indirectly in K by means of an intermediate transient state.

Example 3. For the RKS described in Example 2, the quiescent reduction $Q(K)$ has initial states $Q(S_0) = \{(V_{est}, V_{MRSP}, \ell, \mathsf{W}, \mathsf{EB}) \mid V_{est} \le V_{MRSP} \wedge \ell = \mathsf{NS} \wedge \mathsf{W} = 0 \wedge \mathsf{EB} = 0\} \cup \{(V_{est}, V_{MRSP}, \ell, \mathsf{W}, \mathsf{EB}) \mid V_{est} > V_{MRSP} \wedge \neg(g_{ebi_1} \vee g_{ebi_2}) \wedge \ell = \mathsf{WS} \wedge \mathsf{W} = 1 \wedge \mathsf{EB} = 0\} \cup \{(V_{est}, V_{MRSP}, \ell, \mathsf{W}, \mathsf{EB}) \mid (g_{ebi_1} \vee g_{ebi_2}) \wedge \ell = \mathsf{IS} \wedge \mathsf{W} = 1 \wedge \mathsf{EB} = 1\}$. The transition relation is given by

$$Q(R)((V_{est}, V_{MRSP}, \ell, \mathsf{W}, \mathsf{EB}), (V'_{est}, V'_{MRSP}, \ell', \mathsf{W}', \mathsf{EB}')) \equiv$$
$$\bigvee_{i=0}^{7} \psi_i((V_{est}, V_{MRSP}, \ell, \mathsf{W}, \mathsf{EB}), (V'_{est}, V'_{MRSP}, \ell', \mathsf{W}', \mathsf{EB}'))$$
$$\psi_0 \equiv (\ell = \mathsf{NS} \wedge V'_{est} \le V'_{MRSP} \wedge \ell' = \mathsf{NS} \wedge \mathsf{W}' = 0 \wedge \mathsf{EB}' = 0)$$
$$\psi_1 \equiv (\ell = \mathsf{NS} \wedge V'_{est} > V'_{MRSP} \wedge \neg(g'_{ebi_1} \vee g'_{ebi_2}) \wedge \ell' = \mathsf{WS} \wedge \mathsf{W}' = 1 \wedge \mathsf{EB}' = \mathsf{EB})$$
$$\psi_2 \equiv (\ell = \mathsf{NS} \wedge (g'_{ebi_1} \vee g'_{ebi_2}) \wedge \ell' = \mathsf{IS} \wedge \mathsf{W}' = 1 \wedge \mathsf{EB}' = 1)$$
$$\psi_3 \equiv (\ell = \mathsf{WS} \wedge V'_{est} \le V'_{MRSP} \wedge \ell' = \mathsf{NS} \wedge \mathsf{W}' = 0 \wedge \mathsf{EB}' = 0)$$
$$\psi_4 \equiv (\ell = \mathsf{WS} \wedge V'_{est} > V'_{MRSP} \wedge \neg(g'_{ebi_1} \vee g'_{ebi_2}) \wedge \ell' = \mathsf{WS} \wedge \mathsf{W}' = 1 \wedge \mathsf{EB}' = \mathsf{EB})$$
$$\psi_5 \equiv (\ell = \mathsf{WS} \wedge (g'_{ebi_1} \vee g'_{ebi_2}) \wedge \ell' = \mathsf{IS} \wedge \mathsf{W}' = \mathsf{W} \wedge \mathsf{EB}' = 1)$$
$$\psi_6 \equiv (\ell = \mathsf{IS} \wedge V'_{est} > 0 \wedge \ell' = \mathsf{IS} \wedge \mathsf{W}' = \mathsf{W} \wedge \mathsf{EB}' = 1)$$
$$\psi_7 \equiv (\ell = \mathsf{IS} \wedge V'_{est} = 0 \wedge \ell' = \mathsf{NS} \wedge \mathsf{W}' = 0 \wedge \mathsf{EB}' = 0)$$

□

2.3   Traces

Traces of K are finite sequences of states related by R, including the empty sequence ε, $\mathrm{Traces}(K) = \{\varepsilon\} \cup \{s_0 \ldots s_n \in S^* \mid n \in \mathbb{N}_0 \wedge s_0 \in S_0 \wedge \bigwedge_{i=0}^{n-1} R(s_i, s_{i+1})\}$. The last state of a finite sequence of states is denoted by $last(s_0 \ldots s_n) = s_n$, and $tail(s_0 \ldots s_n) = (s_1 \ldots s_n)$, $tail(s_0) = \varepsilon$. Given trace $s_0 \ldots s_n$ we define its *restriction* to symbols from $X \subseteq V$ by $(s_0 \ldots s_n)|_X = (s_0|_X) \ldots (s_n|_X)$.

Given an RKS $K = (S, S_0, R, L)$, we consider input traces on states in K's quiescent reduction $Q(K)$: an *input trace* $\iota = c_0.c_1 \ldots$ is a finite sequence of input vectors $c_i \in D_I$, that is, $\iota \in (D_I)^*$. The application of an input trace ι to a quiescent state $s \in Q(S)$ is written as s/ι and yields a trace of $Q(K)$ which is recursively defined by $s/\varepsilon = s$, $s/(c_0.\iota) = s.(T(s \oplus \{\boldsymbol{x} \mapsto c_0\})/\iota)$.

As in the definitions above, T denotes the function mapping quiescent K-states to themselves and transient ones to their quiescent post-states. Obviously each pair of consecutive states in trace s/ι is related by transition relation $Q(R)$. We will be frequently interested in the last element of an input trace application to a state; therefore the abbreviation $s//\iota = last(s/\iota)$ is used. Since RKSs are deterministic with respect to their reactions on input changes, $s//\iota$ is uniquely determined.

2.4   I/O Equivalence

Model-based testing always investigates some notion of I/O conformance: stimulating the SUT with an input trace ι, the observable behaviour should be consistent with the behaviour expected for ι according to the model. The following definitions specify aspects of I/O equivalence, as they are relevant in the context of Reactive Kripke Structures.

Definition 2. *Given the quiescent reduction $Q(K)$ of some RKS K, and quiescent states $s_0, s_1 \in Q(S)$.*

1. *States s_0 and s_1 are called I/O equivalent, written as $s_0 \sim s_1$, if and only if $(s_0/\iota)|_O = (s_1/\iota)|_O$ holds for all input traces ι.*
2. *States s_0 and s_1 are called ι-equivalent, written as $s_0 \overset{\iota}{\sim} s_1$, if and only if ι is an input trace satisfying $(s_0/\iota)|_O = (s_1/\iota)|_O$.* □

Definition 3. *Two RKSs K, K' over the same variable symbols V are called I/O equivalent (written $K \sim K'$) if their quiescent reductions are equivalent in the sense that $\forall (s_0, s_0') \in Q(S_0) \times Q(S_0') : (s_0|_I = s_0'|_I \Rightarrow s_0 \sim s_0')$.* □

3   Input Equivalence Class Partitionings over Reactive Kripke Structures with Finite Outputs

In the remainder of this paper we study the special case where our specification models K and implementations K' may have infinite input domains, but have output and internal variables with finite domains only. The term "finite" is to be interpreted here in the sense that these values can be enumerated with reasonable effort. This contrasts with the domains of input variables, which we allow to have infinite range (such as real values) or to have "very large" finite cardinality (such as floating point or large integer types), where an enumeration would be impossible, due to time and memory restrictions. As a consequence, it is possible to further restrict the sets AP of atomic propositions under consideration. Since all possible values of internal states and output variables can be explicitly enumerated, AP can be structured into disjoint sets

$$AP = AP_I \cup AP_M \cup AP_O$$
$$AP_I \subseteq \{p \mid p \text{ is atomic and } var(p) \subseteq I\}$$
$$AP_M = \{m = \alpha \mid m \in M \wedge \alpha \in D_m\}$$
$$AP_O = \{y = \beta \mid y \in O \wedge \beta \in D_y\}$$

Example 4. Consider a SysML state machine transition

$$\boxed{C_0} \xrightarrow{[x<m+y]} \boxed{C_1}$$

with $x \in I, m \in M, y \in O$, where $D_x = \mathbb{R}, D_y = \{0,1\}, D_m = \{10, 11\}$. When transforming this machine into an RKS, the atomic propositions AP can be strictly separated according to their free variables being from I, M, or O, respectively. For example, $AP = \{\ell = C_0, m = 10, y = 0, x < 10, x < 11, x < 12\}$. □

Definition 4. *Given RKS $K = (S, S_0, R, L, AP)$ with finite outputs and internal states, and AP partitioned into $AP = AP_I \cup AP_M \cup AP_O$ as described above. If and only if*

$$\forall s_0, s_1 \in S : (L(s_0) = L(s_1) \Rightarrow L(T(s_0)) = L(T(s_1)))$$

then AP is called an input equivalence class partitioning (IECP) *of K, and its* input classes *are specified by*

$$\mathcal{I} = \{\{ \, c \in D_I \mid \bigwedge_{p \in M} p[c/x] \wedge \bigwedge_{p \in AP_I - M} \neg p[c/x] \, \} \mid M \subseteq AP_I\} \setminus \{\varnothing\}$$

$\square$

In order to understand the essence of Definition 4, consider an IECP AP and alternative input changes $\{x \mapsto c\}$ and $\{x \mapsto d\}$ applied to some state s. The input vectors c, d belong to the same input class from $\mathcal{I}$, if and only if they satisfy the same input-related propositions, that is, if

$$\{p \in AP_I \mid p[c/x]\} = \{p \in AP_I \mid p[d/x]\}$$

As a consequence, s, when changed by either c or d, will satisfy the same propositions from AP; this means

$$L(s \oplus \{x \mapsto c\}) = L(s \oplus \{x \mapsto d\})$$

Now, since AP is an IECP, Definition 4 implies that

$$L(T(s \oplus \{x \mapsto c\})) = L(T(s \oplus \{x \mapsto d\}))$$

Therefore the post states $T(s \oplus \{x \mapsto c\})$ and $T(s \oplus \{x \mapsto d\})$ will be in the same internal state and produce the same outputs. Recall that T maps quiescent states to themselves, so the IECP property is only non-trivial for the transient states of an RKS.

Example 5. For the ceiling speed monitoring function, whose RKS K has been constructed in Example 2, atomic propositions

$$AP = \{V_{est} = 0, V_{est} > V_{MRSP}, V_{MRSP} > 110, V_{est} > V_{MRSP} + 7.5, V_{est} > V_{MRSP} + 15,$$
$$\ell = \mathsf{NS}, \ell = \mathsf{WS}, \ell = \mathsf{IS}, \mathsf{W}, \mathsf{EB}\}$$

introduce an IECP for K. Consider, for example, the states s_0 labelled by $L(s_0) = \{V_{est} > V_{MRSP}, \ell = \mathsf{NS}\}$. Each of these s_0 is transient and has a post state s_1 satisfying $V'_{est} = V_{est} \wedge V'_{MRSP} = V_{MRSP} \wedge \ell' = \mathsf{WS} \wedge \mathsf{W}$. As a consequence, all of these post-states are labelled by $L(s_1) = \{V_{est} > V_{MRSP}, \ell = \mathsf{WS}, \mathsf{W}\}$.

$\square$

The following Lemma shows that input traces applied to the same state and passing through the same sequences of input equivalence classes produce identical outputs.

Lemma 1. *Given RKS $K = (S, S_0, R, L, AP)$ with finite outputs and internal state as described above, so that AP is an IECP for K with input classes $\mathcal{I}$. Let $\iota = c_1 \ldots c_k$, $\tau = d_1 \ldots d_k$, $c_i, d_i \in D_I, i = 1, \ldots, k$, such that*

$$\forall i = 1, \ldots, k, \exists X_i \in \mathcal{I} : \{c_i, d_i\} \subseteq X_i$$

Then $\forall s \in S_Q : (s/\iota)|_{M \cup O} = (s/\tau)|_{M \cup O}$.

Proof. Let $X_i \in \mathcal{I}$ satisfying $\{c_i, d_i\} \subseteq X_i, \forall i = 1, \ldots, k$. Let $s \in S_Q$. Denote $s/\iota = s_0.s_1 \ldots s_k$, $s/\tau = r_0.r_1 \ldots r_k$, where $s = s_0 = r_0$. We prove by induction over $i = 0, \ldots, k$ that $s_i|_{M \cup O} = r_i|_{M \cup O}$. For $i = 0$ it is trivial, since $s = s_0 = r_0$. Suppose that the induction hypothesis holds for $i < k$, $s_i|_{M \cup O} = r_i|_{M \cup O}$. Since $s_i \oplus \{x \mapsto c_{i+1}\}|_{M \cup O} = r_i \oplus \{x \mapsto d_{i+1}\}|_{M \cup O}$ and, according to the assumptions of the lemma, $\{c_{i+1}, d_{i+1}\} \subseteq X_{i+1}$, we conclude that $L(s_i \oplus \{x \mapsto c_{i+1}\}) = L(r_i \oplus \{x \mapsto d_{i+1}\})$.The IECP property of AP now implies that also $L(T(s_i \oplus \{x \mapsto c_{i+1}\})) = L(T(r_i \oplus \{x \mapsto d_{i+1}\}))$, and by definition $T(s_i \oplus \{x \mapsto c_{i+1}\}) = s_{i+1}, T(r_i \oplus \{x \mapsto d_{i+1}\}) = r_{i+1}$, therefore $s_{i+1}|_{M \cup O} = r_{i+1}|_{M \cup O}$. This proves the lemma. $\qquad\square$

Lemma 2. *Given RKS K with finite outputs and internal state as described above, and AP an IECP. Let $p_1, \ldots, p_n$ be a set of fresh atomic propositions not contained in AP, with $var(p_i) \subseteq I, i = 1, \ldots, n$. Then $AP_2 = AP \cup \{p_1, \ldots, p_n\}$ is another IECP, called the* refinement *of AP. The input classes of AP_2, constructed according to Definition 4, are denoted by $\mathcal{I}_2$.* $\qquad\square$

Observe that IECP refinement according to Lemma 2 introduces new propositions in AP_I only, while AP_M and AP_O remain unchanged.

4   Test Hypotheses and Proof of Exhaustiveness

The input equivalence class testing strategy to be introduced in this section yield exhaustive tests, provided that the following two test hypotheses are met.

(TH1) Testability Hypothesis. There exists an RKS $K' = (S, S_0', R', L', AP')$ with finite internal states and output as introduced in Section 3 describing the true behaviour of the SUT, and its state space S consists of valuation functions $s : V \to D$ for variables from V as specified for the reference model $K = (S, S_0, R, L, AP)$.

(TH2) Existence of Refined Equivalence Class Partitioning. For specification model $K = (S, S_0, R, L, AP)$ and SUT $K' = (S, S_0', R', L', AP')$, both atomic proposition sets AP, AP' are IECP of K and K' with input classes $\mathcal{I}, \mathcal{I}'$, respectively, and $AP_M = AP_M'$, $AP_O = AP_O'$. Moreover, there exists an input partition refinement $AP_2 = AP_{2I} \cup AP_M \cup AP_O$, in the sense of Lemma 2, such that

$$\forall X \in \mathcal{I}, X' \in \mathcal{I}' : \exists X_2 \in \mathcal{I}_2 : (X \cap X' \neq \varnothing \Rightarrow X_2 \subseteq X \cap X')$$

Validity of (TH2) induces a finite input alphabet to K and K' which will be shown below to suffice for uncovering any violation of I/O equivalence between K and K'.

Definition 5. *Given RKSs K, K' with finite internal state and outputs, and input equivalence class partitionings AP, AP' and AP_2 according to test hypothesis (TH2). Let $\mathcal{A}_I$ denote a finite subset of input vectors $c \in D_I$ satisfying $\forall X \in \mathcal{I}_2 : \exists c \in \mathcal{A}_I : c \in X$. Then $\mathcal{A}_I$ is called an* input alphabet *for equivalence class partition testing of K' against K. For any nonnegative integer k, $\mathcal{A}_I^k$ is the set of all $\mathcal{A}_I$-sequences of length less than or equal to k (including the empty trace ε).* $\qquad\square$

Example 6. Let K be the RKS of the ceiling speed monitor model constructed in Example 2, with IECP AP as given in Example 5. Now suppose that the SUT implementing the monitor model has an error, as indicated in Figure 2: it uses a faulty guard condition $\overline{g}_{ebi_1} \vee g_{ebi_1}$ instead of $g_{ebi_1} \vee g_{ebi_1}$. Its IECP (which, of course, would be unknown in a black box test) is $AP' = \{V_{est} = 0, V_{est} > V_{MRSP}, V_{MRSP} > 110, V_{est} > V_{MRSP} + 7.5, V_{est} > V_{MRSP} + 20, \ell = \mathsf{NS}, \ell = \mathsf{WS}, \ell = \mathsf{IS}, \mathsf{W}, \mathsf{EB}\}$. The IECP refinement of AP, $AP_2 = \{V_{est} = 0, V_{est} > V_{MRSP}, V_{MRSP} > 110, V_{est} > V_{MRSP} + 7.5, V_{est} > V_{MRSP} + 15, V_{est} > V_{MRSP} + 18.75, V_{est} > V_{MRSP} + 22.5, \ell = \mathsf{NS}, \ell = \mathsf{WS}, \ell = \mathsf{IS}, \mathsf{W}, \mathsf{EB}\}$ fulfils test hypothesis (TH2). Consider, for example the intersection of K input class $X = \{(V_{est}, V_{MRSP}) \mid V_{MRSP} > 110 \wedge V_{est} > V_{MRSP} + 15\}$ and the K' input class $X' = \{(V_{est}, V_{MRSP}) \mid V_{MRSP} > 110 \wedge V_{est} > V_{MRSP} + 7.5 \wedge \neg(V_{est} > V_{MRSP} + 20)\}$. Then the input class $X_2 = \{(V_{est}, V_{MRSP}) \mid V_{MRSP} > 110 \wedge V_{est} > V_{MRSP} + 15 \wedge \neg(V_{est} > V_{MRSP} + 18.75)\}$ of the refined IECP AP_2 is contained in the intersection $X \cap X'$. Indeed, any input from X_2 applied to the SUT in control state WS would reveal the erroneous guard condition, because K transits into IS, while K' remains in WS.

For practical application (since the IECP of the SUT is unknown), the input space D_I is systematically partitioned by intersecting the input-related propositions from AP with interval vectors, partitioning D_I into $|I|$-dimensional cubes. $\square$

Theorem 1. *Given RKSs $K = (S, S_0, R, L, AP)$, $K' = (S, S_0', R', L', AP')$, such that AP, AP' are IECP of K and K' with input classes $\mathcal{I}, \mathcal{I}'$, respectively, and AP_2 is a refinement of AP according to test hypothesis (TH2). $\mathcal{I}_2$ contains the input classes associated with AP_2. Let $\mathcal{A}_I$ be an input alphabet derived from $\mathcal{I}_2$ according to Definition 5. Then for any quiescent states $s \in S_Q$, $s' \in S_Q'$ and any input trace ι, there exists an input trace $\tau \in \mathcal{A}_I^*$ with the same length, such that $s/\iota|_O = s/\tau|_O$ and $s'/\iota|_O = s'/\tau|_O$. Hence, $s \overset{\iota}{\sim} s'$ if and only if $s \overset{\tau}{\sim} s'$.*

Proof. If ι is empty, there is nothing to prove, since $\varepsilon \in \mathcal{A}_I$. Suppose therefore, that $\iota = c_1 \ldots c_k$ with $k \geq 1$ and let $s/\iota = s_0.s_1 \ldots s_k$, and $s'/\iota = s_0'.s_1' \ldots s_k'$, where $s_0 = s, s_0' = s'$.

Consider the associated sequences of input classes $X_1 \ldots X_k \in \mathcal{I}$ and $X_1' \ldots X_k' \in \mathcal{I}'$, where $c_i \in X_i$ and $c_i \in X_i'$, for all $i = 1, \ldots, k$. Since $c_i \in X_i \cap X_i' \neq \varnothing$, $i = 1, \ldots, k$, (TH2) implies the existence of $X_{21}, \ldots, X_{2k} \in \mathcal{I}_2$ such that

$$X_{2i} \subseteq X_i \cap X_i', \quad i = 1, \ldots, k \quad (*)$$

According to Definition 5, we can select $d_1, \ldots, d_k \in \mathcal{A}_I$, such that $d_i \in X_{2i}$ for all $i = 1, \ldots, k$. (*) implies $d_i \in X_i \cap X_i'$ $i = 1, \ldots, k$. Therefore, setting $\tau = d_1 \ldots d_k$, Lemma 1 may be applied to conclude that $(s/\iota)|_O = (s/\tau)|_O$ and $(s'/\iota)|_O = (s'/\tau)|_O$. Therefore $s \overset{\iota}{\sim} s' \Leftrightarrow s \overset{\tau}{\sim} s'$, and this completes the proof. $\square$

5   Test Strategy

5.1   Application of the W-Method

Given specification model $K = (S, S_0, R, L, AP)$ and SUT $K' = (S, S'_0, R', L', AP')$, and the refined IECP AP_2 with input classes $\mathcal{I}_2$ according to test hypothesis (TH2). Let $\mathcal{A}_I$ be the input alphabet constructed from $\mathcal{I}_2$ as specified in Definition 5. Then AP, $\mathcal{A}_I$ and each $s_0 \in Q(S_0)$ induce a deterministic finite state machine (DFSM) abstraction $M(K, s_0) = (\mathcal{Q}, q_0, \mathcal{A}_I, D_O, \delta, \omega)$ of K with state space $\mathcal{Q} = \{[s] \mid s \in S_Q\}$, initial state $q_0 = [s_0]$, and input alphabet $\mathcal{A}_I$, where $[s] = \{r \in S_Q \mid r \sim s\}$. Let O be the set of output variables of K. The output alphabet of $M(K, s_0)$ is defined by $D_O = D_{y_1} \times \ldots \times D_{y_{|O|}}$. The state transition function $\delta : \mathcal{Q} \times \mathcal{A}_I \to \mathcal{Q}$ of $M(K, s_0)$ is defined by

$$\delta(q, c) = q_1 \text{ if and only if } \exists s \in S_Q : q = [s] \wedge q_1 = [s//c]$$

The output function $\omega : \mathcal{Q} \times \mathcal{A}_I \to D_O$ of $M(K, s_0)$ is defined by

$$\omega(q, c) = e \text{ if and only if } \exists s \in S_Q : q = [s] \wedge (s//c)|_O = \{y \mapsto e\}$$

We extend the domain of the state transition function to input traces, $\overline{\delta} : \mathcal{Q} \times \mathcal{A}_I^* \to \mathcal{Q}^*$ by setting recursively $\overline{\delta}(q, \varepsilon) = q$, $\overline{\delta}(q, c.\iota) = q.\overline{\delta}(\delta(q, c), \iota)$. The output function can be extended to $\overline{\omega} : \mathcal{Q} \times \mathcal{A}_I^* \to D_O^*$ by setting $\overline{\omega}(q, \iota) = e_0 \ldots e_k$, if and only if $\overline{\delta}(q, \iota) = [s_0] \ldots [s_k]$ and $s_i|_O = \{y \mapsto e_i\}$, $i = 0, \ldots, k$.

Lemma 3. *The DFSMs $M(K, s_0) = (\mathcal{Q}, q_0, \mathcal{A}_I, D_O, \delta, \omega)$ introduced above are well-defined.*

Proof. Let $q = [s]$ and $[r] = [s]$ for some $s, r \in S_Q$. Then $r \sim s$, and therefore $s//c \sim r//c$, and this shows that $\delta(q, c)$ is well-defined. Since all members of $[s//c]$ coincide on O, this also shows that ω is well-defined. □

By construction, the DFSMs are minimal, because each pair of different states $[s_0] \neq [s_1]$ can be distinguished by an input trace resulting in different outputs when applied to $[s_0]$ or $[s_1]$, respectively. Since AP is an IECP, all K-states s_0, s_1 carrying the same label $L(s_0) = L(s_1)$ are I/O-equivalent, so $\{s_1 \mid L(s_1) = L(s)\} \subseteq [s]$ for all quiescent states of K. It may be the case, however, that some states carrying different labels are still I/O-equivalent, that is, $L(s_0) \neq L(s_1)$, but $\{s \mid L(s) = L(s_0)\} \cup \{s \mid L(s) = L(s_1)\} \subseteq [s_0] = [s_1]$. In analogy to $M(K, s_0)$, DFSMs $M(K', s'_0)$ can be constructed from $K', AP', s_0 \in Q(S'_0)$, and the same input alphabet $\mathcal{A}_I$ as has been used for the DFSMs $M(K, s_0)$.

We write $M(K, s_0) \sim M(K', s'_0)$ and $q_0 \sim q'_0$, if and only if $\overline{\omega}(q_0, \iota) = \overline{\omega}'(q'_0, \iota)$ for every $\iota \in \mathcal{A}_I^*$. Note that this differs from I/O equivalence between K and K', where $s_0 \sim s'_0$ if and only if $(s_0/\iota)|_O = (s'_0/\iota)_O$ for every $\iota \in D_I^*$. The following theorem states that I/O equivalence between specification model K and an implementation K' can be established by investigating the equivalence of their associated DFSM, that is, using $\iota \in \mathcal{A}_I^*$ only.

Theorem 2. *With the notation above, the following statements are equivalent.*

- *K and K' are I/O equivalent, $K \sim K'$.*
- *$\forall s_0 \in Q(S_0), s_0' \in Q(S_0') : (s_0|_I = s_0'|_I \Rightarrow M(K, s_0) \sim M(K', s_0'))$.*

Proof. Obviously, $M(K, s_0) \sim M(K', s_0') \Leftrightarrow q_0 \sim q_0' \Leftrightarrow (\forall \tau \in \mathcal{A}_I^* : s_0 \overset{\tau}{\sim} s_0')$. By Theorem 1, we have $(\forall \iota \in D_I^* : s_0 \overset{\iota}{\sim} s_0') \Leftrightarrow (\forall \tau \in \mathcal{A}_I^* : s_0 \overset{\tau}{\sim} s_0')$. Hence $s_0 \sim s_0' \Leftrightarrow M(K, s_0) \sim M(K', s_0')$. Now the assertion follows directly from the definition of $K \sim K'$ (Definition 3). □

Definition 6. *With the terms introduced above, a transition cover of $M(K, s_0)$ is a set of input traces $\iota \in \mathcal{A}_I^*$ satisfying the following condition: for any reachable state $q \in Q$ and any $\mathbf{c} \in \mathcal{A}_I$, there is an input trace $\iota \in TC$ such that $\bar{\delta}(q_0, \iota) = q$ and $\iota.\mathbf{c} \in TC$.* □

Definition 7. *With the terms introduced above and minimal $M(K, s_0)$, define a characterisation set W of $M(K, s_0)$ as a set of traces $\iota \in \mathcal{A}_I^*$, such that for all $q_1, q_2 \in Q$, there exists an input trace $\iota \in W$ such that $\overline{\omega}(q_1, \iota) \neq \overline{\omega}(q_2, \iota)$.* □

On DFSM $M(K, s_0)$ we can apply Chow's W-method [2] to conclude that the following finite test suite is exhaustive for testing I/O equivalence between K and K'.

Theorem 3. *Let $s_0 \in Q(S_0), s_0' \in Q(S_0')$ with $s_0|_I = s_0'|_I$, and $TC(s_0), W(s_0)$ the transition cover and characterisation set of $M(K, s_0)$ as introduced above. Assume that $M(K, s_0)$ has n states and that $M(K', s_0')$ has at most m states and $m_0 = \max(n, m)$. Then*

$$\mathcal{W}(K) = \bigcup_{[s_0] \in Q(S_0)/\sim} (TC(s_0).\mathcal{A}_I^{m_0 - n}.W(s_0))$$

is an exhaustive test suite for testing SUT K' against specification model K.

Proof. $M(K, s_0)$ and $M(K', s_0')$ are two minimal DFSMs with the same input alphabet $\mathcal{A}_I$. Applying Chow's W-method [2] to $M(K, s_0)$ and $M(K', s_0')$, $M(K, s_0)$ and $M(K', s_0')$ are I/O equivalent if and only if they are $TC(s_0).\mathcal{A}_I^{m_0 - n}.W(s_0)$ equivalent.[6] Hence the assertion follows directly from Theorem 2. □

For the example of the ceiling speed monitor introduced in this paper, a detailed description of the test cases resulting from application of Theorem 3 can be found in [6, Section 7.5].

---

[6] Observe that in [2], the author uses a slightly different notation, where $\mathcal{A}_I^i$ denotes the set of input traces with length i, while we use this term to denote the traces of length less or equal i.

5.2 Complexity Considerations

Definition 5 determines the size of the input alphabet $\mathcal{A}_I$ as the number $k_2 = |\mathcal{A}_I| \leq 2^{|AP_{2I}|}$ of input classes in the refined equivalence partitioning AP_2 according to test hypothesis (TH2).

The number n of states in the DFSM associated with K is less or equal to the number $\bar{n}$ of labels $L(s), s \in S_Q$ (we get $n < \bar{n}$, if different labels $L(s_0) \neq L(s_1)$ are associated with I/O equivalent states). Let $m_0 = \max(n, m)$, where n is the number of states in $M(K, s_0)$, and m the number of states in $M(K', s_0')$. Then according to [2,16], the number of input traces contained in $TC(s_0).\mathcal{A}_I^{m_0-n}.W(s_0)$ is bounded by $n^2 \cdot k_2^{m_0-n+1}$. We have to execute several test suites of this type, their number is equal to $k = |Q(S_0)/\sim|$, the number of equivalence classes derived from initial states of the quiescent reduction of K. In the worst case, all classes of K can be reached from some transient initial state, so $k \leq n$. This results in an upper bound of $k \cdot n^2 \cdot k_2^{m_0-n+1} \leq n^3 \cdot k_2^{m_0-n+1}$ test cases (that is, input traces) to be performed.

5.3 Summary of SUT-Related Estimates

While parameters n, k are calculated from the known representation of K, the following hypotheses about the SUT influence the complexity parameters m, m_0, k_2 introduced above. (1) The size k_2 of the input alphabet relies on (TH2) (Section 4); we assume that $\mathcal{A}_I$ is sufficiently fine-grained, such that one $c \in \mathcal{A}_I$ can be found in every intersection of input classes X, X' associated with K and K', respectively. (2) The number m of $M(K', s_0')$-states is bounded by $\bar{m} = |\{L'(s) \mid s \in S \text{ and } s \text{ reachable in } K'\}|$. The finite number of reachable internal states and output states is bounded by $\prod_{v \in M \cup O} |D_v|$, the product of finite value ranges for internal state variables and output variables. The number of different proposition sets $M' \subset AP_I'$ fulfilled by reachable states of K' is bounded by the number k_2 of elements in $\mathcal{A}_I$, because this set contains one element per input equivalence class of AP_2 refining AP'. As a consequence, $m \leq \bar{m} \leq k_2 \cdot \left(\prod_{v \in M \cup O} |D_v| \right)$. (3) This also determines $m_0 = \max(n, m)$.

6 Related Work

Notable examples for exhaustive test methods have been given in [2,12,9,14]. There exists a large variety of research results related to testing against hierarchic state machines similar to Harel's Statecharts or to UML state machines. We mention [4] as one representative and refer to the references given there. These contributions, however, mainly deal with the state machine hierarchy and do not tackle the problem of attributes from large input domains, which is the main motivation for the results presented here. In [1, pp. 205] large data domains in the context of state machine testing are addressed, but no formal justification of the heuristics presented there are given.

In model-based testing, the idea to use data abstraction for the purpose of equivalence class definition has been originally introduced in [5], where the classes are denoted as *hyperstates*, and the concept is applied to testing against abstract state machine models. Our results presented here surpass the findings described in [5] in the following ways: (1) while the authors of [5] introduce the equivalence class partitioning technique for abstract state machines only, our approach extracts partitions from the models' semantic representation. Therefore an exhaustive equivalence class testing strategy can be elaborated for any formalism whose semantics can be expressed by Kripke Structures. (2) The authors sketch for white box tests only how an exhaustive test suite could be created [5, Section 4]: the transition cover approach discussed there is only applicable for SUT where the internal state (respectively, its abstraction) can be monitored during test execution. (3) The authors only consider finite input sets whose values have been fixed *a priori* [5, Section 2], whereas our approach allows for inputs from arbitrary domains.

Our notion of I/O equivalence (Definition 2) corresponds to the well-known **ioco** relation, when translating the Reactive Kripke Structures into input/output transition systems (IOTS) as defined in [14]. To this end, however, the requirement [14, Definition 1] that LTL should only have countably many states and labels has to be dropped, since RKS deal with potentially uncountable input data types. IOTS traces restricted to input actions correspond to our input traces, and IOTS suspension traces to our traces revealing inputs and outputs. Our test strategy is based on quiescent reduction, that is, only outputs in quiescent states are visible. The resulting suspension traces are therefore of the form $\sigma = c_1.y_1.\delta.c_2.y_2.\delta \ldots$, where c_i are input actions, y_i are outputs, and δ is the special output action denoting quiescence. This restricted type of suspension traces occurs naturally in test applications where test data is exchanged between test environment and SUT via shared variables, and not via events.

7   Conclusion and Future Work

In this paper, a novel exhaustive test strategy for input equivalence class testing has been established. The main result (Theorem 1) shows that even in presence of infinite input data domains, a finite input alphabet can be identified, so that for every trace performed by specification model or implementation, there exists a trace using inputs from this finite alphabet only, but producing the same outputs as the original one. This result holds for arbitrary modelling formalisms, whose semantics may be expressed by Reactive Kripke Structures with input domains that may be infinite (or too large to be explicitly enumerated), but with internal states and outputs having a sufficiently small range to be enumerated in an explicit way. With the main theorem at hand, the well-known W-Method can be applied to identify a finite and at the same time exhaustive test suite. Using an abstraction of the Kripke Structures under consideration to deterministic finite state machines, we have proven that this method is applicable.

Further research will focus on the generalisation of the test strategy to Reactive Kripke Structures with arbitrary data domains for internal states and outputs. According to our conjecture, a result similar to Theorem 1 should hold in the general case. The equivalence classes under consideration, however, will no longer refer to system inputs only, but will be characterised by more general atomic propositions with inputs, internal state and outputs as free variables.

References

1. Binder, R.V.: Testing Object-Oriented Systems: Models, Patterns, and Tools. Addison-Wesley (2000)
2. Chow, T.S.: Testing software design modeled by finite-state machines. IEEE Transactions on Software Engineering SE-4(3), 178–186 (1978)
3. Clarke, E.M., Grumberg, O., Peled, D.A.: Model Checking. The MIT Press, Cambridge (1999)
4. Gnesi, S., Latella, D., Massink, M.: Formal test-case generation for uml statecharts. In: Ninth IEEE International Conference on Engineering Complex Computer Systems (ICECCS 2004), pp. 75–84. ICECCS (2004)
5. Grieskamp, W., Gurevich, Y., Schulte, W., Veanes, M.: Generating finite state machines from abstract state machines. ACM SIGSOFT Software Engineering Notes 27(4), 112–122 (2002)
6. Huang, W., Peleska, J., Schulze, U.: Comprehensive modelling for advanced systems of systems – specialised test strategies. Public Document D34.2, COMPASS (October 2013), http://www.compass-research.eu/deliverables.html
7. ISO/DIS 26262-4: Road vehicles – functional safety – part 4: Product development: system level. Tech. rep., International Organization for Standardization (2009)
8. Object Management Group: OMG Systems Modeling Language (OMG SysML^{TM}). Tech. rep., Object Management Group (2010), OMG Document Number: formal/2010-06-02
9. Peleska, J., Siegel, M.: Test automation of safety-critical reactive systems. South African Computer Jounal 19, 53–77 (1997)
10. RTCA,SC-167: Software Considerations in Airborne Systems and Equipment Certification, RTCA/DO-178B. RTCA (1992)
11. Spillner, A., Linz, T., Schaefer, H.: Software Testing Foundations. Dpunkt Verlag, Heidelberg (2006)
12. Springintveld, J., Vaandrager, F., D'Argenio, P.: Testing timed automata. Theoretical Computer Science 254(1-2), 225–257 (2001)
13. European Committee for Electrotechnical Standardization: EN 50128 – Railway applications – Communications, signalling and processing systems – Software for railway control and protection systems. CENELEC, Brussels (2001)
14. Tretmans, J.: Model based testing with labelled transition systems. In: Hierons, R.M., Bowen, J.P., Harman, M. (eds.) FORTEST. LNCS, vol. 4949, pp. 1–38. Springer, Heidelberg (2008)
15. UNISIG: ERTMS/ETCS SystemRequirements Specification, ch. 3, Principles, vol. Subset-026-3 (2012), issue 3.3.0
16. Vasilevskii, M.P.: Failure diagnosis of automata. Kibernetika (Transl.) 4, 98–108 (1973)

Remote Testing of Timed Specifications*

Alexandre David[1], Kim G. Larsen[1], Marius Mikučionis[1],
Omer L. Nguena Timo[2], and Antoine Rollet[2]

[1] Department of Computer Science, Aalborg University, Denmark
{adavid,kgl,marius}@cs.aau.dk
[2] LaBRI, University of Bordeaux - CNRS, France
{nguena,rollet}@labri.fr

Abstract. We present a study and a testing framework on black box remote testing of real-time systems using Uppaal-TIGA. One of the essential challenges of remote testing is the communication latency between the *tester* and the *system under test* (SUT) that may lead to interleaving of inputs and outputs. This affects the generation of inputs for the SUT and the observation of outputs that may trigger a wrong test verdict. We model the overall test setup using Timed Input-Output Automata (TIOA) and present an adapted asynchronous semantics with explicit communication delays. We propose the Δ-testability criterion for the requirement model where Δ describes the communication latency. The test case generation problem is then reduced into a controller synthesis problem. We use Uppaal-TIGA for this purpose to solve a timed game with partial observability between the tester and the communication media together with the SUT. The objective of the game corresponds to a test purpose.

1 Introduction

This paper deals with black box conformance testing of remote real-time systems. Usually, conformance black-box testing is an activity where a tester executes selected *test cases* on a system (implementation) under test (SUT) and emits a test verdict (**pass, fail,** etc.). This verdict indicates the conformance between SUTs and the specification. It is computed according to the specification and a conformance relation between SUTs and the specification. Usually, the assumption of zero delay and synchronous communication between the tester and the SUT is done, but this is not realistic in many situations, such as network applications, or systems when time matters. In some cases, it may provide an erroneous verdict, potentially implying catastrophic situations. Our goal is to study the impact of explicit propagation delays between the implementation and the tester on test case generation and execution, and to provide a general testing framework for remote testing of real-time systems modeled with timed automata.

ioco *Based Theory.* In the case of untimed systems, the most common approaches are based on the Labeled Transition Systems (LTS) model, which is used as a semantics for many standardized languages such as SDL [1] or LOTOS [2]. The ioco relation theory [3] proposes a complete testing approach for LTS with inputs and outputs, using the

---

* This work has been partially supported by the French research project ANR VACSIM.

H. Yenigün, C. Yilmaz, and A. Ulrich (Eds.): ICTSS 2013, LNCS 8254, pp. 65–81, 2013.

idea that any output of the implementation should be authorized by the specification. They also introduce the notion of *quiescence* permitting to consider blocking states as a special output which should be explicitly specified. A complete framework based on this theory has been proposed in [4], especially providing the possibility to use Test Purposes in order to lead the testing process.

Testing with Time. The ioco theory has inspired many testing approaches. [5] proposes an extension of the Finite States Machines with Time (TEFSM) and defines adapted conformance relations. [6], [7] and [8] propose extensions of ioco relation with time (tioco) including delays in the set of observable actions, leading to infinite systems. They propose non deterministic test generation algorithms based on Timed Input/Output Automata (TIOA). [8] also shows how to use the Uppaal tool suite in order to generate offline test cases using coverage criteria for timed models. More recently, [9] proposes a formal framework permitting to use Test Purpose and non-deterministic Timed Automata thanks to a determinization algorithm.

Remote Testing. These works introduce conformance relations and test selection algorithms based on synchronous test execution algorithms. However, in the untimed setting, [10] and [11] point out the fact that synchronous execution of tests cases is not realistic when there is a significant distance between testers and SUTs. Under this remoteness assumption, the adequate communication mode should be asynchronous. [10] considers that SUTs and testers communicate via input and output queues, and asynchronous points of control of observation (PCOs). [10] also shows that simply using logical stamps permits to obtain the "same power" of testing than in a synchronous environment. In a more general way, [12] proposes a study revisiting asynchronous testing and showing possibilities (or not) to synchronize asynchronous testing.

Usually, the works done on this topic consider this as a "distributed" testing, implying several entities in a "system" of components. In this case, most effort is done for solving the problem of relative order between events induced by the communication process without state space explosion. [13] proposes a test generation framework using several Input Output State Machines (IOSM) and perfect FIFO queues between them. Then the author uses the Prime Event Structure in order to fix the problems of interleaving in the test generation process. Still using queues, but with Input Output Transition Systems (IOTS), [11] proposes a method to generate sound test cases with test purposes. They apply a transformation of the test purpose allowing to consider all possible distortions induced by the queues. The problem of interleaving is also addressed in [14] where authors focus on testing of concurrent systems. They propose to use Labeled Event Structures and partial order semantics in order to handle lightly concurrency aspects in the conformance relation. [15] proposes to add local clocks in each component and timestamps directly included in the exchanged messages. They propose different strategies depending on assumptions regarding how the clocks relate and give adapted conformance relations.

Contributions. The related works described above provide testing techniques for untimed systems. To the best of our knowledge, there is no explicit work that considers remote testing of timed specifications. Our contribution is two-fold. Firstly and based on a real example, we show how remote testing can be performed by modelling the communication channels with processes that delay the actions and synchronize with the SUT and its environment. We discuss the drawback of this general approach. Then, after considering timed asynchronous behaviours, we provide a Δ-testability criterion ensuring remote testing with the same detecting properties as local one.

The paper is organised as follows. Section 2 recalls well-known concepts of the model-based testing theory with TIOA. In Section 3, we address the challenges for the remote testing. We present the disadvantages of using asynchronous timed traces in general. Asynchronous semantics described the observations of a remote tester. Section 4 relates observed traces with the traces of the implementation. We define the Δ-testable criterion and present some interesting properties. The remote testing framework with Uppaal-TIGA is described in Section 5 and it is followed by a case study in Section 6.

2 The tioco-Based Testing Theory

The tioco-testing theory is based on the representation of the specifications and the implementations with deterministic TIOA. Let us now present formal notations and concepts for the tioco-testing theory that we extend later for remote testing.

Timed Word, Timed Sequence, and Timed Trace. In the sequel, $\mathbb{R}_{\geq 0}$ denotes the set of non negative real-numbers that we will often call *delays*. A *timed word* over an alphabet of actions Γ is an element $w = w_1 \cdot w_2 \cdot \ldots \cdot w_n$ of $(\mathbb{R}_{\geq 0} \cup \Gamma)^*$. We define $w[i] = w_i$ and $w[i..j] = w_i \cdot w_{i+1} \cdot \ldots \cdot w_{j-1} \cdot w_j$, and $|w| = n$ denotes the length of w. We consider the causal/dependency relation between the actions in w and we say that w_j *depends on* w_i when $i < j$ and we write $w_i \prec_\rho w_j$. The timed word w is a *timed sequence* if the projection of w over $\mathbb{R}_{\geq 0}$ is empty or an increasing sequence of real-numbers i.e $\forall 0 \leq i \leq j \leq |n|$ such that $w_i, w_j \in \mathbb{R}_{\geq 0}$, it holds that $w_i \leq w_j$. A timed sequence is called a *timed trace* if it is a sequence of timestamped actions followed with a delay i.e it belongs to $(\mathbb{R}_{\geq 0} \times \Gamma)^* \times \mathbb{R}_{\geq 0}$. We will consider that the behaviours of real-time systems can be described with timed traces. Each delay in a timed sequence refers to the time that has elapsed since the system started.

2.1 Input/Output Timed Transition Systems (IOTTS)

Definition 1 (IOTTS). *An* input/output timed transition system (IOTTS) *is a tuple* $S = \langle S, s^0, I, O, \Lambda, M \rangle$ *where* S *is the set of* states, s^0 *is the* initial state, I *is a finite set of* input actions, O *is a finite set of* output actions, Λ *is a finite set of* silent actions, $M \subseteq S \times (I \cup O \cup \Lambda \cup \mathbb{R}_{\geq 0}) \times S$ *is the set of* moves. *We will write* $s \xrightarrow{\alpha} s'$ *with* $\alpha \in (I \cup O \cup \Lambda \cup \mathbb{R}_{\geq 0})$ *to represent a move* $(s, \alpha, s') \in M$.

Moreover, we require the following standard properties for IOTTS : *time-Determinism* (if $s \xrightarrow{d} s'$ and $s \xrightarrow{d} s''$ with $d \in \mathbb{R}_{\geq 0}$, then $s' = s''$) , *0-Delay* ($s \xrightarrow{0} s$), *additivity* (if $s \xrightarrow{d} s'$ and $s' \xrightarrow{d'} s''$ with $d, d' \in \mathbb{R}_{\geq 0}$, then $s \xrightarrow{d+d'} s''$), *continuity* (if $s \xrightarrow{d} s'$, then for every d' and d'' in $\mathbb{R}_{\geq 0}$ such that $d = d' + d''$, there exists s'' such that $s \xrightarrow{d'} s'' \xrightarrow{d''} s'$).

We denote by IOTTS(I, O, Λ), the class of IOTTS of which the input actions, the output actions and the silent actions belong to I, O and Λ, respectively. For $S \in$ IOTTS(I, O, Λ), we define $Act(S) = I \cup O \cup \Lambda$.

Notations. In the sequel we write $s \xrightarrow{\alpha}$ with $\alpha \in Act(S) \cup \mathbb{R}_{\geq 0}$ when there exists $s' \in Q$ such that $s \xrightarrow{\alpha} s'$. We write $s \xrightarrow{\alpha_1.\alpha_2....\alpha_n} s'$ with $\alpha_i \in Act(S) \cup \mathbb{R}_{\geq 0}$ when there exists $s_1, s_2, \ldots s_{n-1} \in S$ such that $s \xrightarrow{\alpha_1} s_1 \xrightarrow{\alpha_2} s_2 \to \cdots \to s_{n-1} \xrightarrow{\alpha_n} s'$.

Executions and Timed Traces. A *run* of S starting at $s \in S$, is a finite sequence $\pi = s.(\alpha_i.s_i)_{i=1..n} \in S \times ((Act(S) \cup \mathbb{R}_{\geq 0}) \times S)^*$ such that $s \xrightarrow{\alpha_1} s_1$ and $s_i \xrightarrow{\alpha_i} s_{i+1}$. We denote Runs($s$) the set of *runs* of S starting from s and Runs(S) = Runs(s^0). The execution sequence of π is the sequence Seq(π) = $\alpha_1.\alpha_2.\ldots.\alpha_n \in ((Act(S) \cup \mathbb{R}_{\geq 0})^*$, and we naturally extend the notation with Seq(s) = $\{\text{Seq}(\pi) \mid \pi \in \text{Runs}(s)\}$ and Seq(S) = Seq(s^0). As usual, a move $s \xrightarrow{\alpha} s'$ with $a \in Act(S)$ means that s' is reached when the action a is executed on s (discrete move). A move $s \xrightarrow{d} s'$ with $d \in \mathbb{R}_{\geq 0}$ means that the state s' is reached after d time units has elapsed from s; so d is interpreted as the time distance between s and s' (time elapse).

The environment cannot observe the executions of silent actions in Λ. Moreover delays in executions are time distances between states. A timed trace corresponding to an execution is a timed sequence consisting of time-stamps and visible actions and such that the time-stamps indicate the dates of occurrences of the actions. Given an execution sequence $\rho = (\alpha_i)_{i=1..n} \in (Act(S) \cup \mathbb{R}_{\geq 0})^*$, the timed trace associated with ρ is denoted ttrace(ρ) and it is defined by ttrace(ρ) = obs($0, \rho$) where

$$\text{obs} : \mathbb{R}_{\geq 0} \times (I \cup O \cup \Lambda \cup \mathbb{R}_{\geq 0})^* \to (\mathbb{R}_{\geq 0} \times (I \cup O))^* \times \mathbb{R}_{\geq 0}$$

is a function that removes silent action from execution actions and that computes the date of the occurrence of the input and output actions. We propose the following recursive definition of obs: $obs(d, \varepsilon) = d$ with $d \in \mathbb{R}_{\geq 0}$; then $obs(d, \alpha.w)$ equals $obs(d + \alpha, w)$ if $\alpha \in \mathbb{R}_{\geq 0}$, otherwise it equals $obs(d, w)$ if $\alpha \in \Lambda$, otherwise it equals $d.\alpha.obs(d, w)$ if $\alpha \in (I \cup O)$.

In the sequel, TTraces(S) = $\{\text{ttrace}(\rho) \mid \rho \in \text{Seq}(S)\}$ denotes the set of *timed traces* of S. Note that since $\sigma = (\delta_i \cdot a_i)_{i=1..m}.\delta_{m+1} \in \text{TTraces}(S)$ is a timed sequence, it implies that $\delta_i \leq \delta_{i+1}$ for every $i \in [1..m]$. Given a timed trace $\sigma \in (\mathbb{R}_{\geq 0} \times (I \cup O))^* \times \mathbb{R}_{\geq 0}$, we consider as usual the after operator: s after $\sigma = \{s' \in S \mid \exists \rho \in \text{Seq}(s') \text{ s.t } s \xrightarrow{\rho} s' \wedge \sigma = \text{ttrace}(\rho)\}$ represents the set of states that can be reached from s and after observing the behaviour σ. Then we define elapse(s) = $\{\delta \in \mathbb{R}_{\geq 0} \mid s \xrightarrow{\delta}\}$ (Notice that elapse(s) = $\mathbb{R}_{\geq 0}$ when there is no restriction on the elapse of the time in s), S after $\sigma = s^0$ after σ; and out(s) = $\{a \in O \mid \exists \rho \in \text{Seq}(s) \text{ s.t ttrace}(\rho) = (0 \cdot a) \cdot 0\} \cup \text{elapse}(s)$ denotes the set of delays augmented with the set of outputs that can be observed from s without any delay, possibly preceded by the execution of silent actions. Illustrations of all these notations can be found in Example 1.

Complete and Deterministic IOTTS. We say that S is *deterministic* if it has no silent transition and $s' = s''$ whenever there exists $s, \alpha \in Act(S), s \xrightarrow{\alpha} s'$ and $s \xrightarrow{\alpha} s''$. IOTTS S is *input-complete* if all the inputs can be executed (observed) in each state.

2.2 Timed Input/Output Automata (TIOA)

A clock is a real-valued variable. Let X denote a set of clocks. A (clock) valuation over X is a function $v : X \to \mathbb{R}_{\geq 0}$ that assigns a non negative real value to each clock.

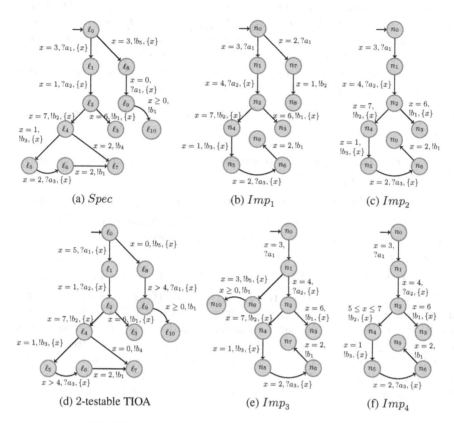

Fig. 1. Models of one specification and four implementations

The set of valuations over X is denoted by $\mathbb{R}^X_{\geq 0}$. As usual, we consider two operations on valuations: the reset of the clocks and the elapse of the time. Given a valuation v, a real number $t \in \mathbb{R}_{\geq 0}$ and a subset of clocks $Y \subseteq X$, the valuation $v[Y := 0]$ is obtained from v by resetting every clock in Y and the valuation $v + t$ increases by t the value $v(x)$ of each clock $x \in X$. Formally, $v[Y := 0](x) = 0$ when $x \in Y$, otherwise $v[Y := 0](x) = v(x)$; and $(v + t)(x) = v(x) + t$. The valuation $\mathbf{0}$ assigns the zero value to every clock. A clock constraint over X is a boolean combination of equations of the form $n \preceq x$ where $n \in \mathbb{Q}$ is a rational number, $\preceq \in \{<, >, =, \leq, \geq\}$ and $x \in X$. We will denote by $\mathcal{C}(X)$ the set of clock constraints over X. The truth value of a clock constraint is computed w.r.t a valuation and this notion is standard. We say that $v \in \mathbb{R}^X_{\geq 0}$ satisfies $g \in \mathcal{C}(X)$ and we write $v \models g$ if g evaluates to true w.r.t to v.

Definition 2 (TIOA). *A timed input/output automaton (TIOA) is a tuple* $A = \langle L, \ell^0, I, O, \Lambda, X, E \rangle$ *where* L *is a finite set of* locations, ℓ^0 *is the* initial *location,* X *is a finite set of* clocks, I *is a finite set of* input *actions,* O *is a finite set of* output *actions,* Λ *is a finite set of* silent *actions,* $E \subseteq L \times (\mathcal{C}(X) \times (I \cup O) \times 2^X) \times L$ *is the set of edges.*

Definition 3 (Semantics of TIOA). *Let* $A = \langle L, \ell^0, I, O, \Lambda, X, E \rangle$ *be a TIOA. The semantics of A is the* IOTTS$(I, O, \emptyset)$ $[\![A]\!] = \langle S_A, s_A^0, I, O, \emptyset, M_A \rangle$ *where:* $S_A = L \times \mathbb{R}_{\geq 0}^X$ *is the set of states of A,* $s_A^0 = (\ell^0, \mathbf{0})$ *is the initial state of A, I is the set of inputs of A, O is the set of outputs of A,* $M_A \subseteq S_A \times (I \cup O \cup \mathbb{R}_{\geq 0}) \times S_A$ *is the set of moves of A defined such that:* $((\ell, v), d, (\ell, v+d))$ *for every* $d \in \mathbb{R}_{\geq 0}$, $(\ell, v) \in S_A$; *and* $((\ell, v), a, (\ell', v[Y := 0]))$ *whenever* $(\ell, g, a, Y, \ell') \in E$ *and* $v \models g$.

We define $\mathsf{TTraces}(A) = \mathsf{TTraces}([\![A]\!])$ and A after $\sigma = [\![A]\!]$ after σ with $\sigma \in \mathsf{TTraces}(A)$.

Deterministic TIOA. We say that A is deterministic if $[\![A]\!]$ is deterministic. Similarly, A is input-complete if $[\![A]\!]$ is input-complete.

Example 1. The TIOA *Spec* in Fig. 1a is composed of a single clock x, the inputs are $?a_1, ?a_2, ?a_3$ and the outputs are $!b_1, !b_2, !b_3, !b_4, !b_5$. The edge $\ell_0 \xrightarrow{x=3, ?a_1, \{x\}} \ell_1$ is *passed* provided that x equals 3, the input $?a_1$ is received and x set to 0 just after the passing of the edge. An execution of *Spec* is $\pi_1 = (\ell_0, 0) \xrightarrow{0.5} (\ell_0, 0.5) \xrightarrow{2.5} (\ell_0, 3) \xrightarrow{?a_1} (\ell_1, 0) \xrightarrow{0.7} (\ell_1, 0.7) \xrightarrow{0.3} (\ell_1, 1) \xrightarrow{?a_2} (\ell_2, 0) \xrightarrow{2} (\ell_2, 2) \xrightarrow{1} (\ell_2, 3) \xrightarrow{4} (\ell_2, 7) \xrightarrow{!b_2} (\ell_4, 0) \xrightarrow{1} (\ell_4, 1) \xrightarrow{!b_3} (\ell_5, 0) \xrightarrow{1} (\ell_5, 1) \xrightarrow{1} (\ell_5, 2) \xrightarrow{?a_3} (\ell_6, 0)$, and the execution sequence associated with π_1 is $\mathsf{Seq}(\pi_1) = 0.5 \cdot 2.5 \cdot ?a_1 \cdot 0.7 \cdot 0.3 \cdot ?a_2 \cdot 2 \cdot 1 \cdot 4 \cdot !b_2 \cdot 1 \cdot !b_3 \cdot 1 \cdot 1 \cdot ?a_3$ and the associated timed trace is $\mathsf{TTraces}(\mathsf{Seq}(\pi_1)) = (3 \cdot ?a_1) \cdot (4 \cdot ?a_2) \cdot (11 \cdot !b_2) \cdot (12 \cdot !b_3) \cdot (14 \cdot ?a_3) \cdot 0$. We have that *Spec* after $(3 \cdot ?a_1) \cdot (4 \cdot ?a_2) \cdot (11 \cdot !b_2) \cdot 0 = \{(\ell_4, 0)\}$, *Spec* after $(3 \cdot ?a_1) \cdot (4 \cdot ?a_2) \cdot (10 \cdot !b_1) \cdot 0 = \{(\ell_3, 0)\}$, $\mathsf{out}(Spec$ after $(3 \cdot ?a_1) \cdot (4 \cdot ?a_2) \cdot 9) = \mathbb{R}_{\geq 0}$, $\mathsf{out}(Spec$ after $(3 \cdot ?a_1) \cdot (4 \cdot ?a_2) \cdot 10) = \{!b_1\} \cup \mathbb{R}_{\geq 0}$ and $\mathsf{out}(Spec$ after $(3 \cdot ?a_1) \cdot (4 \cdot ?a_2) \cdot 11) = \{!b_2\} \cup \mathbb{R}_{\geq 0}$.

2.3 The Relation tioco and Synchronous Testing

As usual, the SUT is represented with an input-complete TIOA. We recall the tioco conformance relation definition, a common extension of **ioco**. In the following, we use this relation for conformance between the SUT and the specification.

Definition 4 (tioco). *Let* S *and* $\mathcal{I}$ *be in* TIOA(I, O) *where* $\mathcal{I}$ *is input-complete.*

$$\mathcal{I} \text{ tioco } S \text{ iff } \forall \sigma \in \mathsf{TTraces}(S), \mathsf{out}(\mathcal{I} \text{ after } \sigma) \subseteq \mathsf{out}(S \text{ after } \sigma)$$

Example 2. Consider *Spec* and the four implementations depicted in Figure 1. We can verify that Imp_1 conforms with *Spec* even though Imp_1 can receive $?a_1$ when $x = 2$. The same, Imp_2 tioco *Spec*. But Imp_3 does not because $\mathsf{out}(Imp_3$ after $(3 \cdot ?a_1)) = \{!b_5\} \cup \mathbb{R}_{\geq 0}$ and $\mathsf{out}(Spec_1$ after $(3 \cdot ?a_1)) = \mathbb{R}_{\geq 0}$ and Imp_4 does not conform with *Spec* because $\mathsf{out}(Imp_4$ after $(3 \cdot ?a_1) \cdot (4 \cdot ?a_2) \cdot 9) = \{!b_2\} \cup \mathbb{R}_{\geq 0}$ whereas $\mathsf{out}(Spec$ after $(3 \cdot ?a_1) \cdot (4 \cdot ?a_2) \cdot 9) = \mathbb{R}_{\geq 0}$.

An on-line tester for an SUT simulates the specification either by sending an input to the SUT or by letting the time elapses, while checking that the outputs emitted by the SUT are expected. Upon the reception of an unexpected output (outputs that are not specified or that arrive at bad instants), the tester emits the verdict **fail** indicating that

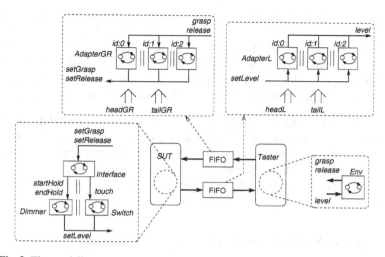

Fig. 2. The modeling pattern and how our example of the light controller is modeled

the SUT does not conform to the specification. The communications between the tester and the SUT are synchronous meaning that the tester blocks upon transmitting an input to (receiving an output from) the implementation. There is no latency. Consequently, the time instant at which the tester sends available inputs or receives expected outputs should be exactly those described by the specification. Local and synchronous testers control the tests i.e each time a tester observes an output, that output depends on all the inputs it has sent before. The controllability of the test is an important property giving the possibility to lead the SUT into a particular situation.

3   Introduction to Remote Testing and Challenges

The main idea is that the SUT and the tester are not located at the same site and communications may be delayed. Fig. 2 illustrates our framework for remote testing. The model is centered around a $2FIFO(\bowtie, \Delta)$ architecture that consists of:

1. One FIFO for each direction of the communication between the SUT and the tester.
2. A communication latency bounded by Δ. The symbol $\bowtie$ stands for either $\leq$ or $=$.

3.1   Remote Testing Challenges

Remote test cases are different from the test cases designed for local testers. When the transmission of an input depends on the reception of an output, a remote tester should not wait to receive the output before sending the input since there is a latency. The experimentation with Uppaal-TIGA highlights this point. Let us now consider simple specification models to provide a theoretical point of view of remote testing.

Example 3. Consider the specification *Spec* in Fig. 1a and assume that the latency is exactly 2 time units. If the tester wants that SUT receives a_1 at global time 3, it should send a_1 at time 1. When SUT sends b_2 at time 11, the tester receives it at time 13. etc. So a tester shall observe the timed trace $\sigma'_1 = (1 \cdot ?a_1) \cdot (2 \cdot ?a_2) \cdot (12 \cdot ?a_3) \cdot (13 \cdot !b_2) \cdot (14 \cdot !b_3) \cdot 0$ and the SUT executes the timed trace $\sigma_1 = (3 \cdot ?a_1) \cdot (4 \cdot ?a_2) \cdot (11 \cdot !b_2) \cdot (12 \cdot !b_3) \cdot (14 \cdot ?a_3).0$. Note that the outputs $!b_2$ and $!b_3$ follow $?a_3$ in σ'_1 contrary to the trace $\sigma_1 \in \mathsf{TTraces}(Spec)$. This means that the tester does not wait for $!b_2$ and $!b_3$ before sending $?a_3$ despite the fact that the SUT sends $!b_2$ and $!b_3$ before receiving $?a_3$.

Remote testing introduces two news challenges: managing the **signal propagation delay** between the tester and the SUT; and managing the **input/output interleaving** caused by the asynchronous communication: the actions are not always received in the order they are transmitted and received.

In the next subsection we study the asynchronous traces and we will study the impact of the propagation delay and the interleaving on the tests cases.

3.2   Testing with Asynchronous Traces

We introduce the asynchronous semantics for TIOA and we present results on using asynchronous traces for testing. The asynchronous semantics for TIOA takes into account the queues and the latency; it describes the influence of the latency on the transmissions and the receptions of the actions.

Definition 5 (Asynchronous semantics for TIOA). *Let $A = \langle L, \ell^0, I, O, \emptyset, X, E \rangle$ be a TIOA(I, O) with no silent action. Let $\bowtie \in \{\leq, =\}$ and $\Delta \in \mathbb{N}$. The asynchronous semantics for A is an IOTTS$(I, O, \Lambda_{I \cup O})$,*

$$\langle\!\langle A \rangle\!\rangle^{\bowtie \Delta} = \langle (L \times \mathbb{R}_{\geq 0}^X) \times (\mathbb{R}_{\geq 0} \times (I \cup O))^* \times (\mathbb{R}_{\geq 0} \times (I \cup O))^*, (\ell_0, \mathbf{0}), I, O, \Lambda_{I \cup O}\}, M_{\bowtie \Delta}\rangle$$

where $\Lambda_{I \cup O} = \{\tau_a \mid a \in I \cup O\}$ is the set of silent actions. An asynchronous state is of the form $((\ell, v), p, q)$ where p and q are input and output queues respectively. The set of asynchronous moves, $M_{\bowtie \Delta}$ is defined by the following five rules:

$$\frac{}{((\ell, v), p, q) \xrightarrow{?a} ((\ell, v), p.(0 \cdot ?a), q)}(r1) \qquad \frac{((\ell, v), (\delta \cdot ?a).p, q) \xrightarrow{\tau_a} ((\ell', v[Y := 0]), p, q)}{\ell \xrightarrow{g, ?a, Y} \ell' \wedge v \models g \wedge \delta \bowtie \Delta}(r2)$$

$$\frac{}{((\ell, v), p, q) \xrightarrow{t} ((\ell, v + t), p + t, q + t)}(r3)$$

$$\frac{((\ell, v), p, (\delta \cdot !b).q) \xrightarrow{!b} ((\ell, v), p, q)}{\delta \bowtie \Delta}(r4) \qquad \frac{((\ell, v), p, q) \xrightarrow{\tau_b} ((\ell', v[Y := 0]), p, q.(0 \cdot !b))}{\ell \xrightarrow{g, !b, Y} \ell' \wedge v \models g}(r5)$$

The rules r1 and r2 (resp r5 and r4) are dual and they correspond to the transmission and the reception of an input (resp. output). The rule r3 corresponds to the time elapsing. The time elapsing operation on a queue is defined by $((\delta \cdot a).p) + t = (\delta + t, a).(p + t)$. Notice that $\langle\!\langle A \rangle\!\rangle^{\bowtie \Delta}$ is input-complete because the transmissions of the inputs do not require to check the clock constraints. The receptions of the pending inputs require to check for the validity of clock constraints. The length of each queue is unbounded. Based on $\langle\!\langle A \rangle\!\rangle^{\bowtie \Delta}$, we can define asynchronous runs, asynchronous execution sequences and asynchronous timed traces in $\mathsf{ATTraces}_{\bowtie \Delta}(A) = \mathsf{TTraces}(\langle\!\langle A \rangle\!\rangle^{\bowtie \Delta})$.

On Asynchronous tioco. Given an implementation $\mathcal{I}$ and a specification $\mathcal{S}$ modelled with a $TIOA(I, O)$, one could try to adapt the relation tioco based on the asynchronous semantics. Such an adaptation has been studied in [10] for untimed systems. A quick adaptation of tioco that we call atioco$_{\bowtie\Delta}$ can be defined as follows:

$$\mathcal{I} \text{ atioco}_{\bowtie\Delta} \mathcal{S}$$
$$\text{iff}$$
$$\forall \sigma \in \text{ATTraces}_{\bowtie\Delta}(\mathcal{S}), \text{out}((\langle\!\langle\mathcal{I}\rangle\!\rangle^{\bowtie\Delta}) \text{ after } \sigma) \subseteq \text{out}((\langle\!\langle\mathcal{S}\rangle\!\rangle^{\bowtie\Delta}) \text{ after } \sigma).$$

Designing a remote testing algorithm as a simple adaptation of the local and synchronous testing algorithm with asynchronous traces can be the source of differences between local testing verdicts and remote testing verdicts. The following example highlights three relevant problems: the non preservation of conformance, the permissiveness and the lack of control during the test.

Permissiveness. The relation atioco$_{\bowtie\Delta}$ is permissive in the way that there exists an implementation $\mathcal{I}$ of a specification $\mathcal{S}$, a delay Δ and $\bowtie\in\{<=, =\}$ such that $\neg(\mathcal{I} \text{ tioco } \mathcal{S})$ but $\mathcal{I}$ atioco$_{\bowtie\Delta}$ $\mathcal{S}$.

For example, consider Fig. 1 and $2FIFO(=, 2)$. We check that Imp_3 atioco$_{\bowtie\Delta}$ $Spec$ because out$(\langle\!\langle Imp_3\rangle\!\rangle^{\bowtie\Delta}$ after $(1\cdot?a_1) \cdot 2) = \{!b_5\} \cup \mathbb{R}_{\geq 0}$ and out$(\langle\!\langle Spec\rangle\!\rangle^{\bowtie\Delta}$ after $(1\cdot?a_1) \cdot 2) = \{!b_5\} \cup \mathbb{R}_{\geq 0}$. But, as we discussed earlier, $\neg(Imp_3 \text{ tioco } Spec)$.

Non Preservation of Conformance. The relation atioco$_{\bowtie\Delta}$ does not preserve the conformance in the way that there exists an implementation $\mathcal{I}$ of a specification $\mathcal{S}$, a delay Δ and $\bowtie\in\{<=, =\}$ such that $\neg(\mathcal{I} \text{ atioco}_{\bowtie\Delta} \mathcal{S})$ but $\mathcal{I}$ tioco $\mathcal{S}$.

For example, consider Fig. 1 and $2FIFO(=, 2)$. Because out$(\langle\!\langle Imp_1\rangle\!\rangle^{\bowtie\Delta}$ after $(0\cdot?a_1) \cdot 1) = \{!b_2\} \cup \mathbb{R}_{\geq 0}$ and out$(\langle\!\langle Spec\rangle\!\rangle^{\bowtie\Delta}$ after $(0\cdot?a_1) \cdot 1) = \mathbb{R}_{\geq 0}$ it comes that $\neg(Imp_1 \text{ atioco}_{\bowtie\Delta} Spec)$. But we can check that Imp_1 tioco $Spec$.

Controllability of the Test. We say that a specification is *controllable* if in the case a tester observes an input, this means that any output it has sent before has already been received by the implementation. When performing remote testing, signal propagating delay needs to be managed, especially when the tester sends the inputs early and receives the outputs lately. An output received after the transmission of an input it does not depend on forces the tester to change the test case it was executing. For example, consider the specification in Figure 1, and assume that the implementation is the same as the specification. Also assume that we want to test the path up to ℓ_7 through ℓ_6. For that purpose a tester may observe the asynchronous timed trace $\sigma'_1 = (1\cdot?a_1) \cdot (2\cdot?a_2) \cdot (12\cdot?a_3) \cdot (13\cdot!b_2) \cdot (14\cdot!b_3) \cdot 0$. This trace means that the tester sends $?a_3$ before it receives $!b_3$. But, the implementation can change the test purpose by sending $!b_4$ at the time 13. So a tester should remind that it already has sent $?a_3$ and it should pursue the test by following a new trajectory where $?a_3$ follows $!b_4$.

It is not reasonable that testing verdicts vary depending on the distance and the communication mode between tester and implementation. In order to return correct verdict whatever the distance and the communication mode, we can equip the implementations with an additional mechanisms, like logical stamping mechanism [10], that will help the testers to recover the causal order of the interleaved actions. But, that mechanism cannot allow the remote testers to control the test.

4   Input/Output Interleaving and Δ-Testability Criterion

Asynchronous timed traces are remote observations of local timed traces executed by the implementation. The execution order of actions may differ from the observation order: this happens when inputs and outputs interleave in the communication channels. We intend to characterize remote observations that may lead to action interleaving. Thanks to the timing information, we introduce Δ-testable specifications of which asynchronous traces can be used for remote testing without using costly mechanisms.

4.1   Local Timed Traces and Action-Interleaving in Asynchronous Timed Traces

We address the derivation of local timed traces from asynchronous traces. Let $\mathcal{S} \in$ TIOA(I, O) and let $\rho = (\alpha_i)_{i=1..n}$ in $Seq(\langle\!\langle \mathcal{S} \rangle\!\rangle^{\bowtie\Delta})$ be an asynchronous execution sequence. Each occurrence of a silent action τ_a in an asynchronous execution sequences can be interpreted as the reception/transmission of input/output a. For $\rho[i] = \alpha_i \in I \cup O$, let us denote by $\zeta_{\rho[i]}$ the unique silent action associated with the visible action $\rho[i]$, when it exists. Notice that either $\rho[i]$ is an input action and $\rho[i] \prec_\rho \zeta_{\rho[i]}$ or $\rho[i]$ is an output action and $\zeta_{\rho[i]} \prec_\rho \rho[i]$: this is because the actions in a queue are delivered according to their positions in the queue. Moreover, $\zeta_{\rho[i]} \prec_\rho \zeta_{\rho[j]}$ whenever $\rho[i], \rho[j]$ are both either inputs or outputs and $\rho[i] \prec_\rho \rho[j]$. We say that ρ is *regular* if for every $\rho[i] \in I \cup O$, $\zeta_{\rho[i]}$ exists in ρ. A *regular asynchronous timed trace* is constructed from a regular asynchronous execution sequence. The local execution sequence associated with a regular asynchronous execution sequence $\rho = (\alpha_i)_{i=1..n}$, denoted by apply$(\rho)$, is the timed word obtained from ρ by deleting the visible actions in $I \cup O$ and replacing each silent action $\zeta_{\rho[i]}$ ($1 \le j \le n$) with the corresponding visible action $\rho[i]$.

Example 4. Let $\rho = 1 \cdot ?a_1 \cdot 1 \cdot ?a_2 \cdot 1 \cdot \tau_{a_1} \cdot 1 \cdot \tau_{a_2} \cdot 5 \cdot 2 \cdot \tau_{b_2} \cdot 1 \cdot \tau_{b_3} \cdot 0 \cdot ?a_3 \cdot 1 \cdot !b_2 \cdot 0.6 \cdot 0.4 \cdot !b_3 \cdot 0 \cdot \tau_{a_3}$ be in ATTraces$_{\bowtie\Delta}(Spec)$. We have that $|\rho| = 22$. We have that $\zeta_{\rho[2]} = \rho[6] = \tau_{a_1}$ because τ_{a_1} corresponds to the remote execution of $?a_1$ that is transmitted at the time 1. $\zeta_{\rho[17]} = \rho[11] = \tau_b$ because this occurrence of τ_{b_2} corresponds to the transmission of $!b_2$ and $!b_2$ is observed later at the position 17. We can check that $\zeta_{\rho[15]} = \rho[22] = \tau_{a_3}$. Then apply$(\rho) = 1 \cdot 1 \cdot 1?a_1 1 \cdot ?a_2 \cdot 5 \cdot 2 \cdot !b_2 \cdot 1 \cdot !b_3 \cdot 0 \cdot 1 \cdot 0.6 \cdot 0.4 \cdot 0 \cdot ?a_3$. We can also compute ttrace$(\rho) = (1 \cdot ?a_1) \cdot (2 \cdot ?a_2) \cdot (12 \cdot ?a_3) \cdot (13 \cdot !b_2) \cdot (14 \cdot !b_3) \cdot 0$ and ttrace$($apply$(\rho)) = (3 \cdot ?a_1) \cdot (4 \cdot ?a_2) \cdot (11 \cdot !b_2) \cdot (12 \cdot !b_3) \cdot (14 \cdot ?a_3).0$. We remark that $?a_3$ occurs before $!b_2$ in ttrace(ρ) but $!b_2$ occurs before $?a_3$ in ttrace$($apply$(\rho))$ which is a timed traces of $Spec$.

The causal order of the action in an asynchronous timed trace may not be respected by a remote implementation. The order of execution of two actions may be inverted by the remote SUT. For example this situation happens in asynchronous sequence ρ that contains a pattern[1] of the form $\cdots \rho[i] \cdots \zeta_{\rho[j]} \cdots \zeta_{\rho[i]} \cdots \rho[j] \cdots$ where $\rho[i]$ and

---

[1] Note that there are three more patterns.

$\rho[j]$ are visible actions and $i < j$. When such a situation happens, we say that ρ is action-interleaving. For example, ρ presented in Example 4 is action-interleaving.

Definition 6. *A regular sequence $\rho \in Seq(\langle\!\langle S \rangle\!\rangle^{\bowtie\Delta})$ is action interleaving if there exists i, j s.t $\rho[i] \prec_\rho \rho[j]$ and $\zeta_{\rho[j]} \prec_\rho \zeta_{\rho[i]}$.*

Proposition 1 states that the causal order of the actions in a non interleaving asynchronous trace is preserved at the implementation site. Let us denote by $\mathsf{Proj}_{vis}(\rho)$ the projection of ρ over $I \cup O \cup \mathbb{R}_{\geq 0}$. Given a state $s = ((l, v), p, q)$ of $\langle\!\langle A \rangle\!\rangle^{\bowtie\Delta}$, let us denote by $p(s) = p$ and $q(s) = q$ the content of the input and output queues at s.

Proposition 1. *Let $\rho = (\alpha_i)_{i=1..n}$ in $Seq(\langle\!\langle S \rangle\!\rangle^{\bowtie\Delta})$ be a regular execution sequence. ρ is not action-interleaving iff $\mathsf{Proj}_{vis}(\mathsf{apply}(\rho)) = \mathsf{Proj}_{vis}(\rho)$.*

Proposition 2. *Let $\rho = (\alpha_i)_{i=1..n} \in Seq(\langle\!\langle S \rangle\!\rangle^{\bowtie\Delta})$ be a regular asynchronous execution sequence. ρ is action-interleaving iff $p(s)$ and $q(s)$ are non empty for some state s, some $k \leq n$ such that $s^0 \xrightarrow{\rho[1..k]} s$.*

4.2 Δ-Testable TIOA

We provide a Δ-testability criterion permitting to test remotely while preserving properties of local testing. Action-interleaving does not occur in Δ-testable specifications.

Definition 7 (Δ-testability). *Let $A \in \mathrm{TIOA}(I, O)$ and $\sigma \in \mathsf{TTraces}(A)$ such that $\sigma = (t_i \cdot a_i)_{i=1..n}.t_{n+1}$. The timed trace σ is Δ-testable if,*

- *either $n = 0$,*
- *or $(t_i \cdot a_i)_{i=1..n-1}$ is Δ-testable and $a_n \in O$,*
- *or $(t_i \cdot a_i)_{i=1..n-1}$ is Δ-testable and if $a_n \in I$, then for every $t_b \in \mathbb{R}_{\geq 0}$, every $b \in O$, and every $k \in [1..n-1]$ such that $!b \in \mathsf{out}(\llbracket A \rrbracket$ after $\sigma[1..k] \cdot t_b)$, it holds that $t_n - t_b > 2\Delta$.*

A is Δ-testable if every $\sigma \in \mathsf{TTraces}(A)$ is Δ-testable.

Example 5. $Spec$ is 1-testable. $Spec$ is not 2-testable. Indeed, one can consider the subspecification rooted at ℓ_4. The delay between $!b_4$ and $?a_3$ equals 1 and it is not greater than $2 \times \Delta = 4$. The specification obtained in Fig. 1d that is obtained from $Spec$ by changing some constants is 2-testable.

The causal order of the observed actions is the same as the causal order of the actions executed by the remote implementation when the specification is Δ-testable.

Proposition 3. *Let A be a $\mathrm{TIOA}(I, O)$. If A is Δ-testable then $Seq(\langle\!\langle A \rangle\!\rangle^{\bowtie\Delta})$ contains no action-interleaving sequence.*

Putting Proposition 2 and Proposition 3 together, we get Proposition 4.

Proposition 4. *Let A be a* $\text{TIOA}(I, O)$. *Let* $s, \rho \in Seq(\langle\! A \rangle\!^{\bowtie\Delta})$ *such that* $s^0 \xrightarrow{\rho} s$. *A is Δ-testable iff $p(s)$ is non empty implies $q(s)$ is empty.*

According to Proposition 4, Δ-testability implies that at most one queue is non empty at every reachable state. However, Δ-testability does not guarantee that the sizes of the queues are bounded. A fast environment can increase the size of the input queue by sending repetitively the inputs faster than the latency.

We can show that Δ-testable specifications are controllable. Indeed, Δ-testable specifications have no action-interleaving sequences. Consequently a regular asynchronous timed trace ρ is such that $\rho[i] \prec_\rho \rho[j]$ iff $\zeta_{\rho[i]} \prec_\rho \zeta_{\rho[j]}$ for every $1 \leq i, j \leq |\rho|$. W.l.o.g, assume that $\rho[i] \in O$ and $\rho[j] \in I$. Then, $\zeta_{\rho[i]} \prec_\rho \rho[i]$, $\rho[j] \prec_\rho \zeta_{\rho[j]}$. Since the specification is Δ-testable, the delay between $\zeta_{\rho[i]}$ and $\zeta_{\rho[j]}$ is strictly greater than 2Δ. But since the delay between $\rho[k]$ and $\zeta_{\rho[k]}$ with $k \in \{i, j\}$ is bounded with Δ, we get the delay between $\rho[i]$ and $\rho[j]$ is strictly positive. This implies that the output $\rho[i]$ is observed before the input $\rho[j]$. This means that the outputs transmitted earlier are received before the transmission of new inputs. Thus, each observed output depends on input transmitted earlier and the specification is controllable.

In brief, Δ-testability criterion takes advantage of the timing information that are not available in untimed models. We claim that if the specification is Δ-testable then, the asynchronous execution of the synthesized test cases is as simple as the synchronous execution, the tioco conformance is preserved and the tester can control the test.

5   Remote Testing Framework with Uppaal-TIGA

In this section we present our general framework using Uppaal-TIGA with partial observability [16]. We model the SUT, the communication channels, and the actual tester as a timed game with the twist that only some states or clocks are visible. The tester changes its states according to the output from the SUT (via the delayed FIFOs) and the goal is that given a test objective expressed as a formula (using an extra observer automaton or not), find a strategy using the actions of the tester and a fixed set of observations to reach that objective. This matches the situation that the tester can only observe the delayed output from the SUT and cannot see its state. The framework is an extension of [17].

Modelling Pattern. Fig. 2 presents our modelling pattern. The originality of the model is how the FIFOs are encoded. We want to transmit a message with optional data with a delay that may be non-deterministic. In general, this may change the order of the outputs of the "FIFO" if the delays overlap. Each *cell* of the FIFO buffer is modeled as an automaton with its own identifier (*id*) as shown in Fig. 2. Only the automaton with the right identifier that matches the head of the FIFO (a global variable) reacts to the communication. The head and tail of the FIFOs are simple counters managed by the automata. Each automaton has its own clock to delay the output of the incoming message. We rename the channels to do the delayed transmission. For our light controller example of Section 6, *grasp* becomes *setGrasp*, and *release setRelease*.

Then we compose the SUT in parallel with the FIFOs and the tester. The tester automaton is free to generate outputs with possibly some constraints. The next step is to solve the game to decide which outputs should be generated, and when.

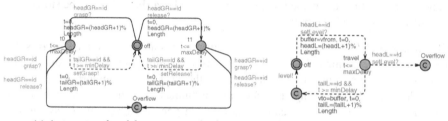

(a) Automaton that delays *grasp* and *release*.

(b) Automaton that delays *level* and its value.

Fig. 3. Automata for the FIFOs

Solving the Game. To generate the test, Uppaal-TIGA solves a two-player game between the tester and the implementation. The implementation (together with the FIFO) plays *uncontrollable* transitions and the tester plays *controllable* transitions. In addition, observations together with the test purpose are specified. To play the game an *action label* is associated with the transitions and the tester plays one given controllable action until its *observation changes*. In the meantime, the implementation can play its uncontrollable transitions. It is only when an observation changes that the tester can change its action. We refer to [16] and [17] for more details. The result is that Uppaal-TIGA will find a strategy for the tester to fulfil the test purpose under the specified observations *iff* there exists such a strategy.

POCO Conformance. Uppaal Tiga with partial observability [17] assumes poco$_P$ conformance relation constructed similarly to tioco, except that in addition to outputs the observations also contain a partial information about the system state defined by a set of predicates P. In theory the discrete changes in the partial state observation can be identified as special outputs and therefore emulated by tioco. In general, poco$_P$ is most useful to relate to the SUT as a continuous observation of its partial state which might be difficult to achieve in practice. In this paper we assume that only the state of environment (the model of test assumptions or a tester) is observable and thus only observable I/O is communicated with the black-box SUT and media and therefore tioco is sufficient for our purposes.

6 Light Controller Example

To apply our remote testing framework we consider the example of a light controller [18]. A user can grasp or release a trigger rod. Grasping and holding makes the intensity of the light vary. Grasping and releasing have the effect of switching off or on to the previous light level.

Encoding Delayed Communications. We specialize the FIFOs presented in Section 3 to send *grasp* and *release* to the SUT, and *level* together with a value to the tester. Fig. 3a shows the automaton used to delay *grasp* and *release*, and Fig. 3b the one to delay *level* with the value of the light level. The pattern for both automata is that upon synchronization on a given channel, a transition is taken to a state where the delay occurs and then a renamed output is produced. Data (Fig. 3b) may be stored and forwarded thanks to a local buffer.

SUT, *Tester, and Test Purpose.* The light controller has an interface that receives the grasp and release commands. It controls two components to respectively dimmer or switch on or off the light. The actual details of the SUT are not important here since we are doing black-box testing. The internal communication is not visible to the tester or the FIFOs. The tester is an automaton that can generate *grasp* or *release* at any time. We can constrain the outputs and to illustrate this, we use two types of testers to generate test strategies. Our testers are shown in Fig. 4a and 4b. They restrict the tests to one or two grasp and release. The test purpose is a monitor automaton put in parallel together with the tester automaton to specify interesting sequences of outputs that we want to observe. Fig. 4c specifies that the light level should increase to its maximum level and then decrease monotonically. Fig. 4d specifies that the light level should increase monotonically to its maximum level and then be switched off.

Playing the Game to Generate Tests. To generate the tests, Uppaal-TIGA solves a two-player game between the tester and the implementation. In the automata shown for the tester, purpose, and the FIFO, the *uncontrollable* transitions played by the implementation are *dashed*. The *controllable* transitions played by the tester are not dashed. In addition, we need to specify what is observable, which is done together with the formula giving the test purpose.

We specify the following test purposes:

1. {user.x>=0 && user.x<1} control: A[forall(s:slot_t)
   !adapterGR(s).Overflow U user.Released and envLevel==Max]
2. {user.x>=0 && user.x<2, envLevel==Max, envLevel==0} control:
   A[!purpose.Error && forall(s:slot_t) !adapterGR(s).Overflow
   U purpose.Goal]

Purpose 1 specifies to turn the light on to its maximum intensity level without having a buffer overflow in the FIFO[2]. In addition, the user must have released the trigger. We do not need an extra automaton for this purpose. To achieve this, the user has a clock x that can be reset (Fig. 4a or 4b) and can observe if $x \in [0, 1[$ or not. In addition, overflow and the released state together with the maximum light intensity are observable[3].

Purpose 2 specifies that the goal state of our monitor automaton should be reached while avoiding overflow or the error state in the monitor. To do so the user can observe if his clock $x \in [0, 2[$ or not, if the light is at its maximum level (or not), or if it is switched off (or not). This can be checked for both our purpose automata, though we need the user of Fig. 4b to fulfil the goal of the purpose of Fig. 4d.

It is important to notice that the observations that are given are only from the tester's side and we do not see the internal state of the SUT, thus respecting the black-box testing principle. We show one strategy generated in a few second[4] for purpose 2 with a deterministic communication delay of 4 time units. We sanitized and minimized it (the raw output has 16 states).

---

[2] We model-checked that the 2nd FIFO cannot overflow.

[3] The winning and losing conditions are always implicitly observable.

[4] Using the pre-release version 0.17.

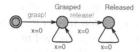

(a) Tester that can generate one grasp and release.

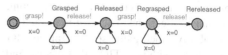

(b) Tester that can generate two grasps and releases.

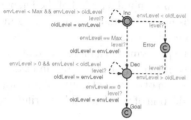

(c) Test purpose to increase and then decrease the intensity of the light.

(d) Test purpose to increase the intensity of the light and then switch it off.

Fig. 4. Tester and test purpose automata

State 0: GRASP until $x \notin [0, 2[$. Goto state 1.
State 1: delay until $envLevel \neq 0$. Goto state 2.
State 2: RESET until $x \in [0, 2[$. Goto state 3.
State 3: RELEASE until $x \notin [0, 2[$. Goto state 4.
State 4: GRASP until $x \in [0, 2[$. Goto state 5.
State 5: delay until $x \notin [0, 2[$. Goto state 6.
State 6: RESET until either $x \in [0, 2[$ and then goto state 7
  or $envLevel = Max$ and then goto state 12.
State 7: RESET until $envLevel = Max$. Goto state 8.
State 8: RELEASE until $x \notin [0, 2[$. Goto state 9.
State 9: delay until $envLevel = 0$ and $envLevel \neq Max$. Goto state 10.
State 10: delay until $purpose.Goal$. Goto state 11.
State 11: $envLevel = 0$ and $purpose.Goal$, goal reached.
State 12: RESET until $x \in [0, 2[$. Goto state 8.

Δ-*Testability*. The model is general and does not enforce minimal delays between inputs and outputs. We can constrain the environment model or add another purpose automaton to constrain the strategy. For example, if the delay between *grasp* and *release* exceeds the longest duration for registering a touch, then there is no strategy to satisfy purpose 2. This delay is the Δ of our example.

7 Conclusion

We addressed conformance testing of remote SUTs specified with timed input/output automata. Our testing architecture is composed of two queues with a communication latency threshold. Testers and SUTs communicate in an asynchronous way. We introduced the Δ-testability criterion allowing remote testing to be as powerful as local testing without any additional mechanism. The Δ-testability criterion ensures that input/output interleaving never occurs, controllability of the test and a remote verdict similar to local one. Then we presented a test selection approach with the partial observability timed game solver Uppaal-TIGA. The method has consisted in modelling the queues with new TIOA that receive and delay the actions. Then the test generation was reduced to synthesis of winning strategies in the game provided that the sizes of the queues are bounded. However the limitation of the size of the queue restricts the number of consecutive inputs/outputs the tester/SUT may send within the period of the latency threshold. Moreover, using one clock per cell leads to exponential blow up during the generation of the test cases whether the latency is deterministic or not.

We believe that testing Δ-testable criterion can be performed in a more efficient way and with less constraints on the size of the queues. Promising results hold in case of deterministic latencies. Further works include the design of dedicated testing algorithms for Δ-testable specifications and the automatic verification of the Δ-testability criterion.

References

1. Mammeri, Z.: Introduction au langage de description et de spécification (sdl). Technical report, Université Paul Sabatier - Toulouse (2001)
2. ISO: Information processing systems – open systems interconnection – LOTOS – a formal description technique based on the temporal ordering of observational behaviour ISO/TC97/SC21/N DIS8807 (1987)
3. Tretmans, J.: Test generation with inputs, outputs and repetitive quiescence. Software - Concepts and Tools 17, 103–120 (1996)
4. Jard, C., Jéron, T.: TGV: theory, principles and algorithms. International Journal on Software Tools for Technology Transfer 7, 297–315 (2005)
5. Núñez, M., Rodríguez, I.: Conformance testing relations for timed systems. In: Grieskamp, W., Weise, C. (eds.) FATES 2005. LNCS, vol. 3997, pp. 103–117. Springer, Heidelberg (2006)
6. Krichen, M., Tripakis, S.: Black-box conformance testing for real-time systems. In: Graf, S., Mounier, L. (eds.) SPIN 2004. LNCS, vol. 2989, pp. 109–126. Springer, Heidelberg (2004)
7. Mikučionis, M., Larsen, K.G., Nielsen, B.: T-uppaal: Online model-based testing of real-time systems. In: 19th IEEE International Conference on Automated Software Engineering, pp. 396–397. IEEE Computer Society (2004)
8. Hessel, A., Larsen, K.G., Mikucionis, M., Nielsen, B., Pettersson, P., Skou, A.: Testing real-time systems using uppaal. In: Hierons, R.M., Bowen, J.P., Harman, M. (eds.) FORTEST. LNCS, vol. 4949, pp. 77–117. Springer, Heidelberg (2008)
9. Bertrand, N., Jéron, T., Stainer, A., Krichen, M.: Off-line test selection with test purposes for non-deterministic timed automata. In: Abdulla, P.A., Leino, K.R.M. (eds.) TACAS 2011. LNCS, vol. 6605, pp. 96–111. Springer, Heidelberg (2011)
10. Jard, C., Jéron, T., Tanguy, L., Viho, C.: Remote testing can be as powerful as local testing. Formal Desciption Techniques and Protocol Specification, Testing and Verification FORTE XI/PSTV XVIII 99 (1999)
11. Simao, A., Petrenko, A.: Generating asynchronous test cases from test purposes. Information and Software Technology 53, 1252–1262 (2011)
12. Noroozi, N., Khosravi, R., Mousavi, M.R., Willemse, T.A.: Synchronizing asynchronous conformance testing. In: Barthe, G., Pardo, A., Schneider, G. (eds.) SEFM 2011. LNCS, vol. 7041, pp. 334–349. Springer, Heidelberg (2011)

13. Henniger, O.: On test case generation from asynchronously communicating state machines. In: Kim, M., Kang, S., Hong, K. (eds.) IFIP The International Federation for Information Processing, pp. 255–271. Springer (1997)
14. Ponce de León, H., Haar, S., Longuet, D.: Conformance relations for labeled event structures. In: Brucker, A.D., Julliand, J. (eds.) TAP 2012. LNCS, vol. 7305, pp. 83–98. Springer, Heidelberg (2012)
15. Hierons, R.M., Merayo, M.G., Núñez, M.: Using time to add order to distributed testing. In: Giannakopoulou, D., Méry, D. (eds.) FM 2012. LNCS, vol. 7436, pp. 232–246. Springer, Heidelberg (2012)
16. Cassez, F., David, A., Larsen, K.G., Lime, D., Raskin, J.F.: Timed control with observation based and stuttering invariant strategies. In: Namjoshi, K.S., Yoneda, T., Higashino, T., Okamura, Y. (eds.) ATVA 2007. LNCS, vol. 4762, pp. 192–206. Springer, Heidelberg (2007)
17. David, A., Larsen, K.G., Li, S., Nielsen, B.: Timed testing under partial observability. In: 2nd IEEE International Conference on Software Testing, Verification, and Validation, pp. 61–70. IEEE Computer Society (2009)
18. Larsen, K.G., Mikučionis, M., Nielsen, B.: Uppaal TRON User Manual. CISS. BRICS, Aalborg University (2009)

An Implementation Relation and Test Framework for Timed Distributed Systems*

Christophe Gaston[1], Robert M. Hierons[2], and Pascale Le Gall[3]

[1] CEA, LIST, Point Courrier 174, 91191, Gif-sur-Yvette, France
christophe.gaston@cea.fr
[2] Brunel University, Uxbridge, Middlesex, UK, UB8 3PH
rob.hierons@brunel.ac.uk
[3] Laboratoire MAS, Grande Voie des Vignes, 92195 Châtenay-Malabry, France
pascale.legall@ecp.fr

Abstract. Many systems interact with their environment at physically distributed interfaces and the distributed nature of any observations made is known to complicate testing. This paper concerns distributed testing, where a separate tester is placed at each localised interface and may only observe what happens at this interface. Most previous work on distributed model based testing has used models that are either finite state machines or input output transition systems. In this paper we define a framework for distributed testing from timed input output transition systems along with corresponding test hypotheses and a distributed conformance relation.

Keywords: distributed systems, timed systems, model based testing, symbolic input output transition systems.

1 Introduction

Most approaches to model based testing (MBT) assume that a single tester interacts with the system under test (SUT) and this tester observes all inputs and outputs. However, many systems such as web services and wireless sensor networks interact with the environment at multiple physically distributed interfaces. This has led to interest in distributed testing, where there is a separate local tester at each interface, a tester only observes events at its interface, and there is no global clock. This approach to distributed testing was formalised by ISO as the *distributed test architecture* [1]. It is known that the use of the distributed test architecture affects software testing [2–7]. However, only recently has the effect been formalised as implementation relations for FSMs [8] and IOTSs[1] [10, 11].

---

* This work was partially supported by the French Program "Investissements d'Avenir" in the IRT/SystemX/FSF project and the SesamGrid project, and by the ITEA2 project openETCS.

[1] The implementation relation *mioco* [9] has also been defined for testing systems with distributed interfaces but this assumes that a single tester makes global observations.

H. Yenigün, C. Yilmaz, and A. Ulrich (Eds.): ICTSS 2013, LNCS 8254, pp. 82–97, 2013.
© IFIP International Federation for Information Processing 2013

Previous work showed that the distributed test architecture causes additional controllability and observability problems. A controllability problem is a situation where a local tester does not know when to apply an input [2]. Consider, for example, a test case where tester t_1 at interface 1 applies input i_1?, this should lead to output o_1! at 1, and tester t_2 at interface 2 should then send input i_2?. Here t_2 cannot know when to send i_2? since it does not observe the previous input and output. Observability problems refer to situations where one cannot distinguish between the global trace produced by the SUT and that expected despite these being different [3]. Let us suppose, for example, that the specification contains global trace σ where the response to a first i_1? at interface 1 leads to output o_1! at 1, and a second i_1? leads to output o_1! at 1 and output o_2! at 2. Here, the tester at 1 expects to observe $i_1?o_1!i_1?o_1!$ and the tester at 2 expects to observe o_2! and this observation is made if the SUT produces global trace σ' in which o_2! is output in response to the first input rather than the second. While σ and σ' are different they have the same projections at the interfaces and so it is not possible to distinguish between them in distributed testing.

This paper explores distributed testing from systems described by means of cooperating timed input output transition systems (TIOTS): IOTS extended with time. We assume that testers have local clocks that are not synchronised but clocks progress at the same rate; it should be straightforward to adapt this to the case where the clocks can drift. As far as we are aware only two previous papers have explored the role of clocks/time in distributed testing and these consider different problems. One paper uses timestamps and bounds on clock differences to strengthen implementation relations for IOTSs [12] but did not consider timed models. A second looked at coordinating distributed testing from an FSM through the testers exchanging messages when we have bounds on message latency [13]. While this considered timed models it assumed that the model is an FSM with time and concentrated on overcoming controllability problems.

The previously defined implementation relation *dioco* for distributed testing against an IOTS compares global traces of the SUT against global traces of the specification using $\sim$ where $\sigma \sim \sigma'$ denotes σ and σ' having the same local projections. In order to ensure that the observations at the interfaces are all projections of the same global trace, it considers either global traces of the SUT that end in quiescence[2] or infinite traces of the SUT [10,12].

This paper uses an alternative approach in which an observation is a tuple $(\sigma_1, \ldots, \sigma_n)$ where the tester at p observes σ_p and we call such an observation a *multitrace*. Instead of defining the implementation relation with some projection mechanisms, we directly use the notion of multitraces to define a new implementation relation *dtioco* for distributed testing. We also provide a compositionality result, which says that *dtioco* holds if and only if all multitraces of the SUT are such that exchanged messages respect some communication rules and also that the local projections of the SUT conform to the local components of the

---

[2] The SUT is quiescent if it cannot produce output without receiving input.

specification under *tioco*. This allows standard techniques for *tioco* [14,15] to be used in distributed testing.

Having defined a new implementation relation we describe a test architecture for TIOTSs such that test cases can be denoted as multitraces. In distributed testing we have to bring together observations made by the local testers in order to determine whether the SUT has passed a test case. Solving the oracle problem mainly becomes a multitrace analysis problem and is described as a two step process, in which a test case is run and then a verdict is produced based on the set of local (timed) traces observed. We then describe how timed testing can be carried out and provide an algorithm for checking that communication rules are verified; the compositionality result tells us that we can derive a verdict using such an algorithm along with standard methods for *tioco*.

The paper is structured as follows. Section 2 defines the terminology and notation used in this paper and in Section 3 we describe TIOTSs. In Section 4, we present specifications of timed distributed systems as a collection of cooperating TIOTSs. Section 5 gives the test framework, defines the new implementation relation *dtioco* and provides an example. Section 6 then explains how distributed timed testing can be carried out. Finally, Section 7 draws conclusions and discusses possible avenues for future work.

2   Preliminaries

We will use a carrier set D (for *Duration*) isomorphic to the set of strictly positive real numbers[3]. We may use classical operations $+, - : D \times D \to D, <, \leq: D \times D \to bool...$ on durations[4], provided by default with their usual meanings. Variables having their values in D are called *clocks*.

A *Labelled Transition Systems* (LTS) $\mathbb{G}$ over a set of labels L is a triple (Q, q_{in}, T) where Q is a set of states, $q_{in} \in Q$ is the *initial state*, and $Tr \subseteq Q \times L \times Q$ is a set of transitions. For transition $tr = (q, a, q')$, also denoted $q \xrightarrow{a} q'$, $source(tr)$ stands for q, $target(tr)$ stands for q' and $act(t)$ stands for the action a. $Paths(\mathbb{G}) \subseteq T^*$ is[5] the set of *paths of* $\mathbb{G}$ which contains the empty sequence ε and all sequences of transitions $tr_1 \cdots tr_n$ with $n \geq 1$ such that $source(tr_1) = q_{in}$ and for all i satisfying $1 < i \leq n$, we have $source(tr_i) = target(tr_{i-1})$. For any p in path $Paths(\mathbb{G})$, the *trace of* p, denoted $trace(p)$, is inductively defined as ε for $p = \varepsilon$, and $act(tr).trace(p')$ for $p = tr.p'$ with tr a transition and p' a path. $Traces(\mathbb{G})$ stands for the set of traces of all paths of $Paths(\mathbb{G})$.

3   Timed Input Output Transition Systems

In this section we define Timed Input Output Transition Systems (TIOTSs) and associated notation. We then discuss and formalise as multitraces the

---

[3] In practice, any set of values used in a constraint solver for approaching real numbers.
[4] $d_1 - d_2$ is defined if and only if $d_1 > d_2$.
[5] Given a set A, A^* denotes the set of finite sequences of elements of A, ε denotes the empty sequence, and '.' is used for concatenation.

observations that may be made in distributed testing. TIOTSs are labelled transition systems whose labels represent either Outputs, Inputs or durations.

Definition 1 (TIOTS). *A TIOTS-signature is a tuple* $\Sigma = (C, I, O)$ *with* $I \cap O = \emptyset$, *where* C *is a set of* channels, I *is a set of* inputs *and* O *is a set of* outputs. *Moreover* C *can be partitioned as* $C_{in} \coprod C_{out}$ *where* C_{in} *and* C_{out} *are a set of* input channels *and a set of* output channels *respectively. Accordingly,* I *and* O *can be partitioned as* $\coprod_{c \in C_{in}} I_c$ *and* $\coprod_{c \in C_{out}} O_c$ *respectively, where for channel* c *we have that* I_c *is the set of inputs that can be received on* c *and* O_c *is the set of outputs that can be sent through* c. *A TIOTS over* Σ *is an LTS* (Q, q_{in}, T) *over* $I \cup O \cup D$.

In the sequel, for any TIOTS $\mathbb{A}$ over $\Sigma = (C, I, O)$, $Sig(\mathbb{A})$ stands for Σ, $C(\mathbb{A})$ or $C(\Sigma)$ stand for C, $I(\mathbb{A})$ or $I(\Sigma)$ stand for I, and $O(\mathbb{A})$ or $O(\Sigma)$ stands for O. Moreover, in a slight abuse of notation we use Σ^* for $(I \cup O \cup D)^*$. Inputs (respectively Outputs) occuring in I_c (respectively O_c) are sometimes denoted $c?a$ (respectively $c!a$) where a is a value received (sent) through channel c. We also use $c?$ or $c!$ for simple signals received or sent through channel c. Executions of TIOTS are called *Timed Traces*, which are defined as follows:

Definition 2 (Timed Traces). *The set* $TTraces(\mathbb{A})$ *of timed traces of the TIOTS* $\mathbb{A}$ *is the smallest set that satisfies the following:*

- *for any* $\sigma \in Traces(\mathbb{A})$ *(with* $\mathbb{A}$ *viewed as a simple LTS), if* σ *is of the form* $\nabla . \sigma'$ *where[6]* $\nabla = d_1 \ldots d_n$, $n \geq 0$, *for all* $i \leq n$, $d_i \in D$, *and* σ' *is either* ε *or of the form* $a.\sigma''$ *with* $a \in I \cup O$, *then* $\sigma' \in TTraces(\mathbb{A})$.
- *for any* d_1, d_2 *and* d_3 *in* D *satisfying* $d_1 + d_2 = d_3$, *for any* σ, σ' *in* Σ^*, $\sigma.d_3.\sigma' \in TTraces(\mathbb{A})$ *iff* $\sigma.d_1.d_2.\sigma' \in TTraces(\mathbb{A})$.

Given timed trace σ and action a in $I \cup O$, $|\sigma|_a$ will denote the number of instances of a in σ.

The first point of the definition prevents us from having timed traces beginning with durations. This is because in black box testing we cannot differentiate between the SUT not being initialised from the SUT being initialised but not having interacted with its environment. Thus, if d is a duration then we cannot distinguish between traces $d.\sigma$ and σ. In a distributed context, this problem is even more pronounced since we cannot even expect that the tester and SUT are initially synchronised via a reset. The second point says that durations can be composed and decomposed provided that cumulative sums of consecutive durations are maintained. The definition of timed traces makes no assumption on how durations are sampled in testing (it allows all possible choices).

4   Specifications of Timed Distributed Systems

We specify systems as a collection of localized parts (described as TIOTSs) communicating through a network. In particular, each localisation l is identified by its

---

[6] If $n = 0$, then $\nabla = \varepsilon$.

interface, given as a TIOTS signature Σ_l. The next definition characterises communications between a collection of interfaces, that is *a system signature*. They are given as a set of consistency conditions defining tuples of local executions (timed traces) corresponding to compatible visions of some global execution:

Definition 3 (System communications). *A system signature Σ_{Sys} is a tuple $(\Sigma_1, \ldots, \Sigma_n)$ of TIOTS signatures. The set of multitraces over Σ_{Sys}, denoted $MTraces(\Sigma_{Sys})$, is the subset of $\Sigma_1^* \times \ldots \times \Sigma_n^*$ defined as follows:*

Empty Trace: $(\varepsilon \ldots \varepsilon)$ *is in* $MTraces(\Sigma_{Sys})$,

Inputs from the environment: *for any* $i \leq n$, $c \in C(\Sigma_i) \setminus \cup_{j \neq i} C(\Sigma_j)$, $a \in I(\Sigma_i)_c$, *and* $(\sigma_1 \ldots \sigma_i, \ldots \sigma_n) \in MTraces(\Sigma_{Sys})$ *we have* $(\sigma_1 \ldots \sigma_i.a, \ldots \sigma_n) \in MTraces(\Sigma_{Sys})$.

Non Blocking Outputs: *for any* $i \leq n$, $a \in O(\Sigma_i)$, *and* $(\sigma_1 \ldots \sigma_i, \ldots \sigma_n) \in MTraces(\Sigma_{Sys})$, *we have* $(\sigma_1 \ldots, \sigma_i.a, \ldots \sigma_n) \in MTraces(\Sigma_{Sys})$.

Causality of communication: *for any* $i \leq n$, $a \in I(\Sigma_i)_c$ *where c is a channel of at least two TIOTS-signatures of Sys, and* $(\sigma_1 \ldots, \sigma_i, \ldots \sigma_n) \in MTraces(\Sigma_{Sys})$, *let us denote by* $O_a \subseteq \{1, \ldots, n\}$ *the set of all indexes j such that* $a \in O(\Sigma_j)_c$. *If* $|\sigma_i|_a < \Sigma_{j \in O_a} |\sigma_j|_a$, *then* $(\sigma_1 \ldots, \sigma_i.a, \ldots, \sigma_n) \in MTraces(\Sigma_{Sys})$.

Consistent Time Elapsing: *for any* $d \in D$ *and* $(\sigma_1, \ldots, \sigma_n) \in MTraces(\Sigma_{Sys})$, *we have* $(\sigma'_1, \ldots, \sigma'_n) \in MTraces(\Sigma_{Sys})$ *where for any* $i \leq n$, σ'_i *is equal to* ε *if* $\sigma_i = \varepsilon$ *and equal to* $\sigma_i.d$ *otherwise.*

A multitrace is a tuple, each element being a sequence of inputs, outputs or durations that is an execution that may be observed on a localised interface. The multitrace whose sequences are all ε (Item *Empty Trace*) corresponds to no interaction having occurred. A multitrace can be extended by adding to any component either an input from the environment (Item *Inputs from the environment*) or an output (Item *Non Blocking Outputs*). Outputs are non-blocking, when sent to the environment and when sent to other parts of the system. Internal communications are on shared channels. A channel may be shared by an arbitrary number of localised TIOTSs. Internal communication is multicast: a message sent can be received by several recipients (all those who listen on the channel of interest). Messages are never lost but the time to reach a recipient is not quantifiable since it travels between interfaces and there is no global clock (we cannot measure it). If we focus on a thread of execution (*i.e.* a sequence in a multitrace), a message cannot be received more often than the total number of emissions of this message in the system (Item *Causality of communication*). Finally, we require that time elapses in the same way for all interfaces whose corresponding trace is not empty (Item *Consistent Time Elapsing*).

In distributed testing there is a separate localised tester at each interface and there is no global clock. Thus, we cannot make any suppositions on the different moments at which the different testers stop observing their associated interfaces. To reflect this, we accept as admissible observations multitraces made of trace prefixes, which we call observable multitraces.

Definition 4 (Observable Multitraces). *The set of observable multitraces of* $\Sigma_{Sys} = (\Sigma_1 \ldots \Sigma_n)$, *denoted* $OTraces(\Sigma_{Sys})$, *is the smallest set containing* $MTraces(\Sigma_{Sys})$ *and such that for any a in* Σ_i, *we have:*

$(\sigma_1, \ldots, \sigma_i.a, \ldots, \sigma_n) \in OTraces(\Sigma_{Sys}) \Rightarrow (\sigma_1, \ldots, \sigma_i, \ldots, \sigma_n) \in OTraces(\Sigma_{Sys})$

On each localised subsystem, the observer only observes a prefix of the whole (local) timed trace if it does not wait long enough. Now, system specifications are defined as tuples $(\mathbb{A}_1, \ldots, \mathbb{A}_n)$ of TIOTSs whose associated observable multitraces $(\sigma_1 \ldots, \sigma_i, \ldots \sigma_n)$ are those such that σ_i is a timed trace of $\mathbb{A}_i$.

Definition 5 (System). *A system* Sys *over* $\Sigma_{Sys} = (\Sigma_1, \ldots, \Sigma_n)$ *is a tuple* $(\mathbb{A}_1, \ldots, \mathbb{A}_n)$ *of TIOTS,* $\mathbb{A}_i$ *being defined on* Σ_i *($1 \leq i \leq n$).* $OTraces(Sys)$ *is the set of multitraces:*

$$(TTraces(\mathbb{A}_1) \times \ldots \times TTraces(\mathbb{A}_n)) \cap OTraces(\Sigma_{Sys})$$

Each TIOTS corresponds to a view of the system from one interface. Its timed traces denote possible observations of system executions from this interface. Observable traces denote tuples of consistent views of system executions.

5   Testing Framework

5.1   A Conformance Relation for Timed Distributed Systems

In this section we define our new implementation relation *dtioco*. In MBT it is normal to assume that certain test hypotheses hold [16], the most basic hypothesis being that the SUT can be described using the same formalism as the specification. We assume that the following classical test hypotheses hold.

Definition 6 (*LUT and SUT*). *Let* $\Sigma = (C, I, O)$ *be a TIOTS signature and* $C' \subseteq C$. *A TIOTS* $\mathbb{A} = (Q, q_{in}, Tr)$ *over* Σ *satisfies the so-called* Input Enableness *property over* C' *iff* $\forall q \in Q, \forall c \in C', \forall a \in I_c, \exists q' \in Q, (q, a, q') \in Tr$.

A Localized System Under Test (LUT) over (Σ, C') *is a TIOTS over* Σ, *satisfying the input enableness property over* C'.

A System Under Test (SUT) over $\Sigma_{Sys} = (\Sigma_1, \ldots, \Sigma_n)$ *is a tuple* $(\mathbb{LS}_1, \ldots, \mathbb{LS}_n)$ *such that for each* $1 \leq i \leq n$, $\mathbb{LS}_i$ *is an LUT over* $(\Sigma_i, I(\Sigma_i) \backslash (\cup_{j \in 1..n} O(\Sigma_j)))$.

Input-enabledness adapts the traditional hypothesis to distributed testing by requiring that the system is input-enabled on its public interface made of channels shared with the environment. We base our new conformance relation on *tioco* [14, 17–19]. In fact, we use a slightly modified version of *tioco* since, as stated in Definition 2, our timed traces start with an input or an output (we remove durations occuring at the beginning of traces).

Definition 7 (tioco). *Let* $\mathbb{LS}$ *be an LUT and* $\mathbb{A}$ *a TIOTS both defined on the same signature* (C, I, O). $\mathbb{LS}$ *conforms to* $\mathbb{A}$, *denoted* $\mathbb{LS}$ tioco $\mathbb{A}$, *if and only if for any* σ *in* $TTraces(\mathbb{A})$ *and* r *in* $O \cup D$, *we have:*

$$\sigma.r \in TTraces(\mathbb{LS}) \implies \sigma.r \in TTraces(\mathbb{A})$$

Our conformance relation for distributed systems is an extension of *tioco* to observable multitraces, except that observable multitraces introduce some constraints (Definition 3), typically on internal receptions that should be preceded by internal emissions. However, it may happen that an observation of an SUT $\mathbb{S}$ does not satisfy those constraints. For example, the network might create a spurious message in a channel between localised systems, a localised system $\mathbb{LS}_i$ receiving a message (input) on a channel c that connects it to another localised system $\mathbb{LS}_j$ without $\mathbb{LS}_j$ sending this message. Let us note that there exists no specification to which such systems conform according to Definition 8 since they do not meet consistency conditions of Definition 3. Although our implementation relation will consider such behaviours to be erroneous, we cannot assume that the possible executions of the SUT are in $OTraces(\Sigma_{Sys})$. In fact, we will only suppose that each local execution is a timed trace of some localised system $\mathbb{LS}_i$ under test. In the sequel any SUT $\mathbb{S} = (\mathbb{LS}_1, \ldots, \mathbb{LS}_n)$ has a set $Sem(\mathbb{S}) \subseteq TTraces(\mathbb{LS}_1) \times \ldots \times TTraces(\mathbb{LS}_n)$ that denotes the set of all observations that can be made in testing; this allows the network to introduce messages on channels as discussed earlier. We further suppose, as in the case of observable traces, that for any a we have that: $((\sigma_1, \ldots, \sigma_i.a, \ldots, \sigma_n) \in Sem(\mathbb{S})) \Rightarrow ((\sigma_1, \ldots, \sigma_i, \ldots, \sigma_n) \in Sem(\mathbb{S}))$.

Definition 8 (dtioco). *Let $\mathbb{S} = (\mathbb{LS}_1, \ldots, \mathbb{LS}_n)$ and $Sys = (\mathbb{A}_1, \ldots, \mathbb{A}_n)$ be resp. an SUT and a system both on the signature $\Sigma_{Sys} = (\Sigma_1, \ldots, \Sigma_n)$. $\mathbb{S}$ conforms to Sys, denoted $\mathbb{S}$ dtioco Sys, if and only if $Sem(\mathbb{S}) \subseteq OTrace(\Sigma_{Sys})$ and for any $(\sigma_1 \ldots, \sigma_i, \ldots, \sigma_n) \in OTraces(Sys)$ and $r \in (\cup_{i \leq n} O(\Sigma_i)) \cup D$, we have:*

$$(\sigma_1 \ldots, \sigma_i.r, \ldots \sigma_n) \in Sem(\mathbb{S}) \implies (\sigma_1 \ldots, \sigma_i.r, \ldots \sigma_n) \in OTraces(Sys)$$

The first part of the definition requires that any observation of the SUT is valid. The second part follows an approach similar to *tioco* in that it says that for any observable multitrace $(\sigma_1 \ldots \sigma_i, \ldots, \sigma_n)$ of the specification, every possible next observation of the SUT after $(\sigma_1 \ldots \sigma_i, \ldots, \sigma_n)$ is also an observation that might be made after $(\sigma_1 \ldots \sigma_i, \ldots, \sigma_n)$ in the specification.

In the sequel, we introduce a compositionality result that allows us to reuse testing algorithms dedicated for *tioco* in a distributed system testing process. We begin by introducing a definition allowing us to identify which part of an LUT is stimulated in a distributed SUT.

Definition 9. *Let $\mathbb{S} = (\mathbb{LS}_1, \ldots, \mathbb{LS}_n)$ be an SUT with $\mathbb{LS}_i = (Q_i, q_i, Tr_i)$ for i in $1..n$. The projection of $\mathbb{LS}_i$ on $\mathbb{S}$, denoted $\mathbb{LS}_i|_{\mathbb{S}}$ is the TIOTS (Q_i, q_i, Tr_i') where Tr_i' is the subset of Tr_i that contains all transitions tr such that there exists a path of the form $p'.t$ in $Paths(\mathbb{LS}_i)$, a timed trace σ in $TTraces(p'.tr)$ and a tuple $(\sigma_1, \ldots, \sigma_n)$ in $Sem(\mathbb{S})$ such that $\sigma = \sigma_i$.*

The set of timed traces of $\mathbb{LS}_i|_{\mathbb{S}}$ contains all timed traces of $\mathbb{LS}_i$ that $\mathbb{LS}_i$ can produce when interacting with the other LUTs. Thus, if a tester interacts with $\mathbb{S}$ only through the channels of $\mathbb{LS}_i$, he/she interacts with a real system that may be represented by $\mathbb{LS}_i|_{\mathbb{S}}$ (except that the tester does not control inputs received on channels between LUTs). By construction, $\mathbb{LS}_i|_{\mathbb{S}}$ need not be input enabled over all internal channels since all configurations over the localised part are not exercised in the context of $\mathbb{S}$.

Property 1. Let $\mathbb{S} = (\mathbb{LS}_1, \ldots, \mathbb{LS}_n)$ and $Sys = (\mathbb{A}_1, \ldots, \mathbb{A}_n)$ be resp. an SUT and a system with both having signature $\Sigma_{Sys} = (\Sigma_1, \ldots, \Sigma_n)$.

If for all i in $1..n$, $\mathbb{A}_i$ is input enabled over $C(\Sigma_i)$, the following result holds: $(\mathbb{S} \; dtioco \; Sys) \Leftrightarrow ((\forall i \leq n, \mathbb{LS}_i|_{\mathbb{S}} \; tioco \; \mathbb{A}_i) \wedge Sem(\mathbb{S}) \subseteq OTraces(\Sigma_{Sys}))$

Proof. First consider the left-to-right implication. The fact that $Sem(\mathbb{S}) \subseteq OTraces(\Sigma_{Sys})$ is part of the definition of *dtioco*.

Now let us suppose that there exists i in $1, \ldots, n$ such that $\neg(\mathbb{LS}_i|_{\mathbb{S}} \; tioco \; \mathbb{A}_i)$. If so, there exists $\sigma_i \in TTraces(\mathbb{A}_i)$ and $r \in O(\Sigma_i) \cup D$ such that $\sigma_i.r \in TTraces(\mathbb{LS}_i|_{\mathbb{S}})$ and $\sigma_i.r \notin TTraces(\mathbb{A}_i)$.

Since $\sigma_i.r \in TTraces(\mathbb{LS}_i|_{\mathbb{S}})$, there exists $(\sigma_1, \ldots, \sigma_i.r, \ldots, \sigma_n) \in Sem(\mathbb{S})$. As $Sem(\mathbb{S}) \subseteq OTraces(\Sigma_{Sys})$, we have that $(\sigma_1, \ldots \sigma_i.r, \ldots, \sigma_n) \in OTraces(\Sigma_{Sys})$. Assume that i, r and $(\sigma_1 \ldots, \sigma_i, \ldots \sigma_n)$ are chosen to be minimal and so $\sigma_j \in TTraces(\mathbb{A}_j)$ for all $1 \leq j \leq n$. Thus, since $(\sigma_1, \ldots \sigma_i, \ldots, \sigma_n) \in OTraces(\Sigma_{Sys})$, we have that $(\sigma_1 \ldots, \sigma_i, \ldots \sigma_n) \in OTraces(Sys)$. By Definition 8, since $\mathbb{S} \; dtioco \; Sys$ we have that $(\sigma_1 \ldots, \sigma_i.r, \ldots \sigma_n) \in OTraces(Sys)$. Thus, $(\sigma_1, \ldots \sigma_i.r, \ldots, \sigma_n) \in TTraces(\mathbb{A}_1) \times \ldots \times TTraces(\mathbb{A}_n)$, and so we can deduce that $\sigma_i.r \in TTraces(\mathbb{A}_i)$. This contradicts our hypothesis.

Now consider the right-to-left implication. The first condition of Definition 8 (*dtioco*) holds immediately from the hypotheses. We assume that we have been given $(\sigma_1 \ldots \sigma_i, \ldots, \sigma_n) \in OTraces(Sys)$, $r \in \Sigma_i \cup D$ and $(\sigma_1 \ldots, \sigma_i.r, \ldots \sigma_n) \in Sem(\mathbb{S})$ and are required to prove that $(\sigma_1 \ldots, \sigma_i.r, \ldots \sigma_n) \in OTraces(Sys)$.

Since $(\sigma_1 \ldots, \sigma_i.r, \ldots \sigma_n) \in Sem(\mathbb{S})$ we have that $\sigma_i.r \in TTraces(\mathbb{LS}_i|_{\mathbb{S}})$. Further, since $(\sigma_1 \ldots \sigma_i, \ldots, \sigma_n) \in OTraces(Sys)$ we know that $\sigma_i \in TTraces(\mathbb{A}_i)$. Thus, since $\mathbb{LS}_i|_{\mathbb{S}} \; tioco \; \mathbb{A}_i$, we have that $\sigma_i.r \in TTraces(\mathbb{A}_i)$. Since $Sem(\mathbb{S}) \subseteq OTraces(\Sigma_{Sys})$ we have that $(\sigma_1 \ldots \sigma_i.r, \ldots, \sigma_n) \in OTraces(\Sigma_{Sys})$. We thus have that $(\sigma_1 \ldots, \sigma_i.r, \ldots, \sigma_n) \in OTraces(\Sigma_{Sys})$, $\sigma_i.r \in TTraces(\mathbb{A}_i)$ and $\sigma_j \in TTraces(\mathbb{A}_j)$ for all $1 \leq j \leq n$ with $j \neq i$. From the definition of $OTraces(Sys)$, we conclude that $(\sigma_1 \ldots, \sigma_i.r, \ldots \sigma_n) \in OTraces(Sys)$ as required. $\square$

5.2 TIOSTSs as Symbolic Denotation of TIOSTs

Now, we briefly present symbolic versions of TIOTSs that will be used to illustrate our test framework with a reasonable example. Indeed, generally, for expressiveness sake, we do not directly use TIOTSs, which are appropriate to theoretically reason about conformance, but do not permit real time constraints to be expressed. Here, we use TIOSTS (Timed Input Output Symbolic Transition Systems) [14, 15] which are automata that have variables to abstractly denote system states (we call them data variables) and variables to capture timing constraints (we call them clocks) on system executions.

TIOSTS introduce transitions of the form $(q, \mathcal{T}, \phi, \psi, act, \rho, q')$ where (i) q and q' are states, ϕ and ψ are guards on time and data respectively, (ii) $\mathcal{T}$ is a set of clocks to be reset to 0 when the action *act* occurs, (iii) *act* may be receptions of the form $c?x$ $(c?)$ where c is a channel and x is a data variable or emissions of the form $c!t$ $(c!)$ where t is a term and (iv) ρ is an assignment of data variables denoting updates of variable values. Such a transition can be executed from q if ψ holds and at any moment for which values of the clocks are such that ϕ holds (as for timed automata). At this moment, the action occurs (signals $c?$ or $c!$ or a reception of a value on x if the action is $c?x$ or emission of the current value of t if the action is $c!t$). Clocks of $\mathcal{T}$ are reset and data variables are updated according to ρ. Finally, by successively executing all consecutive transitions, one may form all timed traces of a TIOST.

5.3 Example

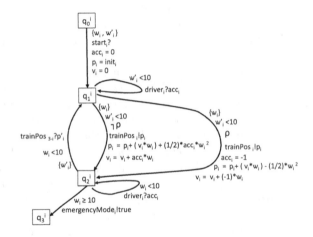

With: $init_1 = 42$ and $init_2 = 300$ and $\rho \equiv p_i < p'_i \le (v_i * 20) + 200$

Fig. 1. Train Control System Example: TLC_i for $i = 1, 2$

Figure 1 gives a simplified model of the functional requirements of Train Local Controllers (TLCs) that forms part of the European Train Control System[7]. Similar specifications can found, e.g. in [20] and in [21]. The overall Train Control System (TCS) contains two Train Local Controllers (TLCs), one per train (say train 1 and train 2), going in the same direction on a rolling stock.

The symbol i in Figure 1 should be replaced by two possible values, 1 and 2. The system $TCS = (TLC_1, TLC_2)$ ensures that the train on the rear side automatically decreases speed as soon as the one in front of it is too close. The relative position of trains is given by their positions, which can be accessed by consulting the value of variable p_i: if $p_1 < p_2$, then train 1 is behind train 2.

---

[7] Interested readers can consult http://www.uic.org/spip.php?rubrique850

The TLC_i are automata containing 4 states (q_0^i the initial state, q_1^i, q_2^i and q_3^i), communicating through channels ($start_i$, $driver_i$, $emergencyMode_i$ for communicating with the environment, $trainPos_i$ for sending internal messages and $trainPos_{3-i}$ for receiving internal messages) and having 4 data variables (acc_i in $\{-1,0,1\}$ for the acceleration of the train, v_i for the speed of the train, p_i for the position value of the train, p_i' for the estimation of the position of the other train) and 2 clocks (w_i, which is reset at each emission of the position and w_i', which is reset at each reception of the position of the second train).

TLC_i specifies the following behaviour: after an initialisation phase, the train of interest sends its position to the other train, and in return, the other train is supposed to send its position. In this loop, two consecutive communication actions are supposed to be separated by a delay of less than 10 units of time. If the remote train does not send its position on time, the local train goes into an emergency mode (not detailed here). At any moment in the loop, the driver may ask to modify the train acceleration. The new value is taken into account only if it does not affect the safety of the system (safety is threatened if condition ρ holds, that is, the distance between trains is less than the distance that can be covered by the rear train with the current acceleration). If safety is threatened, than the acceleration of the rear train is set to -1 in order to reduce its speed. Here are some examples of couples (σ_1, σ_2) with σ_i a trace of TLC_i for i in $1, 2$:

- $(\sigma_1^1 = start_1?.(2).(1).driver_1?1.(1).(2).trainPos_1!42.(2).(3).trainPos_2?300.(2).(1)$,
  $\sigma_2^1 = start_2?.(1).(1).trainPos_2!300.(2).(2).trainPos_1?42.(3).(2).trainPos_2!300.(1))$
  is a multitrace with the convention that numbers between parentheses are durations, numbers without parentheses are messages and the punctuation symbol "." separates durations and actions. Note that train 1 is the rear train and train 2 does not move. This multitrace corresponds to a situation in which all local testers have observed until the end of the behaviour of TLC_i: in particular, all receptions have been preceded by an emission, and except the first duration (2) occurring in σ_1^1, all following durations (1).(1).(2).(2).(3).(2).(1) are the same in both traces (time elapsing property).
- $(\sigma_1^2 = start_1?.(2).(1).driver_1?1$,
  $\sigma_2^2 = start_2?.(1).(1).trainPos_2!300.(2).(2).trainPos_1?42.(3).(2).trainPos_2!300.(1))$
  is such that σ_1^2 is a prefix of σ_1^1 and $\sigma_2^2 = \sigma_2^1$. (σ_1^2, σ_2^2) is thus an observable multitrace. The observation of TLC_1 is stopped just after the driver asked to accelerate. Since the tester at TLC_2 observes for longer, TLC_2 receives the value 42. So, TLC_1 sent its position (42), but the observer associated with TLC_1 did not wait long enough to record this action.
- $(\sigma_1^3 = start_1?.(2).(1).driver_1?1.(1).(2).trainPos_1!42.(1).trainPos_2?300.(1).$
       $trainPos_1!60.(1).TrainPos_2?300$,
  $\sigma_2^3 = start_2?.(1).(1).trainPos_2!300.(2).(2).trainPos_1?42.(3).(2).trainPos_2!300.(1))$
  does not constitute an observable multitrace. Indeed, in σ_1^3, $trainPos_1!42$ is emitted and 3 units of time later, $trainPos_2?300$ is received a second time. This reception corresponds to the second emission $trainPos_2!300$ in σ_2^3. Now, in σ_2^3, the second emission $trainPos_2!300$ occurs 5 units of time after

the reception $trainPos_1?42$. This contradicts the time elapsing property: indeed, for TLC_1, time elapses of only 3 units of time between emission of 42 and reception of 300, but, meanwhile, for TLC_2, it elapses for at least 5 units of time since it comprises the duration separating the reception of 42 and the emission of 300.

6   Implementing Distributed Timed Testing

This section describes how testing for *dtioco* can be carried out in a manner that reflects our underlying assumptions and also utilises our compositionality result.

6.1   Architecture

Fig. 2. Distributed testing Architecture

Figure 2 illustrates the architecture used. The SUT $\mathbb{S}$ is composed of LUTs $\mathbb{LS}_1$, $\mathbb{LS}_2$ and $\mathbb{LS}_3$. Each LUT $\mathbb{LS}_i$ has channels connected to the environment (dark connections) and internal channels to exchange values with other LUTs $\mathbb{LS}_i$ (light connections). A tester $\mathbb{T}_i$ is associated with each LUT $\mathbb{LS}_i$ and $\mathbb{T}_i$ may control inputs and observe outputs occurring on channels connected to the environment. The tester may also observe values sent through internal channels (represented by the magnifying glasses). Each $\mathbb{LS}_i$ executes in a centralised way, so that the local tester can observe the order of actions occurring on its channels and can measure durations between consecutive actions. Therefore, behaviours observed by each $\mathbb{T}_i$ can be viewed as timed traces and may be analysed with respect to the set of timed traces of the model specifying the LUT. We cannot directly combine the timed traces observed at different LUTs since there is no global clock. Internal communications, represented by a cloud, are observed twice, at the emission and at the reception, by different testers. Recall, however, that we assume that all testers use clocks progressing at the same rate.

6.2   Process

Consider SUT $\mathbb{S} = (\mathbb{LS}_1, \ldots, \mathbb{LS}_n)$ with tester $\mathbb{T}_i$ at each $\mathbb{LS}_i$ (i in $1..n$), that we want to test against system $Sys = (\mathbb{A}_1, \ldots, \mathbb{A}_n)$. Based on Definition 8, and Property 1, we see that any fault of the whole system can be identified either at the level of one LUT, or at the level of internal communications:
$$(\mathbb{S} \; dtioco \; Sys) \iff ((\forall i \leq n, \mathbb{LS}_i|_{\mathbb{S}} \; tioco \; \mathbb{A}_i) \wedge Sem(\mathbb{S}) \subseteq OTraces(\Sigma_{Sys}))$$

So, if a local tester $\mathbb{T}_i$ exhibits timed trace σ_i contradicting $\mathbb{LS}_i|_{\mathbb{S}} \; tioco \; \mathbb{A}_i$, or if $(\sigma_1, \ldots, \sigma_n)$ (σ_i observed by tester $\mathbb{T}_i$) does not form an observational trace, then $(\mathbb{S} \; dtioco \; Sys)$ does not hold. Moreover, as these conditions are sufficient to ensure that $\mathbb{S} \; dtioco \; Sys$, this suggests a two step testing process:

(1) **Timed unitary testing of each $\mathbb{LS}_i$ w.r.t. $\mathbb{A}_i$.** Tester $\mathbb{T}_i$ associated with $\mathbb{LS}_i$ checks that the timed trace it observes is allowed by $\mathbb{A}_i$ under *tioco*. If one of the testers reveals an error, then $(\mathbb{S} \; dtioco \; Sys)$ does not hold;

(2) **Testing of internal communications.** All the $\mathbb{T}_i$ keep track of the localised timed traces σ_i observed. Tuple $(\sigma_1, \ldots, \sigma_n)$ of timed traces is analysed to check whether or not it constitutes an observational trace. If not, then $(\mathbb{S} \; dtioco \; Sys)$ does not hold.

For the first step, the test execution process corresponds to classical unitary testing since $\mathbb{T}_i$ interacts with $\mathbb{LS}_i$ in the context of the whole system (modeled as $\mathbb{LS}_i|_{\mathbb{S}}$). The only slight difference is that inputs on internal channels are not controlled by the tester but by the remaining part of the system (the $\mathbb{LS}_j$ with $j \neq i$) and the cloud network. This kind of test architecture has already been addressed, typically in the context of *orchestrations*, a particular class of web services compositions. An orchestrator can be seen as a main localised module that orchestrates exchanges between a user and some web services. In [22], we proposed an (untimed) algorithm to test an orchestrator in the context of the system in which they are plugged. In such a test architecture, the orchestrator receives inputs from a user and web services: typically, the latter are not controlled by the tester. An orchestrator is an LUT and a whole orchestration can be seen as a special case of systems addressed in this paper. The algorithm in [22] can be adapted to be used in Step (1) to incorporate timed aspects, for example by considering the on-line test generation algorithm given in [14], or an off-line alternative [15] and by adapting them in order to ignore any duration that occurs before the first action of a timed trace. In fact, in our test framework, the off-line approach should be preferred, since for the moment, we have not addressed the question of test case generation, but focus mainly on the oracle problem. So, as we only need an algorithm for analysing trace conformance, it can be obtained for free from an off-line testing architecture.

Due to the lack of space, we do not fully present Step (1), and rather focus on the analysis of the system multitraces to check the observational trace property, and thus to achieve Step (2).

6.3   Observational Multitrace Checking

The algorithm (Figure 3) checking the observable multitrace property follows the points of Definitions 3 and 4. In the sequel we assume that any duration observed in any timed trace consists of sequences of 1 unit (which implies that we can see all delays between communication actions as integers). This is exactly what is done in practice in a timed testing process, when using a clock to measure time between actions in a testing process (the clock itself imposes the basic delay defining the unity). The main idea is to store a multitrace $(\sigma_1^c, \ldots, \sigma_n^c)$ that is observed at the end of a run, to read it from the beginning and to store the elements already read in a multitrace $ot = (\mu_1, \ldots, \mu_n)$ while keeping the elements still to be read in a multitrace $mt = (\sigma_1, \ldots, \sigma_n)$. The algorithm $check(mt, ot)$ ends with success (**return** $True$) when the current multitrace $mt = (\sigma_1, \ldots, \sigma_n)$ to be analysed is the empty multitrace $(\varepsilon, \ldots, \varepsilon)$ (line 5) and the read multitrace $ot = (\mu_1, \ldots, \mu_n)$ corresponds to the complete initial multitrace $(\sigma_1^c, \ldots, \sigma_n^c)$. There are two ways of reading a multitrace $(\sigma_1, \ldots, \sigma_n)$: either there exists a trace σ_i beginning with an action a_i (Case (1)) (line 8), or a duration d can be read on all admissible traces (Case (2)) (line 13):

Case (1). An action a_i can be read by the algorithm from σ_i (line 12), that is, removed from the trace still to be read ($replace(mt, i, tail(\sigma_i))$) and added to the trace already read ($replace(ot, i, addEnd(\mu_i, a_i))$) if one of the following conditions is fulfilled: (1) a_i is an emission towards the environment or other subsystems ($isOuptut(a_i)$), (2) a_i is a reception from the environment ($isInputEnv(a_i)$), (3) a_i is a reception of a message m on the channel c coming from one of the other subsystems ($isInputInt(a_i)$) and the number of occurrences of a_i in μ_i (elements already read by the algorithm for the subsystem $\mathbb{LS}_i$) is strictly less than the number of emissions already read by the algorithm, i.e. the number of $c!m$ occurring in $(\mu_1, \ldots, \mu_n)$ ($Nb\_I(\mu_i, a_i) < Nb\_O(ot, a_i)$), provided that none of the subsystems $\mathbb{LS}_j$ ($i \neq j$) that can emit on the channel c has a trace fully read, i.e. $\forall j \mid \mathbb{LS}_j$ can emit on c ,$\sigma_j \neq \varepsilon$, and lastly, (4) a_i is a reception of a message m on the channel c coming from one of the other subsystems and there exists a subsystem $\mathbb{LS}_j$ ($i \neq j$) that can emit on the channel c whose trace is already fully read, i.e. $\exists j \mid \mathbb{LS}_j$ can emit on c ,$\sigma_j = \varepsilon$.
In the algorithm, the predicate $FullR(Chan(a_i), mt)$ is $True$ when for all j such that $\mathbb{LS}_j$ can emit on $Chan(a_i)$, σ_j (occurring in $mt = (\sigma_1, \ldots, \sigma_n)$) is equal to ε. The predicate is used both for subcases (3) and (4).

Case (2). A duration $d = 1$ can be read by the algorithm if one of the non empty traces σ_i starts with a duration $d_i > 0$ and if for all traces σ_i starting with an action, the reading of the trace has not been started, i.e. $\mu_i = \varepsilon$ ($TimeElapsing(mt, ot)$). In this case, the duration d is subtracted from all durations d_i occurring at the beginning of traces σ_i (d_i is simply removed if $d_i = 1$) and added to the corresponding μ_i ($time\_elapse\_of\_1(mt, ot)$).

If the reading cannot be continued until reaching the empty multitrace, then the initial multitrace does not meet the targeted observable multitrace property ($check(mt, ot)$ returns the value *False*, initialised at line 7). As the underlying principle consists of considering all possible configurations for interleaving emissions and receptions of different subsystems, its complexity is clearly high. However, as the algorithm is applied only once the local traces are completely stored (off-line algorithm), a good efficiency is not of primary necessity.

Algorithm 1. Checking of the observable multitrace property

```
1  check(mt, ot):        (* initial call : check((σ₁ᶜ, ..., σₙᶜ), (ε, ..., ε)) *)
2  (σ₁, ..., σₙ) = mt
3  (μ₁, ..., μₙ) = ot
4  if  mt = (ε, ..., ε) then
5  ⌊ return True

6  else
7  │  Cond = False
8  │  for i in [1, .., n] do
9  │  │  if notEmpty(σᵢ) then
10 │  │  │  aᵢ = first(σᵢ)
11 │  │  │  if isOutput(aᵢ) or  isInputEnv(aᵢ) or
       │  │  │  (isInputInt(aᵢ) and Nb_I(μᵢ, aᵢ) < Nb_O(ot, aᵢ) and not(FullR(Chan(aᵢ), mt)))
       │  │  │  or (isInputInt(aᵢ) and FullR(Chan(aᵢ), mt)) then
12 │  │  │  │  Cond =
       │  │  │  ⌊ Cond or check(replace(mt, i, tail(σᵢ)), replace(ot, i, addEnd(μᵢ, aᵢ)))

13 │  if TimeElapsing(mt, ot) then
14 │  │  (mt', ot') = time_elapse_of_1(mt, ot)
15 │  ⌊ Cond = Cond or check(mt', ot')

16 ⌊  return Cond;
```

Fig. 3. Checking Observable Trace property

7   Conclusions

There has been growing interest in distributed testing where the SUT has physically distributed interfaces, there is a separate tester at each interface and a tester only observes the interactions at its interface. This paper extends previous work by investigating distributed testing from specifications based on TIOTSs that interact through an implicit distributed protocol. We assume that the SUT and specification are both composed of separate components at the interfaces and that the sending and receiving of messages between components is observed during testing. Components themselves are described as TIOTS. We define the semantics of such systems as a sets of tuples containing a local trace for each interface. Such tuples, called observational multitraces, have to respect consistency conditions ensuring that all local traces together reflect correct interactions between components. Having defined observations, we defined an implementation relation *dtioco* for distributed testing. This implementation relation is an extension of *tioco* (timed version of *ioco*). It captures two things: tuples resulting from distributed interactions with the system under test are valid (*i.e.* are observational multitraces), and all reactions of the system under test after a specified multitrace should also be specified.

We also provide a compositionality result, which shows that an SUT conforms to a specification under *dtioco* if and only if all of the observations of the SUT that can be made are valid and the local projections of the SUT conform to the corresponding components of the specification under *tioco*. This result allows us to reuse techniques developed for *tioco*. We then describe how testing can be implemented and give an algorithm that checks that an observation is valid.

Since this is the first work to define an implementation relation for distributed timed testing, there are several lines of future work. First, there is a need to define and implement suitable test generation algorithms. In particular, it is necessary to define distributed test purposes, and to find test generation strategies to drive system executions so that they follow those test purposes. Recent work has shown that for untimed systems it is undecidable whether there is a distributed test case guaranteed to force a model M into a given state s or to distinguish two states and that this holds even if we restrict M to being a deterministic finite state machine (DFSM) [4]. Thus, general test generation problems are likely to be undecidable but we will investigate conditions under which they are decidable. Such test generation problems become tractable if we restrict attention to controllable test cases and DFSM models [8] and so it would be interesting to investigate notions of controllability for timed models. Second, we assume that local clocks progress at the same rate; it should be possible to generalise the results to the case where the clocks can drift but, for example, we have upper bounds on the rate of drift. We also intend to consider the case where the sending and receiving of internal messages are hidden.

References

1. ISO/IEC JTC 1, J.T.C.: International Standard ISO/IEC 9646-1. Information Technology - Open Systems Interconnection - Conformance testing methodology and framework - Part 1: General concepts. ISO/IEC (1994)
2. Dssouli, R., von Bochmann, G.: Error detection with multiple observers. In: Protocol Specification, Testing and Verification V, pp. 483–494. Elsevier Science, North Holland (1985)
3. Dssouli, R., von Bochmann, G.: Conformance testing with multiple observers. In: Protocol Specification, Testing and Verification VI, pp. 217–229. Elsevier Science, North Holland (1986)
4. Hierons, R.M.: Reaching and distinguishing states of distributed systems. SIAM Journal on Computing 39(8), 3480–3500 (2010)
5. Luo, G., Dssouli, R., von Bochmann, G.: Generating synchronizable test sequences based on finite state machine with distributed ports. In: The 6th IFIP Workshop on Protocol Test Systems, pp. 139–153. Elsevier, North-Holland (1993)
6. Sarikaya, B., von Bochmann, G.: Synchronization and specification issues in protocol testing. IEEE Transactions on Communications 32, 389–395 (1984)
7. Ural, H., Wang, Z.: Synchronizable test sequence generation using UIO sequences. Computer Communications 16(10), 653–661 (1993)

8. Hierons, R.M., Ural, H.: The effect of the distributed test architecture on the power of testing. The Computer Journal 51(4), 497–510 (2008)
9. Brinksma, E., Heerink, L., Tretmans, J.: Factorized test generation for multi-input/output transition systems. In: FIP TC6 11th International Workshop on Testing Communicating Systems (IWTCS). IFIP Conference Proceedings, vol. 131, pp. 67–82. Kluwer (1998)
10. Hierons, R.M., Merayo, M.G., Núñez, M.: Implementation relations for the distributed test architecture. In: Suzuki, K., Higashino, T., Ulrich, A., Hasegawa, T. (eds.) TestCom/FATES 2008. LNCS, vol. 5047, pp. 200–215. Springer, Heidelberg (2008)
11. Hierons, R.M., Merayo, M.G., Núñez, M.: Implementation relations and test generation for systems with distributed interfaces. Distributed Computing 25(1), 35–62 (2012)
12. Hierons, R.M., Merayo, M.G., Núñez, M.: Using time to add order to distributed testing. In: Giannakopoulou, D., Méry, D. (eds.) FM 2012. LNCS, vol. 7436, pp. 232–246. Springer, Heidelberg (2012)
13. Khoumsi, A.: A temporal approach for testing distributed systems. IEEE Transactions on Software Engineering 28(11), 1085–1103 (2002)
14. Escobedo, J.P., Gaston, C., Le Gall, P.: Timed Conformance Testing for Orchestrated Service Discovery. In: Arbab, F., Ölveczky, P.C. (eds.) FACS 2011. LNCS, vol. 7253, pp. 133–150. Springer, Heidelberg (2012)
15. Bannour, B., Escobedo, J., Gaston, C., Gall, P.L.: Off-line test case generation for timed symbolic model-based conformance testing. In: Nielsen, B., Weise, C. (eds.) ICTSS 2012. LNCS, vol. 7641, pp. 133–150. Springer, Heidelberg (2012)
16. Gaudel, M.C.: Testing can be formal too. In: Mosses, P.D., Nielsen, M. (eds.) CAAP 1995, FASE 1995, and TAPSOFT 1995. LNCS, vol. 915, pp. 82–96. Springer, Heidelberg (1995)
17. Krichen, M., Tripakis, S.: Black-box time systems. In: Proc. of Int. SPIN Workshop Model Checking of Software. Springer (2004)
18. Bohnenkamp, H.C., Belinfante, A.: Timed Testing with TorX. In: Fitzgerald, J.S., Hayes, I.J., Tarlecki, A. (eds.) FM 2005. LNCS, vol. 3582, pp. 173–188. Springer, Heidelberg (2005)
19. Schmaltz, J., Tretmans, J.: On Conformance Testing for Timed Systems. In: Cassez, F., Jard, C. (eds.) FORMATS 2008. LNCS, vol. 5215, pp. 250–264. Springer, Heidelberg (2008)
20. Meyer, R., Faber, J., Hoenicke, J., Rybalchenko, A.: Model checking duration calculus: a practical approach. Formal Asp. Comput. 20(4-5), 481–505 (2008)
21. Andres, C., Yevtushenko, N., On, A.R.C.: modeling and testing the european train control system. Technical Report TechRca 14-03-2013, Telecom Sudparis (2013)
22. Escobedo, J., Gaston, C., Gall, P.L., Cavalli, A.R.: Testing web service orchestrators in context: A symbolic approach. In: Int. Conf. SEFM. IEEE (2010)

Unfolding-Based Test Selection
for Concurrent Conformance

Hernán Ponce de León[1], Stefan Haar[1], and Delphine Longuet[2]

[1] INRIA and LSV, École Normale Supérieure de Cachan and CNRS, France
ponce@lsv.ens-cachan.fr, stefan.haar@inria.fr
[2] Univ Paris-Sud, LRI UMR8623, 91405 Orsay, France
longuet@lri.fr

Abstract. Model-based testing has mainly focused on models where currency is interpreted as interleaving (like the *ioco* theory for labeled transition systems), which may be too coarse when one wants concurrency to be preserved in the implementation. In order to test such concurrent systems, we choose to use Petri nets as specifications and define a concurrent conformance relation named *co-ioco*. We propose a test generation algorithm based on Petri net unfolding able to build a complete test suite w.r.t our *co-ioco* conformance relation. In addition we propose a coverage criterion based on a dedicated notion of complete prefixes that selects a manageable test suite.

Model-Based Testing. The aim of testing is to execute a software system, the *implementation*, on a set of input data selected so as to find discrepancies between actual behavior and intended behavior described by the *specification*. The testing process is usually decomposed into three phases: selection of relevant input data, called a *test suite*, among the possible inputs of the system; submission of this test suite to the implementation, its *execution*; and decision of the success or the failure of the test suite submission, known as the *oracle problem*. We focus here on the selection phase, crucial for relevance and efficiency of testing.

Model-based testing requires a behavioral description of the system under test. One of the most popular formalisms studied in conformance testing is that of *input output labeled transition systems* (IOLTS). In this framework, the correctness (or conformance) relation the system under test (SUT) and its specification must verify is formalized by the *ioco* relation [1]. This relation has become a standard, and is used as a basis in several testing theories for extended state-based models: restrictive transition systems [2, 3], symbolic transition systems [4, 5], timed automata [6], multi-port finite state machines [7].

Model-Based Testing of Concurrent Systems. Systems composed of concurrent components are naturally modeled as a *network of finite automata*, a formal class of models that can be captured equivalently by *safe Petri nets*. Concurrency in a specification can arise for different reasons. First, two events may be physically localized on different components, and thus be "naturally" independent of one another; this distribution is then part of the system construction. Second, the specification may not care about the order in which two actions are performed *on the same component*, and thus leave the

H. Yenigün, C. Yilmaz, and A. Ulrich (Eds.): ICTSS 2013, LNCS 8254, pp. 98–113, 2013.

choice of their ordering to the implementation. Depending on the nature of the concurrency specified in a given case, and thus on the intention of the specification, the *implementation relations* have to allow or disallow ordering of concurrent events. The kind of systems that we consider is of the first type, where concurrency comes from the distribution of components. Therefore, we want concurrency of the specification to be preserved in the implementation.

Model-based testing of concurrent systems has been studied for a long time [8–10], however it is most of the time studied in the context of interleaving, or trace, semantics, which is known to suffer the state space explosion problem. While the passage to models with explicit concurrency has been successfully performed in other fields of formal analysis such as model checking or diagnosis, testing has embraced such models somewhat more recently. Ulrich and König propose in [11] a framework for testing concurrent systems specified by communicating labeled transition systems. The specification is translated into a Petri net, and a complete prefix of its unfolding is used to construct a *behavior machine*. The conformance relation proposed in [11] is a generalization of trace equivalence relation; their work does not include a test selection procedure, or how the choice of complete prefix impacts selection. Since our goal is to include *conflict* relations as well, we will use *event structures* and their properties.

Haar et al [12, 13] generalize the basic notions and techniques of I/O-sequence based conformance testing via a generalized I/O-automaton model where partially ordered patterns of input/output events are admitted as transition labels. However, these models still maintain a sequential automaton as the system's skeleton, and include synchronization constraints, e.g. all events in the course of a transition must be completed before any other transition can start.

Our Contribution. In order to enlarge the application domain, and at stronger benefits from concurrency modeling, we have introduced in [14] a concurrent conformance relation named *co-ioco*, as a generalization of *ioco*. In [15], we dropped the input enabledness assumption and enlarged the conformance relation in order to observe refusals. Extra causality between outputs specified as concurrent is also allowed.

This paper extends [14, 15] with a conformance relation where actions specified as concurrent must occur independently, on different processes, in any conformant implementation. While sufficient conditions for soundness and exhaustiveness of test suites have been given in [15], we need more: in practice, only a finite number of test cases can be executed; hence we need a method to select a finite set of relevant test cases covering as many behaviors as possible (thus finding as many anomalies as possible).

The main contributions of this paper are the following: an algorithm to construct a complete test suite; a selection criterion that stipulates which behaviors of the system should be tested in order to have a good coverage of the specification; and an algorithm to construct a sound test suite based on this criterion.

Outline. The paper is organized as follows. Section 1 recalls basic notions about Petri nets, occurrence nets and labeled event structures. Section 2 introduces our testing hypotheses and our *co-ioco* conformance relation. In Section 3, we define the notion of complete test suite, we give sufficient conditions for a test suite to be complete and an algorithm producing such a test suite. Finally, we define in Section 4 our notion of coverage criterion and we adapt the complete finite prefix algorithm of [16] to build a sound test suite satisfying this criterion.

1   I/O Petri Nets and Their Semantics

We choose to use *Petri nets* as specifications to have explicit concurrency. The semantics associated to a Petri net is given by its unfolding to an *occurrence net*, which can also be seen as an *event structure*. We will present both notions since we use them in different contexts in the following. The execution traces for this semantics are not sequences but *partial orders*, which keep concurrency explicit. We recall here these basic notions.

I/O Petri Nets. A *net* is a tuple $N = (P, T, F)$ where *(i)* $P \neq \emptyset$ is a set of *places*, *(ii)* $T \neq \emptyset$ is a set of *transitions* such that $P \cap T = \emptyset$, *(iii)* $F \subseteq (P \times T) \cup (T \times P)$ is a set of *flow arcs*. A *marking* is a multiset M of places, i.e. a map $M : P \to \mathbb{N}$. A *Petri net* is a tuple $\mathcal{N} = (P, T, F, M_0)$, where *(i)* (P, T, F) is a finite net, and *(ii)* $M_0 : P \to \mathbb{N}$ is an *initial marking*. Elements of $P \cup T$ are called the *nodes* of $\mathcal{N}$. For a transition $t \in T$, we call ${}^\bullet t = \{p \mid (p, t) \in F\}$ the *preset* of t, and $t^\bullet = \{p \mid (t, p) \in F\}$ the *postset* of t. In figures, we represent as usual places by empty circles, transitions by squares, F by arrows, and the marking of a place p by black tokens in p. A transition t is *enabled* in marking M, written $M \xrightarrow{t}$, if $\forall p \in {}^\bullet t$, $M(p) > 0$. This enabled transition can *fire*, resulting in a new marking $M' = M - {}^\bullet t + t^\bullet$. This firing relation is denoted by $M \xrightarrow{t} M'$. A marking M is *reachable* from M_0 if there exists a *firing sequence*, i.e. transitions $t_0 \ldots t_n$ such that $M_0 \xrightarrow{t_0} M_1 \xrightarrow{t_1} \ldots \xrightarrow{t_n} M$. The set of markings reachable from M_0 (in $\mathcal{N}$) is denoted $\mathbf{R}_\mathcal{N}(M_0)$ (we drop the subscript referring to $\mathcal{N}$ when it is clear from the context). A Petri net $\mathcal{N} = (P, T, F, M_0)$ is *(1-)safe* iff for all reachable markings $M \in \mathbf{R}(M_0)$, $M(p) \in \{0, 1\}$ for all $p \in P$.

Let $\mathcal{I}$ and $\mathcal{O}$ be two disjoint non-empty sets of *input* and *output* labels, respectively. For a net $N = (P, T, F)$, a mapping $\lambda : T \to (\mathcal{I} \uplus \mathcal{O})$ is called an *I/O-labeling*. Denote by $T^\mathcal{I}$ and $T^\mathcal{O}$ the input and output transition sets, respectively; that is, $T^\mathcal{I} \triangleq \lambda^{-1}(\mathcal{I})$ and $T^\mathcal{O} \triangleq \lambda^{-1}(\mathcal{O})$. An *I/O Petri net* is a pair $\Sigma = (\mathcal{N}, \lambda)$, where $\mathcal{N} = (P, T, F, M_0)$ is a 1-safe Petri net and $\lambda : T \to (\mathcal{I} \uplus \mathcal{O})$ an I/O-labeling. Σ is called *deterministically labeled* iff no two transitions with the same label are simultaneously enabled, i.e. for all $t_1, t_2 \in T$ and $M \in \mathbf{R}(M_0)$:

$$(M \xrightarrow{t_1} \wedge M \xrightarrow{t_2} \wedge \lambda(t_1) = \lambda(t_2)) \Rightarrow t_1 = t_2$$

Note that 1-safeness of the Petri net is not sufficient for guaranteeing deterministic labeling. Deterministic labeling ensures that the system behavior is locally discernible through labels, either through distinct inputs or through observation of different outputs.

When testing reactive systems, we need to differentiate situations where the system can still produce some outputs and those where the system can not evolve without an input from the environment. Such situations are captured by the notion of *quiescence* [17]. A marking is said quiescent if it does not enable output transitions, i.e. $M \xrightarrow{t}$ implies $t \in T^\mathcal{I}$. The observation of quiescence is usually instrumented by timers. Jard and Jéron [18] present three different kinds of quiescence: *output quiescence* when the

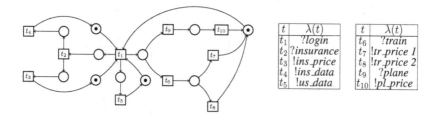

t	$\lambda(t)$
t_1	?login
t_2	?insurance
t_3	!ins_price
t_4	!ins_data
t_5	!us_data

t	$\lambda(t)$
t_6	?train
t_7	!tr_price 1
t_8	!tr_price 2
t_9	?plane
t_{10}	!pl_price

Fig. 1. A travel agency specified by an I/O Petri net

system is waiting for an input from the environment, *deadlock* when the system can not evolve anymore, and *livelock* when the system diverges by an infinite sequence of silent actions.

Occurrence Nets and Unfoldings. Occurrence nets can be seen as Petri nets[1] with a special acyclic structure that highlights *conflict* between transitions that compete for resources. Formally, let $N = (P, T, F)$ be a net, $<_N$ the transitive closure of F, and $\leqslant_N$ the reflexive closure of $<_N$. We say that transitions t_1 and t_2 are in *structural conflict*, written $t_1 \#^\omega t_2$, if and only if $t_1 \neq t_2$ and $^\bullet t_1 \cap {}^\bullet t_2 \neq \emptyset$. Conflict is inherited along $<_N$, that is, the conflict relation $\#$ is given by

$$a \# b \Leftrightarrow \exists t_a, t_b \in T : t_a \#^\omega t_b \wedge t_a \leqslant_N a \wedge t_b \leqslant_N b$$

Finally, the *concurrency relation* **co** holds between nodes $a, b \in P \cup T$ that are neither ordered nor in conflict, i.e. $a \, \mathbf{co} \, b \Leftrightarrow \neg (a \leqslant b) \wedge \neg (a \# b) \wedge \neg (b < a)$.

Definition 1. *A net $ON = (B, E, G)$ is an* occurrence net *if and only if*

1. $\leqslant_{ON}$ *is a partial order;*
2. *for all $b \in B$, $|^\bullet b| \in \{0, 1\}$;*
3. *for all $x \in B \cup E$, the set $[x] = \{y \in E \mid y \leqslant x\}$ is finite;*
4. *no self-conflict, i.e. there is no $x \in B \cup E$ such that $x \# x$;*
5. $\perp \in E$ *is the only $\leqslant$-minimal node (event $\perp$ creates the initial conditions)*

Call the elements of E *events*, those of B *conditions*. An ON can also be given as a tuple $(B, E \backslash \{\perp\}, F, cut_0)$, where $cut_0 = \perp^\bullet$ is the set of minimal conditions. Occurrence nets are the mathematical form of the *partial order unfolding semantics* [16]. A *branching process* of a 1-safe Petri net $\mathcal{N} = (N, M_0)$ is given by a pair $\Phi = (ON, \varphi)$, where $ON = (B, E, G)$ is an occurrence net, and $\varphi : B \cup E \to P \cup T$ is such that:

1. it is a homomorphism from ON to N, i.e.
   - $\varphi(B) \subseteq P$ and $\varphi(E) \subseteq T$, and
   - for every $e \in E$, the restriction of φ to $^\bullet e$ is a bijection between the set $^\bullet e$ in ON and the set $^\bullet \varphi(e)$ in N, and similarly for $e^\bullet$ and $\varphi(e)^\bullet$;

---

[1] When one allows Petri nets to be *infinite*.

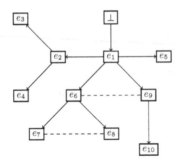

e	$\varphi(e)$	$\lambda(e)$
e_1	t_1	*?login*
e_2	t_2	*?insurance*
e_3	t_3	*!ins_price*
e_4	t_4	*!ins_data*
e_5	t_5	*!us_data*
e_6	t_6	*?train*
e_7	t_7	*!tr_price 1*
e_8	t_8	*!tr_price 2*
e_9	t_9	*?plane*
e_{10}	t_{10}	*!pl_price*

Fig. 2. Part of the unfolding of the PN from Figure 1 represented as an IOLES. Causality is represented by arrows and immediate conflict by dashed lines.

2. the restriction of φ to cut_0 is a bijection from cut_0 to M_0; and
3. for every $e_1, e_2 \in E$, if $\bullet e_1 = \bullet e_2$ and $\varphi(e_1) = \varphi(e_2)$ then $e_1 = e_2$.

The unique (up to isomorphism) maximal branching process $\mathcal{U} = (ON_{\mathcal{U}}, \varphi_{\mathcal{U}})$ of $\mathcal{N}$ is called the *unfolding* of $\mathcal{N}$.

Input/Output Labeled Event Structures. Occurrence nets give rise to event structures in the sense of Winskel et al [19]; as usual, we will use both the event structure and the occurrence net formalism, whichever is more convenient. An *input/output labeled event structure (IOLES)* over an alphabet $L = \mathcal{I} \uplus \mathcal{O}$ is a 4-tuple $\mathcal{E} = (E, \leq, \#, \lambda)$ where *(i)* E is a set of events, *(ii)* $\leq \subseteq E \times E$ is a partial order (called *causality*) satisfying the property of *finite causes*, i.e. $\forall e \in E : |\{e' \in E \mid e' \leq e\}| < \infty$, *(iii)* $\# \subseteq E \times E$ is an irreflexive symmetric relation (called *conflict*) satisfying the property of *conflict heredity*, i.e. $\forall e, e', e'' \in E : e \# e' \wedge e' \leq e'' \Rightarrow e \# e''$, *(iv)* $\lambda : E \to (\mathcal{I} \uplus \mathcal{O})$ is a labeling mapping. In addition, we assume every IOLES $\mathcal{E}$ has a unique minimal event $\perp_{\mathcal{E}}$. We denote the class of all input/output labeled event structures over L by $\mathcal{IOLES}(L)$. Given event e, its *local configuration* is $[e] \triangleq \{e' \in E \mid e' \leq e\}$, and its set of *causal predecessors* is $\langle e \rangle \triangleq [e] \backslash \{e\}$. Two events $e, e' \in E$ are said to be concurrent (e **co** e') iff neither $e \leq e'$ nor $e' \leq e$ nor $e \# e'$ hold; $e, e' \in E$ are in *immediate conflict* ($e_1 \#^\mu e_2$) iff $[e_1] \times [e_2] \cap \# = \{(e_1, e_2)\}$. A *configuration* of an IOLES is a non-empty set $C \subseteq E$ that is *(i)* causally closed, i.e. $e \in C$ implies $[e] \subseteq C$, and *(ii) conflict-free*, i.e. $e \in C$ and $e\#e'$ imply $e' \notin C$. Note that we define, for technical convenience, all configurations to be non-empty; the initial configuration of $\mathcal{E}$, containing only $\perp_{\mathcal{E}}$ and denoted by $\perp_{\mathcal{E}}$, is contained in every configuration of $\mathcal{E}$. We denote the set of all the configurations of $\mathcal{E}$ by $\mathcal{C}(\mathcal{E})$.

Labeled Partial Orders. We are interested in testing distributed systems where concurrent actions occur in different components of the system. For this reason, we want to keep concurrency explicit, i.e. specifications do not impose any order of execution between concurrent events. Labeled partial orders can then be used to represent executions of such systems. A *labeled partial order* (lpo) is a tuple $lpo = (E, \leq, \lambda)$ where E is a set of events, $\leq$ is a reflexive, antisymmetric, and transitive relation, and $\lambda : E \to L$ is a labeling mapping to a fix alphabet L. We denote the class of all labeled partial orders over

L by $\mathcal{LPO}(L)$. Consider $lpo_1 = (E_1, \leq_1, \lambda_1)$ and $lpo_2 = (E_2, \leq_2, \lambda_2) \in \mathcal{LPO}(L)$. A bijective function $f : E_1 \rightarrow E_2$ is an isomorphism between lpo_1 and lpo_2 iff (i) $\forall e, e' \in E_1 : e \leq_1 e' \Leftrightarrow f(e) \leq_2 f(e')$ and (ii) $\forall e \in E_1 : \lambda_1(e) = \lambda_2(f(e))$. Two labeled partial orders lpo_1 and lpo_2 are isomorphic if there exists an isomorphism between them. A *partially ordered multiset* (pomset) is an isomorphism class of lpos. We will represent such a class by one of its objects. Denote the class of all non empty pomsets over L by $\mathcal{POMSET}(L)$. The evolution of the system is captured by the following definition: pomsets are observations.

Definition 2. *For* $\mathcal{E} = (E, \leq, \#, \lambda) \in \mathcal{IOLES}(L), \omega \in \mathcal{POMSET}(L)$ *and* $C, C' \in \mathcal{C}(\mathcal{E})$, *define*

$$C \overset{\omega}{\Longrightarrow} C' \triangleq \exists lpo = (E_\omega, \leq_\omega, \lambda_\omega) \in \omega : E_\omega \subseteq E \backslash C, C' = C \cup E_\omega,$$
$$\leq \cap (E_\omega \times E_\omega) = \leq_\omega \text{ and } \lambda_{|E_\omega} = \lambda_\omega$$
$$C \overset{\omega}{\Longrightarrow} \quad \triangleq \exists C' : C \overset{\omega}{\Longrightarrow} C'$$

We can now define the notions of traces and of configurations reachable from a given configuration by an observation. Our notion of traces is similar to the one of Ulrich and König [11].

Definition 3. *For* $\mathcal{E} \in \mathcal{IOLES}(L), \omega \in \mathcal{POMSET}(L), C, C' \in \mathcal{C}(\mathcal{E})$, *define*

$$traces(\mathcal{E}) \triangleq \{\omega \in \mathcal{POMSET}(L) \mid \perp_\mathcal{E} \overset{\omega}{\Longrightarrow}\}$$
$$C \text{ after } \omega \triangleq \{C' \mid C \overset{\omega}{\Longrightarrow} C'\}$$

Note that for deterministically labeled I/O Petri nets, the corresponding IOLES is deterministic and the set of reachable configurations is a singleton.

2   Testing Framework for IOPNs

Testing Hypotheses. We assume that the specification of the system under test is given as a 1-safe and deterministically labeled I/O Petri net $\Sigma = (\mathcal{N}, \lambda)$ over alphabet $L = \mathcal{I} \uplus \mathcal{O}$ of input and output labels. To be able to test an implementation against such a specification, we make a set of testing assumptions. First of all, we make the usual testing assumption that the behavior of the SUT itself can be modeled by a 1-safe I/O Petri net over the same alphabet of labels. We also assume as usual that the specification does not contain cycles of outputs actions, so that the number of expected outputs after a given trace is finite.

Assumption 1. *The net* $\mathcal{N}$ *has no cycle containing only output transitions.*

Third, in order to allow the observation of both the outputs produced by the system and the inputs it can accept, markings where conflicting inputs and outputs are enabled should not be reachable. As a matter of fact, if conflicting input and output are enabled in a given marking, once the output is produced, the input is not enabled anymore, and

vice versa. Such markings prevent from observing the inputs enabled in a given configuration, which we will see is one of the key points of our conformance relation. For this
reason, we restrict the form of the nets we consider via the following assumption on the
unfolding:[2]

Assumption 2. *The unfolding of the net $\mathcal{N}$ has no immediate conflict between input
and output events, i.e. $\forall e_1 \in E^{\mathcal{I}}, e_2 \in E^{\mathcal{O}} : \neg(e_1 \#^{\mu} e_2)$.*

Conformance Relation. A formal testing framework relies on the definition of a conformance relation to be satisfied by the SUT and its specification. In the LTS framework,
the *ioco* conformance relation compares the outputs and blockings in the implementation after a trace of the specification to the outputs and blockings authorised after this
trace in the specification. Classically, the produced outputs of the system under test are
elements of $\mathcal{O}$ (single actions) and blockings are observable by a special action $\delta \notin L$
which represents the expiration of a timer.

By contrast, in partial order semantics, we need any set of outputs to be entirely
produced by the system under test before we send a new input; this is necessary to
detect outputs depending on extra inputs. Suppose two concurrent outputs o_1 and o_2
depending on input i_1 and another input i_2 depending on both outputs. Clearly, an
implementation that accepts i_2 before o_2 should not be considered as correct, but if i_2 is
sent too early to the system, we may not know if the occurrence of o_2 depends or not on
i_2. For this reason we define the expected outputs from a configuration C as the pomset
of outputs leading to a quiescent configuration. Such a configuration always exists, and
must be finite by Assumption 1.

The notion of quiescence is inherited from nets, i.e. a configuration C is quiescent iff
$C \xRightarrow{\omega}$ implies $\omega \in \mathcal{POMSET}(\mathcal{I})$. We assume as usual that quiescence is observable
by a special δ action, i.e. C is quiescent iff $C \xRightarrow{\delta}$.

Definition 4. *For $\mathcal{E} \in \mathcal{IOLES}(L)$, $C \in \mathcal{C}(\mathcal{E})$, the outputs produced by C are*

$$out_{\mathcal{E}}(C) \triangleq \{!\omega \in \mathcal{POMSET}(\mathcal{O}) \mid C \xRightarrow{!\omega} C' \wedge C' \xRightarrow{\delta}\} \cup \{\delta \mid C \xRightarrow{\delta}\}$$

The *co-ioco* theory assumes the input enabledness of the implementation [1], i.e. in
any state of the implementation, every input action is enabled. This assumption is made
to ensure that no blocking can occur during the execution of the test until its end and
the emission of a verdict. However, as explained by Heerink, Lestiennes and Gaudel
in [2, 3] even if many realistic systems can be modeled with such an assumption, there
remains a significant portion of realistic systems that can not be modeled as such. In
order to overcome these difficulties, Lestiennes and Gaudel enrich the system model by
refused transitions and a set of possible actions is defined in each state. Any possible
input in a given state of the specification should be possible in a correct implementation.

Definition 5. *For $\mathcal{E} \in \mathcal{IOLES}(L)$ and $C \in \mathcal{C}(\mathcal{E})$, the possible inputs in C are*

$$poss_{\mathcal{E}}(C) \triangleq \{?\omega \in \mathcal{POMSET}(\mathcal{I}) \mid C \xRightarrow{?\omega}\}$$

---

[2] Gaudel et al [3] assume a similar property called *IO-exclusiveness*.

Our *co-ioco* conformance relation for labeled event structures can be informally described as follows. The behavior of a correct *co-ioco* implementation after some observations (obtained from the specification) should respect the following restrictions: (1) the outputs produced by the implementation should be specified; (2) if a quiescent configuration is reached, this should also be the case in the specification; (3) any time an input is possible in the specification, this should also be the case in the implementation. These restrictions are formalized by the following conformance relation.

Definition 6. *Let* $\mathcal{E}_i, \mathcal{E}_s \in \mathcal{IOLES}(L)$, *then*

$$\mathcal{E}_i \ \textbf{\textit{co-ioco}} \ \mathcal{E}_s \Leftrightarrow \forall \omega \in traces(\mathcal{E}_s) :$$
$$poss_s(\bot \ \textbf{\textit{after}} \ \omega) \subseteq poss_i(\bot \ \textbf{\textit{after}} \ \omega)$$
$$out_i(\bot \ \textbf{\textit{after}} \ \omega) \subseteq out_s(\bot \ \textbf{\textit{after}} \ \omega)$$

When several outputs in conflicts are possible, our conformance relation allows implementations where at least one of them is implemented. Extra inputs are allowed in any configuration, but extra outputs, extra quiescence and extra causality between events specified as concurrent are forbidden.

Consider Figure 3. In the *ioco* theory where concurrency is interpreted as interleaving, the concurrency between outputs $!b$ and $!d$ of system S_2 would be described allowing either $!b$ before $!d$ or $!d$ before $!b$. S_1 would be a correct implementation w.r.t *ioco* because one of the two possible orders between the outputs is observed, even if process P_2 interferes in the behavior of process P_1 ($!b$ depends on $!d$). We want to prevent implementations like S_1 introducing extra dependency

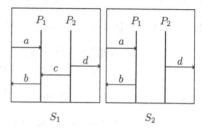

Fig. 3. Message sequence charts showing two implementations of concurrency

between events specified as concurrent. Therefore actions specified as concurrent must be implemented as such, meaning that they must occur on different processes and must be independent from each other.

3   Complete Test Suites

A test case is a specification of the tester's behavior during an experiment carried out on the SUT. It must be controllable, i.e. the tester must not have choices to make during the execution of the test. That is, tests must be deterministic, and at any stage, the next input to be proposed by the tester must be unique, i.e. there are no immediate conflicts between inputs. Finally, we require the experiment to terminate, i.e. the resulting event structure to be finite.

Definition 7. *A test case is a finite deterministic IOLES* $\mathcal{E}_t = (E_t, \leq_t, \#_t, \lambda_t)$ *where* $(E_t^{\mathcal{I}} \times E_t^{\mathcal{I}}) \cap \#_t^{\mu} = \emptyset$. *A test suite is a set of test cases.*

The *success* of a test is determined by the verdict associated to the result of its execution on the system, *pass* or *fail*, the pass verdict meaning that the result of the test is consistent with the specification according to the conformance relation. As IOLES can be seen as occurrence nets, we can model the test execution as the parallel composition of labeled nets [20]. This execution leads to a fail verdict in the following situations: (1) the implementation produces a pomset of outputs that the test case can not accept, (2) the test case can accept such a pomset of outputs, but the reached configuration is not quiescent, (3) a quiescent configuration is reached in the implementation, but not in the test case, or (4) the test case proposes an input that the implementation is not prepared to accept. These situations corresponds to a deadlock in the parallel composition, but not in the test case. If the test case deadlocks (and therefore the execution), the SUT passes the test case.

We expect our test suite to be *sound*, i.e. if the implementation fails the test, then it does not conform to the specification. A test suite is *exhaustive* iff it contains, for every non conforming implementation, a test that detects it. The existence of a *complete* (sound and exhaustive) test suite ensures *testability* of the conformance relation, since success of the SUT under such a test suite proves the SUT's conformance. For obtaining sound and exhaustive test suites, we give in [15] the following sufficient conditions. First, for a test suite to be sound, each test must produce only traces of the specification, and preserve all possible outputs for each such trace.

Theorem 1 ([15]). *Let $\mathcal{E}_s \in \mathcal{IOLES}(L)$ and T a test suite such that*[3]

1. *$\forall \mathcal{E}_t \in T : traces(\mathcal{E}_t) \subseteq traces(\mathcal{E}_s)$*
2. *$\forall \mathcal{E}_t \in T, \omega \in traces(\mathcal{E}_t) : out_t(\bot \text{ after } \omega) = out_s(\bot \text{ after } \omega)$*

then T is sound for $\mathcal{E}_s$ w.r.t co-ioco.

A test suite is exhaustive if each trace of the specification appears in at least one test and if tests preserve quiescence.

Theorem 2 ([15]). *Let $\mathcal{E}_s \in \mathcal{IOLES}(L)$ and T a test suite such that*

1. *$\forall \omega \in traces(\mathcal{E}_s), \exists \mathcal{E}_t \in T : \omega \in traces(\mathcal{E}_t)$;*
2. *$\forall \mathcal{E}_t \in T, \omega \in traces(\mathcal{E}_t) : (\bot_t \text{ after } \omega)$ is quiescent implies $(\bot_s \text{ after } \omega)$ is quiescent;*

then T is exhaustive for $\mathcal{E}_s$ w.r.t co-ioco.

The algorithm below builds a test case from an IOLES by resolving immediate conflicts between inputs, while accepting several branches in case of conflict between outputs (note that "mixed" immediate conflicts between inputs and outputs have been ruled out by Assumption 2). At the end of the algorithm, all such conflicts have been resolved in one way, following one fixed strategy of resolution of immediate input conflicts; the resulting object, the test case, is thus one branching prefix of the IOLES. In order to cover the other branches, the algorithm must be run several times with *different* conflict resolution schemes, to obtain a test suite that represents every possible event in at least one test case. Each such scheme can be represented as a linearization of the causality relation that specifies in which order the events are selected by the algorithm. By the

---

[3] The inclusion of possible inputs follows from point 1.

Algorithm 1. Constructs a test case from $\mathcal{E}$

Require: A finite and deterministically labeled $\mathcal{E} = (E, \leq, \#, \lambda) \in \mathcal{IOLES}(L)$ such that
$\quad \forall e \in E^\mathcal{I}, e' \in E^\mathcal{O} : \neg(e \#^\mu e')$ and a linearization $\mathcal{R}$ of $\leq$

Ensure: A test case $\mathcal{E}_t$ such that
$\quad \forall \omega \in \text{traces}(\mathcal{E}_t) : \text{out}_{\mathcal{E}_t}(\bot \text{ after } \omega) = \text{out}_{\mathcal{E}}(\bot \text{ after } \omega)$

1: $E_t := \emptyset$
2: $E_{temp} := E$
3: **while** $E_{temp} \neq \emptyset$ **do**
4: $\quad e_m := \min_{\mathcal{R}}(E_{temp})$
5: $\quad E_{temp} := E_{temp} \setminus \{e_m\}$
6: $\quad$ **if** $(\{e_m\} \times E_t^\mathcal{I}) \cap \#^\mu = \emptyset \wedge [e_m] \subseteq E_t$ **then**
7: $\qquad E_t := E_t \cup \{e_m\}$
8: $\quad$ **end if**
9: **end while**
10: $\leq_t := \leq \cap (E_t \times E_t)$
11: $\#_t := \# \cap (E_t \times E_t)$
12: $\lambda_t := \lambda_{|E_t}$
13: **return** $\mathcal{E}_t = (E_t, \leq_t, \#_t, \lambda_t)$

---

above, we need to be sure that the collection of linearizations that we use considers all resolutions of immediate input conflict, i.e. is rich enough such that there is a pair of linearizations that reverses the order in a given immediate input conflict.

Definition 8. *Fix $\mathcal{E} \in \mathcal{IOLES}(L)$, and let $\mathcal{L}$ be a set of linearizations of $\leq$. Then $\mathcal{L}$ is an* immediate input conflict saturated *set, or* iics *set, for $\mathcal{E}$ iff for all $e_1, e_2 \in E^\mathcal{I}$ such that $e_1 \#^\mu e_2$, there exist $\mathcal{R}_1, \mathcal{R}_2 \in \mathcal{L}$ with $\forall e \in [e_1] : e\mathcal{R}_1 e_2$ and $\forall e \in [e_2] : e\mathcal{R}_2 e_1$.*

Proposition 1. *Let $\mathcal{L}$ be an iics set for $\mathcal{E}$, and T the test suite obtained using Algorithm 1 with $\mathcal{L}$. Then every event $e \in E$ is represented by at least one test case $\mathcal{E}_t \in T$.*

Proof. Let T be the test suite obtained by the algorithm and $\mathcal{L}$ and suppose e is not represented by any test case in T. We have then that for every $\mathcal{E}_t \in T$ either *(i)* $e \in E^\mathcal{I}$ and $\{e\} \times E_t^\mathcal{I} \cap \#^\mu \neq \emptyset$ or *(ii)* $[e] \not\subseteq E_t$. If *(i)*, we have that there exists $e' \in E_t^\mathcal{I}$ such that $e \#^\mu e'$ and $e'\mathcal{R}_1 e$ (where $\mathcal{R}_1$ is the linearization used to build $\mathcal{E}_t$). By Proposition 1 we know there exist $\mathcal{R}_2 \in \mathcal{L}$ such that $\forall e'' \in [e] : e''\mathcal{R}_2 e'$ and then we can use $\mathcal{R}_2$ to construct $\mathcal{E}'_t \in T$ such that e is represented by $\mathcal{E}'_t$ which leads to a contradiction. If *(ii)*, then there exists $e' \in [e]$ such that $\{e'\} \times E_t^\mathcal{I} \cap \neq \emptyset$ and the analysis is analogous to the one in *(i)*. $\qquad\square$

Note that the size of $\mathcal{L}$ and hence of T can be bounded by the number of input events in immediate conflict, i.e. $|T| \leq 2^\mathcal{K}$, where $\mathcal{K} = |\#^\mu \cap (E^\mathcal{I} \times E^\mathcal{I})|$. Note that in the case where several input events are two by two in immediate conflict, we need fewer test cases than one per pair. For example if $e_1 \#^\mu e_2, e_2 \#^\mu e_3$ and $e_3 \#^\mu e_1$, we only need three linearizations, each having a different event e_i preceding the two others whose order does not matter, and therefore only three cases. Moreover, for any pair of concurrent events $e \textbf{ co } e'$, the order in which they appear in any $\mathcal{R} \in \mathcal{L}$ is irrelevant; it suffices therefore to have in $\mathcal{L}$ only one representative for any class of permutations of some set of pairwise concurrent events in $\mathcal{E}$. Therefore, the size of $\mathcal{L}$ and thus of T depends on the degree of input conflict in $\mathcal{E}$ and not on the degree of concurrency. It is known that such a performance is characteristic of methods based on partial order unfoldings.

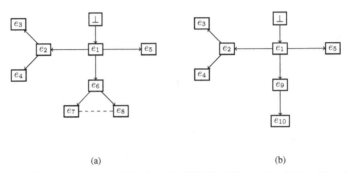

(a)   (b)

Fig. 4. Two test cases build using the IOLES in Figure 2 and Algorithm 1

Example 1. The test cases (a) and (b) in Figure 4 can be obtained using Algorithm 1 and any linearizations $\mathcal{R}_1, \mathcal{R}_2$ such that $e_6 \mathcal{R}_1 e_9$ and $e_9 \mathcal{R}_2 e_6$.

Let $\mathcal{PREF}(\mathcal{E})$ be the set of all prefixes of $\mathcal{E}$, we show now that Algorithm 1 is general enough to produce a complete test suite from it.

Theorem 3. *From $\mathcal{PREF}(\mathcal{E})$ and an iics set $\mathcal{L}$ for $\mathcal{E}$, Algorithm 1 yields a complete test suite T.*

Proof. Soundness: By Theorem 1 we need to prove: (1) the traces of every test case are traces of the specification; (2) the outputs following a trace of the test case are preserved. (1) Trace inclusion is immediate as the test case is a prefix of the unfolding of the specification. (2) For a test $\mathcal{E}_t$ and a trace $w \in \text{traces}(\mathcal{E}_t)$, if an output in $\text{out}_s(\perp \textit{ after } w)$ is not in $\text{out}_t(\perp \textit{ after } w)$, it means either that it is in conflict with an input in $\mathcal{E}_t$, which is impossible by Assumption 2, or that its past is not already in $\mathcal{E}_t$, which is impossible since w is a trace of $\mathcal{E}_t$.

Exhaustiveness: By Theorem 2 we need to prove that every trace is represented in at least one test case, and that the algorithm does not introduce extra quiescence. Clearly, for all $w \in \text{traces}(\mathcal{E}_s)$ there exists at least one complete prefix $c \in \mathcal{PREF}(\mathcal{E})$ such that $w \in \text{traces}(c)$. By Proposition 1 we can find $\mathcal{R} \in \mathcal{L}$ such that this trace remains in the test case obtain by the algorithm, i.e. $\exists t \in T : w \in \text{traces}(t)$. If we only consider the prefixes $c \in \mathcal{PREF}(\mathcal{E})$ such that $(\perp_c \textit{ after } w)$ is quiescent implies $(\perp_s \textit{ after } w)$ is quiescent, it follows that any test case built with the algorithm from c inherits this property. $\qquad\square$

4   Coverage Criteria for Labeled Event Structures

In the **ioco** framework and its extensions, the selection of test suites is achieved by different methods. Tests can be built in a randomized way from a canonical tester, which is a completion of the specification representing all the authorized and forbidden behaviors [1]. Closer to practice is the selection of tests according to test purposes, which represent a set of behaviors one wants to test. [18]. Another method, used for symbolic transition systems for instance, is to unfold the specification until a certain testing criterion is fulfiled, and then to build a test suite covering this unfolding. Criteria for stopping the unfolding can be a given depth or state inclusion for instance [21].

The behavior of the system described by the specification consists usually of infinite traces. However, in practice, these long traces can be considered as a sequence of (finite) "basic" behaviors. For example, the travel agency offers few basic behaviors: (1) interaction with the server; (2) selection of insurance; and (3) selection of tickets. Any "complex" behavior of the agency is built from such basic behaviors. We choose a criterion allowing to cover each basic behavior described by the specification once, using a proper notion of *complete prefixes*.

Complete Prefixes as Testing Criteria. The dynamic behavior of a Petri net is entirely captured by its unfolding, but this unfolding is usually infinite. There are several different methods of truncating an unfolding. The differences are related to the kind of information about the original unfolding one wants to preserve in the prefix. Our aim is to use such a prefix to build test cases, therefore obtaining a finite prefix can be seen as defining a testing criterion.

As it is shown above, if the information about the produced outputs (and quiescence) is preserved in the test cases, we can prove the soundness of the test suite. Hence we aim at truncating the unfolding following an inclusion criterion, while preserving information about outputs and quiescence.

We say that a branching process β of an I/O Petri net Σ is *complete* if for every reachable marking M there exists a configuration C in β such that

1. $Mark(C) = M$ (i.e. M is represented in β), and
2. for every transition t enabled by M there exists $C \cup \{e\} \in C(\beta)$ such that e is labeled by t.

A complete prefix Fin can be obtained modifying the unfolding algorithm. The *complete finite prefix algorithm* is presented in [16] and depends on the notion of *cut-off event*: how long the net is unfolded. The following notion corresponds to our inclusion criterion: every cycle is unfolded once.

Definition 9. *Let Fin be a branching process. An event e is a cut-off event iff Fin contains an event $e' \leq e$ such that $Mark([e']) = Mark([e])$.*

Nevertheless, as explained in Example 2, completeness does not imply that the information about outputs and quiescence is preserved.

Example 2. Consider Figure 5, we have that Fin is complete, but the expected outputs are not part of the prefix. We expect that o_1 is produced by the system after i_2 and i_4, i.e. $out_{\mathcal{E}}(\perp \textbf{\textit{after}} (i_2 \cdot i_4)) = \{o_1\}$, but this is not the case in Fin, i.e. $o_2 \notin out_{Fin}(\perp \textbf{\textit{after}} (i_2 \cdot i_4)) = \{\delta\}$.

In order to preserve this information, we follow [21] and modify the complete finite prefix algorithm adding all the outputs from the unfolding that the complete prefix

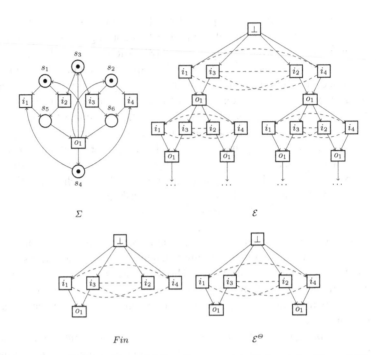

Fig. 5. I/O Petri net Σ, part of its unfolding $\mathcal{E}$, a complete finite prefix Fin and its quiescent closure $\mathcal{E}^{\ominus}$

enables. As there exists no cycles of outputs in the original net, this procedure terminates, yielding a finite prefix. The procedure to compute the *quiescent closure* $\mathcal{E}^{\ominus}$ of
the complete finite prefix is described by Algorithm 2.

As in [16], we implement a branching process of an I/O Petri net Σ as a list of nodes.
A node is either a condition or an event. A condition is a pair (s, e), where s is a place
of Σ and e its preset. An event is a pair (t, B), where t is a transition in Σ, and B is its
preset. The possible extensions of a branching process β are the pairs (t, B) where the
elements of B are pairwise in **co** relation, t is such that $\varphi(B) = {}^{\bullet}t$ and β contains no
event e satisfying $\varphi(e) = t$ and ${}^{\bullet}e = B$. We denote the set of possible extensions of β
by $PE(\beta)$. The following result is central and will help proving soundness of the test
suites proposed below.

Theorem 4. *Let $\mathcal{E} \in \mathcal{IOLES}(L)$ and $\mathcal{E}^{\ominus}$ the quiescent closure of its complete finite
prefix. Then*

1. *$traces(\mathcal{E}^{\ominus}) \subseteq traces(\mathcal{E})$*
2. *$\forall \omega \in traces(\mathcal{E}^{\ominus}) : out_{\mathcal{E}^{\ominus}}(\bot \text{ after } \omega) = out_{\mathcal{E}}(\bot \text{ after } \omega)$*

Proof. 1) is immediate since $\mathcal{E}^{\ominus}$ is a prefix of $\mathcal{E}$. Since only the outputs produced after
the traces of $\mathcal{E}^{\ominus}$ are considered, 2) follows by its construction.   □

The test suite build based on the inclusion criteria is sound:

Algorithm 2. The quiescent closure of the complete finite prefix algorithm

Require: A 1-safe I/O Petri net $\Sigma = (T, P, F, M_0, \lambda)$ where $M_0 = \{s_1, \ldots, s_k\}$.
Ensure: A complete finite prefix $\mathcal{E}^\Theta$ of the unfolding $\mathcal{E}$ of Σ such that
$\quad \forall w \in \text{traces}(\mathcal{E}^\Theta) : \text{out}_{\mathcal{E}^\Theta}(\perp \textbf{ after } w) = \text{out}_{\mathcal{E}}(\perp \textbf{ after } w)$
1: $\mathcal{E}^\Theta := (s_0, \emptyset), \ldots, (s_k, \emptyset)$
2: $pe := PE(\mathcal{E}^\Theta)$
3: $cut\text{-}off := \emptyset$
4: **while** $pe \neq \emptyset$ **do**
5:     choose an event $e = (t, B)$ in pe such that e is minimal w.r.t $\leq$;
6:     **if** $[e] \cap cut\text{-}off = \emptyset$ **then**
7:         append to $\mathcal{E}^\Theta$ the event e and a condition (s, e) for every place s in $t^\bullet$
8:         $pe := PE(\mathcal{E}^\Theta)$;
9:         **if** e is a *cut-off* event of $\mathcal{E}^\Theta$ **then**
10:             $cut\text{-}off := cut\text{-}off \cup \{e\}$
11:         **end if**
12:     **else**
13:         $pe := pe \backslash \{e\}$
14:     **end if**
15: **end while**
16: $pe := PE(\mathcal{E}^\Theta)$
17: **while** $pe \cap T^O \neq \emptyset$ **do**
18:     choose an event $e = (t, B)$ in $pe \cap T^O$ such that e is minimal w.r.t $\leq$;
19:     append to $\mathcal{E}^\Theta$ the event e and a condition (s, e) for every place s in $t^\bullet$
20:     $pe := PE(\mathcal{E}^\Theta)$;
21: **end while**
22: **return** $\mathcal{E}^\Theta$

Theorem 5. *Let Σ_s be the specification of a system and $\mathcal{E}_s$ the IOLES of its unfolding. Any test suite constructed using Algorithm 1 and $\mathcal{E}_s^\Theta$ as an input is sound for $\mathcal{E}_s$ w.r.t co-ioco.*

Proof. By Theorem 1 we need to prove that any trace of a test case $\mathcal{E}_t$ is a trace of $\mathcal{E}_s$ (which is trivial as $\mathcal{E}_t$ is a prefix of $\mathcal{E}_s^\Theta$ and therefore of $\mathcal{E}_s$) and that outputs and quiescence produced after any trace w of such a test are preserved. The events of $\mathcal{E}_s^\Theta$ that are added to $\mathcal{E}_t$ are all the events whose past is already in $\mathcal{E}_t$ and which are not in immediate conflict with an input. An output cannot be in immediate conflict with an input by Assumption 2, so all the outputs whose past is already in $\mathcal{E}_t$ are added. So all the outputs from $\mathcal{E}_s^\Theta$ after a trace w are preserved and by Theorem 4 we have $\forall w \in \text{traces}(\mathcal{E}_t) : \text{out}_t(\perp \textbf{ after } w) = \text{out}_s(\perp \textbf{ after } w)$. $\qquad\square$

Example 3. The IOLES of Figure 2 is a complete prefix of the unfolding of the net in Figure 1 and can be obtained using Algorithm 2. We saw in Example 1 how to build test cases that cover such a complete prefix. Thus the test cases of Figure 4 form a sound test suite that covers the specification according to our inclusion criterion.

5   Conclusion and Future Work

We have presented a testing framework and a test generation algorithm for true concurrency specifications of distributed and concurrent systems. Our test selection criterion is based on the quiescent closure of the complete finite prefix of the unfolding of the specification; it allows to select, among all possible test cases, those covering the behaviors traversing each cycle once. As in the case of McMillan's complete prefixes, the size of our prefixes can be exponential in the number of reachable markings in worst case (see for example [16]). However, for several families of nets, the resulting prefix is smaller than the reachability graph. Full information about the behavior of the net can be reconstructed with only a finite marking-complete prefix whose size is bounded by the number of states in the reachability graph. However such reconstruction is not straight forwards.

Future technical studies include the question whether it is possible to drop assumptions 1 and 2 under a fairness assumption, meaning that in a given configuration, all the different events will eventually occur if the experiment is repeated enough times. However under such an assumption, controllability of test cases must be ensured during their construction.

The present testing approach here is global, meaning that a global control and observation of the distributed system is assumed, and tests are performed in a centralized way. The next step of our work is to distribute control and observation over several concurrent components. This will necessarily weaken the conformance relation, since dependencies between events occurring on different components cannot be observed anymore. The local test cases should, roughly speaking, be projections of the global test cases onto the different components, since concurrency of the specification was preserved in the test cases. We still have to investigate how distribution affects the power of testing, and how the resulting methods compares to others, such as the **dioco** framework of Hierons et al. [7] for multi-port IOTS.

Acknowledgment. This work was funded by the DIGITEO / DIM-LSC project TEC-STES, convention DIGITEO Number 2011-052D - TECSTES.

References

1. Tretmans, J.: Test generation with inputs, outputs and repetitive quiescence. Software - Concepts and Tools 17(3), 103–120 (1996)
2. Heerink, L., Tretmans, J.: Refusal testing for classes of transition systems with inputs and outputs. In: Formal Description Techniques for Distributed Systems and Communication Protocols. IFIP Conference Proceedings, vol. 107, pp. 23–38. Chapman & Hall (1997)
3. Lestiennes, G., Gaudel, M.C.: Test de systèmes réactifs non réceptifs. Journal Européen des Systèmes Automatisés 39(1-2-3), 255–270 (2005)
4. Faivre, A., Gaston, C., Le Gall, P., Touil, A.: Test purpose concretization through symbolic action refinement. In: Suzuki, K., Higashino, T., Ulrich, A., Hasegawa, T. (eds.) TestCom/FATES 2008. LNCS, vol. 5047, pp. 184–199. Springer, Heidelberg (2008)
5. Jéron, T.: Symbolic model-based test selection. Electronic Notes in Theoretical Computer Science 240, 167–184 (2009)
6. Krichen, M., Tripakis, S.: Conformance testing for real-time systems. Formal Methods in System Design 34(3), 238–304 (2009)
7. Hierons, R.M., Merayo, M.G., Núñez, M.: Implementation relations for the distributed test architecture. In: Suzuki, K., Higashino, T., Ulrich, A., Hasegawa, T. (eds.) TestCom/FATES 2008. LNCS, vol. 5047, pp. 200–215. Springer, Heidelberg (2008)

8. Hennessy, M.: Algebraic Theory of Processes. MIT Press (1988)
9. Peleska, J., Siegel, M.: From testing theory to test driver implementation. In: Gaudel, M.-C., Wing, J.M. (eds.) FME 1996. LNCS, vol. 1051, pp. 538–556. Springer, Heidelberg (1996)
10. Schneider, S.: Concurrent and Real Time Systems: The CSP Approach, 1st edn. John Wiley & Sons, Inc., New York (1999)
11. Ulrich, A., König, H.: Specification-based testing of concurrent systems. In: Formal Description Techniques for Distributed Systems and Communication Protocols. IFIP Conference Proceedings, vol. 107, pp. 7–22. Chapman & Hall (1998)
12. von Bochmann, G., Haar, S., Jard, C., Jourdan, G.-V.: Testing systems specified as partial order input/output automata. In: Suzuki, K., Higashino, T., Ulrich, A., Hasegawa, T. (eds.) TestCom/FATES 2008. LNCS, vol. 5047, pp. 169–183. Springer, Heidelberg (2008)
13. Haar, S., Jard, C., Jourdan, G.-V.: Testing input/output partial order automata. In: Petrenko, A., Veanes, M., Tretmans, J., Grieskamp, W. (eds.) TestCom/FATES 2007. LNCS, vol. 4581, pp. 171–185. Springer, Heidelberg (2007)
14. Ponce de León, H., Haar, S., Longuet, D.: Conformance relations for labeled event structures. In: Brucker, A.D., Julliand, J. (eds.) TAP 2012. LNCS, vol. 7305, pp. 83–98. Springer, Heidelberg (2012)
15. Ponce de León, H., Haar, S., Longuet, D.: Model-based testing for concurrent systems with labeled event structures (2012), http://hal.inria.fr/hal-00796006
16. Esparza, J., Römer, S., Vogler, W.: An improvement of McMillan's unfolding algorithm. In: Margaria, T., Steffen, B. (eds.) TACAS 1996. LNCS, vol. 1055, pp. 87–106. Springer, Heidelberg (1996)
17. Segala, R.: Quiescence, fairness, testing, and the notion of implementation. Information and Computation 138(2), 194–210 (1997)
18. Jard, C., Jéron, T.: TGV: theory, principles and algorithms. International Journal on Software Tools for Technology Transfer 7, 297–315 (2005)
19. Nielsen, M., Plotkin, G.D., Winskel, G.: Petri nets, event structures and domains, part I. Theoretical Computer Science 13, 85–108 (1981)
20. Winskel, G.: Petri nets, morphisms and compositionality. In: Applications and Theory in Petri Nets, pp. 453–477 (1985)
21. Gaston, C., Le Gall, P., Rapin, N., Touil, A.: Symbolic execution techniques for test purpose definition. In: Uyar, M.Ü., Duale, A.Y., Fecko, M.A. (eds.) TestCom 2006. LNCS, vol. 3964, pp. 1–18. Springer, Heidelberg (2006)

Predicting the Size of Test Suites from Use Cases: An Empirical Exploration

Mourad Badri, Linda Badri, and William Flageol

Software Engineering Research Laboratory
Department of Mathematics and Computer Science
University of Quebec, Trois-Rivières, Quebec, Canada
{Mourad.Badri,Linda.Badri,William.Flageol}uqtr.ca

Abstract. Software testing plays a crucial role in software quality assurance. Software testing is, however, a time and resource consuming process. It is, therefore, important to estimate as soon as possible the effort required to test software. Unfortunately, little is known about the prediction of the testing effort. The study presented in this paper aims at exploring empirically the prediction of the testing effort from use cases. We address the testing effort from the perspective of test suites size. We used four metrics to characterize the size and complexity of use cases, and three metrics to quantify different perspectives of the size of corresponding test suites. We used the univariate logistic regression analysis to evaluate the individual effect of each use case metric on the size of test suites. The multivariate logistic regression analysis was used to explore the combined effect of the use case metrics. The performance of the prediction models was evaluated using receiver operating characteristic analysis. An experimental study, using data collected from five Java case studies, is reported providing evidence that some of the use case metrics are significant predictors of the size of test suites.

Keywords: Software Testing, Testing Effort, Test Suite Size, Use Cases, Metrics, Relationship, Prediction, Logistic Regression Analysis.

1   Introduction

Software testing is an important part of the software development lifecycle. It plays a crucial role in software quality assurance. Software testing is, however, a time and resource consuming process. It is, therefore, absolutely necessary to estimate as soon as possible the effort required to test software, so that activities can be planned and resources can be optimally allocated. However, estimating the testing effort is not an easy task. Indeed, the overall effort spent on testing depends on many different factors including human factors, testing techniques, used tools, characteristics of the software development artifacts, and so forth. Many studies focusing on software development size and effort estimation (prediction) have been published in the literature. Unfortunately, only a few proposals have addressed problems of the software testing effort prediction. Often, the testing effort is estimated as a part of the overall software development. Software testing effort prediction is a key open issue.

H. Yenigün, C. Yilmaz, and A. Ulrich (Eds.): ICTSS 2013, LNCS 8254, pp. 114–132, 2013.

Software metrics, or models based on software metrics, can be used to predict (estimate) the testing effort required to test a software. Software metrics have, in fact, a number of interesting characteristics for providing effort prediction (estimation) support. In practice, such prediction (estimation) support can, in fact, be used to guide the decision-making of software development managers seeking to produce high quality software. Particularly, it can help software managers, developers, and testers to allocate testing resources, plan and monitor testing activities, and especially determine the critical parts of the software which require more testing effort to ensure software quality. One effective way to deal with this important issue is to develop prediction models that can be used in early stages of software development lifecycle to provide high-level estimates of the effort required to test software. Testing effort prediction at early stages of software development is a challenge. Typical inputs available at early stages of software development lifecycle are functional requirements, which describe what a software system is expected to do. Use cases describe the functional requirements of a software system, so they can be basis for testing effort prediction.

We explored in [6] the relationship between use cases and the size of test suites in object-oriented (OO) software systems. The size of test suites was measured in terms of lines of test code. The performed study was, however, limited to a correlation analysis between use cases size and complexity and the size of test suites. Results provide evidence that there is a significant relationship between use cases and the size of test suites. The present paper aims at exploring empirically, more deeply than the study presented in [6], the relationship between use cases and the size of test suites in OO software systems. The goal is to explore the potential of using use cases to predict the testing effort. Using use cases may be, indeed, a simple and good way to predict early the testing effort. Use cases have gained popularity and are widely used for many years. In addition, use cases are the axis of the unified process, which employs a use case driven approach. In particular, use cases may be used to generate test cases. Use cases have, in fact, already been used to estimate (predict) the testing effort [e.g., 2, 15, 28, 35, 36]. These approaches consider actor ranking, use case points, normal and exceptional scenarios and various technical and environmental factors which may be difficult to measure.

We propose in this paper a simple alternative approach. We used four metrics to characterize the size and complexity of use cases. We also used three metrics to quantify different perspectives of the size of test suites. In order to evaluate the relationship between use case metrics and the size of test suites, we used logistic regression methods. The research question we attempt to answer is how accurately do use case metrics predict the testing effort in terms of size of test suites. In a first step, and in order to understand the underlying orthogonal dimensions captured by the proposed use case and test case metrics, we performed a Principal Component Analysis (PCA). In a second step, we used the univariate logistic regression analysis to evaluate the individual effect of use case metrics on the size of test suites. The multivariate logistic regression analysis was used to explore the combined effect of use case metrics. The performance of the prediction models was evaluated using Receiver Operating Characteristic analysis. An experimental study, using data collected from five Java case studies, is reported providing evidence that some of the use case metrics are significant predictors of the size of test suites.

The rest of this paper is organized as follows: Section 2 gives a brief survey of related work. The use case metrics are introduced in Section 3. Section 4 presents the test suite metrics we used to quantify test cases. Section 5 presents the empirical study we performed to evaluate the capacity of use case metrics to predict the testing effort. Finally, Section 6 concludes the paper and outlines some future work directions.

2   Related Work

Recent years have seen an increasing interest in the testability of OO software systems. Many OO metrics, related to different OO software attributes such as size, complexity, coupling, and cohesion have been used to predict (assess) testability of OO software systems [e.g., 3, 4, 13, 14, 19, 32-34]. Bruntink and Van Deursen [13, 14] investigate factors of testability of OO software systems. The authors studied five open source Java software systems in order to explore the relationship between OO design metrics and some characteristics of JUnit test classes. Testability was measured (inversely) by the number of lines of test code and the number of *assert* statements in the test code. The study was limited to a correlation analysis between OO design metrics and testability of classes. Singh et *al.* [32] use OO metrics and neural networks to predict the testing effort. The testing effort in this work is measured in terms of lines of code added or changed during the lifecycle of a defect. Singh et *al.* conclude that the performance of the developed model is to a large degree dependent on the data used. In [34], Singh and Saha attempt to predict the testability of Eclipse at the package level. This study was limited to a correlation analysis between source code metrics and test metrics. Badri et *al.* [3] explore the relationship between lack of cohesion metrics and testability of OO software systems. In [4], Badri et *al.* investigate the capability of lack of cohesion metrics to predict testability of classes using logistic regression methods. Here also, testability was measured by the number of lines of test code and the number of *assert* statements in the test code. More recently, Badri and Toure [5] explore the capacity of OO metrics to predict the testing effort of classes using logistic regression analysis. Results indicate, among others, that multivariate regression models based on OO design metrics are able to accurately predict the unit testing effort of classes. Most of these studies are, however, code-based. Using the code to estimate the effort required to test software is a little late. It is better to do so as soon as possible, ideally in early phases of software development lifecycle.

Some model-based approaches [e.g., 8-10, 23, 25] have been proposed to deal with testing effort (or testability) estimation. Most of these approaches are based on data or control flow designs or on UML design models. Baudry et *al.* [8-10] address testability measurement (and improvement) of OO designs. The authors focus on design patterns as coherent subsets in the architecture, and explain how their use can provide a way for limiting the severity of testability weaknesses. The proposed approach supports the detection of undesirable configurations in UML class diagrams.

Le Traon et *al.* [25] propose testability measures for data flow designs. Khan and Mustafa [23] focus on testability at the design level and propose a model for predicting testability of classes from UML class diagrams. Unfortunately, only a few approaches used use cases to estimate the testing effort. Use cases have, however, been used in many studies to estimate the software development effort (cost) [e.g., 18, 22, 27, 29-31]. Nageshwaran [28] presents a use cases based approach for test effort estimation considering weight and environmental factors. Yi et *al.* [36] present an experience-based approach for the test suites size estimation. The proposed model is based on use case verification points. The authors found a linear relationship between use case verification points and test case number. Zhu Xiaochun et *al.* [35] present an empirical study on early test execution effort estimation based on test case number prediction and test execution complexity. Almeida et *al.* [2] propose a method to estimate test activity effort based on information obtained from use cases. The information used is the actors and the number of scenarios, in addition to technical and environmental factors available for the tests. The method separates, in fact, the quantities of normal scenarios of a use case from exceptional ones, arguing that they have different influences in the effort. Chaudhary and Yadav [15] propose an approach for estimating the size and effort required in the testing projects using test case points. The test case point analysis is an approach for doing estimation of functional testing projects that emphasizes on key testing factors that determine the complexity of the testing cycle.

3   Use Case Metrics

Use cases are used for capturing and describing functional requirements of a system. Informally, a use case is a collection of related success and failure scenarios that describe actors using a system to support a goal [24]. A use case model defines the functional scope of the system to be developed. Use cases describe, in fact, how external actors interact with the software system. The interactions between actors and the software system generate events to the software system, known as input system events, which are usually associated with system operations. A scenario, also called a use case instance, is a specific sequence of actions and interactions between actors and the system. It is one particular story of using the system, or one path through the use case. The development (testing) process is driven by use cases. In particular, use case realizations drive the design. A use-case realization (scenario) describes how a particular use case is realized within the design model, in terms of collaborating objects. We present, in what follows, the metrics we used to characterize use cases size and complexity.

Number of Scenarios (NS): This metric gives the total number of scenarios of a use case. One use case can, in fact, have one or more transactions. The NS metric is related to the cyclomatic complexity of the use case.

Number of External Operations (NEO): This metric defines the number of system operations associated with the system events related to a use case. The entire set of system operations defines the public system interface. During the design, the system operations identified during system behavior analysis are assigned to one or more (controller) classes, which usually should delegate to other objects (classes) the work that needs to be done.

Number of Involved Methods (NIM): The system events represent messages that initiate interaction diagrams, which illustrate how objects interact to fulfill the required tasks (the use case realization). This metric defines the total number of methods that are involved in the execution of a use case, across all of its scenarios, including the methods that are invoked by other methods.

Number of Involved Classes (NIC): This metric defines the total number of classes involved in the realization of a use case (all of its scenarios). It includes the main classes that are involved in the realization of the use case and collaborating classes.

4   Test Suite Metrics

To indicate the testing effort required for a use case (noted UC_i), we used three metrics to quantify the corresponding JUnit test cases (noted TC_i). JUnit (www.junit.org) is a simple framework for writing and running automated unit tests for Java classes. Test cases in JUnit are written by testers in Java. We used in our experiments each pair $<UC_i, TC_i>$ to explore the relationship between the characteristics of a use case and the characteristics of the corresponding test cases. We used the following metrics to quantify the test cases required to test a use case:

Number of lines of test code (TLOC): This metric defines the cumulative number of lines of code of the JUnit test cases related to a use case (all of its scenarios). This number includes only the test cases related to classes/methods involved in the realizations of the use case. It is used to indicate the total size, in terms of lines of test code, of the test cases corresponding to a use case.

Number of assert statements (TASSERT): This metric defines the cumulative number of invocations of JUnit *assert* methods that occur in the code of the test cases related to a use case (all of its scenarios). The set of JUnit *assert* methods are used by the testers to compare the expected behavior of the classes (methods) to their current behavior. This metric is used to indicate another perspective of the size of the test cases corresponding to a use case.

Number of test cases (NBTESTS): This metric gives the total number of JUnit test cases related to a use case (all of its scenarios). This number includes only the test cases related to classes/methods involved in the realizations of the use case. This metric is used to indicate another perspective of the size of the test cases corresponding to a use case.

The first two metrics have already been used (at the class level) in several studies [e.g., 3, 4, 13, 14, 34] to indicate the size of a test suite corresponding to a class.

5   An Experimental Evaluation

We used in our experiment five Java case studies from different domains. UML models have been generated by reverse engineering the source code of the applications. We have also developed the necessary JUnit test cases for each of the five case studies. In order to explore the relationship between use case metrics and the size of test suites, we related to each use case the corresponding JUnit test cases. For each use case, we calculated the values of the four use case metrics. We also used the suite of test case metrics to quantify the corresponding JUnit test cases.

Table 1. Some statistics on the used case studies

	Use Cases	Classes	Methods	Lines of code
ATM	7	68	158	2 474
NextGen	10	17	95	795
CommonsExec	7	29	150	4 376
CommonsEmail	4	10	128	3 737
CommonsIO	13	22	298	8 969

5.1   Selected Case Studies

The selected case studies are: ATM, NextGen, CommonsExec, CommonsEmail and CommonsIO. Table 1 summarizes some statistics on the case studies. It gives, for each case study, the number of use cases, the number of classes, the number of methods and the total number of lines of code. The first case study ATM is a simulator system allowing performing basic banking operations (withdrawal, deposit, transfer, balance, etc.). We adapted the case study for our purposes. The second case study NextGen is an extension of the application developed in the book by Larman [24]. The original application has been extended for our purposes. We have added features about accounts receivable management, suppliers, and employees. We also added features to support billing and rental payments by debit and credit. The third case study Commons Exec is an API for dealing with external process execution and environment management in Java. It allows executing a shell command on a variety of operating systems. The fourth case study Commons Email aims to provide an API for sending email. It is built on top of the Java Mail API, which it aims to simplify. The fifth case study Commons IO is a library of utilities to assist with developing IO functionality. We used only a part of this system that is related to reading, writing and files comparison functionalities. In order to have a significant sample of data, we combined the use cases of the five case studies. We have then a total of 41 use cases. Table 2 lists the descriptive statistics for use case and test case metrics.

Table 2. Descriptive statistics for use case and test case metrics

Metrics	Obs.	Min.	Max.	Mean	Sigma
NIC	41	1,000	12,000	2,244	2,245
NEO	41	1,000	12,000	2,024	2,242
NIM	41	1,000	23,000	3,585	4,796
NS	41	1,000	8,000	2,488	1,938
TLOC	41	14,000	1556,000	201,561	347,010
TASSERT	41	1,000	284,000	21,878	49,865
NBTESTS	41	1,000	36,000	5,780	7,761

5.2   Correlation Analysis

In order to assess the relationship between use case metrics (noted UC_m) and test case metrics (noted TC_m), we performed statistical tests using correlation. The null and alternative hypotheses that our study have tested were:

- H0: There is no significant correlation between a use case metric UC_m and a test case metric TC_m.

- H1: There is a significant correlation between a use case metric UC_m and a test case metric TC_m.

In this experiment, rejecting the null hypothesis indicates that there is a statistically significant relationship between a use case metric UC_m and a test case metric TC_m. For the analysis of the collected data, and in order to test the correlation between a use case metric and a size test case metric, we used three correlation analysis techniques (Pearson, Spearman and Kendall). The Pearson r correlation is widely used in statistics to measure the degree of the relationship between linear related variables. The variables should be normally distributed. The Spearman rank correlation is a non-parametric test that is used to measure the degree of association between two variables. Spearman rank correlation test does not assume anything about the distribution. The Kendall rank correlation is also a non-parametric test that does not assume anything about the distribution (like Spearman's correlation). Correlation is a bivariate analysis that measures the strengths of association between two variables. In statistics, the value of the correlation coefficient varies between +1 and -1. A positive correlation is one in which the variables increase together. A negative correlation is one in which one variable increases as the other variable decreases. A correlation of +1 or -1 will arise if the relationship between the variables is exactly linear. A correlation close to zero means that there is no linear relationship between the variables. We used the XLSTAT software tool (http://www.xlstat.com/) to measure the three types of correlations. We applied the typical significance threshold ($\alpha = 0.05$) to decide whether the correlations where significant. For each pair $<UC_m, TC_m>$ we analyzed the collected data set by calculating the (Pearson's, Spearman's and Kendall's) correlation coefficients for each pair of metrics. Tables 3, 4 and 5 summarize the results of the correlation analysis (respectively Pearson's, Spearman's and Kendall's correlation coefficients). These tables show the values for the three correlation coefficients between each distinct pair of use case and test case metrics. The correlation coefficients that are significant (at $\alpha=0.05$) are set in boldface in the three tables. This means that for the corresponding pairs of metrics there exist a correlation at the 95 % confidence level.

Table 3. Pearson's correlation values between use case and test case metrics

Metrics	NIC	NEO	NIM	NS	TLOC	TASSERT	NBTESTS
NIC	1	0,267	**0,892**	0,213	**0,844**	**0,366**	0,851
NEO	0,267	1	**0,573**	-0,066	**0,557**	0,168	**0,499**
NIM	**0,892**	**0,573**	1	0,237	**0,958**	**0,409**	**0,923**
NS	0,213	-0,066	0,237	1	**0,329**	**0,340**	**0,333**
TLOC	**0,844**	**0,557**	**0,958**	**0,329**	1	**0,560**	**0,944**
TASSERT	**0,366**	0,168	**0,409**	**0,340**	**0,560**	1	**0,489**
NBTESTS	**0,851**	**0,499**	**0,923**	**0,333**	**0,944**	**0,489**	1

Table 4. Spearman's correlation values between use case and test case metrics

Metrics	NIC	NEO	NIM	NS	TLOC	TASSERT	NBTESTS
NIC	1	**0,541**	**0,639**	-0,062	**0,329**	0,234	**0,382**
NEO	**0,541**	1	**0,535**	-0,180	**0,334**	0,269	**0,386**
NIM	**0,639**	**0,535**	1	0,148	**0,652**	**0,556**	**0,575**
NS	-0,062	-0,180	0,148	1	**0,497**	**0,655**	**0,437**
TLOC	**0,329**	**0,334**	**0,652**	**0,497**	1	**0,872**	**0,794**
TASSERT	0,234	0,269	**0,556**	**0,655**	**0,872**	1	**0,816**
NBTESTS	**0,382**	**0,386**	**0,575**	**0,437**	**0,794**	**0,816**	1

Table 5. Kendall's correlation values between use case and test case metrics

Metrics	NIC	NEO	NIM	NS	TLOC	TASSERT	NBTESTS
NIC	1	**0,490**	**0,573**	-0,058	**0,277**	0,203	**0,319**
NEO	**0,490**	1	**0,468**	-0,157	**0,250**	0,198	**0,305**
NIM	**0,573**	**0,468**	1	0,128	**0,562**	**0,485**	**0,482**
NS	-0,058	-0,157	0,128	1	**0,382**	**0,539**	**0,375**
TLOC	**0,277**	**0,250**	**0,562**	**0,382**	1	**0,733**	**0,654**
TASSERT	0,203	0,198	**0,485**	**0,539**	**0,733**	1	**0,727**
NBTESTS	**0,319**	**0,305**	**0,482**	**0,375**	**0,654**	0,727	1

The first global observation that we can make is that there is a significant relationship between the majority of use case and test case metrics. Only few correlations that are not significant are observed, particularly in the case of the pair (NEO, TASSERT) according to the three correlation coefficients and the pair (NIC, TASSERT) according to the Spearman's and Kendall's correlation coefficients. The second global observation that we can make is that the use case metrics NIM and NS are correlated to the three test case metrics. The obtained correlation coefficients, according to the three techniques we used, between NIM and NS and the test case metrics are all significant (at $\alpha=0.05$, and for all the pairs of metrics). The four use case metrics are, however, correlated to the size test case metrics TLOC and NBTESTS. Moreover, the measures have positive correlation. As mentioned previously, a positive correlation indicates that one variable (use case metric value in our case) increases as the other variable (size test case metric value in our case) increases. These results are plausible knowing that the more a use case is complex, in terms of size and complexity, the more it is difficult to test. So, the effort required in terms of developing corresponding test cases will be relatively high.

Furthermore, it can also be seen that the correlation values between the use case metrics are overall not uniform. The correlations change from one pair to another. In some cases, the correlations are not significant. This suggests that even if there is an overlap between the metrics in terms of provided information, according to the correlation values, these metrics seem capturing different dimensions. This issue must, however, be validated. From the same tables, it can also be seen that the test case metrics are also correlated between themselves. Unlike use case metrics, test case metrics are better correlated between themselves, which suggest that the overlap (in terms of provided information) between the metrics is more important than in the case of use case metrics. This is plausible given that these metrics are all related to the size of test suites. According to the obtained results, we can therefore reasonably reject the null hypothesis H0.

5.3   Use Cases Ranking

In order to deepen our analysis and better understand the relationship between use cases and the size of test suites, we wanted to explore in a first step the use of clustering techniques for classifying (ranking) use cases into three categories: simple, medium and complex. Clustering provides, indeed, a natural way for identifying clusters of related objects (use cases in our case) based on their similarity (use case metrics in our case). The resulting clusters (three in our case), are to be built so that use cases within each cluster are more closely related to one another than use cases assigned to different clusters. We wanted, in fact, to investigate if test case features will reflect the complexity level of the corresponding use cases. Indeed, we can intuitively expect that test cases corresponding to complex use cases will be (relatively) complex, and test cases corresponding to simple use cases will be (relatively) simple. Let UC be a use case and $P = \{ UC_{mi} \}$ be the set of its properties (use case metrics). In this paper, as a first attempt, we used the K-means clustering, which is a method of cluster analysis that aims to partition n observations (use cases in our study) into k clusters (three in our study) in which each observation belongs to the cluster with the nearest mean. We used the Weka (Waikato Environment for Knowledge Analysis) tool, which is a comprehensive suite of Java class libraries that implement many state-of-the-art machine learning and data mining algorithms. We obtain three clusters of use cases. Tables 6, 7 and 8 give the descriptive statistics for test case metrics of the JUnit test cases corresponding respectively to complex, medium and simple use cases.

Table 6. Descriptive statistics for test cases metrics corresponding to complex use cases

Variables	Obs.	Mean	Sigma
TLOC	3	595,000	145,523
TASSERT	3	32,000	5,292
NBTESTS	3	12,333	3,786

Table 7. Descriptive statistics for test cases metrics corresponding to medium use cases

Variables	Obs.	Mean	Sigma
TLOC	13	293,000	549,852
TASSERT	13	21,769	42,165
NBTESTS	13	8,154	11,936

Table 8. Descriptive statistics for test cases metrics corresponding to simple use cases

Variables	Obs.	Mean	Sigma
TLOC	25	106,800	120,531
TASSERT	25	20,720	56,910
NBTESTS	25	3,760	3,908

The first cluster, corresponding to complex use cases, includes 3 use cases. The mean values of the corresponding TLOC, TASSERT and NBTESTS metrics are respectively 595, 32 and 12.33. The second cluster, corresponding to medium use cases, includes 13 use cases. The mean values of the corresponding TLOC, TASSERT and NBTESTS metrics are respectively 293, 21.77 and 8.15. The third cluster, corresponding to simple use cases, includes 25 use cases. The mean values of the corresponding TLOC, TASSERT and NBTESTS metrics are respectively 106.8, 20.72 and 3.76. Results show clearly that the mean value of the TLOC, TASSERT and NBTESTS metrics of complex use cases are higher than the mean value of the same metrics of medium use cases, which are higher than the mean value of the same metrics of simple use cases. The descriptive statistics of the test case metrics reflect properly the ranking in terms of complexity level of corresponding use cases. These results seem suggesting that the more use cases are complex, the more the effort required to develop corresponding test cases is higher. This issue must, however, be validated.

5.4   Evaluating the Effect of Use Case Metrics on the Size of Test Suites

We present, in this section, the empirical study we conducted in order to evaluate the individual and combined effect of use case metrics on the size of test suites. The goal here is to evaluate how accurately do use case metrics predict the testing effort in terms of size of test suites. We used both univariate and multivariate Logistic Regression (LR) analysis. The univariate LR analysis is used to find the individual effect of each use case metric, identifying which metrics are significantly related to the size of test suites. The multivariate LR analysis is used to investigate the combined effect of use case metrics on the size of test suites, indicating which metrics may play a more dominant role in predicting the testing effort in terms of test suites size.

5.4.1 Principal Component Analysis

Results of correlation analysis suggest that there is an overlap between the metrics (use case and test case metrics) in terms of provided information. So, in order to better understand the underlying orthogonal dimensions captured by these metrics, we performed a Principal Component Analysis (PCA). PCA is a technique that has been widely used in software engineering to identify important underlying dimensions captured by a set of metrics. We used this technique to find whether the used metrics are independent or are capturing the same underlying dimensions (properties) of the object being measured. In a first step, the PCA was performed on the data set consisting of use case metrics values. The PCA identified three Principal Components (PCs), which capture about 99% of the data set variance (see Table 9). Based on the analysis of the coefficients associated with each use case metric within each of the components, the PCs are interpreted as follows: (1) PC1: NIM, (2) PC2: NS, and (3) PC3: NEO. So, we used in the following section the suite of metrics (NIM, NS and NEO) to characterize use cases.

Table 9. Results of PCA analysis (use case metrics)

	PC1	PC2	PC3	PC4
Prop (%)	56,169	26,693	16,087	1,052
Cumul (%)	56,169	82,862	**98,948**	100,000
NIC	0,594	0,125	-0,522	-0,599
NEO	0,418	-0,542	**0,671**	-0,284
NIM	**0,656**	-0,027	-0,115	0,745
NS	0,204	**0,830**	0,513	-0,071

Table 10. Results of PCA analysis (test case metrics)

	PC1	PC2	PC3
Prop (%)	88,493	7,308	4,199
Cumul (%)	**88,493**	95,801	100,000
TLOC	**0,580**	-0,496	-0,646
TASSERT	0,585	-0,298	0,754
NBTESTS	0,567	0,816	-0,117

We also performed a PCA using the three test case metrics (TLOC, TASSERT and NBTESTS). The goal was here also to find whether the test case metrics are independent or are capturing the same underlying dimensions of the object being measured. The PCA was performed on the data set consisting of test case metrics values. The PCA identified one Principal Components (PCs), which captures more than 88% of the data set variance (see Table 10). Based on the analysis of the coefficients associated with each test case metric within each of the components, the first PC is interpreted as a size component. Moreover, knowing that the three test case metrics are size related metrics, we decided to use in what follows the TLOC metric as a test case metric. We assume that the effort necessary to write test cases corresponding to a use case is proportional to the TLOC metric.

5.4.2 Dependent and Independent Variables

In this section, we used LR analysis to explore empirically the relationship between use case metrics (independent variables) and the testing effort in terms of size of test suites (dependent variable). We used the test case metric TLOC to identify the use cases which required a (relatively) high testing effort. In order to simplify the process of testing effort categorization, we provide only two categorizations: use cases which required a high testing effort and use cases which required a (relatively) low testing effort.

Category 1: includes the JUnit test cases corresponding to use cases for which the following condition is satisfied: large number of lines of test code (corresponding TLOC >= mean value of TLOC). We affect the value 1 to this category.

Category 2: includes all the other JUnit test cases. We affect the value 0 to this category.

Table 11 summarizes the distribution of use cases according to the adopted categorization. From Table 11, it can be seen that 9 (22%) use cases have been categorized as use cases having required a high testing effort, and 32 (78%) use cases have been categorized as use cases having required a (relatively) low testing effort.

Table 11. Distribution of use cases

1	0
9(22%)	32(78%)

5.4.3 Hypotheses

The study tested two hypotheses, which relate the use case metrics to the testing effort. For each use case metric UC_m, the hypothesis was:

A use case with a high UC_m value is more likely to require a high testing effort than a use case with a low UC_m value.

The null hypothesis was:

A use case with a high UC_m value is no more likely to require a high testing effort than a use case with a low UC_m value.

5.4.4 Logistic Regression Analysis: Research Methodology

LR is a standard statistical modeling method in which the dependent variable can take on only one of two different values. It is suitable for building software quality classification models. It is used to predict the dependent variable from a set of independent variables to determine the percent of variance in the dependent variable explained by the independent variables [1, 7, 37]. This technique has been widely applied to the prediction of fault-prone classes [e.g., 11, 12, 20, 26, 33, 37]. LR is of two types: univariate LR and multivariate LR. A multivariate LR model is based on the following equation:

$$P(X_1, \ldots X_n) = \frac{e^{\left(a+\Sigma_{i=1}^{i=n} b_i X_i\right)}}{1+e^{\left(a+\Sigma_{i=1}^{i=n} b_i X_i\right)}} \qquad (1)$$

The X_is are the independent variables and the (normalized) b_is are the estimated regression coefficients (approximated contribution) corresponding to the independent variables X_is. The larger the absolute value of the coefficient, the stronger the impact of the independent variable on the probability of detecting a high testing effort. P is the probability of detecting a use case requiring a high testing effort. The univariate LR analysis is, in fact, a special case of the multivariate LR analysis, where there is only one independent variable. The *p-value* (related to the statistical hypothesis) is the probability of the coefficient being different from zero by chance and is also an indicator of the accuracy of the coefficient estimate. To decide whether a metric is a statistically significant predictor of testing effort, we used the $\alpha = 0.05$ significance level to assess the *p-value*. R^2 (Nagelkerke) is defined as the proportion of the total variance in the dependent variable that is explained by the model. The higher R^2 is, the higher the effect of the independent variables, and the more accurate the model.

5.4.5 Model Evaluation

In order to evaluate the performance of the prediction models, we used the ROC (*Receiver Operating Characteristic*) analysis. Indeed, *precision* and *recall*, which are traditional evaluation criteria used to evaluate the prediction accuracy of LR models, are subject to change as the selected threshold changes. The ROC curve, which is defined as a plot of sensitivity on the y-coordinate versus its 1-specificity on the x-coordinate, is an effective method of evaluating the performance of prediction models [16, 17]. The optimal choice of the cutoff point that maximizes both sensitivity and specificity can be selected from the ROC curve. This will allow avoiding an arbitrary selection of the cutoff. In order to evaluate the performance of the models, we used particularly the AUC (*Area Under the Curve*) measure. It is a combined measure of sensitivity and specificity. It allows appreciating the model without subjective selection of the cutoff value. The larger the AUC measure, the better the model is at classifying use cases. A perfect model that correctly classifies all use cases has an AUC measure of 1. An AUC value close to 0.5 corresponds to a poor model. An AUC value greater than 0.7 corresponds to a good model [21].

5.4.6 Univariate LR Analysis: Results and Discussion

In this section, we present the results of the univariate LR analysis. The results, summarized in Table 12, show that the b-coefficient of the metrics NIM (1.825) and NEO (1.310) are significantly different from zero according to their p-values (respectively 0.015 and 0.021). This is not the case of the metric NS. The b-coefficient of the metric NS (0.313) is not significantly different from zero according to its p-value (0.108). Moreover, the metric NIM has the highest (and significant) R^2 value (53.7%). According to these results, the metrics NIM and NEO are significantly related to the testing effort compared to the metric NS. The AUC values (0.816 for NIM and 0.802 for NEO) confirm that univariate LR models based on the metrics NIM and NEO are more predictive of the testing effort than the univariate LR model based on the metric NS. These results are also confirmed by the confusion matrices corresponding to the three univariate LR models (see Table13 – cutoff = 0.5). In fact, we can get a better idea of the performance of the three univariate models, respectively the one based on the metric NS (Table 13, I), the one based on the metric NIM (Table 13, II) and the one based on the metric NEO (Table 13, III), by analyzing the corresponding ROC confusion matrices. These matrices are also excellent indicators of the accuracy of the models (73.17% for NS, 90.24% for NIM and 87.80% for NEO). According to these results, we can reasonably support the hypothesis of the NIM and NEO metrics and reject the one of the NS metric.

Table 12. Results for univariate LR analysis

	NS	NIM	NEO
R^2	9.5%	53.7%	47.9%
2Log	0.106	< 0.0001	< 0.0001
b	0.313	1.825	1.310
p-value	0.108	0.015	0.021
AUC	0.785	0.816	0.802

Table 13. Confusion matrices

I-Univariate model based on NS

	0	1	Total	% Correct
0	30	2	32	Specificity 93,75%
1	9	0	9	Sensitivity 0,00%
Total	39	2	41	73,17%

II-Univariate model based on NIM

	0	1	Total	% Correct
0	32	0	32	Specificity 100,00%
1	4	5	9	Sensitivity 55,56%
Total	36	5	41	90,24%

III- Univariate model based on NEO

	0	1	Total	% Correct
0	32	0	32	Specificity 100,00%
1	5	4	9	Sensitivity 44,44%
Total	37	4	41	87.80%

5.4.7 Multivariate LR Analysis: Results and Discussion

We present, in this section, the results of the multivariate LR analysis. According to the PCA analysis (section 5.4.1), the three use case metrics NIM, NS and NEO are complementary in terms of provided information. As mentioned in section 3, the metric NEO gives the number of system operations associated with the system events related to a use case. The system operations, which are identified in fact during system behavior analysis, are assigned during the design to one or more (controller) classes, which usually should delegate to other objects (classes) the work that needs to be done. The metric NIM defines the total number of methods (operations) that are involved in the execution (realization) of a use case (all of its scenarios), including the methods that are invoked by other methods according to the assignment of responsibilities and design of collaborations. The NS metric gives the total number of scenarios of a use case. The metrics NS and NEO can be calculated early in the software development lifecycle from the use case model. The metric NIM can be calculated from the design model, and can be considered as a refinement of the metric NEO.

The univariate LR analysis showed that the two metrics NIM and NEO are significant predictors of the testing effort. Moreover, despite the fact that the metric NS when taken alone is not a significant predictor of the testing effort (section 5.4.6), it remains that it captures information that is not captured by the NIM and NEO metrics. So, we wanted to explore the potential of the use case metrics, when used in combination, to predict the testing effort. We wanted to explore the two following combinations: (1) multivariate LR model based on the metrics NEO and NS, which can be used in the analysis phase of the software development lifecycle, and (2) multivariate LR model based on the metrics NIM and NS, which can be used in the design phase of the software development lifecycle. In other words, we wanted to investigate if the prediction capacity of the metrics NIM and NEO, as significant predictors of the testing effort, will be improved when combined with the metric NS.

Table 14. Results for multivariate LR analysis

(MLR-I)

R^2	61.3%	
2log	< 0.0001	
	p-value	b
NS	0.024	0.579
NEO	0.031	1.660
AUC	0.906	

(MLR-II)

R^2	60.1%	
2log	< 0.0001	
	p-value	b
NS	0.101	0.453
NIM	0.012	2.262
AUC	0.903	

Table 15. Confusion matrix of the multivariate model

(I)

	0	1	Total	% Correct
0	30	2	32	Specificity 93,75%
1	3	6	9	Sensitivity 66,67%
Total	33	8	41	87,80%

(II)

	0	1	Total	% Correct
0	32	0	32	Specificity 100,00%
1	3	6	9	Sensitivity 66,67%
Total	35	6	41	92,68%

In a first step, we used the two metrics NS and NEO to build the first multivariate LR model. Table 14 MLR-I summarizes the results of the multivariate LR analysis. From this table, it can be seen that the AUC value is 0.906, which is higher than the AUC values obtained with the univariate LR analysis. Moreover, the R^2 value increases (61.3%). This shows that the combined effect of the two metrics NEO and NS is higher than the effect of each metric taken alone. The results also show that the metric NEO has the highest (and significant) contribution (impact of the metric on the probability of detecting a high testing effort). These results are also confirmed by the confusion matrix corresponding to the multivariate model MLR-I (see Table 15, I, cutoff = 0.5). Indeed, the accuracy of the multivariate model (87.80% - Table 15, I) is higher than the accuracy of the univariate model based on the NS metric (73.17% - Table 13, I). It remained equal to the accuracy of the univariate model based on the metric NEO (87.80% - Table 13, II). The sensitivity of the multivariate model is however improved (66.67% - Table 15, I).

In a second step, we used the two metrics NS and NIM to build the second multivariate LR model. Table 14 MLR-II summarizes the results of the multivariate LR analysis. From this table, it can be seen that the AUC value is 0.903, which is higher than the AUC values obtained with the univariate LR analysis. Moreover, the R^2 value increases (60.1%). This shows that the combined effect of the two metrics is higher than the effect of each metric taken alone. The results also show that the metric NIM has the highest (and significant) contribution (impact of the metric on the probability of detecting a high testing effort). These results are also confirmed by the confusion matrix corresponding to the multivariate model MLR-II (see Table15, II, cutoff = 0.5). Indeed, the accuracy of the multivariate model (92.68% - Table 15, II) is higher than the accuracy of the two univariate models (73.17% for the one based on the metric NS and 90.24% for the one based on the metric NIM – Table 13, I and II).

In summary, the multivariate LR analysis shows that the combined effect of the metrics is more significant than when the metrics are considered individually. In addition, as it can be seen from the confusion matrices corresponding to the two multivariate LR models (Table 15, I and II), the accuracy of the second model (based on the metrics NS and NIM – 92.68%) is slightly better than the accuracy of the first model (based on the metrics NS and NEO – 87.80%).

5.5   Threats to Validity

The study presented in this paper should be replicated using many other OO software systems in order to draw more general conclusions about the ability of the use case metrics to predict the testing effort. Indeed, there are a number of limitations that may affect the results of the study or limit their interpretation and generalization. The achieved results are based on the data set we collected from only five case studies. To perform our study, we grouped the use cases of the five case studies to build our data set. Even if the collected data set is statistically significant, we do not claim that our results can be generalized. Moreover, knowing that these use cases are from different case studies, this may bias the results. In order to reduce this threat, we deliberately affected the development of test cases to the same team, two Master students in computer science which are familiar with the JUnit framework. They followed the same methodology in the development of test cases. The findings in this paper should be viewed as exploratory and indicative rather than conclusive. Results show at least that use cases offer a potential way that can be used in early stages of the software development lifecycle to predict the size of test suites. Moreover, the study has been performed on simple case studies. It is necessary to replicate the study on large systems.

6   Conclusions and Future Work

We explored, in this paper, the relationship between use case metrics and the size of test suites. The goal was to evaluate the capacity of use case metrics to predict the size of test suites. We performed an empirical analysis using data collected from five Java case studies for which we developed JUnit test cases. We used logistic regression analysis to evaluate the individual and combined effect of use case metrics on the size of test suites. The univariate LR analysis shows that: (1) the univariate model based on the metric NIM, which is related to the number of involved methods in the realizations of a use case, is a significant predictor of the testing effort, (2) the univariate model based on the metric NEO, which is related to the number of external operations associated to a use case, is also a significant predictor of the testing effort. The multivariate LR analysis shows that: (1) the multivariate model based on the NEO metric combined with the NS metric, which is related to the number of scenarios of a use case, improves the accuracy of the testing effort prediction, (2) the multivariate model based on the NIM metric combined with the NS metric improves also the accuracy of the testing effort prediction. Moreover, the multivariate LR analysis shows that the accuracy of the multivariate LR model based on the metrics NS and NIM is slightly better than the accuracy of the multivariate LR model based on the metrics NS and NEO.

The performed study should, however, be replicated using many other OO software systems in order to draw more general conclusions. The findings in this paper should, in fact, be viewed as exploratory and indicative rather than conclusive. Results show at least that use cases offer a potential way that can be used in early stages of the software development lifecycle to provide high-level estimates of the testing effort (use case ranking). As future work, we plan to extend the present study by using other methods (such as machine learning methods) to explore the individual and combined effect of the metrics on the testing effort, compare our approach to other testing effort prediction (estimation) approaches, and finally replicate the study on various OO software systems to be able to give generalized results.

Acknowledgments. This work was supported by NSERC (Natural Sciences and Engineering Research Council of Canada) grant.

References

[1] Aggarwal, K.K., Singh, Y., Arvinder, K., Ruchika, M.: Empirical Analysis for Investigating the Effect of Object-Oriented Metrics on Fault Proneness: A Replicated Case Study. Software Process: Improvement and Practice 16(1), 39–62 (2009)

[2] de Almeida, É.R.C., de Abreu, B.T., Moraes, R.: An Alternative Approach to Test Effort Estimation Based on Use Cases. In: Proceedings of the International Conference on Software Testing, Verification and Validation. IEEE Computer Society (2009)

[3] Badri, L., Badri, M., Toure, F.: Exploring empirically the relationship between lack of cohesion and testability in object-oriented systems. In: Kim, T.-H., Kim, H.-K., Khan, M.K., et al. (eds.) ASEA 2010. CCIS, vol. 117, pp. 78–92. Springer, Heidelberg (2010)

[4] Badri, L., Badri, M., Toure, F.: An empirical analysis of lack of cohesion metrics for predicting testability of classes. International Journal of Software Engineering and Its Applications 5(2) (2011)

[5] Badri, M., Toure, F.: Empirical Analysis of Object‐Oriented Design Metrics for Predicting Unit Testing Effort of Classes. Journal of Software Engineering and Applications 5(7) (July 2012)

[6] Badri, M., Badri, L., Flageol, W.: On the Relationship between Use Cases and Test Suites Size: An Exploratory Study. ACM SIGSOFT Software Engineering Notes 38(4) (July 2013)

[7] Basili, V.R., Briand, L.C., Melo, W.: A Validation of Object-Oriented Design Metrics as Quality Indicators. IEEE Transactions on Software Engineering 22(10) (1996)

[8] Baudry, B., Le Traon, B., Sunyé, G.: Testability analysis of a UML class diagram. In: Proceedings of the 9th International Software Metrics Symposium. IEEE CS (2003)

[9] Baudry, B., Le Traon, Y., Sunyé, G., Jézéquel, J.M.: Measuring and improving design patterns testability. In: Proceedings of the 9th International Software Metrics Symposium (METRICS 2003). IEEE Computer Society (2003)

[10] Baudry, B., Le Traon, Y., Sunyé, G.: Improving the testability of UML class diagrams. In: Proceedings of the International Workshop on Testability Analysis, Rennes, France (2004)

[11] Briand, L.C., Daly, J., Wuest, J.: A Unified Framework for Cohesion Measurement in Object-Oriented Systems. Empirical Software Engineering—An International Journal 3(1), 65–117 (1998)

[12] Briand, L.C., Wust, J., Daly, J., Porter, V.: Exploring the Relationship between Design Measures and Software Quality in Object-Oriented Systems. Journal of Systems and Software 51(3), 245–273 (2000)

[13] Bruntink, M., Van Deursen, A.: Predicting class testability using object-oriented metrics. In: Proceedings of the 4th IEEE International Workshop on Source Code Analysis and Manipulation (SCAM 2004), pp. 136–145 (September 2004)

[14] Bruntink, M., van Deursen, A.: An empirical study into class testability. Journal of Systems and Software 79(9), 1219–1232 (2006)

[15] Chaudhary, P., Yadav, C.S.: An Approach for Calculating the Effort Needed on testing Projects. International Journal of Advanced Research in Computer Engineering & Technology 1(1) (March 2012)

[16] El Emam, K., Melo, W.: The Prediction of Faulty Classes Using Object-Oriented Design Metrics. National Research Council of Canada NRC/ERB 1064 (1999)

[17] El Emam, K.: A Methodology for Validating Software Product Metrics. National Research Council of Canada NRC/ERB 1076 (2000)

[18] Fan, W., Xiaohu, Y., Xiaochun, Z., Lu, C.: Extended Use Case Points Method for Software Cost Estimation. In: International Conference on Computational Intelligence and Software Engineering (2009)

[19] Gupta, V., Aggarwal, K.K., Singh, Y.: A Fuzzy Approach for Integrated Measure of Object-Oriented Software Testability. Journal of Computer Science 1(2) (2005)

[20] Gyimothy, T., Ferenc, R., Siket, I.: Empirical Validation of Object-Oriented Metrics on Open Source Software for Fault Prediction. IEEE TSE 3(10), 897–910 (2005)

[21] Hosmer, D.W., Lemeshow, S.: Applied Logistic Regression. Wiley, New York (2000)

[22] Karner, G.: Resource Estimation for Objectory Projects (1993)

[23] Khan, R.A., Mustafa, K.: Metric based testability model for object-oriented design (MTMOOD). ACM SIGSOFT Software Engineering Notes 34(2) (2009)

[24] Larman, C.: Applying UML and Design Patterns, An introduction to object-oriented analysis and design and the unified process. Prentice Hall (2004)

[25] Le Traon, Y., Ouabdesselam, F., Robach, C.: Analyzing testability on data flow designs. In: Proceedings of the 11th International Symposium on Software Reliability Engineering (ISSRE 2000), pp. 162–173 (October 2000)

[26] Marcus, D.P., Ferenc, R.: Using the Conceptual Cohesion of Classes for Fault Prediction in Object-Oriented Systems. IEEE Transactions on Software Engineering 34(2), 287–300 (2008)

[27] Mohagheghi, P., Anda, B., Conradi, R.: Effort Estimation of Use Cases for Incremental Large-Scale Software Development. In: Proceedings of the International Conference on Software Engineering (2005)

[28] Nagheshwaran, S.: Test Effort Estimation Using Use Case Points. In: Quality Week 2001, San Francisco, California, USA (2001)

[29] Ochodek, M., Nawrocki, J., Kwarciak, K.: Simplifying effort estimation based on Use Case Points. Information and Software Technology 53, 200–213 (2011)

[30] Robiolo, G., Orosco, R.: Employing use cases to early estimate effort with simpler metrics. Innovations in Systems and Software Engineering 4 (2008)

[31] Robiolo, G., Badano, C., Orosco, R.: Transactions and Paths: two use case based metrics which improve the early effort estimation. In: Proceedings of the Third International Symposium on Empirical Software Engineering and Measurement. IEEE Computer Society (2009)

[32] Singh, Y., Kaur, A., Malhota, R.: Predicting testability effort using artificial neural network. In: Proceedings of the World Congress on Engineering and Computer Science, CA, USA (2008)

[33] Singh, Y., Kaur, A., Malhotra, R.: Empirical validation of object-oriented metrics for predicting fault proneness models. Software Quality Journal 18(1), 3–35 (2009)

[34] Singh, Y., Saha, A.: Predicting testability of eclipse: a case study. Journal of Software Engineering 4(2) (2010)

[35] Xiaochun, Z., Bo, Z., Fan, W., Chen Lu, Q.Y.: Estimate Test Execution Effort at an Early Stage: An Empirical Study. In: International Conference on Cyber World. IEEE CS (2008)

[36] Yi, Q., Bo, Z., Xiaochum, Z.: Early Estimate the Size of Test Suites from Use Cases. In: Proceedings of the 15th Asia-Pacific Software Engineering Conference. IEEE CS (2008)

[37] Zhou, Y., Leung, H.: Empirical Analysis of Object-Oriented Design Metrics for Predicting High and Low Severity Faults. IEEE Transactions on Software Engineering 32(10), 771–789 (2006)

Chaining Test Cases
for Reactive System Testing*

Peter Schrammel, Tom Melham, and Daniel Kroening

University of Oxford
Department of Computer Science
`first.lastname@cs.ox.ac.uk`

Abstract. Testing of synchronous reactive systems is challenging because long input sequences are often needed to drive them into a state to test a desired feature. This is particularly problematic in *on-target testing*, where a system is tested in its real-life application environment and the amount of time required for resetting is high. This paper presents an approach to discovering a *test case chain*—a single software execution that covers a group of test goals and minimises overall test execution time. Our technique targets the scenario in which test goals for the requirements are given as safety properties. We give conditions for the existence and minimality of a single test case chain and minimise the number of test case chains if a single test case chain is infeasible. We report experimental results with a prototype tool for C code generated from SIMULINK models and compare it to state-of-the-art test suite generators.

1 Introduction

Safety-critical embedded software, e.g., in the automotive or avionics domain, is often implemented as a *synchronous reactive system*. These systems compute their new state and their output as functions of old state and the given inputs. As these systems frequently have to satisfy high safety standards, tool support for systematic testing is highly desirable. The completeness of the testing process is frequently measured by defining a set of *test goals*, which are typically formulated as reachability properties. A good-quality test suite is a set of input sequences that drive the system into states that cover a large fraction of those goals.

Test suites generated by random test generators often contain a huge number of redundant test cases. Directed test case generation often requires lengthy input sequences to drive the system into a state where the desired feature can be tested. Furthermore, to execute the test suite, test cases must be chained manually or the system must be reset after executing each test case. This is a serious problem in *on-target testing*, where a system is tested in its real-life application environment and resetting might be very time-consuming [1].

This paper presents an approach to discovering a *test case chain*—a single test case that covers a set of multiple test goals and minimises overall test execution

---

* Supported by the EU FP7 STREP PINCETTE, the ARTEMIS VeTeSS project and ERC project 280053.

H. Yenigün, C. Yilmaz, and A. Ulrich (Eds.): ICTSS 2013, LNCS 8254, pp. 133–148, 2013.
© IFIP International Federation for Information Processing 2013

```
void init(t_state *s) { s->mode = OFF; s->speed = 0; s->enable = FALSE; }
void compute(t_input *i, t_state *s) {
  mode = s->mode;
  switch(mode) {
    case ON: if(i->gas || i->brake) s->mode=DIS; break;
    case DIS:
      if( (s->speed==2 && (i->dec || i->brake)) || (s->speed==0 && (i->acc || i->gas)) )
        s->mode=ON;
      break;
    case OFF:
      if( s->speed==0 && s->enable && (i->gas || i->acc) ||
          s->speed==1 && i->button ||
          s->speed==2 && s->enable && (i->brake || i->dec) )
        s->mode=ON;
      break;
  }
  if(i->button) s->enable = !s->enable;
  if((i->gas || mode!=ON && i->acc) && s->speed<2) s->speed++;
  if((i->brake || mode!=ON && i->dec) && s->speed>0) s->speed--;
}
```

Fig. 1. Code generated for cruise controller example

time. The essence of the problem is to find a shortest path through the system
that covers all the test goals.

Example. To illustrate the problem and our approach, we reuse the classical
cruise controller example given in [2]. There are five Boolean inputs, two for
actuation of the *gas* and *brake* pedals, a toggle *button* to enable the cruise control
and two sensors indicating whether the car is *acc*- or *dec*elerating. There are three
state variables: *speed, enable*, which is true when cruise control is enabled, and
mode indicating whether cruise control is turned *OFF*, actually active (*ON*),
or temporarily inactive, i.e., *DIS*engaged while user pushes the gas or brake
pedal. A C implementation, with the structure typical of code generated from
SIMULINK models, is given in Fig. 1 and its state machine is depicted in Fig. 2.
The function **compute** is executed periodically (e.g. on a timer interrupt). Thus,
there is a notion of *step* that relates to execution time.

We formulate some LTL properties for which we want to generate test cases:

$$p_1: \mathbf{G}\big(mode = ON \wedge speed = 1 \wedge dec \Rightarrow \mathbf{X}(speed = 1)\big)$$
$$p_2: \mathbf{G}\big(mode = DIS \wedge speed = 2 \wedge dec \Rightarrow \mathbf{X}(mode = ON)\big)$$
$$p_3: \mathbf{G}\big(mode = ON \wedge brake \Rightarrow \mathbf{X}(mode = DIS)\big)$$
$$p_4: \mathbf{G}\big(mode = OFF \wedge speed = 2 \wedge \neg enable \wedge button \Rightarrow \mathbf{X}\ enable\big)$$

We observe that each of the properties above relates to a particular transition
in the state machine (shown as bold edge labels in Fig. 2). A *test case* is a
sequence of inputs that determines a (bounded) execution path through the
system. The *length* of a test case is the length of this sequence. A test case
covers a property if it triggers the transition the property relates to. A *test suite*
is a set of test cases that covers all the properties.

Ideally, we can obtain a single test case that covers all properties in a single
execution. We call a test case that covers a sequence of properties a *test case
chain*. Our goal is to synthesise minimal test case chains—test case chains with
fewest transitions. It is not always possible to generate a single test case chain
that covers all properties; multiple test case chains may be required.

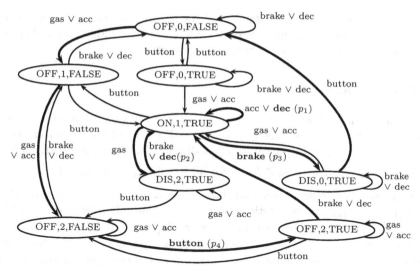

Fig. 2. State machine of the example. Edges are labelled by inputs and nodes by state ⟨*mode, speed, enable*⟩. Properties are in bold, bold arcs show a minimal test case chain.

We compute such a minimal test case chain from a set of start states I via a set of given properties $P = \{p_1, p_2, \ldots\}$ to a set of final states F. For our example, with $I = F = \{mode = OFF \wedge speed = 0 \wedge \neg enable\}$ and $P = \{p_1, p_2, p_3, p_4\}$, for instance, we obtain the test case chain consisting of the bold arcs in Fig. 2. First, this chain advances to p_4, then covers p_1, p_2 and p_3, and finally goes to F. One can assert that this path has the minimal length of 9 steps.

Testing problems similar to ours have been addressed by research on *minimal checking sequences* in conformance testing [3,4,1]. This work analyses automata-based specifications that encode system control and have transitions labelled with operations on data variables. The challenge here is to find short transition paths based on a given coverage criterion that are feasible, i.e. consistent with the data operations. Random test case generation can then be used to discover such a path. In contrast, our approach analyses the code generated from models or the implementation code itself, and it can handle partial specifications expressed as a collection of safety properties. A common example is acceptance testing in the automotive domain. Our solution uses bounded model checking to generate test cases guaranteed to exercise the desired functionality.

Contributions. The contributions of this paper can be summarised as follows:
- We present a new algorithm to compute minimal test chains that first constructs a weighted digraph abstraction using a reachability analysis, on which the minimisation is performed as a second step. The final step is to compute the test input sequence. We give conditions for the existence and minimality of a single test case chain and propose algorithms to handle the general case.
- We have implemented a prototype tool, CHAINCOVER, for C code generated from SIMULINK models, on top of the CBMC bounded model checker and the LKH travelling salesman problem solver.

– We present experimental results to demonstrate that our approach is viable on a set of benchmarks, mainly from automotive industry, and is more efficient than state-of-the-art test suite generators.

2 Preliminaries

Program Model. A *program* is given by (Σ, Υ, T, I) with finite sets of states Σ and inputs Υ, a transition relation $T \subseteq (\Sigma \times \Upsilon \times \Sigma)$ and a set of initial states $I \subseteq \Sigma$. An *execution* of a program is a (possibly) infinite sequence of transitions $s_0 \xrightarrow{i_0} s_1 \xrightarrow{i_1} s_2 \to \dots$ with $s_0 \in I$ and for all $k \geq 0$, $(s_k, i_k, s_{k+1}) \in T$.

Properties. We consider specifications given as a set of safety properties $P = \{p_1, \dots, p_{|P|}\}$. The properties are given as a formula over state variables s and input variables i and are of the form $\mathbf{G}(\varphi \Rightarrow \psi)$ where φ describes an *assumption* and ψ is the *assertion* to be checked. φ specifies a test goal, whereas ψ defines the test outcome; hence, for test case generation, only φ is needed. We denote by Π the set of property assumptions. φ is a temporal logic formula built using the operators $\wedge, \vee, \neg, \mathbf{X}$, i.e., it describes sets of finite paths. An execution $\pi = \langle s_0, s_1, \dots \rangle$ *covers* a property iff it contains a subpath $\langle s_k, \dots s_{k+j} \rangle$ that satisfies φ (j is the nesting depth of $\mathbf{X}$ operators in φ), i.e., $\exists k \geq 0 : \exists i_k, \dots, i_{k+j} : \varphi(s_k, i_k, \dots, s_{k+j}, i_{k+j}) \wedge \bigwedge_{k \leq m \leq k+j} T(s_m, i_m, s_{m+1})$. We call the set of states s_k satisfying φ the *trigger* $\widehat{\varphi}$ of the property.

For our method, it is not essential whether φ describes a set of paths or just a set of states; thus, to simplify the presentation, we assume that the property assumptions do not contain $\mathbf{X}$ operators. Single-step transition properties $\mathbf{G}(\varphi \Rightarrow \mathbf{X}\psi)$ fall into this category, for example. In this case, φ is equivalent to its trigger $\widehat{\varphi}$.

Moreover, we assume that property assumptions are non-overlapping, i.e. the sub-paths satisfying the assumptions do not share any edges. Our minimality results only apply to such specifications. Detecting overlappings is a hard problem [5] that goes beyond the scope of this paper.

Test Cases. A *test case* is an input sequence $\langle i_0, \dots, i_n \rangle$ and generates an execution $\pi = \langle s_0, \dots, s_{n+1} \rangle$. A test case *covers* a property p iff its execution covers the property.

3 Chaining Test Cases

The Problem. We are given a program (Σ, Υ, T, I), properties P, and a set of final states $F \subseteq \Sigma$. A *test case chain* is a test case $\langle i_0, \dots, i_n \rangle$ that covers all properties in P, i.e., its execution $\langle s_0, \dots, s_{n+1} \rangle$ starts in $s_0 \in I$, ends in $s_{n+1} \in F$ and covers all properties in P. A *minimal test case chain* is a test case chain of minimal length. The final states F are used to ensure the test execution ends in a desired state, e.g. "engines off" or "gear locked in park mode".

Our Approach. We now describe our basic algorithm, which has three steps:

(1) *Abstraction:* We construct a *property K-reachability graph* of the system. This is a weighted, directed graph with nodes representing the properties and edges labelled with the number of states through which execution must pass, up to length K, between the properties.

(2) *Optimisation:* We determine the shortest path that covers all properties in the abstraction.

(3) *Concretisation:* Finally, we compute the corresponding concrete test case chain along the abstract path.

We discuss the conditions under which we obtain the *minimal* test case chain. Due to space limitations, we refer to the extended version [6] for the pseudo-code of the algorithms and the proofs omitted in this paper.

3.1   Abstraction: Property K-Reachability Graph

The *property K-reachability graph* is an abstraction of the original program by a weighted, directed graph (V, E, W), with

- vertices $V = \Pi \cup \{I, F\}$, all defining property assumptions, including formulas describing the sets I and F,
- edges $E \subseteq E_{target} \subset V \times V$, as explained below, and
- an edge labelling $W : E \to \mathbb{N}$ assigning to each $(\varphi, \varphi') \in E$ the minimal number of steps bounded by K needed to reach some state satisfying φ' from any state satisfying φ according to the program's transition relation T.

Fig. 3 shows the property 2-reachability graph for our example.

Graph Construction.   The graph is constructed by iteratively calling a function *GetKreachEdges* that returns the subset of edges that have weight k in the set of interesting edges $E_{target} = \left(\bigcup_{\varphi_j \in \Pi} \{(I, \varphi_j), (\varphi_j, F)\} \right) \cup \{(\varphi_j, \varphi_\ell) \mid \varphi_j, \varphi_\ell \in \Pi, j \neq \ell\}$. E_{target} contains all pairwise links between the nodes φ_j, links from I to all nodes φ_j, and from every φ_j to F. *GetKreachEdges* (e.g. implemented using constraint solving) is called for increasing values of k and the obtained edges are added to the graph until a *covering path* exists, i.e., a path from I to F visiting all nodes at least once. If we fail to find a path before reaching a given reachability bound K, or there is no path although the graph contains all edges in E_{target}, then we abort. The constructed graph contains an edge (φ, φ') with weight k iff for the two properties with assumptions φ and φ', a state in φ' is reachable from a state φ in $k \leq K$ steps, and k is the minimal number of steps for reaching φ' from φ.

Existence of a Covering Path.   The existence of a covering path can be formulated as a reachability problem in a directed graph:

Lemma 1. *Let (V, E) be a directed graph of the kind described above. Then, there is a covering path from I to F iff*

(1) all vertices are reachable from I,

(2) F is reachable from all vertices and

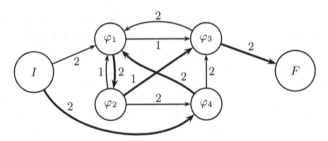

Fig. 3. Test case chaining: property K-reachability graph (for $K = 2$) and minimal test case chain of length $n = 9$ (bold arcs) for our example (Fig. 2)

(3) for all pairs of vertices $(v_1, v_2) \in (V \setminus \{I, F\})^2$,
    (a) v_2 is reachable from v_1 or (b) v_1 is reachable from v_2.

Proof. In the transitive closure (V, E') of (V, E), v_2 is reachable from v_1 iff there exists an edge $(v_1, v_2) \in E'$.

($\Longrightarrow$): conditions (1) and (2) are obviously necessary. Let us assume that we have a covering path π and there are vertices (v_1, v_2) which neither satisfy (3a) nor (3b). Then neither $\langle v_1, \dots, v_2 \rangle$ nor $\langle v_2, \dots, v_1 \rangle$ can be a subpath of π, which contradicts the fact that π is a covering path.

($\Longleftarrow$): Any vertex is reachable from I (1), so let us choose v_1. From v_1 we can reach another vertex v_2 (3a), or, at least, v_1 is reachable from another vertex v_2 (3b), but in the latter case, since v_2 is reachable from I, we can go first to v_2 and then to v_1. Induction step: Let us assume we have a path $\langle I, v_1, \dots, v_k \rangle$. If there is a vertex v' that is reachable from v_k (3a) we add it to our current path π. If v' is unreachable from v_k, then by (3b), v_k must be reachable from v', and there is a $v_i, i < k$ in $\pi = \langle I, \dots, v_k \rangle$ from which it is reachable and in this case we obtain the path $\langle I, \dots, v_i, v', v_{i+1}, \dots, v_k \rangle$; if there is no such v_i then, at last by (1), v' is reachable from I, so we can construct the path $\langle I, v', \dots, v_k \rangle$. F is reachable from any vertex (2), thus, we can complete the covering path as soon as all other vertices have been covered. $\square$

Reachability can be checked in constant time on the transitive closure of the graph. Hence, the overall existence check has complexity $\mathcal{O}(|V|^3)$.

3.2 Optimisation: Shortest Path Computation

The next step is to compute the shortest path covering all nodes in the property K-reachability graph. Such a path is not necessarily Hamiltonian; revisiting nodes is allowed. However, we can compute the transitive closure of the graph using the Floyd-Warshall algorithm (which preserves minimality), and then compute a Hamiltonian path from I to F. If we do not have a Hamiltonian path solver, we can add an arc from F to I and pass the problem to an *asymmetric travelling salesman problem* (ATSP) solver that gives us the shortest circuit that visits all vertices exactly once. We cut this circuit between F and I to obtain the shortest path π.

For our example, the shortest path has length 9, given as bold arcs in Fig. 3.

3.3 Concretisation: Computing the Test Case Chain

Once we have found a minimum covering path π in the property K-reachability graph abstraction, we have to compute the inputs corresponding to it in the concrete program. This is done by the function $CheckPath(\pi, T, W)$ which takes an abstract path $\pi = \langle \varphi_1, \ldots, \varphi_{|V|} \rangle$ and returns the input sequence $\langle i_0, \ldots, i_n \rangle$ corresponding to a concrete path with the reachability distances between each $(\varphi_j, \varphi_{j+1}) \in \pi$ given by the edge weights $W(\varphi_j, \varphi_{j+1})$. Typically, $CheckPath$ involves constraint solving; we will discuss our implementation in §5.

For our example, we obtain, for instance, the sequence $\langle gas, acc, button, dec,$ $dec, gas, dec, brake, button \rangle$ corresponding to the bold arcs in Fig. 2.

3.4 Optimality

Since the (non-)existence or the optimality of a chain in the K-reachability abstraction does not imply the (non-)existence or the optimality of a chain in the concrete program, the success of this procedure can only be guaranteed under certain conditions, which we now discuss.

Lemma 2 (Single-state property triggers). *If (1) the program and the properties admit a test case chain, (2) all triggers of properties in P are singleton sets, and (3) the test case chain computed by our algorithm visits each property once, then the test case chain is minimal.*

If each property is visited once, it is guaranteed that the abstract path contains only edges that correspond to concrete paths of minimal length, and hence the test case chain is optimal for the concrete program. Otherwise, for a subpath $(\varphi, \varphi', \varphi, \varphi'')$, there might exist an edge (φ', φ'') with $W(\varphi', \varphi'') < W(\varphi', \varphi) + W(\varphi, \varphi'')$ that is only discovered for higher values of K. For finite state systems, there is an upper bound for K, the reachability diameter, i.e., the maximum (finite) length d of a path in the set of shortest paths between any pair of states $s_i, s_j \in \Sigma$ [7]. Beyond d we will not discover shorter pairwise links.

Theorem 1 (Minimal test case chain). *Let d be the reachability diameter of the program, then there is a $K \leq d$ such that, under the preconditions (1) and (2) of Lem. 2, the test case chain is minimal.*

In practice, we can stop the procedure if a chain of acceptable length is found, i.e. we do not compute the reachability diameter but use a user-supplied bound.

4   Generalisations

We will now generalise our algorithm in three ways:

- *Multi-state property triggers:* Dropping the assumption that triggers are single-state may make the concretisation phase fail. Under certain restrictions, we will still find a test case chain if one exists, but we lose minimality.

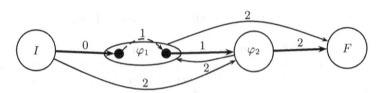

Fig. 4. Broken chain: the path $\langle I, \varphi_1, \varphi_2 \rangle$ is not feasible in a single step, but requires two steps

- Without these restrictions, we might even lose completeness, i.e., the guarantee to find a chain if one exists. We propose an abstraction refinement to *ensure completeness* under these circumstances.
- *Multiple chains:* Dropping the assumption about the existence of a single chain raises the problem of how to generate multiple chains.

We discuss here the first two points and refer to the extended version [6] of this paper for the third one.

4.1   Multi-state Property Triggers

In practice, many properties are multi-state, i.e. precondition (2) of Lem. 2 is not met. In this case, the abstract covering path might be infeasible in the concrete program, and hence, the naive concretisation of §3.3 might fail. We have to extend the concretisation step to fix such broken chains.

Example 1 (Broken chain). Let us consider the following broken chain in our example with the properties:

$p_1 :$ $\mathbf{G}\big(mode = OFF \wedge \neg enable \wedge button \Rightarrow \mathbf{X}\ enable\big)$

$p_2 :$ $\mathbf{G}\big(mode = ON \wedge brake \Rightarrow \mathbf{X}(mode = DIS)\big)$

with $I = F = \{mode = OFF \wedge speed = 0 \wedge \neg enable\}$.

We obtain a shortest covering path $\langle I, \varphi_1, \varphi_2, F \rangle$ in the abstraction with weights $W(I, \varphi_1) = 0$, $W(\varphi_1, \varphi_2) = 1$ and $W(\varphi_2, F) = 2$. However, Fig. 2 tells us that the path $\langle I, \varphi_1, \varphi_2 \rangle$ is not feasible in a single step, but requires two steps, as illustrated in Fig. 4.

A broken chain contains an infeasible subpath *failed_path* $= \langle \varphi_1, \dots, \varphi_k \rangle$ of the abstract path π that involves at least three vertices, such as $\langle I, \varphi_1, \varphi_2 \rangle$ in our example above. We extend the concretisation step with a chain repair capability. The function *RepairPath* iteratively repairs broken chains by incrementing the weights associated with the edges of *failed_path* and checking feasibility of this "stretched" path. We give more details about our implementation in §5.

Example 2 (Repaired chain). For the broken chain in our previous example, we will check whether $\langle I, \varphi_1, \varphi_2 \rangle$ is feasible with $W(\varphi_1, \varphi_2)$ incremented by one. This makes the path feasible and we obtain the chain $\langle button, gas, brake, button \rangle$.

Completeness. The chain repair succeeds if the given path π admits a chain in the concrete program. In particular, this holds when the states in each property trigger are strongly connected:

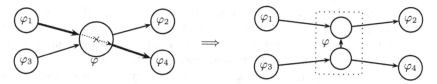

Fig. 5. Abstraction refinement for a failed path $\langle \varphi_1, \varphi, \varphi_4 \rangle$ (bold arrows)

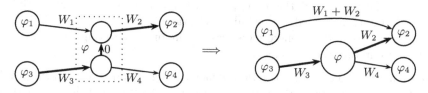

Fig. 6. Collapsing the property refinement group (box) in the refined abstraction to a TSP problem w.r.t. a solution path (bold arrows)

Theorem 2 (Multi-state strongly connected property). *If for each property trigger the states are strongly connected and there exists a test case chain, then our algorithm with chain repair will find it.*

In practice, many reactive systems are, apart from an initialisation phase, strongly connected—but, as stressed above, the test case chain might not be minimal.

4.2 Ensuring Completeness

If the shortest path in the abstraction does not admit a chain in the concrete program, our algorithm with chain repair will fail to find a test case chain even though one exists, i.e., it is not complete.

Example 3 (Chain repair fails). In Fig. 4, we have found the shortest abstract path $\langle I, \varphi_1, \varphi_2, F \rangle$. Now assume that the right state in φ_1 is not reachable from the left state. Then the chain repair fails. In this case, there might still be a (non-)minimal path in the abstraction that admits a chain: in our example in Fig. 4, assuming that the left state in φ_1 is reachable from I via φ_2 and F is reachable from the left state in φ_1, we have the feasible path $\langle I, \varphi_2, \varphi_1, F \rangle$.

To obtain completeness in this situation, we propose the following abstraction refinement method. Suppose a covering path π in the abstraction turns out to be infeasible in the concrete program, with $failed\_path = \langle \varphi_1, \ldots, \varphi_N \rangle$.

1. We refine failed vertices $\varphi_2, \ldots, \varphi_{N-1}$ in $failed\_path$ by splitting them as illustrated in Fig. 5 that rules out the infeasible subpath, as typically done by abstract refinement algorithms. We call the vertices obtained from such splittings that belong to the same property a *property refinement group*.
2. The second part of the proof of Lem. 1 gives us an $\mathcal{O}(n^2)$ algorithm *GetCoveringPath* for finding a (non-minimal) covering path from I to F in the transitive closure of a directed graph, taking into account that a covering path needs to cover only one vertex for each property refinement group.

3. A solution π obtained that way might be far from optimal, so we exploit the TSP solver to give us a better solution π'. However, the refined graph does not encode the desired TSP problem because it is sufficient to cover only one vertex for each property refinement group. Hence, given a path π, we transform the graph by collapsing each property refinement group with respect to π as illustrated by Fig. 6. The obtained graph is handed over to the TSP solver. Note that the transformations do not preserve optimality, because, e.g. in Fig. 6, the arc (φ_1, φ_2) would cover φ in a concrete path but not in the transformed, refined abstract graph.

4. We try to compute a concrete test case chain for the covering path π'. If this fails, we iterate the refinement process.

In each iteration of the abstraction refinement algorithm, a node in the graph is split such that a concrete spurious transition is removed from the abstraction, i.e. the transition system structure of the program inside the property assumptions is made explicit in the abstraction. Since there is only a finite number of transitions, the abstraction refinement will eventually terminate and a covering path will be found that can be concretised to a test case chain.

Example 4 (Abstraction refinement). Assume, as in the previous example, that the right state in φ_1 in Fig. 4 is not reachable from the left state. Then the abstraction refinement will split φ_1 into two vertices. Suppose that *GetCoveringPath* returns the covering path $\pi = \langle I, \varphi_2, \varphi_1, \varphi_2, F \rangle$.[1] Then collapsing the two nodes belonging to φ_1 w.r.t. π will remove the arc from I to φ_1. The TSP solver will optimise π and find the shorter path $\langle I, \varphi_2, \varphi_1, F \rangle$.

5   Test-Case Generation with Bounded Model Checking

The previous sections abstract from the actual backend implementation of the functions *GetKreachEdges*, *CheckPath* and *RepairPath*. In this work, we use bounded model checking to provide an efficient implementation. Alternative instantiations could be based on symbolic execution, for example.

BMC-Based Test Case Generation. Bounded model checking (BMC) [8] can be used to check the existence of a path $\pi = \langle s_0, s_1, \ldots, s_K \rangle$ of increasing length K from ϕ to ϕ'. This check is performed by deciding satisfiability of the following formula using a SAT solver:

$$\phi(s_0) \wedge \bigwedge_{1 \leq k \leq K} T(s_{k-1}, i_{k-1}, s_k) \wedge \phi'(s_K) \tag{1}$$

If the SAT solver returns the answer *satisfiable*, it also provides a satisfying assignment $(s_0, i_0, s_1, i_1, \ldots, s_{K-1}, i_{K-1}, s_K)$. The satisfying assignment represents one possible path $\pi = \langle s_0, s_1, \ldots, s_K \rangle$ from ϕ to ϕ' and identifies the corresponding input sequence $\langle i_0, \ldots, i_{K-1} \rangle$. Hence, a test case $\langle i_0, \ldots, i_{K-1} \rangle$ covering a property with assumption $\varphi(s, i)$ can be generated by checking satisfiability of a path from I to φ.

---

[1] It will actually return the better result for this particular example.

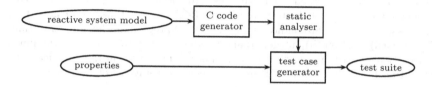

Fig. 7. Tool chain

Instantiation. *CheckPath* corresponds to a SAT query like Eq. (1) with $\phi = I$, $\phi' = F$, conjoined with the formulas for the property assumptions φ_j according to the covering path π. The formula for T includes any assumptions restricting the input domain. If the query is unsatisfiable, the SAT solver can be requested to produce a reason for the failure (e.g. in the form of an unsatisfiable core) from which we can extract *failed_path*.

The function *GetKreachEdges* that returns the K-reachability edges in a set E_{target} is implemented by satisfiability checking the formula:

$$\left(\bigvee_{(\varphi, \varphi') \in E_{target}} \varphi(s_0, i_0) \wedge \varphi'(s_K) \right) \wedge \bigwedge_{1 \leq k \leq K} T(s_{k-1}, i_{k-1}, s_k) \tag{2}$$

We iteratively check this formula, removing the respective terms from the formula each time a solution satisfies (φ, φ'), until the formula becomes unsatisfiable. In addition to assumptions on the inputs, T must also contain a state invariant, obtained, e.g. with a static analyser. This is necessary because, otherwise, the state satisfying φ in Eq. 2 might be unreachable from an initial state.

For the chain repair *RepairPath*, the most efficient method that we tested was to sequentially find a feasible weight for each of the edges in *failed_path*, starting the check for an edge $(\varphi_j, \varphi_{j+1})$ from a concrete state in φ_j obtained from the successful check of the previous edge $(\varphi_{j-1}, \varphi_j)$.

6 Experimental Evaluation

Implementation. For our experiments we have set up a tool chain (Fig. 7) that generates C code from SIMULINK models using the GENE-AUTO[2] code generator. Our prototype test case chain generator CHAINCOVER[3] itself is built upon the infrastructure provided by CBMC[4] [10] with MINISAT[5] as a SAT backend and the LKH TSP solver[6] [11].

The properties are written in C. For instance, property p_1 in our example is stated as follows:

[2] http://geneauto.gforge.enseeiht.fr, version 2.4.9
[3] http://www.cprover.org/chaincover/, version 0.1
[4] http://www.cprover.org/cbmc/, version 4.4
[5] http://minisat.se, version 2.2.0
[6] http://www.akira.ruc.dk/~keld/research/LKH/, version 2.0.2

Table 1. Experimental results: The table lists the number of test cases/chains (tcs), the accumulated length of the test case chains (len) and the time (in seconds) taken for test case generation. Size indicates the size of the program in the number of (minimally encoded) Boolean (b), integer (i) and floating point (f) variables and (minimally encoded) Boolean (b) inputs. "P" is the number of properties in the specification. If the tool timed out ("t/o") after 1 hour the achieved coverage ("cov") is given.

benchmark	size s	i	P	CHAINCOVER tcs	len	time	FSHELL tcs	len	time	random tcs	len	time	KLEE tcs	len	time
Cruise 1	3b	3b	4	1	9	0.77	3	18	3.67	2.8	24.6	0.54	3	27	46.5
Cruise 2	3b	3b	9	1	10	0.71	4	20	3.56	2.4	21.2	0.07	3	30	17.7
Window 1	3b+1i	5b	8	1	24	14.1	4	32	19.0	1.8	40.4	58.9	3	72	155
Window 2	3b+1i	5b	16	1	45	24.9	7	56	28.3	2.0	86.8	18.7	5	225	242
Alarm 1	4b+1i	2b	5	1	26	7.51	1	27	509	80% cov.	t/o		60% cov.	t/o	
Alarm 2	4b+1i	2b	16	1	71	33.5	3	81	690	94% cov.	t/o		63% cov.	t/o	
Elevator 1	6b	3b	4	1	8	22.9	2	15	115	2.2	10.4	0.85	2	16	24.4
Elevator 2	6b	3b	10	1	32	97.3	5	54	789	2.6	49.0	65.8	70% cov.	t/o	
Elevator 3	6b	3b	19	1	48	458	6	54	838	4.0	149	18.0	53% cov.	t/o	
Robotarm 1	4b+2f	3b	4	1	25	185	2	22	362	2.4	49.0	0.07	2	40	10.9
Robotarm 2	4b+2f	3b	10	1	47	113	2	33	532	3.8	72.2	0.21	80% cov.	t/o	
Robotarm 3	4b+2f	3b	18	1	84	427	5	55	731	3.2	160	0.62	67% cov.	t/o	

```
void p_1(t_input* i, t_state* s) {
  __CPROVER_assume(s->mode==ON && s->speed==1 && i->dec);
  compute(i,s);
  assert(s->speed ==1);
}
```

Assumptions on the inputs and the state invariant obtained from the static analysis are written as C code in a similar way.

Benchmarks. Our experiments are based on SIMULINK models, mainly from automotive industry. Our benchmarks are a simple *cruise* control model [2], a *window* controller[7], a car *alarm* system [8], an elevator model [12] and a model of a *robot arm* that can be controlled with a joystick. We generated test case chains for these examples for specifications of different size and granularity. The benchmark characteristics are listed in Table 1. Apart from *Cruise 1* all specifications have properties with multi-state assumptions, thus, the obtained test case chains are not minimal in general. All our benchmarks are (almost) strongly connected (some have an initial transition after which the system is strongly connected), hence, they did not require abstraction refinement.

Comparison. We have compared our prototype tool CHAINCOVER with

- FSHELL[9] [13], an efficient test generator with test suite minimisation,

---

[7] http://www.mathworks.co.uk/products/simulink/examples.html
[8] http://www.mogentes.eu/public/deliverables/
    MOGENTES_3-15_1.0r_D3.4b_TestTheories-final_main.pdf
[9] http://forsyte.at/software/fshell/, version 1.4

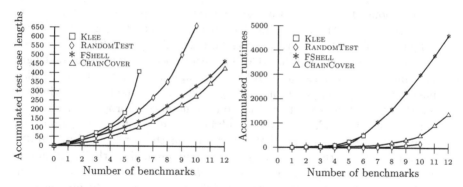

Fig. 8. Experimental results: accumulative graph of test case lengths on the left-hand side, accumulated runtimes on the right-hand side

- an in-house, simple *random* case generator with test suite minimisation and
- KLEE[10] [14], a test case generator based on symbolic execution.

In order to make results comparable, we have chosen F to be equivalent to I (or the state after the initial transition). Hence, test cases generated by FSHELL, random and KLEE can be concatenated (disregarding the initial transition) to get a single test case chain.

Like our prototype, FSHELL is based on bounded model checking. FSHELL takes a coverage specification in form of a query as input. It computes test cases that start in I, cover one or more properties $p_1, \ldots, p_n$ and terminate in F when given the query: `cover (@CALL(p_1) | ... | @CALL(p_n)) -> @CALL(final)`. In the best case, FSHELL returns a single test case, i.e. a test chain. We have run FSHELL with increasing unwinding bounds K until all properties were covered.

For random testing and KLEE, we coded the requirement to finish a test case in F with the help of flags in the test harness. Then we stopped the tools as soon as full coverage was achieved and selected the test cases achieving full coverage while minimising the length of the input sequence using an in-house, weighted-minimal-cover-based test suite minimiser. For random testing we averaged the results over five runs. Unlike CHAINCOVER and FSHELL, which start test chain computation without prior knowledge of how many steps are needed to produce a test case, we had to provide random testing and KLEE with this information. The reason is that the decision when a certain number of steps will not yield a test case can only be taken after reaching a timeout for random testing. Similarly, KLEE may take hours to terminate. Consequently, the results for random testing and KLEE are not fully comparable to those of the other tools.

Results. Experimental results obtained are shown in Table 1 and Fig. 8.

- Our prototype tool CHAINCOVER usually succeeds in finding shorter test case chains than the other tools. It is also in general faster. CHAINCOVER spends more than 99% of its runtime with BMC. The time for solving the ATSP problem is neglible for the number of properties we have in the

---

[10] `http://klee.llvm.org/`, revision 132049

specifications. The runtime ratio for generating the property K-reachability graph ($\mathcal{O}(Kn^2)$ BMC queries for n properties) versus finding and repairing a chain ($\mathcal{O}(Kn)$ BMC queries) varies between 7:92 and 75:24.

- FSHELL comes closest to CHAINCOVER with respect to test case chain length and finds shorter chains on the robot arm example. However, FSHELL takes much longer: the computational cost depends on the number of unwindings and the size of the program and less on the number of properties.
- Random testing yields very good results on some (small) specifications and sometimes even finds chains that are as short as those generated by CHAIN-COVER. However, the results vary and heavily depend on the program and the specification: in some cases, e.g. *Robotarm*, full coverage is achieved in fractions of a second; in other cases, full coverage could not be obtained before reaching the timeout of one hour and generating millions of test cases.
- KLEE found test case chains on a few of the benchmarks in very short time, but did not achieve full coverage within an hour on half of the benchmarks, which suggests that exhaustive exploration is not suitable for our problem.

7   Related Work

Test case generation with model checkers came up in the mid-90s and has attracted continuous research interest since then, especially due to the enormous progress in SAT solver performance. There is a vast literature on this topic, surveyed in [15], for example.

In the model-based testing domain, the problem of finding minimal checking sequences has been studied in *conformance testing* [3,4,1], which amounts to checking whether each state and transition in a given EFSM specification is correctly implemented. First, a minimal checking path is computed, which might be infeasible due to the operations on the data variables. Subsequently, random test case generation is applied to discover such a path, which might fail again. Duale and Uyar [16] propose an algorithm for finding a feasible transition path, but it requres guards and assignments in the models to be linear. Another approach is to use genetic algorithms [3,17] to find a feasible path of minimised length. SAT solvers have also been used to compute (non-minimal) checking sequences in FSM models [18,19]. Our method does not impose restrictions on guards and assignments and implicitly handles low-level issues such as overflows and the semantics of floating-point arithmetic in finding feasible test cases. The fact that minimal paths on the abstraction might not be feasible in the concrete program does not arise due to limited reasoning about data variables, but due to the multi-state nature of the properties we are trying to cover.

Closest to our work is recent work [20] on generating test chains for EFSM models with timers. They use SMT solvers to find a path to the nearest test goal and symbolic execution to constrain the search space. If no test goal is reachable they backtrack to continue the search from an earlier state in the test chain. Their approach represents a greedy heuristics and thus makes minimality considerations difficult. Our method can handle timing information if it is explicitly expressed as counters in the program.

Petrenko et al. [21] propose a method for test optimisation for EFSM models with timers. They use an ATSP solver to find an optimal ordering of a given set of test cases and an SMT solver to determine paths connecting them. The problem they tackle is easier than ours because they do not generate test cases, but just try to chain a given set of test cases in an optimal order. Additionally, they take into account overlappings of test cases during optimisation.

In contrast to all these works, our approach starts from a partial specification given by a set of properties, usually formalised from high-level requirements. The K-reachability graph abstraction can be viewed as the generation of a model from a partial specification and automated annotation of model transitions with timing information in terms of the minimal number of steps required.

8   Summary and Prospects

We have presented a novel approach to discovering a minimal test case chain, i.e., a single test case that covers a given set of test goals in a minimal number of execution steps. Our approach combines reachability analysis to build an abstraction, TSP-based optimisation and heuristics to find a concrete solution in case we cannot guarantee minimality. The test goals might also be generated from an EFSM specification or from code coverage criteria like MC/DC. This flexibility is a distinguishing feature of our approach that makes it equally applicable to model-based and structural coverage-based testing. In our experimental evaluation, we have shown that our prototype tool CHAINCOVER outperforms state-of-the-art test suite generators.

Prospects.   In §4.2 we have proposed an abstraction refinement method in the case of multi-state property triggers. The fundamental problem is that a failed path represents information about at least two edges that we cannot encode as an equivalent TSP because it requires side conditions such as the solution not containing a set of subpaths. Since our experimental results suggest that the bottleneck of the approach lies rather in solving reachability queries than TSPs, we could also opt for using answer set programming (ASP) solvers (e.g. [22]), which are less efficient in solving TSPs, but they allow us to specify arbitrary side conditions.

Test case chains are intended to demonstrate conformance in late stages of the development cycle, especially in acceptance tests when the system can be assumed stable. It is an interesting question in how far they can be used in earlier phases: The test case chains computed by our method are able to continue to the subsequent test goals even if a test fails, as long as the implementation has not changed too much; otherwise the test chain has to be recomputed. In this case, it would be desirable to incrementally adapt the test case chain after bug fixes and code changes.

Acknowledgements. We thank Cristian Cadar for his valuable advice regarding the comparison with KLEE and the anonymous reviewers for their valuable comments.

References

1. Hierons, R., Ural, H.: Generating a checking sequence with a minimum number of reset transitions. ASE 17, 217–250 (2010)
2. Robert Bosch GmbH: Bosch Automotive Handbook. Bentley (2007)
3. Nuñez, A., Merayo, M., Hierons, R., Núñez, M.: Using genetic algorithms to generate test sequences for complex timed systems. Soft Computing 17 (2013)
4. Petrenko, A., da Silva Simão, A., Yevtushenko, N.: Generating checking sequences for nondeterministic finite state machines. In: ICST, pp. 310–319 (2012)
5. Boyd, S., Ural, H.: On the complexity of generating optimal test sequences. Trans. Softw. Eng. 17, 976–978 (1991)
6. Schrammel, P., Melham, T., Kroening, D.: Chaining test cases for reactive system testing (extended version). Research report, University of Oxford (2013), http://arxiv.org/abs/1306.3882
7. Kroning, D., Strichman, O.: Efficient computation of recurrence diameters. In: Zuck, L.D., Attie, P.C., Cortesi, A., Mukhopadhyay, S. (eds.) VMCAI 2003. LNCS, vol. 2575, pp. 298–309. Springer, Heidelberg (2002)
8. Clarke, E., Biere, A., Raimi, R., Zhu, Y.: Bounded model checking using satisfiability solving. Formal Methods in System Design 19, 7–34 (2001)
9. Schrammel, P.: Logico-Numerical Verification Methods for Discrete and Hybrid Systems. PhD thesis, Université de Grenoble (2012)
10. Clarke, E., Kroning, D., Lerda, F.: A tool for checking ANSI-C programs. In: Jensen, K., Podelski, A. (eds.) TACAS 2004. LNCS, vol. 2988, pp. 168–176. Springer, Heidelberg (2004)
11. Helsgaun, K.: An effective implementation of the Lin-Kernighan traveling salesman heuristic. European J. of Operational Research 126, 106–130 (2000)
12. Meinke, K., Sindhu, M.A.: Incremental learning-based testing for reactive systems. In: Gogolla, M., Wolff, B. (eds.) TAP 2011. LNCS, vol. 6706, pp. 134–151. Springer, Heidelberg (2011)
13. Holzer, A., Schallhart, C., Tautschnig, M., Veith, H.: FShell: Systematic test case generation for dynamic analysis and measurement. In: Gupta, A., Malik, S. (eds.) CAV 2008. LNCS, vol. 5123, pp. 209–213. Springer, Heidelberg (2008)
14. Cadar, C., Dunbar, D., Engler, D.: KLEE: Unassisted and automatic generation of high-coverage tests for complex systems programs. In: OSDI, pp. 209–224 (2008)
15. Fraser, G., Wotawa, F., Ammann, P.: Testing with model checkers: a survey. Software Testing, Verification & Reliability 19, 215–261 (2009)
16. Duale, A., Uyar, M.Ü.: A method enabling feasible conformance test sequence generation for EFSM models. IEEE Trans. Computers 53, 614–627 (2004)
17. Kalaji, A.S., Hierons, R.M., Swift, S.: Generating feasible transition paths for testing from an extended finite state machine (EFSM). In: ICST, pp. 230–239 (2009)
18. Jourdan, G.V., Ural, H., Yenigün, H., Zhu, D.: Using a SAT solver to generate checking sequences. In: Int. Sym. on Comp. and Inf. Sciences, pp. 549–554 (2009)
19. Mori, T., Otsuka, H., Funabiki, N., Nakata, A., Higashino, T.: A test sequence generation method for communication protocols using the SAT algorithm. System and Computers in Japan 34, 20–29 (2003)
20. Peleska, J., Vorobev, E., Lapschies, F.: Automated test case generation with SMT-solving and abstract interpretation. In: Bobaru, M., Havelund, K., Holzmann, G.J., Joshi, R. (eds.) NFM 2011. LNCS, vol. 6617, pp. 298–312. Springer, Heidelberg (2011)
21. Petrenko, A., Dury, A., Ramesh, S., Mohalik, S.: A method and tool for test optimization for automotive controllers. In: Software Testing, Verification and Validation Workshops, pp. 198–207 (2013)
22. Gebser, M., Kaufmann, B., Kaminski, R., Ostrowski, M., Schaub, T., Schneider, M.T.: Potassco: The Potsdam answer set solving collection. AI Communications 24, 107–124 (2011)

Variations over Test Suite Reduction

Dennis Güttinger[1], Vitaly Kozyura[2], Dominik Kremer[3],
and Sebastian Wieczorek[2]

[1] Goethe Universität, Frankfurt am Main, Germany
guetting@stud.uni-frankfurt.de
[2] SAP AG, Darmstadt, Germany
{v.kozyura,sebastian.wieczorek}@sap.com
[3] Technische Universität Darmstadt, Germany
kremer@mathematik.tu-darmstadt.de

Abstract. This paper deals with the problem of effective test suite reduction. In its original form this problem is equivalent to the set covering problem, which has already been extensively studied and many strategies such as greedy or branch and bound for computation of an approximative optimal solution to this NP-complete problem are known. All of these algorithms only focus on one objective which is the minimization of the number of action calls within the test suite reduction. However, practical experience shows that balancing out the distribution of action calls is another objective which should be considered when choosing an efficient test suite. We will therefore introduce and evaluate different extensions of the standard techniques which incorporate action call distribution. We will see that these adjusted strategies can compute a reduced test suite with a smoother distribution over function calls within an acceptable amount of additional time in comparison to the classic algorithms.

1 Introduction

Automatically generating tests suites from formal specifications as advertised by Model-based Testing (MBT) is regarded as a potential innovation leap in industrial software quality assurance. Most MBT approaches are running in two phases. In the first phase vast amount of test cases are generated for an inserted model until a coverage of model entities is achieved. In the second phase a subset of these test cases is selected with the aim to preserve the targeted coverage and therefore the assumed fault-uncovering capabilities [11]. This activity is called test suite reduction.

The problem of test suite reduction is largely discussed in the literature. There are papers, where the general test suite reduction activity is described [3,9]. Further work on how to apply 0/1-Integer linear programming to the test suite reduction problem [12] or how to improve the Greedy heuristics [5,6,2] can be found. In [1,14] there are approaches using multi-objective optimization functions, whereas in [8] an approach based on genetic algorithms is introduced. Some empirical results for test suite reductions have been reported in [11].

H. Yenigün, C. Yilmaz, and A. Ulrich (Eds.): ICTSS 2013, LNCS 8254, pp. 149–163, 2013.
© IFIP International Federation for Information Processing 2013

In this paper we propose a test suite reduction approach that aims for a smoother test case distribution, as required by our industrial MBT users. The mathematical definition of the problem as well as proposed algorithmic modifications are the main contributions of this paper. Further we present experimental results that demonstrate the applicability and efficiency of the proposed approaches.

The paper is structured as follows. In Section 2 we briefly introduce the standard algorithms for test suite reduction. Section 3 gives a definition of test case distribution, describes its practical relevance and details how we incorporated it in the standard reduction algorithms. In Section 4 we illustrate the impact of our algorithmic modifications on concrete industrial cases and finally discuss our conclusions in Section 5.

2   Test Suite Reduction

In order to describe the test suite reduction problem, we assume a finite set of coverage requirements $\mathcal{R} = \{r_1, \ldots, r_n\}$ which is guiding the test generation. All requirements have to be met by a complete test suite. Each test case tc either satisfies a given requirement ($r_i(\text{tc})$) or does not, that is $r_i(\text{tc}) \in \{true, false\}$. For convenience we also define

$$\text{cov}(\text{tc}) = \{r_i : r_i(\text{tc}) = \text{True}, 1 \leq i \leq n\}. \tag{1}$$

Now a test suite $\text{TS} = \{\text{tc}_1, \ldots, \text{tc}_m\}$ is *complete*, if $\mathcal{R} = \bigcup_{i=1}^{m} \text{cov}(\text{tc}_i)$ and the test suite reduction problem can be reformulated as follows:

Given: A test suite TS and a set of requirements $\mathcal{R}$, such that TS is complete with respect to these requirements.

Problem: Find a complete test suite $\text{TS}_0 \subseteq \text{TS}$ that is minimal with respect to

$$\text{value}\,(\text{TS}_0) = \sum_{\text{tc} \in \text{TS}_0} |\text{tc}|. \tag{2}$$

In the remainder of this section we present two classical approaches, the *Greedy-* and the *Branch and Bound*-algorithm, to solve this problem. Later we will describe how these algorithms can be modified in order to obtain a better test case distribution.

2.1   Greedy Algorithm

Even though the Greedy algorithm computes an approximation, [4] showed that the result cannot become arbitrarily bad. In fact the upper bound for the error only depends on the number of requirements.

The algorithm stores two objects: An iteratively constructed subset TS_0 of TS, which will be a complete test suite after termination of the algorithm and a set $\mathcal{R}_0$ of all those requirements that are already met by this subset (l. 1–2). While not all requirements are met (l. 3), the algorithm does the following:

It computes the set of all test cases tc, for which the ratio w_{tc} of the number of additionally satisfied requirements and the number of additional action calls is maximal (l. 4–6). Then it picks one of these at random (l. 7). This test case is afterwards added to TS_0 and $\mathcal{R}_0$ is updated appropriately (l. 8–9).

Input: test suite $TS = \{tc_1, \ldots, tc_m\}$, set of requirements $\mathcal{R}$
Output: approximated minimal test suite $TS_0 \subseteq TS$ which is complete
 1: $TS_0 = \emptyset$
 2: $\mathcal{R}_0 = \emptyset$
 3: **while** $|\mathcal{R}_0| < |\mathcal{R}|$ **do**
 4:     **for** tc $\in TS \setminus TS_0$ **do**
 5:         $w_{tc} = \frac{1}{|tc|} \cdot |cov(tc) \setminus \mathcal{R}_0|$
 6:     $TS_0' = \{tc \in TS \setminus TS_0 : w_{tc} \text{ is maximal}\}$
 7:     Pick tc $\in TS_0'$
 8:     $TS_0 = TS_0 \cup \{tc\}$
 9:     $\mathcal{R}_0 = \mathcal{R}_0 \cup cov(tc)$
10: **return** TS_0

Algorithm 1. Greedy

2.2   Branch and Bound – Algorithm

We use the Branch and Bound variation (Balas-algorithm) described in [7] to compute an optimal result.

The algorithm identifies all possible subsets of $TS = \{tc_1, \ldots, tc_m\}$ with arrays $(n_1, \ldots, n_m)$. Here $n_i = 1$ means, that tc_i is part of the subset, while $n_i = 0$ means, that it is not. To check these arrays systematically, they are organized as a binary tree. At the root node no decisions have been made, as any node on level i represents a certain choice of the first i bits. For simplicity it is also denoted as array $(n_1, \ldots, n_i)$ and identified with the test suite $\{tc_j : n_j = 1\}$. We denote the level of a node by $level(n_1, \ldots, n_i) = i$. Now (2) can be extended to nodes by

$$value(n_1, \ldots, n_i) = \sum_{j=1}^{i} |tc_j| \cdot n_j. \tag{3}$$

The Branch and Bound algorithm stores two objects: The best solution found so far, n_{res}, and a stack S of nodes that has to be checked. Obviously n_{res} is initialized with the array that represents whole TS and S with the stack that only contains the root node (l. 1–2). As long as additional nodes have to be checked, one of them is popped from S (l. 3–4). Then child nodes n_0 and n_1 are generated, where n_0 rejects the next test case and n_1 includes it. To decide, whether it is necessary to check these as well, the following rules are applied:

– n_0 is expanded if it has a successor which represents a complete test suite (l. 7) and if appending the smallest remaining test case results in a suite that is smaller than the one represented by n_{res} (l. 8). (To be able to efficiently evaluate the second condition, we presume TS to be sorted ascending by length.)

– n_1 is expanded if it is smaller than n_{res} (l. 11), but not if it is complete (l. 12, 15).

Finally n_{res} is updated, if n_1 is smaller than n_{res} and complete. In this case all nodes bigger than n_1 are removed from S afterwards (l. 11–14).

Input: test suite TS = $\{tc_1, \ldots, tc_m\}$ sorted ascending by length,
   redundant test cases eliminated
Output: exact minimal test suite $TS_0 \subseteq TS$
1: $n_{res} = (1, \ldots, 1)$
2: Stack S = $\{()\}$
3: **while** S $\neq \emptyset$ **do**
4:    $n = S.pop$
5:    **if** level(n) $< m - 1$ **then**
6:       $n_0 = (n, 0)$
7:       **if** $\{tc_i : (n_0)_i = 1 \text{ or } i > level(n_0)\}$ is complete test suite **then**
8:          **if** value(n_0) + $|tc_{i+1}|$ $<$ value(n_{res}) **then**
9:             S.push(n_0)
10:   $n_1 = (n, 1)$
11:   **if** value(n_1) $<$ value(n_{res}) **then**
12:      **if** $\{tc_i : (n_1)_i = 1\}$ is complete test suite **then**
13:         $n_{res} = n_1$
14:         S = $\{n' \in S : value(n') < value(n_1)\}$
15:      **else if** level(n_1) $< m$ **then**
16:         S.push(n_1)
17: **return** $\{tc_i : (n_{res})_i = 1\}$

Algorithm 2. Branch and Bound

3   Test Case Distribution

In this section we formulate the test case distribution problem and describe it mathematically by introducing a sequence of functions that measures distribution quality in terms of variances. Using these functions we show how to modify both Greedy and Branch and Bound algorithms in order to improve test case distribution.

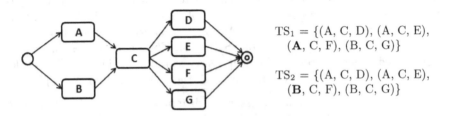

$TS_1 = \{(A, C, D), (A, C, E),$
$\quad (\mathbf{A}, C, F), (B, C, G)\}$

$TS_2 = \{(A, C, D), (A, C, E),$
$\quad (\mathbf{B}, C, F), (B, C, G)\}$

Fig. 1. Test Model Example 1

Let us start with the simple example depicted in Figure 1 together with two test suites TS_1 and TS_2. Both test suites are minimal with respect to action coverage and vary only in one action, which is denoted in bold font. Actions A and B are used an equal number of times in TS_2, while they are not in TS_1.

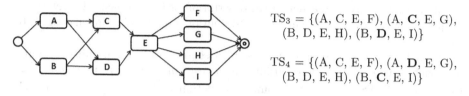

$TS_3 = \{(A, C, E, F), (A, \mathbf{C}, E, G),$
$\quad (B, D, E, H), (B, \mathbf{D}, E, I)\}$

$TS_4 = \{(A, C, E, F), (A, \mathbf{D}, E, G),$
$\quad (B, D, E, H), (B, \mathbf{C}, E, I)\}$

Fig. 2. Test Model Example 2

Let us now move on to the more complex example depicted in Figure 2, which again comes with two test suites TS_3 and TS_4. As before, both test suites are minimal and their difference is marked in bold font. However this time all actions are called the same number of times in TS_3 as in TS_4. Nevertheless the second suite can be regarded as having a smoother test case distribution since it includes four different variations for the first two actions, while the first one only includes two. In a similar fashion one could obtain larger examples, where distribution quality only depends on the number of occurrences of even larger test case subsequences.

3.1   Industrial Relevance

In the last few years, development paradigms like lean and agile, propagating the empowerment of developers [10], have found broad adoption in industrial IT organizations. While previously development processes were defined on a global scale and based on an assumed overall efficiency, todays industrial developers have a much bigger degree of freedom in choosing their development approaches and tools. Based on our experience, on individual level of decision making efficiency is often traded for lower learning effort, better user experience and other partially subjective reasons.

Concretely, in a case study [13] that aimed to validate an MBT framework with industrial testers we observed that uneven test case distribution may cause negative assessments on individual level. In interview sessions, most of the case study participants stated that the distribution resulting from standard test suite reduction made them less confident in the effectiveness of the test suite and the correctness of the test generation approach. While no concrete evidence for superior qualities of evenly distributed test suites were found in our experiments, they assumed that a better distribution may be beneficial in the test data assignment, test maintenance and selection of test cases for regression. As a consequence, most participants required smoothly distributed test suites in order to apply MBT in their test routines.

In summary, from our industrial experience a smooth test suite is more desirable as it increases confidence of MBT users. Whether it also has direct effects on the quality of the test suite remains subject of future investigations.

3.2 Formalization

We now want to give a mathematical description of the problem. Therefore we propose a way how to measure the distribution quality of a given test suite $TS_0 \subseteq TS$.

Given that a test case is composed of a sequence of action calls, a simple approach is to evaluate their variance in a test suite. For any test case $tc = (a_1, \ldots, a_k) \in TS$ we define a counting function $d_{tc}^{(1)}$, which assigns to each action $a \in \mathcal{A}$ the number of times it is called by tc:

$$d_{tc}^{(1)} : \mathcal{A} \to \mathbb{N}, \quad a \mapsto \left| \{ i \in \{1, \ldots, k\} : a_i = a \} \right|. \tag{4}$$

Equivalently for any test suite $TS_0 = \{tc_1, \ldots, tc_m\} \subseteq TS$ we define a counting function $d_{TS_0}^{(1)}$, which assigns to each action $a \in \mathcal{A}$ the number of times it is called by whole TS_0. This can be formalized as

$$d_{TS_0}^{(1)} : \mathcal{A} \to \mathbb{N}, \quad a \mapsto \sum_{i=1}^{m} d_{tc_i}^{(1)}(a). \tag{5}$$

Now the mean number of calls per action in TS_0 is given as

$$\overline{d_{TS_0}^{(1)}} = \frac{1}{|\mathcal{A}|} \sum_{a \in \mathcal{A}} d_{TS_0}^{(1)}(a) \left(= \frac{1}{|\mathcal{A}|} \sum_{i=1}^{m} |tc_i| \right). \tag{6}$$

If TS_0 is well distributed, we would expect $d_{TS_0}^{(1)}(a)$ not to vary much, but to stay near its mean value for all $a \in \mathcal{A}$. Hence, the *variance* of $d_{TS_0}^{(1)}$ or the *variance of action calls in* TS_0 will be our first measure for distribution quality:

$$\text{Var}_1(TS_0) = \frac{1}{|\mathcal{A}|} \sum_{a \in \mathcal{A}} \left(d_{TS_0}^{(1)}(a) - \overline{d_{TS_0}^{(1)}} \right)^2. \tag{7}$$

Let us apply this definition to the examples from above. The values obtained for $d_{TS_i}^{(1)}$ are denoted in table 1. Further calculations show, that for the first example $\text{Var}_1(TS_1) = 1.35$, while $\text{Var}_1(TS_2) = 1.06$. As expected TS_2 has a better distribution quality than TS_1. Nevertheless for the second example we get $\text{Var}_1(TS_3) = \text{Var}_1(TS_4) = 0.84$, i. e we cannot determine the difference between TS_3 and TS_4 by Var_1. This is not surprising, since the counting functions for both test suites are identical.

To circumvent this problem we generalize our ideas in order to construct a *variance of action-sequence calls* for sequences of a fixed length p: Let $\mathcal{A}^{(p)}$ be the set of all action-sequences of length p that are part of at least one test case in TS. To ease notation we will use the symbol **a** to denote such sequences.

Table 1. Values of $d_{\mathrm{TS}_i}^{(1)}$

Example 1							
Suite	A	B	C	D	E	F	G
TS$_1$	3	1	4	1	1	1	1
TS$_2$	2	2	4	1	1	1	1

Example 2									
Suite	A	B	C	D	E	F	G	H	I
TS$_3$	2	2	2	2	4	1	1	1	1
TS$_4$	2	2	2	2	4	1	1	1	1

First for any test case tc $= (a_1, \ldots, a_k) \in$ TS we again define a counting function $d_{\mathrm{tc}}^{(p)}$, which assigns to each action-sequence $\mathbf{a} \in \mathcal{A}^{(p)}$ the number of times it is called by tc:

$$d_{\mathrm{tc}}^{(p)} : \mathcal{A}^{(p)} \to \mathbb{N}, \quad \mathbf{a} \mapsto \left| \{ i \in \{p, \ldots, k\} : (a_{i-p+1}, \ldots, a_i) = \mathbf{a} \} \right|. \tag{8}$$

As before we can use these functions to define a counting function $d_{\mathrm{TS}_0}^{(p)}$ for a whole test suite $\mathrm{TS}_0 = \{\mathrm{tc}_1, \ldots, \mathrm{tc}_m\} \subseteq$ TS, i. e.

$$d_{\mathrm{TS}_0}^{(p)} : \mathcal{A}^{(p)} \to \mathbb{N}, \quad \mathbf{a} \mapsto \sum_{i=1}^{m} d_{\mathrm{tc}_i}^{(p)}(\mathbf{a}). \tag{9}$$

The mean amount of calls per p-action-sequence is given by

$$\overline{d_{\mathrm{TS}_0}^{(p)}} = \frac{1}{|\mathcal{A}^{(p)}|} \sum_{\mathbf{a} \in \mathcal{A}^{(p)}} d_{\mathrm{TS}_0}^{(p)}(\mathbf{a}) \tag{10}$$

and we can finally define the *variance of* $d_{\mathrm{TS}_0}^{(p)}$ or the *variance of p-action-sequences* by

$$\mathrm{Var}_p(\mathrm{TS}_0) = \frac{1}{|\mathcal{A}^{(p)}|} \sum_{\mathbf{a} \in \mathcal{A}^{(p)}} \left(d_{\mathrm{TS}_0}^{(p)}(\mathbf{a}) - \overline{d_{\mathrm{TS}_0}^{(p)}} \right)^2. \tag{11}$$

Let us apply this definition with $p = 2$ to example 2 from above. The values obtained for $d_{\mathrm{TS}_i}^{(2)}$ are denoted in table 2. Further calculation shows, that $\mathrm{Var}_2(\mathrm{TS}_3) = 0.56$, while $\mathrm{Var}_2(\mathrm{TS}_4) = 0.16$. This means that Var_2 rates the second test suite better than the first one, as demanded by the motivation from the beginning of this section.

Table 2. Values of $d_{\mathrm{TS}_i}^{(2)}$

Example 2									
Suite	(A,C)	(A,D)	(B,C)	(B,D)	(C,E)	(D,E)	(E,F)	(E,G)	(E,H)	(E,I)
TS$_3$	2	0	0	2	2	2	1	1	1	1
TS$_4$	1	1	1	1	2	2	1	1	1	1

3.3   Lexicographical Approaches

Greedy. We present concrete implementations that respect distribution quality as described in section 3.2. The approaches proposed here optimize with respect to the total number of action calls first and with respect to distribution quality afterwards.

In order to modify the Greedy algorithm, we have to rate distribution quality not of a complete test suite, but of a partially constructed one. More precisely, we have to determine how well an additional test case $tc = (a_1, \ldots, a_k)$ would fit in a non-complete test suite TS_0. This is done by the quality functions

$$q_{TS_0}^{(p)}(tc) = \sum_{i=p}^{k} d_{TS_0}^{(p)}(a_{i-p+1}, \ldots, a_i). \tag{12}$$

Using them we can modify the Greedy algorithm in order to achieve better distribution quality by exchanging line 7 with the following steps:

for $i = 1 \rightarrow p$ **do**
$\quad TS_i' = \left\{ tc \in TS_{(i-1)}' : q_{TS_0}^{(i)}(tc) \text{ is minimal} \right\}$
Pick $tc \in TS_p'$

Branch and Bound. To modify the Branch and Bound algorithm from section 2.2, just some simple modifications have to be made in lines 8, 11 and 13–14, so that the set of all optimal nodes $N^{(0)}$ is returned instead of just one optimal node n_{res}. For example we have to exchange the sharp inequality ($<$) in line 8 with a weak one ($\leq$). We will come back to this particular replacement when discussing experimental results.

More importantly, we have to choose a single node from $N^{(0)}$ when the main loop is finished. This is done such that the according test suite has optimal distribution quality. Therefore we extend definition (11) to nodes $n = (n_1, \ldots, n_i)$ by

$$\text{Var}_p(n) = \text{Var}_p(\{tc_j : n_j = 1\}) \tag{13}$$

and insert the following steps between lines 16 and 17:

1: **for** $i = 1 \rightarrow p$ **do**
2: $\quad N^{(i)} = \{n \in N^{(i-1)} : \text{Var}_i(n) \text{ is minimal}\}$
3: Pick $n_{res} \in N^{(p)}$

3.4   Multi-objective Greedy Approach

In this subsection we present another approach to the problem, which is based on the Greedy algorithm from section 2.1. The strategy proposed here optimizes with respect to both objectives (test suite size and distribution quality) simultaneously and allows arbitrary weighting between them.

As discussed in 3.2, the requirement of $TS_0 \subseteq TS$ having a good distribution quality is equivalent to the one that its variances are minimal. To simplify matters we will only consider Var_1 here. Therefore this objective can be stated as

$$Var_1(TS_0) = \frac{1}{|\mathcal{A}|} \sum_{a \in \mathcal{A}} \left(d_{TS_0}^{(1)}(a) - \overline{d_{TS_0}^{(1)}} \right)^2 \rightarrow min! \tag{14}$$

To combine it with the goal of minimizing the number of action calls we use a probabilistic approach. The probability of being contained in an optimal test suite with respect to distribution quality is greater for some $tc \in TS \setminus TS_0$, if its distribution variance contribution is small. This contribution can be expressed by the value of Var_1 that would result when including tc into TS_0, $Var_1(TS_0 \cup \{tc\})$, in relation to the sum of variances for all elements in $TS \setminus TS_0$, namely $\sum_{\tilde{tc} \in TS \setminus TS_0} Var_1(TS_0 \cup \{\tilde{tc}\})$.

Thus, we start with an initially empty set of test cases TS_0 and iteratively add test cases $tc \in TS$ to TS_0 such that distribution variance increase is minimized. This leads to the following definition of probabilities for each $tc \in TS \setminus TS_0$:

$$p_{var}(tc) := \frac{1 - \frac{Var_1(TS_0 \cup \{tc\})}{\sum_{\tilde{tc} \in TS \setminus TS_0} Var_1(TS_0 \cup \{\tilde{tc}\})}}{|\{\tilde{tc} \in TS \setminus TS_0\}| - 1}. \tag{15}$$

Obviously, $0 \leq p_{var}(tc) \leq 1$ for all $tc \in TS \setminus TS_0$ by construction and the expressions defined in equation (15) can be interpreted as probabilities.

For our primary objective of minimizing the number of action calls we will construct probabilities in an analogous way by using the same decision criterion as for the Greedy algorithm from section 2.1. Referring to line 5 of the algorithm we denote $w_{tc} = \frac{1}{|tc|} \cdot |cov(tc) \setminus \mathcal{R}_0|$ as the weight for each $tc \in TS \setminus TS_0$. The weight of a test case tc is the total number of requirements $r \in \mathcal{R}$ that are satisfied by tc but not yet covered by any test case in TS_0. This value is normalized by the length of tc. It is clear that test cases with a high weight will more probably be contained in a test suite that is optimal with respect to test suite size than test cases with a lower weight. See [4] for more details. We can thus define probabilities for each $tc \in TS \setminus TS_0$ as follows:

$$p_{rate}(tc) := \frac{w_{tc}}{\sum_{\tilde{tc} \in TS \setminus TS_0} w_{\tilde{tc}}}. \tag{16}$$

So, given a rate proportion coefficient $\delta \in [0, 1]$ we can construct a weighted probability distribution by defining

$$p(tc) := \delta \cdot p_{rate}(tc) + (1 - \delta) \cdot p_{var}(tc) \tag{17}$$

for each $tc \in TS \setminus TS_0$.

A resulting Greedy strategy would be to iteratively sort test cases by their combined probability descending and add the test case with highest probability value to the final solution set. These preliminary considerations yield to a Greedy algorithm like the one presented in section 2.1, except that lines 4 to 6 have to be replaced by the following steps[1]:

for tc $\in$ TS $\setminus$ TS$_0$ **do**
   Compute $p(\text{tc})$
   TS$_0'$ = {tc $\in$ TS $\setminus$ TS$_0$: $p(\text{tc})$ is maximal}

4   Experimental Results

In this section we present experimental results for the optimization techniques described above. Due to computational constraints we only considered $p = 2$ for the lexicographical algorithms. All computations were performed on an AMD Opteron (tm) Quad Core with 2.60 GHz and 32 Gigabytes of RAM. As input we derived 13 different transition state machines which were designed on the basis of industrial case studies. To get realistic statements for the context of our work, most of our use cases are small- or intermediate-sized (I-IX). Nevertheless we included some larger models as well (X-XIII). Actually (XII) and (XIII) have proven to be too large to be optimized with algorithms of the Branch and Bound-type.

Table 3. Use cases

#	|TS|	AC	AC$^{(2)}$	$\|\mathcal{A}\|$	$\|\mathcal{A}^{(2)}\|$
I	15	84	69	13	26
II	21	123	102	10	15
III	32	128	96	13	28
IV	41	164	123	15	31
V	30	189	159	25	35
VI	36	190	154	31	40
VII	46	317	271	40	52
VIII	45	374	329	23	36
IX	120	600	480	15	33
X	132	1306	1174	26	40
XI	512	6656	6144	30	54
XII	284	1600	1316	140	422
XIII	625	4375	3750	23	86

For detailed information about the use cases consider table 3. It contains the number of test cases ($\|$TS$\|$), the number of action calls (AC), the number of action-pair calls (AC$^{(2)}$), the number of actions ($\|\mathcal{A}\|$) and the number of action-pairs ($\|\mathcal{A}^{(2)}\|$) for each of our use cases. Nevertheless the full model definitions must not be published due to legal reasons.

---

[1] Note that for $\delta = 1$ this algorithm is equivalent to the one proposed by [4].

4.1   Greedy Based Approaches

In the following we compare experimental results for the original Greedy algorithm from [4] with our proposed extensions. As parameters we choose $p = 2$ for the lexicographical variation and $\delta = 0.5$ for the multi-objective one. Our results are displayed in Table 4.

The second column (AC) contains the number of action calls in the unmodified test suite TS, while columns 4, 8, and 12 (AC_0) in each case contain the number of action calls in the resulting test suite TS_0. Columns 3, 7, and 11 (Time) denote the computation time in seconds needed to run the specific algorithm and columns 5–6, 9–10, and 13–14 present the variance values as defined by equations (7) and (11) for the corresponding reduced suite TS_0.

Table 4. Results for Greedy algorithms

#	AC	Original				Lexicographical				Multi-objective			
		Time	AC_0	Var_1	Var_2	Time	AC_0	Var_1	Var_2	Time	AC_0	Var_1	Var_2
I	84	0.06	16	0.33	0.00	0.08	16	0.33	0.00	0.09	16	0.33	0.00
II	123	0.06	25	2.65	0.86	0.08	25	2.05	0.56	0.09	25	2.05	0.56
III	128	0.08	32	7.17	1.89	0.09	32	4.40	0.16	0.08	32	4.40	0.89
IV	164	0.08	32	4.78	0.76	0.08	32	3.45	0.08	0.08	32	3.45	0.12
V	189	0.08	41	1.83	0.18	0.08	41	1.83	0.18	0.08	41	1.83	0.18
VI	190	0.08	47	0.64	0.15	0.09	48	0.64	0.21	0.09	48	0.64	0.21
VII	317	0.08	69	1.30	0.40	0.09	69	1.30	0.40	0.09	69	1.30	0.40
VIII	374	0.08	47	2.22	0.45	0.09	47	2.22	0.45	0.08	47	2.22	0.45
IX	600	0.09	25	1.56	0.15	0.13	25	1.16	0.19	0.11	25	1.16	0.19
X	1306	0.14	44	1.37	0.30	0.16	44	1.14	0.17	0.17	44	1.14	0.15
XI	6656	0.50	65	1.87	1.00	0.52	65	1.61	0.72	0.52	65	1.61	0.72
XII	1600	0.28	429	92.66	4.63	0.31	425	90.09	4.37	0.30	425	89.95	4.28
XIII	4375	0.36	35	1.82	0.59	0.39	35	1.82	0.59	0.39	35	1.82	0.59

We can see that the computation time for the lexicographical as well as for the multi-objective approach is always higher than the one for the original Greedy algorithm. This is just as expected, since computation and consideration of action call distribution takes additional time. Nevertheless we also note, that the additional time consumption is usually not very significant. The number of action calls is always equal for all algorithms except for the use cases VI and XII. The variances are usually decreased when running a modified algorithm, although for Var_2 this does not always hold. This is reasonable as well, since the lexicographical Greedy optimizes with respect to Var_1 first and the multi-objective Greedy does not consider Var_2 at all.

Another conclusion one can draw from the results is, that the two modifications of Greedy behave quite similarly except for use cases III and IV, where a significant difference in Var_2 can be noticed.

To sum up this discussion, we present the average values over the eleven first use cases in table 5[2]. Here we can see, that the variance values obtained by the original Greedy algorithm can be reduced by almost about 22% on average when using the lexicographical or the multi-objective approach. The values for Var_2 can be even be improved by almost 50% or 37% on average when using the lexicographical or the multi-objective approach, respectively.

Table 5. Comparison of Greedy algorithms

Algorithm	Avg Time	Avg AC_0	Avg Var_1	Avg Var_2
Original	0.121	40.273	2.338	0.558
Lexicographical	0.135	40.364	1.828	0.283
Multi-objective	0.134	40.364	1.828	0.352

4.2   Branch and Bound Based Approaches

Now let us compare the standard Branch and Bound approach from section 2.2 with our extension from 3.3. As parameter we again choose $p = 2$. The use cases are similar to the ones from the last section except that XII and XIII are excluded since the algorithms did not terminate within a reasonable time constraint. Additionally we have to remark that (in difference to the Greedy algorithms) redundant test cases as described in 2.2 were removed from the test suite prior to running the algorithms.

Our results are displayed in table 6. Here the second column (AC) contains the number of action calls in test suite TS after performing the removal of redundant test cases, but before running the Branch and Bound algorithms. The third column (AC_0) contains the number of action calls in the resulting test suite TS_0, i. e after performing Branch and Bound. By construction of the algorithms these numbers are always minimal and thus equal. Columns 4–6 contain further results for the unmodified standard algorithm, while columns 7–9 contain the further results for the modification discussed in section 3.3.

Considering use cases IX and XI it is evident, that the lexicographical approach is totally outperformed by the original algorithm in time. Analyzing this problem leads to the conclusion, that most of the additional time consumption yields from the change in line 8 of the algorithm, where a sharp inequality ($<$) is replaced with a weak one ($\leq$) in order to return all minimal solutions. Hence, we also tried to use another modified version, which uses sharp inequality ($<$) and therefore does not return all minimal solutions, but only a subset of these. Afterwards, the best suite with respect to distribution quality is chosen out of this subset just as in the lexicographical approach. The results for this modified lexicographical algorithm are displayed in columns 10–12 of table 6.

To compare the algorithms with each other we again computed average values, which are presented in table 7. One can see that standard Branch and Bound

---

[2] The last two examples have been excluded to ensure comparability with Branch and Bound results, see below.

Table 6. Results for Branch and Bound algorithms

#	AC	AC_0	Original			Lexicographical			Lex. Mod.		
			Time	Var_1	Var_2	Time	Var_1	Var_2	Time	Var_1	Var_2
I	78	16	0.06	0.33	0.00	0.09	0.33	0.00	0.09	0.33	0.00
II	123	17	0.06	1.01	0.14	0.09	1.01	0.20	0.11	1.01	0.14
III	128	32	3.66	7.17	1.89	7.55	4.40	0.16	3.78	4.40	0.16
IV	164	32	9.05	5.32	1.25	24.06	3.45	0.08	9.56	3.45	0.08
V	189	38	0.39	1.45	0.16	0.47	1.45	0.16	0.42	1.45	0.16
VI	190	44	10.25	1.08	0.44	11.28	1.08	0.44	10.28	1.08	0.44
VII	317	64	239.61	0.89	0.28	271.66	0.89	0.27	234.02	0.89	0.27
VIII	185	47	0.06	2.22	0.31	0.11	2.22	0.28	0.11	2.22	0.28
IX	600	25	77.49	1.56	0.31	1755.37	1.16	0.05	81.72	1.16	0.10
X	1089	43	198.68	1.38	0.40	230.98	1.15	0.15	198.94	1.38	0.40
XI	4368	52	19.00	1.13	0.52	484.06	1.00	0.37	19.38	1.00	0.37

and the modified lexicographical version have almost equal computation time on average (about 50 seconds). Nevertheless the average variance values for the latter one are considerably better than those for standard Branch and Bound (about 20% for Var_1 and almost 60% for Var_2). The average variance values for the "exact" lexicographical version are of course even smaller, but do not advance very much (only about 2% for Var_1 and 10% for Var_2). However, this benefit comes with the cost of a significant increase in computation time (about 400%).

Table 7. Comparison of Branch and Bound algorithms

Algorithm	Avg Time	Avg AC_0	Avg Var_1	Avg Var_2
Original	50.755	37.273	2.139	0.518
Lexicographical	253.248	37.273	1.648	0.197
Lex. Mod.	50.765	37.273	1.669	0.218

4.3   Comparison of Results

We can see that for the Greedy as well as for the Branch and Bound approaches taking distribution of action calls into account can yield to considerably smaller variances than for the standard versions. Nevertheless except for the lexico-graphical Branch and Bound algorithm computational effort for the extended approaches is not significantly higher.

When comparing the results for the extended Branch and Bound with the extended Greedy approaches we see that the number of action calls for all Branch and Bound approaches is about 7.5% less on average than the corresponding numbers for the Greedy strategies. Furthermore, the variance of action calls can be decreased by about 10% and the variance of action-pair calls even by 22% up to 43% on average when using an extended Branch and Bound algorithm instead of lexicographical or multi-objective Greedy. However, for the most examples this is dearly bought with a dramatically higher computation time in comparison to the Greedy strategies.

5   Conclusion

In this paper we presented two classical solutions for the test suite reduction problem, namely the Branch and Bound algorithm, which computes an exact solution in exponential time, and the Greedy heuristic, which yields the best approximation possible in polynomial time. Based on these algorithms we introduced modifications to advance distribution quality.

A main contribution of this paper is the formalization of the term "distribution quality" itself. With the variances Var_p at hand a mathematical description of the problem can easily be given. Our modifications of the algorithms introduce simple but effective ways to use this description in order to solve the problem.

Experimental results support these approaches. At no time the result of a modified algorithm was outperformed by the result of its unmodified counterpart in distribution quality. Conversely the variances shrunk in most use cases, at times tremendously. Both variations of the Greedy algorithm performed almost equally and were only marginally slower than the unmodified version. On the other hand it showed that our first modification of Branch and Bound was significantly slower, such that we would not advice to use it. Nevertheless we also introduced a variation that comes with nearly the full advantage of a better distribution quality, but computes insignificant longer compared to standard Branch and Bound.

References

1. Black, J., Melachrinoudis, E., Kaeli, D.: Bi-criteria models for all-uses test suite reduction. In: Proceedings of the 26th International Conference on Software Engineering, ICSE 2004, pp. 106–115. IEEE Computer Society, Washington, DC (2004)
2. Chen, T.Y., Lau, M.F.: A new heuristic for test suite reduction 40(5-6), 347–354 (1998)
3. Chen, T.Y., Lau, M.F.: Dividing strategies for the optimization of a test suite. Information Processing Letters 60, 135–141 (1996)
4. Chvatal, V.: A greedy heuristic for the set-covering problem. Mathematics of Operations Research 4(3), 233–235 (1979)
5. Gupta, R., Soffa, M.L.: Compile-time techniques for improving scalar access performance in parallel memories. IEEE Trans. Parallel Distrib. Syst. 2, 138–148 (1991)
6. Harrold, M.J., Unwersity, C., Gupta, R., Soffa, M.L.: A methodology for controlling the size of a test suite. ACM Transactions on Software Engineering and Methodology 2, 270–285 (1993)
7. Chinneck, J.W.: Practical Optimization: A Gentle Introduction (2003), http://www.sce.carleton.ca/faculty/chinneck/po.html (Chapter 13)
8. Mansour, N., El-Fakih, K.: Simulated annealing and genetic algorithms for optimal regression testing. Journal of Software Maintenance 11, 19–34 (1999)
9. Offutt, A.J., Pan, J., Voas, J.M.: Procedures for reducing the size of coverage-based test sets. In: Proc. Twelfth Int. Conf. Testing Computer Software, pp. 111–123 (1995)
10. Poppendieck, M., Poppendieck, T.: Lean software development: An agile toolkit. Addison-Wesley Professional (2003)

11. Rothermel, G., Harrold, M.J., von Ronne, J., Hong, C.: Empirical studies of test-suite reduction. Journal of Software Testing, Verification, and Reliability 12, 219–249 (2002)
12. Wang, H.S., Hsu, S.R., Lin, J.C.: A generalized optimal path-selection model for structural program testing. Journal of Systems and Software 10(1), 55–63 (1989)
13. Wieczorek, S., Stefanescu, A.: Improving Testing of Enterprise Systems by Model-Based Testing on Graphical User Interfaces. In: 2010 17th IEEE International Conference and Workshops on Engineering of Computer-Based Systems, pp. 352–357. IEEE (2010)
14. Yoo, S., Harman, M.: Pareto efficient multi-objective test case selection. In: Proceedings of the 2007 International Symposium on Software Testing and Analysis, ISSTA 2007, pp. 140–150. ACM, New York (2007)

Case Studies in Learning-Based Testing

Lei Feng[1], Simon Lundmark[4], Karl Meinke[2], Fei Niu[2],
Muddassar A. Sindhu[5], and Peter Y.H. Wong[3]

[1] Machine Design Department,
Royal Institute of Technology, Stockholm 10044, Sweden
feng@kth.se
[2] School of Computer Science and Communication,
Royal Institute of Technology, Stockholm 10044, Sweden
{karlm,niu}@csc.kth.se
[3] SDL Fredhopper, Amsterdam, The Netherlands
peter.wong@fredhopper.com
[4] TriOptima AB, Stockholm, Sweden
simon.lundmark@trioptima.com
[5] Computer Science Department, Quaid i Azam University, Islamabad, Pakistan
masindhu@qau.edu.pk

Abstract. We present case studies which show how the paradigm of learning-based testing (LBT) can be successfully applied to black-box requirements testing of industrial reactive systems. For this, we apply a new testing tool *LBTest*, which combines algorithms for incremental black-box learning of Kripke structures with model checking technology. We show how test requirements can be modeled in propositional linear temporal logic extended by finite data types. We then provide benchmark performance results for *LBTest* applied to three industrial case studies.

1 Introduction

Learning-based testing (LBT) [7] is an emerging paradigm for *black-box requirements testing* that automates the three basic steps of: (1) automated test case generation (ATCG), (2) test execution, and (3) test verdict (the oracle step).

The basic idea of LBT is to automatically generate a large number of high-quality test cases by combining a model checking algorithm with an *incremental model inference* or *learning algorithm*. These two algorithms are integrated with the *system under test* (SUT) in an iterative feedback loop. On each iteration of this loop, a new test case can be generated either by: (i) model checking a learned model M_i of the system under test (SUT) against a formal user requirement *req* and choosing any counterexample to correctness, (ii) using the learning algorithm to generate a membership query, or (iii) random generation. An LBT tool must *interleave* these three TCG methods to achieve an overall testing strategy that is efficient. Whichever TCG method is chosen, the new test case t_i is then executed on the SUT, and the outcome is judged as a pass, fail or warning. This is done by comparing a predicted output p_i (obtained from M_i) with the observed output o_i (from the SUT). The new input/output pair (t_i, o_i) is also used to update the

H. Yenigün, C. Yilmaz, and A. Ulrich (Eds.): ICTSS 2013, LNCS 8254, pp. 164–179, 2013.

current model M_i to a refined model M_{i+1}, which ensures that the iteration can proceed again. If the learning algorithm can be guaranteed to correctly learn in the limit, given enough information about the SUT, then LBT is a sound and complete method of testing. In practice, real-world systems are often too large for complete learning to be accomplished within a feasible timescale. By using incremental learning algorithms, that focus on learning just that part of the SUT which is relevant to the requirement *req*, LBT becomes much more effective.

While algorithms for LBT have been analyzed and benchmarked on small academic case studies (see [9] and [12]), there has so far been no published evaluation of this technology on real-world case studies. So the scalability of this approach is unclear. The work presented here therefore has two aims:

1. to describe the problems and potential of using LBT on real world systems from a variety of industrial domains;
2. to show that learning-based testing is scalable to large industrial case studies, by measuring concrete performance parameters of the LBT tool *LBTest*.

The organization of this paper is as follows: In Section 3, we give an introduction to requirements testing with the *LBTest* tool focussing on its requirements language. In Section 4, we describe industrial case studies with the *LBTest* tool from three different industrial domains: *web, automotive* and *finance*. Finally in Section 5, we give some conclusions and future directions of research.

2   Related Work

A tutorial on the basic principles of LBT and their application to different types of SUTs can be found in [10]. The origin of some of these ideas can be traced perhaps as far back as [17]. Experimental studies of LBT using different learning and model checking algorithms include [12], [7], [8] and [9]. These experiments support the thesis that LBT can substantially outperform random testing as a black-box requirements testing method.

Several previous works, (for example Peled et al. [13], Groce et al. [5] and Raffelt et al. [14]) have also considered a combination of learning and model checking to achieve testing and/or formal verification of reactive systems. Within the model checking community, the verification approach known as *counterexample guided abstraction refinement* (CEGAR) also combines learning and model checking (see e.g. Clarke et al. [3] and Chauhan et al. [1]). The LBT approach can be distinguished from these other approaches by: (i) an emphasis on testing rather than verification, and (ii) use of *incremental learning algorithms*, as well as other optimisations, specifically chosen to make testing more effective and scalable. This related research does not yet seem to have lead to practical testing tools. *LBTest* is the first LBT tool to be used in industrial environments.

Inductive testing (Walkinshaw et al. [16]) is a black-box testing technique that also uses automata learning algorithms. However, this approach is more focussed on finding untrapped exceptions then testing formal user requirements (model checking is not used). Despite its different aim, [16] confirms our own findings that learning algorithms give more efficient search methods than random testing.

In contrast with *model-based testing tools*, such as *Conformiq Designer* [4] or *ModelJUnit* [15], which perform test case generation using a design model (such as a UML model), *LBTest* reverse engineers its own models for testing purposes. Thus *LBTest* is advantageous in agile development since its models do not have to be manually designed or re-synchronised with code changes.

3   Requirements Testing with *LBTest*

A platform for learning-based testing known as *LBTest* [11] has been developed within the EU project HATS FP7-231620. This platform supports black-box requirements testing of fairly general types of reactive systems. The main constraint on applying *LBTest* is that it must be possible to model a particular SUT by a deterministic finite state machine.

The inputs to *LBTest* are a black-box SUT and a set of formal user requirements to be tested. The tool is capable of generating, executing and judging a large number of tests cases within a short time. In large case studies, the main limitation on test throughput is the average execution time of a single test case on the SUT. (This will be seen in case study 3 of Section 4.3.)

For user requirements modeling, the formal language currently supported in *LBTest* is *propositional linear temporal logic* (PLTL) extended by *finite data types*. PLTL formulas can express both: (i) *safety properties* which are invariants that may not be violated, and (ii) *liveness properties*, including *use cases*, which specify intended dynamic behaviors. A significant contribution of *LBTest* is its support for liveness testing. Our case studies in Section 4 will provide examples of both safety and liveness testing.

Currently in *LBTest*, only one (external) model checker is supported, which is NuSMV [2]. Further interfaces are planned in the future. The learning algorithm currently available in *LBTest* is the IKL algorithm [12], which is an algorithm for incremental learning of deterministic Kripke structures. New learning algorithms are also in development for future evaluation.

3.1   PLTL as a Requirements Modeling Language

In the context of reactive systems analysis, temporal logics have been widely used to formally model user requirements. From a testing perspective, *linear time temporal logic* (LTL) with its emphasis on the properties of paths or execution sequences, is a natural choice. The design philosophy of *LBTest* is to generate, execute and judge as many test cases as possible within a given time limit. This requirement places stringent requirements on the efficiency of model checking LTL formulas. Therefore, only model checking of *propositional linear temporal logic* (PLTL) formulas is currently considered. However, in an effort to make PLTL more user-friendly (by hiding low-level Boolean encodings) *LBTest* supports an extended PLTL with user-defined symbolic finite data types.

To use *LBTest* correctly it is important to understand the precise syntax of the requirements modeling language. Our data type model is based on the well known algebraic model of *abstract data types*, involving many-sorted signatures and algebras (see e.g. [6]).

3.1.1   Definition

A *finite data type signature* Σ consists of a finite set S of *sorts* or types, and for each sort $s \in S$, a finite set Σ_s of *constant symbols* all of the same type s.

3.1.2   Definition

Let S be a finite set of sorts containing a distinguished sort $in \in S$, and let Σ be a finite data type signature. The syntax of the language $PLTL(\Sigma)$ of *extended propositional linear temporal logic* over Σ has the following BNF definition:

$$\phi ::= \perp \mid \top \mid s = c \mid s \neq c \mid (\neg\phi) \mid (\phi_1 \wedge \phi_2) \mid (\phi_1 \vee \phi_2) \mid (\phi_1 \rightarrow \phi_2) \mid (X\phi) \mid$$
$$(F\phi) \mid (G\phi) \mid (\phi_1 U \phi_2) \mid (\phi_1 W \phi_2) \mid (\phi_1 R \phi_2)$$

where $s \in S$ and $c \in \Sigma_s$. This logic has a simple but strict typing system.

The atomic formulas of $PLTL(\Sigma)$ are equations and inequations over the data type signature Σ for defining input and output operations. Only a single variable symbol of each type is allowed, to support a *simple black-box interface* to the SUT. We overload each type symbol $s \in S$ to also name a unique SUT read or write variable of type s. The distinguished sort $in \in S$ denotes the single *SUT write variable*, while every other type $s \in S$ denotes an *SUT read variable*.

The language $PLTL(\Sigma)$ can be given a formal Kripke semantics, in a routine way, over any algebra that interprets the data type signature Σ. A precise definition is omitted for brevity. Informally, the symbols $\perp$, $\top$, $\neg$, $\wedge$, $\vee$ and $\rightarrow$ denote the usual Boolean constants and connectives. The symbols X, F, G, U, W and R denote the temporal operators. Thus, $X\phi$ means that ϕ is true in the next state, $F\phi$ means that ϕ is true sometime in the future, $G\phi$ means that ϕ is always true in the future and U is the binary operator which means that ϕ_1 will remain true until a point in the future when ϕ_2 becomes true. The two operators W and R stand for *weak until* and *release* respectively.

4   Case Studies in Learning-Based Testing

We can now present three industrial case studies which were tested with *LBTest*. These were: (i) an *access server* (FAS) from Fredhopper , (ii) a *break-by-wire system* (BBW) from Volvo Technology, and (iii) a *portfolio compression service* (triReduce) from TriOptima . These case studies represent mature applications from the domains of web, automotive and finance. The tool was able to find errors in each of them, which is a promising achievement. These case studies have the following basic characteristics:

– FAS is an e-commerce application which has been developed and evolved over 12 years. Its various modules have been tested with automated and manual techniques. Requirements modeling involved events and finite data types.

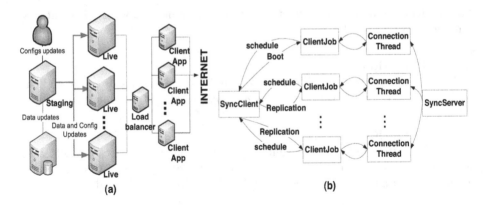

Fig. 1. (a) an FAS Deployment and (b) Interactions in the Replication System

- BBW is relatively new embedded application from the automobile industry, which has not yet been widely adopted. It has strict timing constraints to ensure the safety of the vehicle. Requirements modeling involved events and infinite data types.
- triReduce service has been developed using Django, a popular web framework for the Python programming language. It involves significant use of dynamically changing databases, so test set-up and tear-down are non-trivial. Requirements modeling involved events and finite data types.

Requirements modeling for the BBW case study was particularly challenging due to the presence of the infinite floating point data type. This required an extension of *LBTest* to support *partition testing* by *discretising* each floating point domain.

4.1   Case Study 1: Access Server

The Fredhopper Access Server (FAS) is a distributed, concurrent OO system developed by Fredhopper that provides search and merchandising services to e-Commerce companies, including structured search capabilities within the client's data. Fig. 1(a) shows the deployment architecture used to deploy an FAS to a customer. An FAS consists of a set of live environments and a single staging environment. A live environment processes queries from client web applications via web services. A staging environment is responsible for receiving data updates in XML format, indexing the XML, and distributing the resulting indices across all live environments according to the Replication Protocol. The Replication Protocol is implemented by the Replication System which consists of a SyncServer at the staging environment and one SyncClient for each live environment. The SyncServer determines the schedule of replication jobs, as well as their contents, while SyncClient receives data and configuration updates according to the schedule. Fig. 1(b) shows the interactions in the Replication System. Informally, the

Replication Protocol is as follows: the SyncServer begins by listening for connections from SyncClients. A SyncClient creates and schedules a ClientJob object with job type Boot that connects immediately to the SyncServer. The SyncServer then creates a ConnectionThread to communicate with the SyncClient's ClientJob. The ClientJob asks the ConnectionThread for replication schedules, notifies the SyncClient about the schedules, receives a sequence of file updates according to the schedule from the ConnectionThread and terminates.

The existing QA practise at Fredhopper is to run a daily QA process. The core component (˜160,000 LoC) of FAS, including the Replication System has 2500+ unit tests (more with other parts of FAS). There is also a continuous build system that runs the unit tests and a set of 200+ black box test cases automated using the WebDriver Selenium for every code change / 3rd library change to FAS. Moreover, for every bug fix or feature addition, specific manual test cases are run by a QA team and for every release, a subset of standard manual test cases (900+) is executed by the QA team.

The SUT was a Java implementation of the SyncClient, consisting of about 6400 lines of Java code organized into 44 classes and 2 interfaces. Specifically, we were interested to test the interaction between a SyncClient and a ClientJob by learning the SyncClient as a Kripke structure over the input data type

$$\Sigma_{in} = \{setAcceptor,\ schedule,\ searchjob,\ businessJob,\ dataJob,$$

$$connectThread,\ noConnectionThread\}$$

Four relevant output data types were identified as follows:

$$\Sigma_{schedules} = \{\phi,\ \{search\},\ \{business\},\ \{business,\ search\},\ \{data\},$$

$$\{data,\ search\},\ \{data,\ business\},\ \{data,\ business,\ search\}\}.$$

$$\Sigma_{state} = \{Start,\ WaitToBoot,\ Boot,\ WaitToReplicate,\ WorkOnReplicate,$$

$$WorkOnReplicate,\ End\},$$

$$\Sigma_{jobtype} = \{nojob, Boot, SR, BR, DR\},\quad \Sigma_{files} = \{readonly, writeable\}.$$

Eleven informal user requirements were then formalized in $PLTL(\Sigma)$. Below, for brevity, we only reproduce some of these requirements formally.

Requirement 1: *If the SyncClient is at state Start and receives an acceptor, the client will proceed to state WaitToBoot and execute a boot job.*

$$G(state = Start \wedge in = setAcceptor \rightarrow X(state = WaitToBoot \wedge jobtype = Boot))$$

Requirement 2: *If the SyncClient's state is either WaitToBoot or Booting then it must have a boot job (Jobtype = Boot), and if it has a boot job, its state can only be one of WaitToBoot, Booting, WaitToReplicate or End.*[1]

$$G(state \in \{WaitToBoot,\ Booting\} \rightarrow jobtype = Boot \wedge$$

---

[1] The membership relation $\in$ used in Requirement 2 and elsewhere does not belong to PLTL(Σ) but is a macro notation that can be replaced automatically.

$jobtype = Boot \rightarrow state \in \{WaitToBoot,\ Booting,\ WaitToReplicate,\ End\})$

Requirement 3: *If the SyncClient is executing a Boot job (Jobtype = Boot) and is in state WaitToBoot and receives a connection to a connection thread, it will proceed to state Booting.*

Requirement 4: *If the SyncClient is executing a Boot job (Jobtype = Boot) and is in state Booting and receives schedules (schedule), it will proceed to state WaitToReplicate and it will queue all schedules (schedules = { data, business, search }).*

Requirement 5: *If the SyncClient is executing a replication job jobtype ∈ { SR, BR, DR} and is in state WaitToReplicate and receives a connection to a connection thread, the client will proceed to state WorkOnReplicate*

Requirement 6: *If the SyncClient is waiting either to replicate or boot and there is no more connection, the client proceeds to the End state.*

Requirement 7: *Once the SyncClient is in the End state, it cannot go to another different state.*

Requirement 8: *If it is not in the End state then every schedule that the SyncClient possesses will eventually be executed as a replication job.*

$$G(state \neq End \rightarrow$$

$$search \in schedules \rightarrow (F(jobtype = SR\ U\ state = End)) \land$$

$$business \in schedules \rightarrow (F(jobtype = BR\ U\ state = End)) \land$$

$$data \in schedules \rightarrow (F(jobtype = DR\ U\ state = End)))$$

Requirement 9: *The SyncClient cannot modify its underlying file system (files = readonly) unless it is in state WorkOnReplicate.*

Requirement 10: *If the SyncClient is executing a replication job for a particular type of schedule, then that job can only receive schedules for that particular type of schedule.*

Requirement 11: *If the SyncClient has committed to a schedule of a particular type and eventually that schedule is executed as a replication job then that schedule will be removed from the queue.*

Table 1 gives the results obtained by running *LBTest* to test these 11 user requirements on the FAS SyncClient. For each requirement, Table 1 breaks down the *total number* of test cases used into three figures (columns 5, 6 and 7) which count the test cases generated by each of the three different TCG methods: *model checker*, *learner* and *random*. The total testing time (column 3) is the time taken to execute all three types of test cases. For each requirement, Table 1 gives the final verdict (column 2) i.e. *pass/fail/warning*. Column 4 gives the size of the learned hypothesis model at test termination. To terminate each experiment, a maximum time bound of 5 hours was chosen. However, if the hypothesis model size had not changed over 10 consecutive random tests, then testing was terminated earlier than this.

Table 1. Performance of *LBTest* on Fredhopper Access Server case study

PLTL Requirement	Verdict	Total Testing Time (hours)	Hypothesis size (states)	Model checker tests	Learning tests	Random tests
Req 1	pass	5.0	8	0	50,897	45
Req 2	pass	5.0	15	2	49,226	13
Req 3	pass	1.7	11	0	16,543	17
Req 4	pass	2.1	11	0	20,114	14
Req 5	pass	2.5	11	0	24,944	17
Req 6	pass	2.3	11	0	23,215	16
Req 7	pass	2.1	11	0	18,287	17
Req 8	warning	1.9	8	15	18,263	12
Req 9	warning	3.8	15	18	35,831	18
Req 10	pass	2.7	11	0	26,596	19
Req 11	pass	4.6	11	0	45,937	21

Thus for example: Requirement 1 was tested for a total of 5 hours using 50,942 test cases, of which 50,897 were generated by the learning algorithm, 45 were generated randomly, and 0 were generated by the model checker. We see that learner generated queries dominate, though generally this is influenced by the kind of learning algorithm used (here IKL [12]). Around 10,000 test cases per hour were generated, executed and evaluated. This test throughput does not vary much across the 11 different requirements. On large SUTs, test throughput is mainly determined by the average execution speed of a single test case. Since Requirement 1 was passed, we can infer that the model checker was called 45 times, but on each occasion it failed to find a counterexample, so that a random test case was used instead.

4.1.1 Discussion of Errors Found

Nine out of eleven requirements were passed. For Requirements 8 and 9, *LBTest* gave warnings (due to a loop in the counterexample) corresponding to tests of liveness requirements that were never passed. The counterexample for both these requirements was "*setAcceptor,Schedule,businessJob,businessJob*". After the first instance of symbol "*businessJob*", a loop occurred in the counterexample which was unfolded just once. This counterexample violated Requirement 8 because if we keep reading the input *businessJob* from the state reached after the first "*businessJob*" the SUT does not go to the end state as specified. It also violates Requirement 9 because the start state is reached after reading this sequence rather than *WaitOnReplicate* or *End* states as specified. Neither of these states is ever reached if we keep reading the input *businessJob* from this state. A careful analysis of these requirements showed that both involved using the U (strong Until) operator. When this was replaced with a W (weak Until) operator no further warnings were seen for Requirement 9. Therefore this was regarded as an

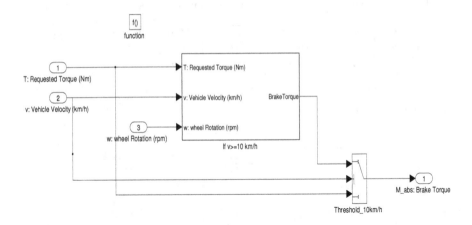

Fig. 2. A High Level Simulink Model of the BBW System

error in the user requirements. However, *LBTest* continued to produce warnings for Requirement 8, corresponding to a true SUT error. So in this case study *LBTest* functioned to uncover errors both in the user requirements and in the SUT.

4.2   Case Study 2: Brake-by-Wire

The Volvo Technology BBW system is an embedded vehicle application with ABS function, where no mechanical connection exists between the brake pedal and the brake actuators applied to the four wheels. A sensor attached to the brake pedal reads the pedal's position percentage, which is used to compute the desired global brake torque. A software component distributes this global brake torque request to the four wheels. At each wheel, the ABS algorithm uses the corresponding brake torque request, the measured wheel speed, and the estimated vehicle speed to compute the actual brake torque on the wheel. For safety purposes, the ABS controller in the BBW system must release the corresponding brake actuator when the slip rate of any wheel is larger than the threshold (e.g., 20%) and the vehicle is moving at a speed of above certain value, e.g., 10 km/h. A Simulink model of the BBW system is shown in Figure 2.

The BBW is a typical distributed system, which is realised by five ECUs (electronic control units) connected via a network bus. The central ECU is connected to the brake and acceleration (gas) pedals. The other four ECUs are connected to four wheels. The software components on the central ECU manage the brake pedal sensor, calculation of the global brake torque from the brake pedal position, and distribution of the global torque to the four wheels. The software components on each wheel ECU measure the wheel speed, control the brake actuator, and implement the ABS controller. The BBW is a hard real-time system with some concrete temporal constraints that could not be modeled in PLTL.

For this it runs 'continuously' with high frequency sampling using two clocks (5 and 20 ms). The BBW has:

- *two real-valued inputs*: received from the brake and gas pedals to identify their positions, denoted by *breakPedalPos* and *gasPedalPos* respectively. The positions of both pedals are bounded by the interval $[0.0, 100.0]$.
- *nine real-valued outputs*: denoting the vehicle speed *vehSpeed*, rotational speeds of the four wheels (front right, front left, rear right and rear left) *wSpeedFR*, *wSpeedFL*, *wSpeedRR* and *wSpeedRL* respectively. These speeds are bounded by the interval $[0.0, 111.0]$. The torque values on these wheels are denoted by *torqueOnFR*, *torqureOnRL*, *torqueOnRR* and *torqueOnRL* respectively. All torque values are bounded by the interval $[0.0, 3000.0]$ Nm.

The SUT consisted of a Java implementation of the BBW consisting of about 1100 lines of code.

The problem of discretely modeling floating point data types was addressed by *partition testing*. For this, the two inputs were discretised into a set of four input events given by $\Sigma_{in} = \{brake, acc, accbrake, none\}$, where the values *brake* and *acc* represented the conditions *brakePedalPos* = 100.0 and *accPedalPos* = 100.0 respectively. Also *accbrake* represented the condition *brakePedalPos* = 100.0 $\wedge$ *accPedalPos* = 100.0 and *none* represented *brakePedalPos* = 0.0 $\wedge$ *accPedalPos* = 0.0 respectively.

Exploiting symmetrical user requirements on all four wheels, four finite output data types for the vehicle speed and one single wheel (front right) were identified as:

$$\Sigma_{speed} = \{vehicleStill, vehicleMove, vehicleDecreased\}$$

$$\Sigma_{wheelRotateFR} = \{zero, nonZero\}$$

$$\Sigma_{torqueFR} = \{zero, nonZero\}$$

$$\Sigma_{slipFR} = \{slipping, notSlipping\}$$

The floating point values of each output variable were mapped to the corresponding set of output events in Σ by using *discretisation formulas*. Effectively, each event represents a partition class. These formulas are defined in Table 2, and they were implemented within the SUT adapter which was used to connect the BBW to *LBTest*.

Note that in Table 2, $vehSpeed_i$ represents the vehicle speed at i-th event and hence the speed change at i-th event is $vehSpeed_i - vehSpeed_{i-1}$. The units of measurement for $vehSpeed_i$ are km/h and the vehicle is considered as still at the i-th event if $vehSpeed_i \leq 10$ otherwise it is considered to be in motion. The vehicle is considered to be decelerating at the i-th event if $vehSpeed_i < vehSpeed_{i-1}$ and $vehSpeed_{i-1} > 0$. The units of angular speed of the wheels are also converted into km/h inside the Java code of the SUT from the usual *rpm*. This was essential to calculate the slip rate of the wheels. The slip rate (denoted by *slip*) of a wheel (e.g front right) is the ratio of the difference of $vehSpeed - wSpeedFR$ and the vehicle speed *vehSpeed*. The vehicle is considered slipping when the slip rate $slip > 0.2$ otherwise the vehicle is considered not

Table 2. BBW Discretisation Formulas

Output Value	Discretisation Formula
vehicleStill	$vehSpeed \leq 10.0$
vehicleMove	$vehSpeed > 10.0$
vehicleDecreased	$vehSpeed_i < vehSpeed_{i-1} \wedge vehSpeed_{i-1} > 0$
nonZero : wheelRotateFR	$wSpeedFR > 0$
Zero : wheelRotateFR	$wSpeedFR = 0$
nonZero : torqueFR	$torqueOnFR > 0$
Zero : torqueFR	$torqueOnFR = 0$
slipping	$10 * (vehSpeed - wSpeedFR) > 2 * vehSpeed$

slipping. After this partitioning of the input and output values, three informal requirements were formalized in $PLTL(\Sigma)$ as follows:

Requirement 1: *If the* brake pedal *is pressed and the* wheel speed *(e.g., the front right wheel) is greater than zero, the value of* brake torque *enforced on the (front right) wheel by the corresponding ABS component will eventually be greater than 0.*

$$G(\, in = brake \rightarrow F(wheelRotateFR = nonZero \rightarrow torqueFR = nonZero) \,)$$

Requirement 2: *If the* brake pedal *is pressed and the actual speed of the vehicle is larger than 10 km/h and the slippage sensor shows that the (front right) wheel is slipping, this implies that the corresponding brake torque at the (front right) wheel should be 0.*

$$G(\, (in = brake \, \wedge \, speed = vehicleMove \, \wedge \, slipFR = slipping) \rightarrow torqueFR = zero \,)$$

Requirement 3: *If both the* brake *and* gas pedals *are pressed, the actual vehicle speed shall be decreased.*

$$G(in = accbrake \rightarrow X(speed = vehicleDecreased))$$

Table 3. Performance of *LBTest* on the Brake-by-Wire case study

PLTL Requirement	Verdict	Total Testing Time (min)	Hypothesis Size (States)	Model Checker Tests	Learning Tests	Random Tests
Req 1	Pass	34.4	11	0	1501038	150
Req 2	Fail	1.0	537	18	34737	2
Req 3	Pass	16.0	22	0	1006275	130

4.2.1   Discussion of Errors Found

Table 3 shows the results of testing BBW with *LBTest* using the three LTL requirements defined above. Noteworthy are the large volumes of test cases and short session times, due to fast execution of individual test cases. Requirements 1 and 3 were passed, while *LBTest* continued to give errors for Requirement 2 with different counterexamples during several testing sessions we ran. The shortest counterexample found during these sessions was "*acc, acc, acc, acc, acc, brake*". This means that when the brake pedal is pressed, after the vehicle has acquired a speed greater than 10 *km/h*, and at that time when the slip rate of a wheel is greater than 20%, then the SUT does not always have zero torque on the slipping wheel. All other counterexamples suggested a similar pattern of behaviour.

4.3   Case Study 3: triReduce

TriOptima is a Swedish IT company in the financial sector which provides post-trade infrastructure and risk management services for the over-the-counter (OTC) derivatives market. Financial markets involve a constantly changing and strict regulatory framework. To keep up with such changes, agile software development methodologies are important. However, short development cycles are difficult without test automation, and ATCG is therefore a valuable addition to quality assurance methods.

A *derivative* is a financial instrument whose value derives from the values of other underlying variables. It can be used to manage financial risk. Millions of derivatives are traded every day. Yet many of these trades are not necessary to maintain a desired risk position versus the market. Financial institutions can participate in *portfolio compression* activities to get rid of unnecessary trades. The triReduce portfolio compression service runs in *cycles*, each cycle focuses on a different product type, for example interest rate swaps or credit default swaps. Each cycle has four main steps:

1. *Preparation.* Before participating, each financial institution must complete a legal process which results in a *protocol adherence*.
2. *Sign up.* Parties can log in to the service to review the schedule for upcoming compression cycles and sign up, indicating they will participate.
3. *Linking.* During this phase, each participating party uploads their portfolio of trades, complementing the other participants in the cycle. The trades are automatically matched, determining which trades are eligible for compression. During linking, each participant sets their parameters for controlling movements in the market and credit risk.
4. *Live execution.* After calculating a multilateral unwind proposal, the different parties verify this and indicate acceptance. When all participants have indicated acceptance, the proposed trades are legally terminated.

TriOptima delivers the triReduce service through a web application that is developed in Python using the Django Framework. Django is based on a Model-View-Controller-like (MVC) software architecture pattern, where the *models* are tightly coupled to relational database models, implemented as Python classes.

In general, testing TriOptima involves *isolating* test case executions so that the ordering of test cases in a suite does not matter. Clearing the databases and caches between test executions would properly isolate them. However, setting up and tearing down the entire database is not feasible in this case since triReduce has a code base almost 100 times larger than the FAS at about 619 000 LoC (including large dependencies like Django). It is a database intensive application with customers uploading trade portfolios containing thousands of trades. Handling this data efficiently takes several hundred database models and relational database tables. Creating these blank database tables and their indexes can take time in the order of minutes. Therefore, a special SUT adapter was written to effectively isolate each test case execution by performing an efficient database rollback between individual test cases. This SUT adapter was implemented in a general way that could be used for any other Django web application.

Authentication solves the problem of deciding *who* a certain user is. Authorization solves the problem of deciding if a certain (authenticated) user is *allowed* to perform a certain operation. A central component of any Django application is its user authentication system. A central and extremely important part of triReduce is deciding what a user may or may not do in the system. For example, a simplified view of the user authorization in triReduce can be described as follows. A *user* is a member of a *party* (a legal entity). There are also user accounts for TriOptima *staff*. To sign up for a triReduce compression cycle, the party must have the correct *protocol adherence* stored in the system. (The protocol can be seen as a legally binding contract between TriReduce and the party.) Only staff users may add or remove protocol adherences for parties. Because of their critical importance for system integrity, requirements related to authentication and authorization were the focus of this *LBTest* case study.

For this specific focus, the input data type was defined by:

$$\Sigma_{in} = \{next\_subject, login, adhere\_to\_protocol\}$$

and four relevant output data types were identified as:

$$\Sigma_{status} = \{ok, client\_error, internal\_error\}$$

$$\Sigma_{subject} = \{none, root, a\_alice, b\_bob\}$$

$$\Sigma_{logged\_in} = \{anonymous, staff, bank\_a, bank\_b\}$$

$$\Sigma_{protocol} = \{not\_adheres, adheres\}, \quad \Sigma_{signup} = \{prohibited, allowed\}.$$

Five functional requirements were then formalised in $PLTL(\Sigma)$:

Requirement 1: *The status must always be okay.*

$$G(status = ok)$$

Requirement 2: *If Bank A is not logged in, and does log in, then Bank A should become logged in.*

$$G(logged\_in \in \{bank\_b, staff, anonymous\} \wedge$$

$$subject = a\_alice \wedge in = login \to X(logged\_in = bank\_a))$$

Requirement 3: *Cycle signup should be prohibited until a bank adheres to the protocol.*

$$G((logged\_in = bank\_a \to cycle\_signup = prohibited)\ U$$

$$(logged\_in = bank\_a \to adheres\_to\_protocol = adheres))$$

Requirement 4: *Cycle signup should be prohibited until a bank adheres to the protocol, and general system status should always be ok, i.e. 3 and 1 together.*

Requirement 5: *If bank A adheres to the protocol, then cycle signup for bank A should always be allowed.*

$$G((logged\_in = bank\_a \to adheres\_to\_protocol = adheres) \to$$

$$G(logged\_in = bank\_a \to cycle\_signup = allowed))$$

4.3.1   Discussion of Errors Found

Three different types of errors were found within four types of experiments, which could be classified as follows.

1. Injected Errors. Injecting errors into the SUT was a way of confirming that *LBTest* was working as intended. Below, we describe some examples of doing this, and the results may be seen in Table 4. Here, three versions of triReduce were used:

– triReduce 1: The standard version.
– triReduce 2: An error is injected, the password of the **b_bob** user was changed.
– triReduce 3: Another error is introduced, switching the meaning of logging in as user **a_alice** and **b_bob**.

2. Errors in the SUT Adapter. While testing Requirement 3 and observing the log output, some SUT output contained **status** states that were not **ok**. Thus internal errors were arising in the SUT, which no requirement had covered. Therefore Requirement 1 and Requirement 3 were combined resulting in Requirement 4. After about 55 minutes of *LBTest* execution it found a counterexample to Requirement 4. This error was easily traced to the SUT adapter, the code connecting *LBTest* to triReduce, and was quickly fixed.

Table 4. Results of injecting errors into triReduce

Req. #	SUT	Verdict	Comment
1	triReduce 1	Pass	Stopped after learning a model of 16 states using 5 hypothesis models, after 18 min.
1	triReduce 2	Warning	Counterexample found in the sixth hypothesis (size 8 states) after only 3.8 min.
2	triReduce 1	Pass	As previously, stopped after learning 5 hypothesis models in 13 min.
2	triReduce 3	Warning	Counterexample found after 98 seconds at a hypothesis size of 4 states.

3. Errors in Requirements. Executions of *LBTest* found an error in the original formalisation of Requirement 3, due to using $\wedge$ instead of $\rightarrow$ (a common mistake for beginners). *LBTest* was able to detect this, by producing a spurious counterexample within a minute on the faulty LTL requirement.

4. Successful Lengthy LBTest Executions. Requirement 5, was tested to see how *LBTest* would behave in much longer testing sessions. Two 7 hour testing sessions were successfully executed with *LBTest*. Both terminated with a "pass" verdict after about 86000 SUT executions and hypothesis sizes of up to 503 states. The log files were manually checked and contained no errors.

5   Conclusions and Future Work

We have applied *LBTest*, a learning-based testing tool, to three industrial case studies from the web, automotive and finance sectors. The tool successfully found errors in all three case studies (albeit injected errors for triReduce). This is despite the fact that one case study (the FAS) had been operational for a relatively long time. The tool supported formal requirements debugging in two case studies, which is often considered to be problematic. The successes of these large case studies suggest that LBT is already a scalable technique, that could be further improved with better learning algorithms.

The third case study (triReduce), is the largest that has been tested using *LBTest* to date. While no SUT errors were found, we note that this study was performed by a test engineer external to the original *LBTest* research team. An early version of *LBTest*, with limited documentation and guidance was used. This suggests that LBT technology should be transferable to industry.

These case studies illustrate the scope and potential for LBT within different industrial domains and problems. They also illustrate the practical difficulties of using LBT within an industrial environment, including requirements modeling and implementing appropriate SUT adapters.

Future research will consider more efficient learning algorithms which can reduce both the number of test cases and the time needed to discover errors. The combination of partition testing with LBT, used in the BBW case study, also merits further research to understand its scope and limits. In [9], we investigated extensions of LBT with more powerful model checkers for full first-order linear temporal logic. However, it remains to be seen whether this approach is competitive with the much simpler but less precise partition testing method used here.

We gratefully acknowledge financial support for this research from the Higher Education Commission (HEC) of Pakistan, the Swedish Research Council (VR) and the European Union under project HATS FP7-231620 and ARTEMIS project 269335 MBAT.

References

1. Chauhan, P., Clarke, E.M., Kukula, J.H., Sapra, S., Veith, H., Wang, D.: Automated abstraction refinement for model checking large state spaces using SAT based conflict analysis. In: Aagaard, M.D., O'Leary, J.W. (eds.) FMCAD 2002. LNCS, vol. 2517, pp. 33–51. Springer, Heidelberg (2002)
2. Cimatti, A., Clarke, E., Giunchiglia, F., Roveri, M.: NuSMV: a new symbolic model verifier. In: Halbwachs, N., Peled, D.A. (eds.) CAV 1999. LNCS, vol. 1633, pp. 495–499. Springer, Heidelberg (1999)
3. Clarke, E.M., Grumberg, O., Peled, D.A.: Model Checking. MIT Press (1999)
4. conformiq. The conformiq designer tool,
   `http://www.conformiq.com/products/conformiq-designer/`
5. Groce, A., Peled, D., Yannakakis, M.: Adaptive model checking. Logic Journal of the IGPL 14(5), 729–744 (2006)
6. Loeckx, J., Ehrich, H.-D., Wolf, M.: Specification of abstract data types. Wiley (1996)
7. Meinke, K.: Automated black-box testing of functional correctness using function approximation. In: ISSTA 2004: Proceedings of the 2004 ACM SIGSOFT International Symposium on Software Testing and Analysis, pp. 143–153. ACM, New York (2004)
8. Meinke, K., Niu, F.: A learning-based approach to unit testing of numerical software. In: Petrenko, A., Simão, A., Maldonado, J.C. (eds.) ICTSS 2010. LNCS, vol. 6435, pp. 221–235. Springer, Heidelberg (2010)
9. Meinke, K., Niu, F.: Learning-based testing for reactive systems using term rewriting technology. In: Wolff, B., Zaïdi, F. (eds.) ICTSS 2011. LNCS, vol. 7019, pp. 97–114. Springer, Heidelberg (2011)
10. Meinke, K., Niu, F., Sindhu, M.: Learning-based software testing: a tutorial. In: Hähnle, R., Knoop, J., Margaria, T., Schreiner, D., Steffen, B. (eds.) ISoLA 2011 Workshops 2011. CCIS, vol. 336, pp. 200–219. Springer, Heidelberg (2012)
11. Meinke, K.: Muddassar A. Sindhu. LBTest: A learning-based testing tool for reactive systems. In: Proc. of the Sixth IEEE Int. Conf. on Software Testing, Verification and Validation, ICST 2013. IEEE Computer Society (to appear, 2013)
12. Meinke, K., Sindhu, M.A.: Incremental learning-based testing for reactive systems. In: Gogolla, M., Wolff, B. (eds.) TAP 2011. LNCS, vol. 6706, pp. 134–151. Springer, Heidelberg (2011)
13. Peled, D., Vardi, M.Y., Yannakakis, M.: Black-box checking. In: Formal Methods for Protocol Engineering and Distributed Systems FORTE/PSTV, pp. 225–240. Kluwer (1999)
14. Raffelt, H., Steffen, B., Margaria, T.: Dynamic testing via automata learning. In: Yorav, K. (ed.) HVC 2007. LNCS, vol. 4899, pp. 136–152. Springer, Heidelberg (2008)
15. Utting, M., Legeard, B.: Practical Model-Based Testing: A Tools Approach. Morgan Kaufmann Publishers Inc., San Francisco (2006)
16. Walkinshaw, N., Bogdanov, K., Derrick, J., Paris, J.: Increasing functional coverage by inductive testing: a case study. In: Petrenko, A., Simão, A., Maldonado, J.C. (eds.) ICTSS 2010. LNCS, vol. 6435, pp. 126–141. Springer, Heidelberg (2010)
17. Weyuker, E.: Assessing test data adequacy through program inference. ACM Trans. Program. Lang. Syst. 5(4), 641–655 (1983)

Techniques and Toolset for Conformance Testing against UML Sequence Diagrams[*]

João Pascoal Faria[1,2], Ana C.R. Paiva[1], and Mário Ventura de Castro[1,2]

[1] Department of Informatics Engineering, Faculty of Engineering, University of Porto, Portugal
{jpf,apaiva,ei06064}@fe.up.pt
[2] INESC TEC, Porto, Portugal

Abstract. Novel techniques and a toolset are presented for automatically testing the conformance of software implementations against partial behavioral models constituted by a set of parameterized UML sequence diagrams (SDs), describing both external and internal interactions. Test code is automatically generated from the SDs and executed on the Java implementation under test, and test results and coverage information are presented back visually in the model. A runtime test library handles internal interaction checking, test stubs, and user interaction testing. Incremental conformance checking is achieved by first translating SDs to non-deterministic acceptance automata with parallelism.

Keywords: conformance testing, UML, sequence diagrams, automata.

1   Introduction

UML sequence diagrams (SDs) [1] allow building partial, lightweight, behavioral models of software systems, focusing on important scenarios and interactions, occurring at system boundaries or inside the system, capturing important requirements and design decisions. Such partial behavioral models may be not sufficient as input for code generation [2], but can be used as input for automatic test generation (as test specifications), using model-based testing (MBT) techniques [3]. However, existing MBT techniques from SDs have several limitations, namely in the final stages of test automation, dealing with the generation of executable tests and conformance analysis, taking into account the features of UML 2 (see Related Work section).

The overcome some of those limitations, in previous work [4], we developed a prototype tool that generates automatically JUnit [5] tests from SDs, to be executed by the user in the development environment with the support of a run-time test library. However, the test code and test results were difficult to interpret by the user and the test library had important limitations in terms of its design and functionality (namely, it lacked the support for weak sequencing). In this paper, we completely redesigned the whole approach, bringing the following contributions for enabling the automatic

---

[*] This work is part-funded by the ERDF – European Regional Development Fund through the COMPETE Programme (operational programme for competitiveness) and by National Funds through the FCT – Fundação para a Ciência e a Tecnologia (Portuguese Foundation for Science and Technology) within project «FCOMP - 01-0124-FEDER-022701».

H. Yenigün, C. Yilmaz, and A. Ulrich (Eds.): ICTSS 2013, LNCS 8254, pp. 180–195, 2013.
© IFIP International Federation for Information Processing 2013

conformance testing of software implementations (currently in Java) against UML SDs, in a modular and extensible way:

- novel techniques for incremental conformance checking, complying with the default weak sequencing semantics of UML SDs [1], based on the translation of SDs to non-deterministic automata with parallelism, that are executed stepwise;
- related techniques for execution tracing and manipulation, namely internal interaction tracing, test stub injection and user interaction tracing, taking advantage of aspect-oriented programming (AOP) techniques and reflection;
- related techniques for test code generation from the model and test results visualization in the model (conformance errors and coverage information), raising the level of abstraction of the user feedback and improving usability.

The rest of the paper is organized as follows: section 2 presents an overview of the approach; section 3 describes the characteristics of test-ready SDs; sections 4, 5 and 6 present the main contributions; section 7 presents a case study; section 8 presents a comparison with related work; section 9 concludes the paper.

2   Approach and Toolset Overview

Our toolset, named UML Checker, comprises two independent tools (see Fig. 1): an add-in for the Enterprise Architect (EA) modeling tool [6], chosen for its accessibility and functionality; and a reusable test library, implemented in Java and AspectJ [7]. The add-in gets the needed information from the model via the EA API and generates JUnit test driver code, including traceability links to the UML model (message identifiers) and expectations about internal interactions. The test code is then compiled and executed over the application under test (AUT). The behavior of the AUT in response to the test inputs (namely internal messages) is traced by the test library using AOP, and compared against the expected behavior. All discrepancies and exceptions occurred and messages effectively executed are listed in the execution result that is processed by the EA add-in, which annotates the model accordingly.

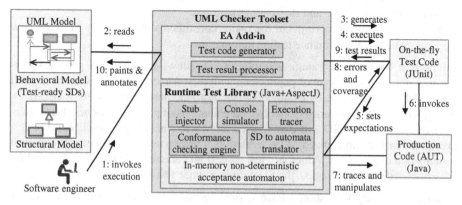

Fig. 1. Communication diagram illustrating the toolset architecture and functioning

3   Test-Ready Sequence Diagrams

This section describes the characteristics that SDs should have to be used as test specifications for automated conformance testing in our approach.

The usual modeling features of SDs [1] are supported, with some restrictions and extensions. As illustrated in Fig. 2, the following types of interactions can be modeled and automatically tested in our approach:

- external interactions with client applications through an API;
- external interactions with users through a user interface (UI);
- internal interactions among objects in the system;
- interactions with objects not yet implemented (marked as «stub»).

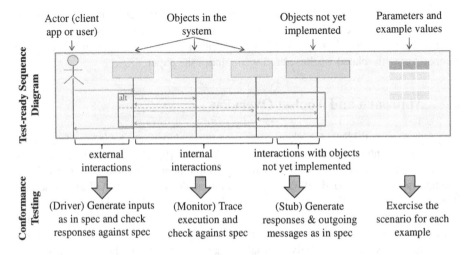

Fig. 2. Major constituents of test-ready sequence diagrams and usage for conformance testing

For example, the SD in Fig. 3 includes external interactions with a client application (messages Account and withdraw), as well as some internal interactions (messages setBalance and Movement).

Next we describe in more detail the major constituents of test-ready SDs and how they are treated in conformance testing automation.

Interaction Parameters. Parameterization of SDs allows defining more generic scenarios in a rigorous way. A set of parameters, with their names and types, may be defined in each SD, accompanied by example values. E.g., the note marked «Parameters» in Fig. 3 defines two parameters and two combinations of parameter values. Parameters have the scope of the SD and can be used anywhere (including as lifelines). For test execution, each parameterized SD is treated as a parameterized test scenario and each combination of parameter values as a test case. If no parameters are defined (i.e., values are hardcoded in the messages), the SD defines a single test case.

Actors. Test-ready SDs should have a single actor, representing a user or a client application that interacts with the AUT through a user interface or API, respectively.

During test execution, the actor is treated as a test driver, responsible to send the specified outgoing messages to the AUT, taking into account any guard conditions defined, and to check the responses against the expected values specified in the diagram.

User Interaction Testing. Since the UML does not prescribe a standard way for that purpose, we adopted a set of keywords (signals) to model user interaction through the console in an abstract way (possibly since the requirements phase):

- `start(args)` – the user starts the application (indicated by its main class);
- `enter(v)` – the user enters the value specified through the standard input;
- `display(v)` – the application displays the value specified to the standard output.

During test execution, the test harness injects the values specified by `enter` messages, simulating a user, and compares the actual AUT responses against the expectations specified by `display` messages.

Internal Interactions Checking. Besides external interactions with client applications or users, test-ready SDs may also describe interactions among objects in the AUT, capturing significant design decisions. During test execution, for each message sent to the AUT, the test harness also checks that internal messages among objects in the AUT occur as specified and internal objects are created and passed as specified. The benefits are improved conformance checking and fault localization.

In order to allow keeping SDs as minimalist as wanted, focusing only on relevant interactions, and enable the scalability of the approach, we support by default a **loose conformance** mode, in which additional messages are allowed in the AUT, besides the ones specified in the diagram (differently from what happens with the other supported conformance mode - **strict** conformance).

Stubs in the Middle. Lifelines may be marked as «stub», to indicate that the corresponding classes (possibly external to the AUT) are not yet implemented or one does not want to use the existing implementation. During test execution, the test harness generates not only the reply messages, but also the outgoing messages (hence "stub in the middle") specified in the SD for any incoming messages. This allows testing partial implementations and simulating additional actors.

Interaction Operators. The most commonly used combined fragments are supported, allowing the specification of more generic scenarios with control flow variants (with the `alt`, `opt`, `loop`, `par`, `seq` and `strict` interaction operators). Conditions of `alt` and `opt` operators may be omitted, to model situations in which the implementation has the freedom to choose the path to follow and to support partial specifications (see, e.g., the inner `alt` fragment in Fig. 3).

Value Specifications. Message parameters, return values and guards may be specified by any computable expression in the context of the interaction (involving constants, interaction parameters, lifelines, etc.), as long as it has no side-effects on participating objects. Otherwise, the evaluation of expected parameter and return values or guards during test execution could change the behavior of the AUT. Looseness in the specification of parameter and return values can be indicated by means of the "-" symbol (matching any value), and by omitting the return value, respectively. During test execution, the semantics of value checking depends on the implementation of `equals` and the comparison precision defined for some data types in the conformance settings.

4   Test Code Generation and Test Results Visualization

This section describes the test code generation and results' visualization techniques. The techniques are illustrated with the running example of Fig. 3, referring to a simple application that exposes an API for creating bank accounts (with an initial balance) and withdrawing money (with alternative execution paths, depending on the money available and the way chosen by the implementation to record movements).

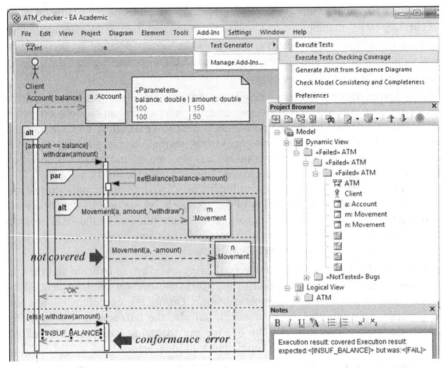

Fig. 3. Sequence diagram of the running example, painted and annotated after test execution

Test Code Generation. A test class is generated from each SD, with the general self-explanatory structure illustrated in Fig. 4, containing a parameterized test method corresponding to the SD and a plain test method for each combination of parameter values. `InteractionTestCase` is a facade [8] that extends JUnit3 `TestCase`. To assure that expressions of message arguments, return values and guards (possibly dependent on the execution state) are evaluated at proper moments, they are encoded with `ValueSpec`. To allow the incremental binding of lifeline names to actual objects (see sec.5), they are encoded with `Lifeline` - a proxy [8] for the actual object.

Test Results Visualization. The results of test execution are presented visually in the model, using a combination of graphical and textual information, as illustrated in Fig. 3. The following color scheme is used for painting each combination of parameter values and each message: black - not exercised, green - exercised without errors, red - exercised with errors. For each message exercised with errors, the error information (plus the AUT stack trace if wanted) is shown in the message notes. Possible error types and locations are shown in Table 1. The information about messages not covered (exercised) is important in the presence of conditional paths, to check the adequacy of test data (parameter values), and in the presence of unconstrained 'opt' or 'alt' fragments, to analyze implementation choices.

Table 1. List of conformance errors and locations in the model where they are signaled

Conformance error	Location in the model
Wrong argument	Call message.
Wrong return value	Reply message, if it exists; call message, otherwise.
Unexpected exception	Method or constructor execution bar.
Unexpected call (strict conformance)	Method or constructor execution bar.
Missing call	Call message or mandatory combined fragment.
Missing or incorrect output	`display` message
Missing input	`enter` message

The behavioral model packages are marked with self-explanatory stereotypes, depending on the status of contained SDs: «Failed», «Passed», «NotTested» and «Incomplete». The stereotypes are visible in the project browser for a quick check of conformance status. The classes and methods in the structural model (class diagrams) that are not covered (exercised) by the behavioral model are also marked as «NotCovered», to help assessing the completeness of the behavioral model.

```
public class ATMTest extends InteractionTestCase {
  private Account a = null; // similar for lifelines m,n
  public void testATM(final double balance,final double amount){
    ValueSpec exp0 = new ValueSpec() {
      public Object get() {return balance-amount;}
    }; // similar for other expressions occurring in SD
    Lifeline aLifeline = new Lifeline() {
      public void set(Object value) {a = (Account)value; }
      public Object get() {return a;}
    }; // similar for other lifelines occurring in SD
    // Declares expected interactions to conform. check. engine:
    expect(/*encoding of SD fragments and messages here*/);
    // Traditional JUnit test driver code (actor messages):
    a = new Account(balance);
    if (amount <= balance)
      assertEquals("OK",a.withdraw(amount));
    else
      assertEquals("INSUF_BALANCE", a.withdraw(amount));
    // Final check of interactions missing:
    finalCheck();
  }
  public void testATM_0() { testATM(100, 150); }
  public void testATM_1() { testATM(100, 50); }
}
```

Fig. 4. Skeleton of test code generated from the SD in Fig. 3

5   Techniques for Incremental Conformance Checking

Translation to Automata. To handle uniformly the variety of interaction operators allowed in SDs, and comply with the default weak sequencing semantics of UML SDs [1] with implicit parallelism between lifelines, SDs are first translated to non-deterministic automata according to the following steps (also illustrated in Fig. 5):

1. **Generate states.** Possible states are generated in each lifeline before and after each message end (including implicit reply messages from synchronous calls), combined fragment boundary and operand boundary. Additionally, a (global) start state and a (global) final state are introduced for the whole diagram. An auxiliary state is also generated for each asynchronous message (see Table 2-j).
2. **Generate transitions.** Transitions linking lifeline states, possibly with multiple source and/or target states (as in parallel finite automata [9]), are generated according to the rules shown in Table 2. A transition is generated for each synchronous message, synchronizing the lifelines involved. Regarding combined fragments, automatic transitions (without events) are generated to enter and exit the combined fragment and its operands along the lifelines covered. Following a common semantic choice [10], the lifelines involved are synchronized in the decision points of 'alt', 'opt' and 'loop'. Otherwise, it is followed the default weak sequencing semantics of SDs (except obviously for 'strict'). Additionally, it is generated a transition linking the start state of the SD to the first state in all lifelines, and another linking the last state in all lifelines to the final state of the SD.
3. **Simplify** (optional). The resulting automaton is simplified by removing transitions with empty labels and redundant states, resulting in an equivalent automaton that accepts the same traces. Another example partially simplified is shown in Fig. 6.

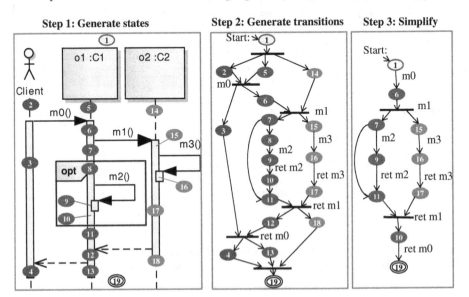

Fig. 5. Three-step translation process (with the 3rd optional) from SD to acceptance automaton

Table 2. Transition generation rules (superimposed in red) for different fragments

a) synchronous messages: synchCall and reply pair	b) synchronous messages: synchCall and reply pair	c) synchronous messages: createMessage & reply pair
m m ... r	m m ... r r	C1(...) o1: C1 C1(...) ... ret o1
d) alternatives	**e) option**	**f) loop**
alt [c_1] $[c_1]$ ... [c_2] $[c_2]$ ...	opt [¬c] [c] [c] ...	loop (n,m) [n=0] /c_i←0 ... [c_i+1<m] /c_i++ [c_i+1≥n]
g) weak sequencing	**h) strict sequencing**	**i) parallel**
seq	strict	par ... ...

j) asynchronous messages: send and receive pair	**Legend:** Transition with single source and target states:	Transition with multiple source and/or target states (notation similar to fork/join in UML):
send -m m rcv-m	event[guard]/action	event[guard]/action ...

a, b, c) Even if not indicated, reply messages are always assumed after synchronous calls.

d, e) In the absence of guards in the SD, all guards are also omitted in the generated transitions.

f) c_i is a counter variable for loop i. Counters are not needed if $n≤1$ and m='*'.

d, e, f, g, h, i) These rules extend trivially to more than two operands and/or lifelines.

i) A coregion can also be treated as a parallel combined fragment over a single lifeline, having as operands the message ends enclosed in the coregion.

j) Currently implemented only for the translation of user interaction messages modeled with the start, enter and display signals. An auxiliary state is introduced for ordering the message sending and receiving events. Even inside loops, given our choice for synchronization at decision points, at most one sent message occurrence may be waiting to be received.

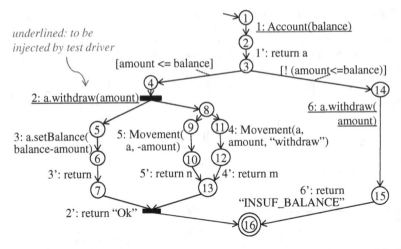

Fig. 6. Automaton generated from the example SD of Fig. 3 (only partially simplified)

Automata Structure. In our approach, a conformance checking automaton is a tuple $\prec S, s_o, F, T \succ$, where S is the set of states, $s_o \in S$ is the initial (start) state, $F \subseteq S$ is the set of final (accepting) states, and T is the set of transitions. Each transition is a tuple $\prec \sigma, \lambda, \tau \succ$, where $\sigma \subseteq S$ is the set of source states of the transition, $\tau \subseteq S$ is the set of target states of the transition, and λ is the transition label. Transitions with multiple source and/or target states are used to handle parallelism and synchronization (see Table 2). A transition label is a triple *event[guard]/action*, all of which components are optional. Transitions without event are automatic. The automaton may be non-deterministic, i.e., different transitions $<\sigma_i, \lambda_i, \tau_i>$ and $<\sigma_j, \lambda_j, \tau_j>$ may exist with $\sigma_i = \sigma_j \wedge \lambda_i = \lambda_j \wedge \tau_i \neq \tau_j$, or with $\lambda_i \neq \lambda_j$ but simultaneously satisfiable (e.g., call specifications $m(1)$ and $m(-)$ are both satisfiable by the occurrence $m(1)$).

Automata Execution. An automaton run state is a tuple $\prec A, \beta, \rho, C \succ$, where:

- A is the set of active automaton states (multiple active states may exist because of parallelism), starting with $\{s_0\}$; each time a transition $\prec \sigma, \lambda, \tau \succ$ is performed, requiring $\sigma \subseteq A$, the new set of active states becomes $(A \backslash \sigma) \cup \tau$;
- $\beta = \beta_P \cup \beta_L \cup \beta_C$ is a binding of variable names to actual values, starting with the binding β_P of interaction parameters to actual values, and incrementally extended with the binding β_L of lifeline names to actual objects and the binding β_C of loop counters to actual values; β_L is extended as message occurrences are encountered involving lifeline names as target, argument or return value; subsequent occurrences of a previously bound lifeline name must refer to the same object;
- ρ is a mapping from identifiers of matched call or send event occurrences to identifiers of corresponding events in the automaton; this is needed to assure that reply or receive occurrences corresponding to ignored call or send occurrences (in loose conformance mode only) are also ignored, and that reply or receive occurrences corresponding to considered call or send occurrences are matched against the

correct event in the automaton; we assume that all call-reply and send-receive pairs have related identifiers, like n and n' (see Fig. 6);

- C is the set of identifiers of messages covered so far, starting with the empty set, for coverage analysis purposes.

Because the same event occurrence may match multiple event specifications (non-determinism), it is kept a set of possible run states $R=\{r_1, ..., r_n\}$. Conformance checking fails when R becomes empty at any point of execution, or, at the end of execution, there is no run state $r_i \in R$ such that all its active states A_i are accepting states (i.e., $\neg \exists r_i \in R \bullet A_i \subseteq F$). An example execution is illustrated in Fig. 7.

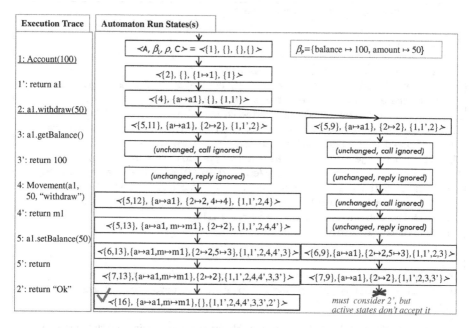

Fig. 7. Example of successful execution of the automaton of Fig. 6 for a possible test case and AUT response in loose conformance mode. The test driver stimuli are underlined in the trace.

6   Techniques for Execution Tracing and Manipulation

In this section we present techniques, based on AOP with load time weaving, to enable execution tracing, stub injection, and user interaction testing in a minimally intrusive way.

Execution Tracing and Stub Injection. Method and constructor invocation and execution in the AUT are intercepted with the AspectJ [7] code depicted in Fig. 8. Method invocations are traced with an `execution` pointcut (line 5), when the control focus is already on the target object, because it also captures reflective invocations. In the case of constructors, operations invoked by super-constructors execute before the self-constructor (and not nested), so we use `call` pointcuts instead (when the control focus is still on the sender object) for proper nesting, with two versions for normal and reflective calls (lines 19 and 20). The invocation and reply occurrences intercepted by the aspect code are sent to the conformance checking engine for incremental checking (lines 6 and 14). Regarding stubs, we assume that objects marked as «stub» in the SD have compilable method skeletons; instead of executing the actual method body, the outgoing messages specified in the SD (constructor and method calls) and enabled in the automaton are issued through reflection (line 12), and it is returned the value specified in the SD and enabled in the automaton (line 13).

```
1:  public priviliged aspect TracingAspect {
2:   // Aux. def. to filter points of interest and avoid infinite recursion:
3:   pointcut mayTrace():  /* definition omitted */ ;
4:   // Intercepts normal and reflective method invocations:
5:   Object around(): mayTrace() && execution(* *(..)) {
6:    Process invocation (call) occurr. by automaton (via synchronized method)
7:     If the automaton failed, throw the failure
8:     If no match was found, proceed with normal execution and return
9:    If target object is not marked as «stub» or this is a constructor call,
10:     Proceed with normal execution and get return value
11:   If target object is marked as «stub», perform stub injection, i.e.,
12:     Execute outgoing calls spec./enabled in SD/automaton via reflection
13:     If this isn't a constructor call, get return value from SD/automaton
14:   Process reply (return) occurrence by automaton (via synchronized method)
15:     If the automaton failed, throw the failure
16:   Return the return value
17:  }
18:  // Intercepts normal and reflective constructor invocations:
19:  Object around(): mayTrace() && call(new(..) {similar template}
20:  Object around():mayTrace()&&call(Object Constructor.newInstance(..)){idem}
21:}
```

Fig. 8. Skeleton of AspectJ code responsible for execution tracing and stub injection

User Interaction Testing. The mechanisms for user interaction testing of console applications are illustrated in Fig. 9. A console simulator (from our test library) starts the AUT in a thread separate from the test driver and creates input and output blocking queues for communication and synchronization between both. AUT calls to read and write operations on `System.in` and `System.out` are intercepted with `around` pointcuts, and replaced by `poll` and `put` operations on the input and output queues, respectively. User interaction messages specified in the SD with the `enter` and `display` keywords originate `put` and `poll` operations that are performed by the test driver on the input and output queues. `Poll` operations are subject to a timeout. Although the test driver already checks displayed values (with `assertEquals`), the relevant events are also sent to the conformance checking automaton for checking their proper ordering with respect to other execution occurrences.

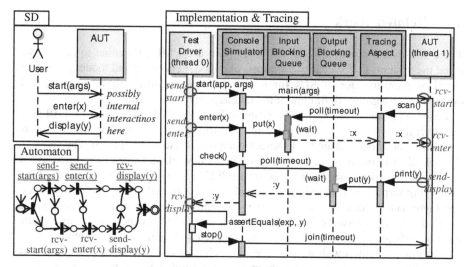

Fig. 9. User interaction specification and conformance testing mechanism for console apps

7   Case Study

To assess our approach we conducted a case study on a Java application, developed at our university and used since 2009 by approximately 200 software engineering students for program size measurement. The application, named "FileDiff", computes the difference with minimum cost between two source files, in terms of lines added (cost 1), modified (cost 1) or deleted (cost 0), ignoring blank lines and comments. An accompanying UML model contains a SD that exercises all classes and methods. Some input files for manual testing purposes also accompany the application.

The goal of the case study was to confirm the main benefits of our approach: the ability to take advantage of existing behavioral models for test automation (hence reducing the test effort); the ability to find discrepancies between the model and the implementation (hence enabling improvements in their quality).

The initial SD ([1], pg.67, not shown here for space limitation reasons) was not test-ready, due to the usage of pseudo-code and a "procedural" feature - attribute assignment ([1], pg.507) - not currently supported by our tool. These problems were solved by making minor changes to the SD. Test parameters and test data were added to exercise the SD for existing test files, resulting in a test-ready SD with 34 messages, 8 lifelines (4 of which instantiated dynamically), and 2 combined fragments ([11], pg.72). Conformance test execution revealed a message not covered (caused by an incorrect loop modeling) and a message exercised with errors (caused by an incorrect sequencing in the implementation), which were fixed in the model and in the implementation, respectively.

Hence, the benefits of our approach could be demonstrated for this case study. Other case studies and acceptance tests performed to validate the approach for all supported modeling features, error types and coverage levels can be found in [11].

8   Related Work

There are several research works that attempt to use UML SDs either to help understand the systems or for quality purposes, like model checking and model-based testing. However, the use of SDs for testing or other rigorous verification methods demands for a rigorous definition of the language semantics [10].

Based on a survey of proposed semantics for UML SDs, Micskei *et al.* [10] point out several problems or challenges with the current natural language semantics, and categorize the choices taken by 13 selected approaches to address them. The semantic choices taken in our approach are inspired by their work and can be classified as follows: execution traces are either valid or invalid, i.e., no inconclusive traces exist; the underlying formalism is based on the encoding of the partial orders into a finite structure (automaton), for efficient processing, with interleaving as the concurrency model (as in the UML standard); both complete (in strict conformance mode) and partial trace specifications (in loose mode) are supported; fragments are combined using standard interpretation with weak sequencing; choices and guards are handled globally, i.e., the involved lifelines synchronize at decision points for evaluating guards and/or choosing a path to follow; the SD is processed by analyzing it as a whole using locations (lifeline states in our case), for higher flexibility.

Currently, we do not support the 'assert', 'neg', 'ignore' and 'consider' operators, but the approach can be easily extended, in particular, 'ignore' and 'consider' operators can be dealt by allowing an explicit conformance mode, besides the loose and strict modes, and 'assert' and 'neg' operators will lead to irrevocable failure states.

As pointed out in [10], the first step of many proposed semantics (e.g., [12]), is to find all the legal cuts of a diagram (global SD states, i.e., combinations of lifeline locations), but finding cuts can get complicated in the presence of complex fragments and asynchronous communication. One advantage of our approach is that, by allowing transitions with multiple source and/or target states, we avoid determining those cuts, as well as the potential explosion of states and transitions. A class of automata with that type of transitions, named parallel finite automata (PFA), was first proposed in [9] as a convenient way to express the interleaving parallelism inherent in Petri net notation without admitting the possibility of an infinite state space (in other words, without admitting multiple tokens per place); the authors also show the equivalence and translation procedure of PFA to deterministic finite automata (DFA). Our conformance checking automata are inspired by the concept and properties of PFA, with the addition of several features found in extended state machines (such as UML state machines [1]), namely state variables and event-guard-action transition labels.

Regarding the representation of execution traces, we follow the approach of [13], which uses a single event to model synchronous (instantaneous) communication and a pair of send and receive events to model asynchronous (non-instantaneous) communication. In [13], it is also proposed a translation procedure of a partially ordered execution trace, containing both synchronous and asynchronous communications (but not interaction operators), into a system of communicating automata, with one automaton per process (lifeline) and one 'message delay' automaton per asynchronous communication, which product yields the possible ways of interleaving events. Despite the different outputs, our translation procedure follows some of the principles of their approach, adding the support for interaction operators and other UML SDs' features.

Despite the challenges with the SD semantics, there are different approaches in the literature that use SD for quality purposes. For instance, [14] translate UML 2 interactions into automata for model checking with respect to specified requirements.

There are also approaches that extract SDs from a dynamic analysis of the system for comparison with design SDs. These approaches are split into four phases: instrumentation; logging; merging (in the case of distributed systems); and comparison. The work of [15] uses AOP to support the instrumentation of Java systems' bytecode. To deal with the fact that SDs are not a straightforward representation of the extracted traces, they define two metamodels (one for traces and another for SDs) and define mapping rules between them using OCL. In our approach, AOP is also used, not only for execution monitoring, but also for user interaction redirection and stub injection.

Other approaches use SDs in the context of model-based testing, either by focusing in test case generation, data generation and/or code generation.

Since SDs show objects and messages exchanged among them along time, test cases generated from them may be adequate to find errors concerning the sequence of executed messages and the values passed [16]. The interaction operators introduced in UML 2 allow the description of a number of traces in a compact and concise manner. Because of that, there are several examples in the literature that use an intermediate notation to represent the set of possible executions within a SD and afterwards, test cases are generated from this representation according to coverage criteria. Some examples of such representations are "sequence dependency graphs" [17], "message dependency graphs" [18], and "structured composite graphs" [19].

Besides generating test sequences, there are some approaches that also generate test data. Nayak *et al.* [19] enrich SDs with attribute and constraint information derived from class diagrams and OCL constraints and use a constraint solver to generate test data to cover paths along scenarios. Samuel *et al.* [18] create dynamic slices according to conditional predicates associated with messages in a SD and generate test data satisfying each slice. Benauttou *et al.* [20] generate test data based on partition analysis of method contracts expressed in the Disjunctive Normal Form.

Another important feature is the generation of test code at the end. There are approaches that generate assertions to check consistency of models with manually derived code at run time [21] and others that generate test code, for instance, as unit tests. These approaches can be used in combination. Some of the latter examples are: a tool generating test code from SDs (SeDiTeC tool [22]); a tool generating functional test drivers from SDs (SCENTOR [23]); a Model-Driven Architecture based approach for generating test code for multiple unit testing frameworks [24].

Javed *et al.* [24] apply a model-to-model transformation from SDs into a xUnit model independent form a particular unit testing framework and, afterwards, apply a model-to-text transformation into JUnit or SUnit. However, their approach has several limitations: the checking of returned values is performed in an intrusive way by constructing additional objects, which is problematic when constructors have side-effects; the gathering of execution traces is not integrated into the approach and they do not automate their verification; they do not deal with the novel features of UML 2.

One advantage of SeDiTeC [22] is the generation of stubs for parts of the AUT not implemented, hence allowing starting testing earlier. As far as we know, they do not deal directly with the novel features of UML 2. However, they combine different SDs which can be used as a way to represent, for instance, alternative blocks of messages.

SCENTOR [23] tool creates functional test drivers for e-business applications from SDs that have test data (parameters and expected values of method calls) embedded in them. However it does not check internal interactions and does not generate test stubs.

Some commercial tools also support conformance testing based on SDs. To our knowledge, the IBM Rational Rhapsody TestConductor Add On [25] is one of the more advanced tools. Having as target real-time embedded applications, it supports many features in common with our approach (like internal interaction checking, visual feedback, etc.) and other features outside the scope of our approach. Despite its powerful features, it does not support several important features of our approach: incremental lifeline instantiation with create messages (all objects must be previously defined in a test architecture); non-deterministic 'alt', 'opt' and 'loop' operators (without guards); strict conformance mode (message types absent from a SD are not traced); stubs in the middle (only normal stubs are supported); user interaction testing.

The implementation of tests derived from SDs or similar formalisms in distributed asynchronous environments poses additional challenges for coordinating test drivers, monitors and stubs. An example of an approach for monitoring the execution of distributed Java applications with AOP was presented in [15]. An approach for coordinating distributed test components (namely test drivers) was presented in [26].

9   Conclusions and Future Work

It were presented a set of techniques and a toolset for the automatic conformance testing of software applications against behavioral models constituted by a set of parameterized UML 2 SDs. With a single click, test cases are automatically generated from the model, executed on the AUT and test results and coverage information presented back visually in the model. The conformance checking approach, based on the translation of SDs to nondeterministic acceptance automata with parallelism that are executed stepwise, provides several advantages over existing SD-based testing techniques, namely regarding the kinds of interactions, operators, conformance modes, and semantics (weak sequencing) supported. The tool was successfully experimented on a set of case studies, one of which was presented. Despite being implemented for specific technologies, the overall approach can be applied for other technologies.

As future work, we plan to: support other modeling environments (reusing the runtime library); support additional modeling features (such as duration constraints and the 'neg', 'ignore', and 'consider' operators); support a semantic option without lifeline synchronization at decision points; extend the abstract user interaction modeling and testing features for GUIs (which, currently, can be handled in a non-abstract way); integrate with approaches for the automatic generation of values for scenario parameters; extend the test execution engine to support the testing of distributed systems; conduct further experiments to assess our approach compared to others.

References

1. OMG Unified Modeling Language™ (OMG UML), Superstructure, v. 2.4.1, OMG (2011)
2. Mellor, S.J., Clark, A.N., Futagami, T.: Model-Driven Development. IEEE Software Magazine 20(5), 14–18 (2003)

3. Uttin, M., Legeard, B.: Practical Model-Based Testing: A Tools Approach. Morgan Kaufmann (2007)
4. Faria, J.P., Paiva, A., Yang, Z.: Test Generation from UML Sequence Diagrams. In: 8th Int. Conf. on the Quality of Information and Communications Technology, pp. 245–250 (2012)
5. JUnit testing framework, http://www.junit.org
6. Enterprise Architect, http://www.sparxsystems.com.au
7. AspectJ, http://www.eclipse.org/aspectj
8. Gamma, E., Helm, R., Johnson, R., Vlissides, J.: Design Patterns: Elements of Reusable Object-Oriented Software. Pearson Education (1994)
9. Stotts, P.D., Pugh, W.: Parallel Finite Automata for Modeling Concurrent Software Systems. J. of Software and Systems 27, 27–43 (1994)
10. Micskei, Z., Waeselynck, H.: The Many Meanings of UML 2 Sequence Diagrams: a Survey. J. of Software and Systems Modeling 10, 489–514 (2011)
11. Castro, M.V.: Automating Scenario Based Testing with UML and AOP, http://www.fe.up.pt/~ei06064/AutomatingSBTwithUMLandAOP.pdf (in Portuguese)
12. Harel, D., Maoz, S.: Assert and Negate Revisited: Modal Semantics for UML Sequence Diagrams. J. of Software and Systems Modeling 7(2), 237–253 (2008)
13. Hallal, H., Boroday, S., Petrenko, A., Ulrich, A.: A Formal Approach to Property Testing in Causally Consistent Distributed Traces. Formal Aspects of Computing 18(1), 63–83 (2006)
14. Knapp, A., Wuttke, J.: Model Checking of UML 2.0 Interactions. In: Kühne, T. (ed.) MoDELS 2006. LNCS, vol. 4364, pp. 42–51. Springer, Heidelberg (2007)
15. Briand, L., Labiche, Y., Leduc, J.: Towards the Reverse Engineering of UML Sequence Diagrams for Distributed Java Software. IEEE Trans. on Soft. Eng. 32(9), 642–663 (2006)
16. Kansomkeat, S., Offutt, J., Abdurazik, A., Baldini, A.: A Comparative Evaluation of Tests Generated from Different UML Diagrams. In: SNPD 2008, pp. 867–872 (2008)
17. Philip, S., Joseph, A.T.: Test Sequence Generation from UML Sequence Diagrams. In: SNPD 2008, pp. 879–887 (2008)
18. Samuel, P., Mall, R.: A Novel Test Case Design Technique using Dynamic Slicing of UML Sequence Diagrams. e-Informatica 2(1), 71–92 (2008)
19. Nayak, A., Samanta, D.: Automatic Test Data Synthesis using UML Sequence Diagrams. J. of Object Technology 9(2), 115–144 (2010)
20. Benattou, M., Bruel, J., Hameurlain, N.: Generating Test Data from OCL Specification. In: ECOOP Workshop Integration and Transformation of UML Models (2002)
21. Engels, G., Güldali, B., Lohmann, M.: Towards Model-Driven Unit Testing. In: Kühne, T. (ed.) MoDELS 2006. LNCS, vol. 4364, pp. 182–192. Springer, Heidelberg (2007)
22. Fraikin, F., Leonhardt, T.: SeDiTeC-testing based on sequence diagrams. In: Proc. of the 17th IEEE Int. Conf. on Automated Software Engineering (ASE 2002). IEEE (2002)
23. Wittevrongel, J., Maurer, F.: SCENTOR: Scenario-Based Testing of E-Business Applications. In: 2nd Int. Workshop on Automation of Software Test (AST) (2007)
24. Javed, A., Strooper, P., Watson, G.: Automated Generation of Test Cases using Model-Driven Architecture. In: 2nd Int. Workshop on Automation of Software Test (AST) (2007)
25. IBM® Rational® Rhapsody® Automatic Test Conductor Add On User Guide, v2.5.2 (2013)
26. Boroday, S., Petrenko, A., Ulrich, A.: Implementing MSC Tests with Quiescence Observation. In: Núñez, M., Baker, P., Merayo, M.G. (eds.) TESTCOM 2009. LNCS, vol. 5826, pp. 49–65. Springer, Heidelberg (2009)

Parallel SMT-Constrained Symbolic Execution for Eclipse CDT/Codan

Andreas Ibing

Chair for IT Security TU München
Boltzmannstrasse 3, 85748 Garching, Germany

Abstract. This paper presents a parallel symbolic execution engine as a plug-in extension to Eclipse CDT/Codan. It uses the CDT parser and the control flow graph builder from CDT's code analysis framework (Codan). Path satisfiability and bug conditions are checked with an SMT solver in the logic of arrays, uninterpreted functions and nonlinear integer and real arithmetic (AUFNIRA). Each worker of the parallel engine keeps the symbolic program states along its current program path in memory, to allow for quick backtracking. Dynamic redistribution of work between workers is enabled by splitting a worker's partition of the execution tree at the partition's top decision node, where a partition is defined by the start path leading to its root control flow decision node. The runtime behaviour of the parallel symbolic execution engine is evaluated by running it on buffer overflow test programs from the NSA's Juliet test suite for static analyzers. Both the speedup of backtracking the symbolic program state over a previous single-threaded implementation with path replay and the speedup with an increasing number of workers are investigated.

1 Introduction

Symbolic execution (SE, [1]) is an attractive approach for automated discovery of common software weaknesses. SE treats program input as variables and translates operations on them into logic equations. For a path through a program, SE builds a path constraint from the control flow decisions. Path satisfiability and the presence of bugs is decided with an automatic theorem prover (constraint solver [2,3]). Current SE tools normally rely on Satisfiability Modulo Theories (SMT, [4]) solvers. A more detailed overview of the current state and available tools is given in [5,6].

Many SE tools first transform the source code into an intermediate representation (IR) and run the symbolic execution on the IR. In [7], C/C++ code is compiled into LLVM [8] bytecode before symbolic execution, while [9] uses CIL [10] as intermediate code. [11] analyzes Java bytecode with symbolic execution.

In order to achieve high code coverage in a limited time, parallelization of SE has been investigated. [12] presents a parallelized version of [11], which initially performs a breadth-first exploration of the symbolic execution tree up to a certain depth, and then runs multiple workers on disjunct static partitions

H. Yenigün, C. Yilmaz, and A. Ulrich (Eds.): ICTSS 2013, LNCS 8254, pp. 196–206, 2013.

of the execution tree. [13] presents a parallelized version of [7] with dynamic redistribution of work between workers.

While SE of intermediate code does have its advantages, there is also a motivation for symbolic execution of source code: an IR loses source information by discarding high-level types and the compiler lowers language constructs and makes assumptions about the evaluation order. However, rich source and type information is needed to explain discovered bugs to the user [14].

In order to detect errors as early as possible, bug detection tools should be integrated into IDEs. The Eclipse IDE is widely used, open source and designed for extensibility (OSGi architecture [15]). For C/C++ development, Eclipse CDT features a code analysis framework (Codan, [16]), which includes a control flow graph (CFG) builder and several code checkers. Codan does not, however, feature path-sensitivity or symbolic execution, which may lead to detection inaccuracies for many analyses (false negative and false positive detections).

This paper presents a parallelized SMT-constrained symbolic execution engine with dynamic work redistribution and backtracking of symbolic program states as plug-in extension for Eclipse CDT. It builds on previous work [17], which developed a sequential SE engine with replay of start paths after backtracking path decisions. The remainder of this paper is organized as follows. Architecture and design are described in section 2. Section 3 evaluates the implementation with buffer overflow test programs from the Juliet test suite [18] and benchmarks both the speedup of backtracking symbolic program states over [17] and the speedup with a varying number of workers. Section 4 discusses the results.

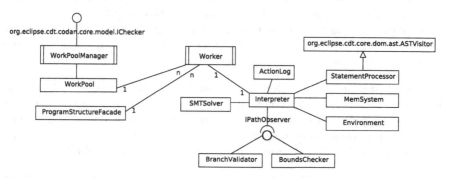

Fig. 1. Overview of main classes. WorkPoolManager and Worker are active classes.

2 Architecture and Design

2.1 Trade-offs in Memory, Computation, Communication and Parallelism

The exploration of (at least a finite) execution tree can in principle be performed in a straight-forward manner with the Worklist algorithm [19], in which unexplored tree nodes (frontier nodes) are put together with the corresponding symbolic program state in a work list (queue-based tree traversal). In practice however, this may lead to memory exhaustion, even in distributed computation setups.

An alternative to reduce memory consumption is to store program paths without symbolic program states. A program path can further be compressed as a sequence of branches. Minimum memory consumption is achieved when only one path and one program state are kept in memory. This approach was used in [17] for a sequential implementation with depth-first exploration of the execution tree (with a configurable loop depth bound). Restoration of a program state for an unexplored (frontier) node, on the other hand, requires redundant computation along the new start path.

The memory versus computation trade-off extends to storing the history of program states along a path (which requires memory) versus the possibility of restoring a program state on this path by backtracking (which avoids redundant computation). The symbolic program state can be backtracked as far as the required information (variable definitions, equations, etc.) is available. Thus, there are effectively three possibilities:

Path replay: only the current symbolic program state is kept in memory, with the possibility for garbage collection of dead symbolic variables. The current path's control flow decisions are used to generate the next path [17].

State cloning: the open symbolic program states (frontier states) are kept in memory. The program state at a decision node is cloned for each child branch node. This is used in a distributed implementation in [13].

State backtracking: program states along the current path are kept in memory. This can be efficiently implemented using single assignment form and not garbage-collecting dead symbolic variables. This approach is used here.

In a parallelized implementation, it is desirable to balance computation complexity and communication complexity. The communication complexity can be rated differently for communication between multiple threads on a shared memory architecture (multi-core and/or hyper-threading CPUs) versus network communication in a distributed setup. There are basically two possibilities:

- symbolic program states are transmitted to new or idle workers (requires state cloning), or
- start paths are transmitted to new or idle workers (less transmitted data, but path replay is needed).

The most adequate parallelization depends on the available hardware resources as well as the size of the software to be analyzed.

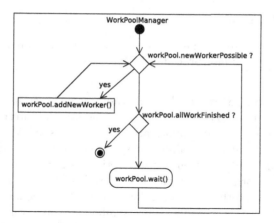

Fig. 2. Activity diagram of WorkPoolManager. WorkPool is used as synchronization object.

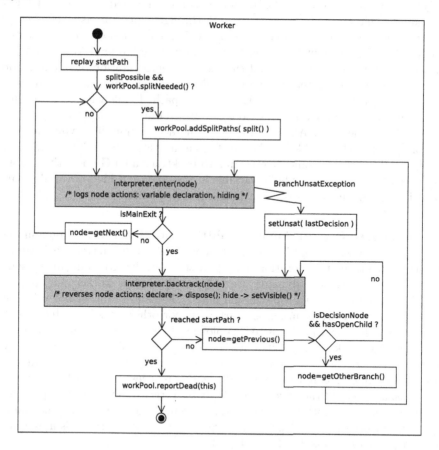

Fig. 3. Activity diagram of Worker. WorkPool is used as synchronization object.

2.2   Design Decisions

The symbolic execution engine performs whole-program analysis with a call string approach [20] for interprocedural analysis.

Symbolic Program State and Backtracking. The translation into SMT logic is the same as in [17]. For program variables, the interpretation generates symbolic variables, whose values are logic formulas in SMTLIB AUFNIRA syntax. The formulas may contain other symbolic variables as terms. Symbolic variables must not be overwritten (no destructive assignments) if they might still be needed in other formulas. A variable is called 'live' if it may still be needed in the future, and 'dead' otherwise. Therefore single assignments are used: for each assignment to a program variable, a new symbolic variable version with unique name is generated. Pointers and structs are not directly translated into SMT logic, they are represented internally during interpretation (e.g. a pointer has a target and an offset formula). Logic equations are generated at pointer dereference and at field access to a struct. A path through a program is a sequence of control flow graph nodes along edges in the CFG, and function calls are treated as edges between different functions' CFGs. A symbolic program state comprises all declared symbolic variables and the internal representation of pointers and structs along a program path. Due to single assignment form, a symbolic program state contains all previous states along the path. To allow for backtracking, an ActionLog keeps track of the actions performed during interpretation of each CFG node on the path. An action may be the declaration of a symbolic variable or hiding stack variables at the exit from a function. Through backtracking, 'dead' variables may become 'live' again. To backtrack a CFG node, the actions are reversed: a declared symbolic variable is disposed, and hidden variables are set visible again (in case of backtracking a function exit).

Execution Tree Exploration and Splitting into Subtrees. A configurable number of workers analyzes disjunct partitions of the execution tree. Each worker performs a depth-first exploration of its partition with backtracking of the symbolic program state. For dynamic work redistribution, a worker can split its partition at the partition's top decision node. The child branches not taken by the current worker are returned as start paths for other workers. After a split, the partition start path is adjusted (prolonged by one branch node). Analysis starts with one worker, who splits until the configured number of workers is busy. A worker is initialized by replaying its partition start path. The maximum loop depth to be explored can be bounded. If a worker reaches an unsatisfiable branch or a satisfiable leaf of the execution tree, it backtracks and changes a path decision according to depth-first tree traversal. If backtracking reaches the end of the partition start path, the partition is exhausted. The algorithm is illustrated in the activity diagrams Fig. 2 and Fig. 3.

2.3 Main Classes

A diagram of the main classes is shown in Fig. 1. The implementation is multi-threaded, where control flow graphs and syntax trees are shared between worker threads.

WorkPoolManager extends Codan at the extension point org.eclipse.cdt.codan.core.model.IChecker. The WorkPoolManager starts workers and reports found errors through the Codan interface to the Eclipse marker framework.

ProgramStructureFacade provides access to control flow graphs.

WorkPool is used as synchronization object (synchronized methods). It is used to track the number of active workers and to exchange split paths.

Worker has a forward and a backward (backtracking) mode. It passes references to control flow graph nodes for entry (forward mode) or backtracking to the Interpreter.

Interpreter follows the tree-based interpreter pattern [21]. SMT syntax is generated by the StatementProcessor (which implements CDT's ASTVisitor) by bottom-up traversal of AST subtrees (visitor pattern), which are referenced by CFG nodes. Symbolic variables are stored in and retrieved from Mem-System. Backtracking additionally relies on ActionLog, which links certain actions to nodes on the current path, like hiding stack variables at function exit. The Environment class provides symbolic models of Standard library functions. The interpreter further offers an interface to BranchValidator and to checker classes.

SMTSolver wraps the interface to the currently used external solver, which is [22].

BranchValidator is triggered when entering a branch node. It generates a satisfiability query for the path constraint. For an unsatisfiable branch it throws an exception, which is caught by the worker.

BoundsChecker is triggered for memory access. It generates satisfiability queries for violation of lower and upper buffer bounds and reports an error in case of satisfiability.

2.4 Communication and Synchronization

Activity diagrams for the active classes are shown in Fig. 2 and Fig. 3. Synchronization of multiple local worker threads for sharing control flow graphs and abstract syntax trees (ASTs) relies on the following methods:

WorkPool all methods are synchronized. The WorkPoolManager waits if the configured number of workers is busy or no further split path is available and is notified for changes (compare Fig. 2).

ProgramStructureFacade offers synchronized methods to retrieve CFG references.

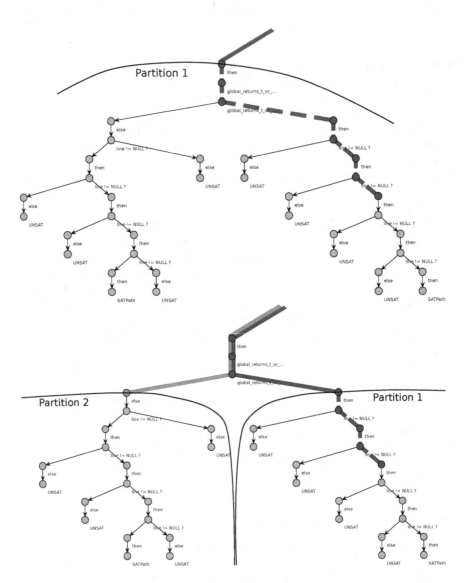

Fig. 4. Illustration of the partition split operation. Red indicates worker 1, green worker 2. Partition start paths are indicated with solid lines, the current worker state with a dashed line. Partition borders are indicated by curves and the text "Partition n". Unexplored parts of the execution tree are shaded.

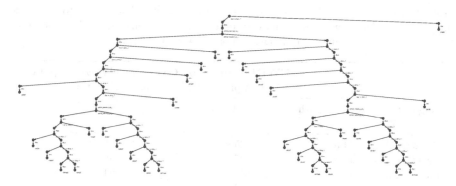

Fig. 5. Example execution tree (showing only decision and branch nodes) for test program CWE121_char_type_overrun_memcpy_12 from the Juliet test suite [18]. The subtree on the lower left was used to illustrate the partition split operation in Fig. 4.

AST nodes are not thread-safe, so Workers lock AST subtrees at the CFG node level (the AST subtree which is referenced by the currently interpreted CFG node).

Index each CDT project has an index, which is the persisted document object model (DOM). Access results in (possibly blocking) I/O operations on a database stored in small files, so that workers acquire a read lock for accesses.

The split operation is illustrated in Fig. 4, which shows part of the execution tree of the Juliet test program CWE121_char_type_overrun_memcpy_12. The tree shows only decision nodes and branch nodes; other CFG node types are not shown. A path through the execution tree normally contains alternating decision nodes and branch nodes. This example tree contains an exception because of a function call expression in a decision node (corresponding to a function call in the condition of an if-statement). This leads to a repetition of the decision node as a call node, so that the interpreter can conveniently continue interpretation with the return value.

The unexplored part of the (sub)tree is shaded. Red lines indicate the paths which have been explored by worker 1, green lines correspond to worker 2. Partition start paths are shown as solid lines, and a dashed line indicates the current position of a worker. Worker 1 splits its partition and generates a split path, which becomes start path for worker 2. After the partition split, worker 1's start path is prolonged by one branch node.

The execution tree is normally not generated during analysis, it is only traversed on-the-fly. The complete execution tree for this example is shown in Fig. 5.

2.5 Visualization

CFGs and explored execution trees can be visualized with the Java Universal Network/Graph library (JUNG, [23]) and exported as vector graphics with Apache Batik [24]. These two libraries are therefore loaded as Eclipse plug-ins. Execution tree visualization has been used for Fig. 4, 5.

Table 1. Duration of analysis for two sets of test programs from Juliet (on a quad-core processor). Shows increase of analysis speed for backtracking the symbolic program state over path replay and for different number of worker threads.

	CWE121_memcpy (18 test programs)	CWE121_CWE129_fgets (30 test programs)
Single-threaded with path-replay [17]	131 s	1026 s
Backtracking, 1 Thread	25 s	102 s
Backtracking, 2 Threads	27 s	58 s
Backtracking, 3 Threads	31 s	54 s
Backtracking, 4 Threads	33 s	54 s

3   Evaluation

The parallelized symbolic execution engine is evaluated with stack based buffer overflow test programs from the Juliet suite [18]. In order to achieve a certain coverage of bugs, language constructs and context depths, Juliet combines 'baseline' bugs with different control and data flow variants into test programs. The test programs contain 'good' functions in addition to 'bad' functions to provide enough possibilities for false positive detections. Juliet contains 39 flow variants for C programs, and the maximum context depth spanned by a flow variant (flow 54) is five functions in five different source files (necessary context depth for accurate bug detection for that flow). The flows are not numbered consecutively.

Two sets of test programs are used, which contain buffer overflows with the *memcpy* (set 1) and *fgets* (set 2) functions. Analyses are run with time measurement as JUnit plug-in tests in Eclipse. Run times are only evaluated for those programs for which bug detection is accurate, i.e. no false positives and no false negatives. Therefore flow 18 is excluded, because it contains a goto statement which leads to an exception in the current version of the CFGBuilder, resulting in a false negative detection. Flow 54 uses unions, which is not yet implemented in the translation to SMT syntax, also resulting in a false negative. A false positive occurs for flow 66, because the current solver version (version 5.1.9 is used) gives an incorrect satisfiability answer for the corresponding mixture of array logic and arithmetic. On the other hand, accurate detection is achieved for flow 12: the solver reports that the contained modulo function is not yet implemented, but luckily guesses the correct satisfiability answer. As in [17], bugs have been accurately detected with 36 of the 39 C flow variants (90%), while the percentage of detectable 'baseline' bugs is unsatisfying, because only a small part of the standard library functions is interpreted.

Table 1 shows benchmarks for single-thread execution with path replay, single-thread execution with backtracking, and multi-threaded execution with partition splitting for a varying number of threads. The plug-in is run in Eclipse 4.2 on a Core 2 Quad CPU Q9550 on 64-bit Linux kernel 3.2.0. Even for the tiny test programs, backtracking already shows a 5-10x speedup over path replay.

The overhead of partition splits and thread creation hampers multi-threading speedup, and actually leads to a setback for the tiny *memcpy* programs. The *fgets* test programs contain several loops, which leads to bigger execution trees and a 2x speedup with 3 threads.

4   Discussion

This paper presented a parallelized symbolic execution engine with Eclipse CDT integration and showed significant speedup over a previous sequential implementation. Workers are run as multiple local threads on shared control flow graphs and syntax trees. While the symbolic execution currently aims at path coverage (with a loop depth bound), less comprehensive coverage criteria also need to be supported in order to scale analyses to bigger programs. Future work includes a straightforward extension to a distributed setup with a dynamic two-level hierarchical partitioning of the execution tree (first over Eclipse processes on different machines, then over local threads).

Acknowledgement. This work has been partially funded by the German Ministry for Education and Research (BMBF) under grant 01IS13020.

References

1. King, J.: Symbolic execution and program testing. Communications of the ACM 19(7), 385–394 (1976)
2. Dechter, R.: Constraint Processing. Morgan Kaufmann Publishers (2003)
3. Harrison, J.: Handbook of Practical Logic and Automated Reasoning. Cambridge University Press (2009)
4. Barrett, C., Stump, A., Tinelli, C.: The SMT-LIB Standard Version 2.0 (December 2010),
   http://goedel.cs.uiowa.edu/smtlib/papers/
   smt-lib-reference-v2.0-r10.12.21.pdf
5. Cadar, C., Sen, K., Godefroid, P., Tillmann, N., Khurshid, S., Visser, W., Pasareanu, C.: Symbolic execution for software testing in practice – preliminary assessment. In: Int. Conf. Software Eng. (2011)
6. Pasareanu, C., Visser, W.: A survey of new trends in symbolic execution for software testing and analysis. Int. J. Software Tools Technology Transfer 11, 339–353 (2009)
7. Cadar, C., Dunbar, D., Engler, D.: KLEE: Unassisted and automatic generation of high-coverage tests for complex systems programs. In: USENIX Symp. Operating Systems Design and Implementation (2008)
8. Lattner, C., Adve, V.: LLVM: A compilation framework for lifelong program analysis and transformation. In: Int. Symp. Code Generation and Optimization (2004)
9. Correnson, L., et al.: FRAMA-C User Manual, release oxygen-20120901. CEA LIST (2012), http://frama-c.com/download/frama-c-user-manual.pdf
10. Necula, G.C., McPeak, S., Rahul, S.P., Weimer, W.: CIL: Intermediate language and tools for analysis and transformation of C programs. In: Nigel Horspool, R. (ed.) CC 2002. LNCS, vol. 2304, pp. 213–228. Springer, Heidelberg (2002), http://dl.acm.org/citation.cfm?id=647478.727796

11. Visser, W., Pasareanu, C., Khurshid, S.: Test input generation with Java Pathfinder. In: Int. Symp. Software Testing and Analysis (2004)
12. Staats, M., Pasareanu, C.: Parallel symbolic execution for structural test generation. In: Int. Symp. Software Testing and Analysis, pp. 183–193 (2010)
13. Bucur, S., Ureche, V., Candea, G.: Parallel symbolic execution for automated real-world software testing. In: EuroSys (2011)
14. Kremenek, T.: Finding software bugs with the Clang static analyzer. LLVM Developers' Meeting (August 2008),
    http://llvm.org/devmtg/2008-08/Kremenek_StaticAnalyzer.pdf
15. Archer, S., VanderLei, P., McAffer, J.: OSGi and Equinox: Creating Highly Modular Java Systems. Addison Wesley (2010)
16. Laskavaia, A.: Codan- C/C++ static analysis framework for CDT. In: EclipseCon (2011)
17. Ibing, A.: SMT-constrained symbolic execution for Eclipse CDT/Codan. In: Workshop on Formal Methods in the Development of Software (2013)
18. United States National Security Agency, Center for Assured Software: Juliet Test Suite v1.1 for C/C++ (December 2011),
    http://samate.nist.gov/SRD/testCases/suites/
    Juliet_Test_Suite_v1.1_for_C_Cpp.zip
19. Nielson, F., Nielson, H., Hankin, C.: Principles of Program Analysis. Springer (2010)
20. Sharir, M., Pnueli, A.: Two approaches to interprocedural data flow analysis. In: Muchnik, S., Jones, N. (eds.) Program Flow Analysis: Theory and Applications, pp. 189–233. Prentice-Hall (1981)
21. Parr, T.: Language Implementation Patterns. Pragmatic Bookshelf (2010)
22. Cimatti, A., Griggio, A., Schaafsma, B.J., Sebastiani, R.: The mathSAT5 SMT solver. In: Piterman, N., Smolka, S.A. (eds.) TACAS 2013 (ETAPS 2013). LNCS, vol. 7795, pp. 93–107. Springer, Heidelberg (2013)
23. Madadhain, J., Fisher, D., Smyth, P., White, S., Boey, Y.: Analysis and visualization of network data using JUNG. J. Statistical Software (2005)
24. Apache: Batik Java svg toolkit, http://xmlgraphics.apache.org/batik/

Challenges of Testing Periodic Messages in Avionics Systems Using TTCN-3

Bernard Stepien and Liam Peyton

University of Ottawa - EECS
800 King Edward Ave Ottawa, ON K1N 6N5, Canada
{Bernard,lpeyton}@eecs.uOttawa.ca

Abstract. The TTCN-3 language was conceived initially for testing telecommunications protocols that consist of sequences of discrete messages between communicating entities. TTCN-3 has a clear model of separation of concerns between an abstract layer, where test behavior is specified, and a concrete layer, where messages are encoded / decoded and sent and received to/from the system under test. This model, however, is cumbersome for testing protocols with periodic messages as used in avionics systems. This paper presents an innovative approach to addressing issues involving periodic messages in TTCN-3, based on our experiences working with avionics systems. Extensions to the TTCN-3 standard are proposed, based on our approach. We also demonstrate how the approach can be used for test system certification and requirements verification for avionics systems.

Keywords: periodic messages, testing, TTCN-3, avionics.

1 Introduction

TTCN-3 [1] is a language and international standard that was initially conceived specifically for testing telecommunications protocols that consist of complex exchanges of messages that offer both alternative and interleaved behaviors. TTCN-3 has a clear model of separation of concerns between an abstract layer that specifies the test behavior of a System Under Test (SUT) and a concrete layer that encodes and decodes messages that are sent to and received from the SUT. The link between the two layers is an abstract representation of data that enables the use of generic tools not requiring any programming effort from the user to perform the matching of received data with test oracles as shown in Fig. 1. The matching mechanism is a central concept in TTCN-3.

Telecommunications system protocols are usually composed of a limited number of discrete messages. However, avionics systems that use periodic messages send or receive possibly very large series of messages with an identical payload at precise time intervals. In contrast to telecommunications protocols, protocols with periodic messages are mostly based on unacknowledged communication using the UDP protocol in broadcast mode. This is mostly due to the fact that the repetition of the same message will ensure that at least a minimum amount of messages will eventually get through and thus maintain the receiving system in a stable state. The periodicity is also verified by the receiving entity to determine if a message is not obsolete and thus

H. Yenigün, C. Yilmaz, and A. Ulrich (Eds.): ICTSS 2013, LNCS 8254, pp. 207–222, 2013.

should be used. Finally, an important feature of periodic messages is that sequence numbers are used to determine if a message is not obsolete since they do not use any confirmation mechanisms. These sequence numbers are the only data element that varies from one message to the next in the otherwise identical payload.

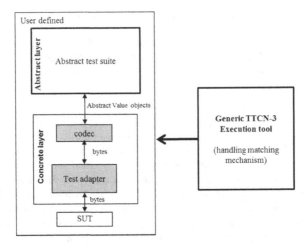

Fig. 1. The TTCN-3 separation of concerns model

This paper presents an innovative approach to addressing issues involving periodic messages in TTCN-3, based on our experiences working with avionics systems. Extensions to the TTCN-3 standard are proposed, based on our approach. We also demonstrate how the approach can be used for test system certification and requirements verification for avionics systems

2   Background

Various extensions to TTCN-3 have already been developed for other application domains. The extension for continuous signals [4] [19] introduces the notions of time, sampling, streams, stream ports, stream variables and the definition of an automaton similar to control flow structure to support the specification of hybrid behavior. The extension for real time requirements [16][17] introduces a test system wide available system clock and means to access the time points of the relevant interaction events between the test system and the system under test (SUT) with precision, namely to avoid delays caused by the test tool's processing. The extension for static test configuration and deployment [14] introduces a concept of special configuration function which can only be called in the control part of a TTCN-3 test suite. This consists in defining static test components that straddle several test case executions and have the result of not resetting timers and message queues. The extension for extended parameterization [17] introduces extended value and type parameterization for the various TTCN-3 parametric language elements. The extension for behavior type [18] allows defining types for altsteps, functions and test case to render them parametric. The extension for extended TRI [20] introduces the capability to pass abstract values from the abstract to the concrete layer, thus bypassing the codec step as shown in Fig. 1. Early use of TTCN-3 is reported for avionics testing in the context of automated test case generation. An approach to periodic messages using the current version of the TTCN-3 language has been attempted using procedure oriented testing [5]. However, avionics systems use messages based on structured data types, similar to telecommunications messages, for which message oriented testing would seem more appropriate.

3   Periodic Messages and the TTCN-3 Model

3.1   Differences between Discrete and Periodic Message Systems

There are conceptual differences between protocols of systems that use discrete messages and those that use periodic messages. In systems with discrete messages each message is unique and usually only occurs once or a limited number of times. Also, messages usually occur in a given sequence that can be strict as shown in Fig. 2 or follow more complex patterns of interleaving.

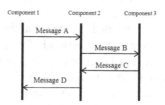

Fig. 2. Discrete message protocol

In systems with periodic messages, such as the ARINC 629 protocol [9], a given message is repeated automatically potentially a large number of times either with identical content or minor differences in content as shown on Fig. 3. Most of these messages are sent to the avionics system by various sensors but less frequent messages are also originating from the avionics equipment side to indicate status. More challenging is the case where heterogeneous messages of different types occur concurrently and over the same communication medium.

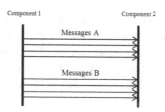

Fig. 3. Periodic messages systems

The typical TTCN-3 separation of concerns requires unnecessary repeated encoding or decoding of identical messages. To avoid this redundancy, we propose a new approach that consists in handling periodicity in the concrete instead of the abstract layer as shown on Fig. 4. Messages are sent only once by the abstract layer until the content needs to be changed and received by the abstract layer only when the data received in the concrete layer has changed. There is a difference between handling messages that are sent and messages that are received. Periodic identical messages being sent need to be encoded only once and are first sent to a scheduler that handles the periodicity. A mechanism updates the data buffer containing the encoded message whenever content changes and controls the scheduler to modify periodicity.

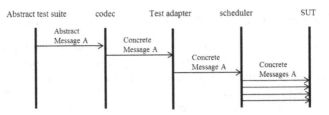

Fig. 4. Separation of concerns for sending periodic messages

Messages being received are handled through traditional asynchronous receiving threads, but, with a major difference that consists in first checking if a newly received message is identical to the previously received message merely by comparing their bytes, i.e. without first decoding the message. If there is a change, the received message is en-queued and presented to the abstract layer for matching with test oracles as shown on Fig. 5. If the content has not changed, the message is discarded.

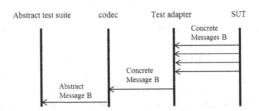

Fig. 5. Separation of concerns for receiving periodic messages

This approach is particularly efficient in the case of concurrent periodic messages of different types which would present enormous interleaving challenges if taken raw. Also, this approach results in the specification of changes of message content that appear in the abstract test suite as if they were discrete messages, thus removing the complexity that concurrent message types would create if their periodicity would be handled in the abstract level.

One of the major features of TTCN-3 is logging. Each message sent or received is logged by the test execution tools and thus enables efficient tracing. Although logging is mostly a feature of TTCN-3 execution tools except for the TTCN-3 explicit log statement, there is no standardization of logging as such. Logging remains the concern of tool providers. However, since each message is logged, periodic messages inevitably would produce a massive amount of logging making analysis of results tedious if not impossible. Various tools provide log filtering features based on parallel test components, but these would not be usable for periodic messages. Solutions have been found by tool providers that produce logs only when messages have changed. These solutions are not portable from one tool to another from different vendors because there are not covered by the standard and each vendor may choose a different approach. Also, the requirement specific to the avionics industry of using a scheduler [8] makes the handling of periodicity by the abstract layer useless by definition. The implementation at the concrete layer requires dispatching messages arriving through the *triSend()* method to the appropriate message type data buffer that is then used by the scheduler as shown on Fig. 6.

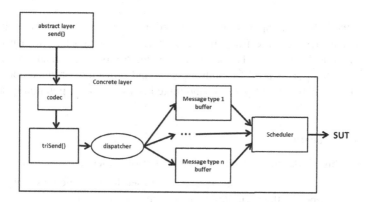

Fig. 6. Concrete layer architecture for periodic messages

In avionics, reducing weight is a prime preoccupation. This includes reducing the needs for equipment of all sorts including networking equipment such as cables. This is achieved by using data concentrators that receive data from nearby sensors or other equipment on a many to one principle and then forward an assembled complex message to the final destination (cockpit) on a single cable. Different message have different periodicity or may even be aperiodic which requires the use of the concept of scheduler that is subject to intense research such as in [11] [22] [23]. It is the scheduler that computes sequence numbers. One of our findings was that the requirement of schedulers naturally eliminates the use of parallel test components that is one of the central concepts of TTCN-3.

3.2   Proposed Changes to the TTCN-3 Language

While a prototype of this model has been fully implemented in the concrete layer with the current version of the TTCN-3 standard and thus using a general purpose object oriented language, some modifications to the TTCN-3 language would provide a more rigorous approach by enabling one to specify the test fully at the abstract level leaving the implementation details as built-in features in the hands of TTCN-3 tool providers rather than the users, thus preserving semantics across TTCN-3 tools. TTCN-3 is a strongly typed language. For periodic messages, there are a number of enhancements that would allow mostly checking the use of operations that are specific to periodic messages and cannot be used for discrete messages protocols. We list our proposed changes here.

Port Declarations

The port declaration for messages needs an additional keyword periodic to indicate that the messages are periodic as for example.

```
port myPort periodic message {
   inout MyPeriodicMesssageType;
}
```

Also, in the industrial applications we studied, there were cases where both periodic and discrete messages are using the same port. This would lead to a need for a mixed communication mode. The keyword mixed, by itself is already reserved for indicating that the port is used for both message and procedure oriented communication. Here the combination of periodic and mixed keyword could potentially solve the problem.

Data Type Declarations

There are three differences in data typing for periodic messages:

- Specify that the data type is to be used for periodic messages only.
- Specify the periodicity and any changes thereof.
- Handling sequence numbers.

Specifying the Periodic Nature of the Message and Its Periodicity

The first two differences for data typing periodic messages involves specifying the time interval between sending two periodic messages and determining if received messages are received at time intervals that exceed the periodicity threshold in which case a timeout event should be reported to the abstract level. This consists in the capability to specify both an initial or default periodicity and also new periodicities in the course of a test sequence. The initial periodicity would be part of the data type declaration itself rather than a port declaration since a port can be used for different message types that could have different periodicities or even aperiodic messages. For example to specify an initial periodicity (default) of 30 ms we would use the following syntax:

```
type record MyType periodic 0.030 {
   // field definitions
}
```

However, one test purpose could be the variation of the periodicity to trigger faults in the SUT and verify that they occur. For that purpose we also need a new abstract language construct in order to be able to specify modifications of the periodicity in a similar way as TTCN-3 enables modifying the values of timers with a fundamental difference that with timers we use a timer instance while with data types we use the data type name only. This is based on the fact that for periodic messages data types we have only one method that handles this periodic data type in the test adapter. We propose the method name *setperiodicity* with a float value that is applied to a data type name for this purpose as for example:

`MyPeriodicType.`**`setperiodicity`**`(0.100);`

Another aspect of periodicity could be that the periodicity would be different whether the messages are sent or received. This issue certainly would arise with concrete telecommunication messages where a given message type is used in both directions but our experience with periodic messages shows that periodic messages have a different data type depending on the direction. Thus, that distinction is not a priority but must be considered as future work. This feature also requires a mirror method in the standard test adapter class: *triSetPeriodicity(Object datatype, double periodicity)*.

Handling Sequence Numbers

Sequence numbers must also be handled differently for periodic messages. Normally, each message has a different sequence number whether the payload is the same or not. Since the periodicity is handled in the concrete layer, the scheduler is responsible for assigning the correct sequence numbers. Thus, when creating a template at the abstract layer, the sequence number field should not be instantiated. This is somewhat similar to the treatment of optional fields. This means that a sequence number field can be omitted without producing a compile time error as for mandatory fields. Here the field is merely ignored in the abstract layer but we still need to declare what the initial and maximal values that the concrete layer should automatically compute are. Thus, we propose the new keyword *concrete* to indicate that a field is computed in the concrete layer and two keywords to indicate its starting and maximal value. The maximal value is used for in fact resetting the value to the starting value when the maximum is reached.

```
type record MyPeriodicMessageType {
  integer myConcreteField concrete startvalue 0
                          maximumvalue 32000,
  // more fields definitions }
```

Here again, methods to access the start and maximum values should be provided by the *triAdapter* class in order for the scheduler to access them.

Updating Individual Field Values

Real time constraints of systems that use periodic messages call for minimizing the amount of data being manipulated especially in the codec. In particular, it is important to avoid having to encode an entire record when only the value of a minimal amount of fields has changed. Thus, there needs to be a separate keyword for sending only a new value for a given field when all the remaining fields remain constant. We propose the keyword update with three parameters, one that indicates the data type, one for the field name and finally one for the new value as for example:

```
myPort.update(MyPediodicDataType, aFieldName, 45000);
```

This abstract layer keyword requires a corresponding method *triUpdate()* in the TriAdapter abstract class defined in the TTCN-3 standard [13] that must be implemented exactly like the *triSend()* method that corresponds to the abstract send() command. However, the update command has another challenge, it requires late coding since it affects only a small portion of the persistent data buffer used by the scheduler. Effectively the traditional model of sequence of actions –abstract send-message encoding-concrete *triSend* cannot be used since only a portion of a message is encoded with the updated value. Thus, the *triUpdate()* method will receive an abstract value in its parameter. The implementation of this method consists in making the appropriate modification to the data buffer corresponding to the specified data type and this remains the responsibility of the user.

Timeout and Out of Sequence Events

For receiving periodic message, we propose a concept of timeout event associated with the data type rather than a concept of timer at the abstract level. This is due partly to the fact that periodicity is an implicit timer that thus does not need to be specified as such but also because periodicity is by definition associated with a specific data type. Thus we propose an abstract language construct with the keyword *periodictimeout* that has a data type as an argument and that is associated with a port instance as follows:

```
myPort.periodictimeout(MyMessageType);
```

However, this timeout is triggered by a timer in the concrete layer that should be built-in and thus implemented by the TTCN-3 execution tool provider specifically for periodic messages only and not by the user.

Consequently, when a timeout occurs in the concrete layer, a timeout event should be en-queued on the message queue.

The setting or checking of out of order sequence numbers can be specified in a similar way. For checking out of sequence messages being received we use an out of sequence indicator event that indicates the data type and the field name in which sequence numbers are stored as follows:

```
myPort.outofsequence(MyMessageType, myFieldName);
```

However, when sending messages, while the periodicity is naturally controlled with the *setperiodicity* construct, provoking out of sequence messages for testing the response to such a situation by the SUT is not as simple. Here we need to specify which sequence numbers need to be interchanged without really knowing at which state the sequence numbers are in since they are computed by the scheduler. Thus we propose a concept of relative position of sequence numbers which really indicates that at the present point, a sequence number that normally would occur only later should be sent immediately. We propose the following syntax for specifying out of order sequence numbers in terms of a relative distance between sequence numbers:

```
myPort.setoutofsequence(MyMessageType, myDistance);
```

For example, a relative distance of 8 would create the following suite of sequence numbers when they have already internally reached the value of 235:

{235, 243, 236, 237, 238, 239, 240, 241, 242, 244, ...}

However, one important aspect of periodic messages is that some field values can be determined only at the concrete layer. This requires a mechanism to specify the encoding or decoding rule of such fields well decoupled from the value assignment mechanism. The user would specify the encoding/decoding rule while the value would be determined by a scheduler. This problem is novel and is future work.

4   Test Certification Using the TTCN-3 Matching Mechanism

Periodic message systems used in the aviation industry require certification by law. For example, no airplane can fly without a certification of navigability which includes certification of each of its components, whether hardware or software including test suites. There are numerous approaches to test certification used by industry. The decision factors for choosing the appropriate approach for testing are described qualitatively in a survey in [3]. They first distinguish the test system for its capacity for abstraction from a code-centric to a model-driven view and second discuss the advantages of test specification languages. TTCN-3 meets these criteria and has the additional advantage of being a standard; being well supported by a number of tool vendors; and by having a clear model. This raises the question of migrating from legacy test systems to TTCN-3. However, in light of the certification requirement, any migration from a legacy test system to TTCN-3 also requires certification of the corresponding new TTCN-3 test suite. Certification is a long and tedious process. Thus, migrating to a new test specification language requires reducing the certification process. Normally, this can be achieved by proving behavior equivalence.

The major advantage of using TTCN-3 as a formal test specification language is the separation of concerns between an abstract level in which test logic is specified and a concrete level in which system specific messages and protocols are parsed. In the case of test certification, this means that the equivalence can be determined at the abstract level only and using the very powerful and simple matching mechanisms that saves the test engineer the actual implementation of message comparisons. This task is handled by the built-in mechanisms in the TTCN-3 execution tool.

Behavior equivalence has been already researched for the case of refactoring TTCN-3 test suites. Makedonski et al [7] studied the equivalence of observable behavior of two TTCN-3 test suites, the latter being the result of refactoring the former.

They define observable behavior by the interactions of the test system running the test case and the SUT and the test verdicts and they came to the conclusion that the test system interface is the best location to observe behavior. More precisely, they state that the possible sequences of observable events define the observable behavior. Basically, behavior equivalence means the same message sequences, the same message content, and the same test verdicts. Practically, they use TTCN-3 logs to evaluate behavior equivalence. TTCN-3 logs have the advantage of providing message content in their abstract form which makes the use of the TTCN-3 matching mechanism possible with a valuable consequence of being able to evaluate the equivalence strictly in abstract terms since the codecs would remain constant by definition. Their study was based on discrete messages systems. In our case we face two new challenges:

- The comparison between a non-TTCN-3 and a TTCN-3 test system.
- Periodic rather than discrete messages.

The first difference makes the use of logs difficult because both the format and the content of these logs are heterogeneous and would require at least a translation prior to any attempt to use them. Thus, as a result, the only solution would be to capture concrete messages on the transport medium instead of abstract messages in logs. With periodic messages, the main problem is precisely the periodicity that produces large quantity of messages that need to be compared to prove equivalence. Here the principle of decoding messages only if their content has changed as shown previously on Fig. 5 can be used efficiently for the purpose of certification because it reduces the number of messages to be compared enormously and also avoids interleaving of different message types. Thus, with this approach we focus on the changes in state of the messages. This results in a more manageable reduced number of messages that is then comparable to what can be found in discrete messages systems.

The approach consists of using the messages from the legacy system as test oracles against the messages produced by the corresponding TTCN-3 implementation. The verification of equivalence can be performed by another TTCN-3 test suite that uses the logs of both the legacy and TTCN-3 migration test suites and re-uses the codecs of the migrated TTCN-3 test suite as shown on Fig. 7. Thus, the TTCN-3 certification test suite is composed of sequences of receive statements only since it checks both captured messages being sent or received either by the legacy or migration test suites as shown on Fig. 8.

Thus, the certification process is performed in five steps using TTCN-3:

- Capture concrete messages produced by the execution of the legacy system using a packet sniffer such as Wireshark [21].
- Transform the concrete legacy messages into a list of abstract TTCN-3 messages templates using the codec.
- Capture concrete messages produced by the execution of the TTCN-3 migrated system using a packet sniffer again.
- Transform concrete messages produced by the TTCN-3 migration test suite into a list of abstract TTCN-3 messages templates using the same codec as in step 2.

- Use a simple comparator implemented in the abstract layer of TTCN-3 that compares an abstract message of the legacy system to its corresponding abstract message of the migrated TTCN-3 system using the basic TTCN-3 matching mechanism.

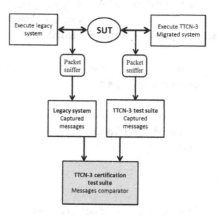

Fig. 7. Using TTCN-3 for certification

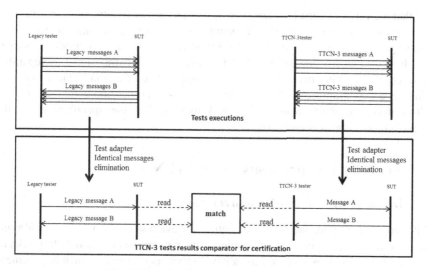

Fig. 8. Test Certification message comparison

Since both test systems use different message types, the TTCN-3 messages comparator test behavior is composed of alternatives (line 04) for each data type on the port handling the legacy messages. A message received on the legacy port (line 05) is stored into a variable (line 06) that is used as a template (line 09) when attempting to receive and match the corresponding message from the port handling the migrated messages as shown below:

```
01 function messageComparator() runs on ComparatorType{
02   var template MessageType_A legacyMessage_A;
03   var template MessageType_B legacyMessage_B;
04   alt { // code handling MessageType_A
05      [] legacyPort.receive(MessageType_A:?)
06                           -> value legacyMessage_A {
07         legacyMessage_A.sequenceNumber := ?;
08         alt {
09            [] migrationPort.receive(legacyMessage_A){
10                setverdict(pass);
11            }
12            [] migrationPort.receive {
13                setverdict(fail);
14                stop;
15         }  }
16         repeat;
17      }
18      // other alternatives for different message types
19 }  }
```

Note that the variable must be a template so that the sequence number of that message can be set to any value using the "?" symbol (line 07) to avoid matching this field since sequence numbers are not handled in the abstract layer for periodic messages. Thus, here we can see that the TTCN-3 language and its central model of separation of concern are used in different ways in the process of certification because this model ensures a maximum flexibility and the high level of abstraction combined with the built-in matching mechanism of TTCN-3 tools makes the specification of this message comparator extremely simple.

5   Verifying Requirements Using TTCN-3

5.1   Defining Verification of Requirements

While most test systems are test case centric, the aviation industry uses an additional level of structuring, the concept of requirements that consists in enumerating selected test cases that should have passed to satisfy a given requirement. Such requirements are described in standards such as in the joint FAA/EASA DO-178C standard [12] and related documents which also cover the quality assurance process (testing) [10]. They target, in particular, model based development and verification using formal methods. The requirements are based on a metric of severity that consists of five different levels ranging from no effect to catastrophic. This means that a system may still be authorized to be put into production even if a requirement with a low severity level is not full-filled, i.e. some test cases composing it have failed. For example, an aircraft may still be authorized to fly if the test for the functioning of the entertainment system is not full-filled. The evaluation of the fulfillment of requirements is performed in two steps: first, all the test cases of a test suite are executed independently from their involvement in a requirement, second, each requirement is evaluated using the subsets of test cases that define them. This means that a given test case could belong to several requirements and thus is evaluated but not executed several times. The failure of a test case could thus have different impacts depending of the severity associated with the requirements it belongs to.

5.2   Implementation Details

The verification of requirements can be easily implemented in TTCN-3 using the verdicts that are returned by test cases that are executed in the control part. First, requirements are defined using sets of records containing two fields, one for the requirement name and the other for the set of test cases containing the test cases names and their corresponding desired verdicts (always pass) as follows:

```
type record TestcaseVerdictType {
  charstring testcaseName,
  verdicttype testcaseVerdict
}
type set of TestcaseVerdictType TestCasesVerdictsType;

type record RequirementType {
    charstring name,
    TestCasesVerdictsType testCasesVerdicts
}
type record of RequirementType RequirementsType;
```

Using the above abstract data types, we can define the requirements using TTCN-3 templates as follows:

```
template RequirementsType requirements := {
  { name:= "requirement_1",
    testCasesVerdicts := {
     {testcaseName:= "TC_1", testcaseVerdict := pass },
     {testcaseName:= "TC_2", testcaseVerdict := pass },
     {testcaseName:= "TC_3", testcaseVerdict := pass }
     }
  },
  { name:= "requirement_2",
    testCasesVerdicts := {
     {testcaseName:= "TC_1", testcaseVerdict := pass },
     {testcaseName:= "TC_3", testcaseVerdict := pass }
} } }
```

Then, we need to execute the test cases independently from the definitions of requirements and collect their returned verdicts in variables of type *verdicttype*. The test case verdicts variables must be initialized to the standard value *none* in order to avoid problems resulting from uninitialized variables in the case of conditionally executed test cases where the actual execution of the test case is not guaranteed. The control section is executed as follows:

```
control {
  var verdicttype verdictTC_1 := none;
  var verdicttype verdictTC_2 := none;
  var verdicttype verdictTC_3 := none;
  verdictTC_1 := execute(TC_1());
  verdictTC_2 := execute(TC_2());
  verdictTC_3 := execute(TC_3());
```

Once all test cases have been executed, we compose a template variable to create a set of TestCaseVerdictType that is defined as a subset and contain the actual verdicts resulting from executing the test cases individually:

```
var template TestCasesVerdictsType tc_verdicts :=
  subset (
    { testcaseName := "TC_1",
      testcaseVerdict := verdictTC_1 },
    { testcaseName := "TC_2",
      testcaseVerdict := verdictTC_2 },
    { testcaseName := "TC_3",
      testcaseVerdict := verdictTC_3 }
  );
```

Finally we can verify the requirements by using the TTCN-3 matching mechanism construct (keyword *match*) for sets using the requirements and test cases verdicts templates that were defined previously, one statically and the later dynamically as follows:

```
var integer i;
for(i:= 0; i < sizeof(requirements); i := i + 1) {
  if(match(requirements[i].testCasesVerdicts,
                                tc_verdicts)) {
    log("requirement " & requirements[i].name &
                        " has been fullfilled");
  }
  else {
    log("requirement " & requirements[i].name &
                        " has NOT been fullfilled");
} }
```

Thus, the principle consists in verifying that the set of test cases verdicts of a requirement is a subset of the entire set of test cases verdicts. The match can occur only if all of the test cases of a given requirement have passed. As a result, test cases that have failed do not influence the evaluation of a requirement if they are not specified for this specific requirement.

5.3   Recommended Change to the TTCN-3 Standard

While the implementation described in the previous section certainly functions correctly and is straightforward, it requires a development effort and this not only on the requirement evaluation activity but also on the test report aspect. Test reports are not covered by the standard and are effectively provided with various levels of details by TTCN-3 tools. Thus, here we can only recommend the specification of requirements at the abstract level leaving responsibility of implementation of the corresponding logging to the tools providers. The abstract language construct can be relatively simple: the keyword *requirement* followed by a requirement identifier and a list of test cases identifiers as follows:

```
requirement myRequirement
                    {myTestcase_1,...,myTestcase_n};
```

The execution of test cases would still have to be specified separately within the control section and could include conditional execution. Although this proposal would be adequate for the industrial avionics systems we have studied because their test cases are not parametric and thus a given test case is executed only once in a test campaign, TTCN-3's parametric test case concept allows the execution of the same test case but with different parameter values. Thus, the TTCN-3 test case name as a way to identify an effective test case is not sufficient. Solutions to this problem are future work.

6   Conclusions

In this paper, we have shown how TTCN-3 can be adapted to provide the same level of efficacy in testing periodic messages in avionics systems as is provided for discrete messages in telecommunications systems. The key insight is to leverage the separation of concerns in the architecture of TTCN-3 between the abstract test specification layer that specifies test behavior and the concrete messaging layer that filters and interprets the periodic messages. This approach can be implemented with the current version of TTCN-3, but we have suggested some simple extensions to the TTCN-3 standard that would support testing of periodic message protocols in a more natural fashion. Test certification and verification of requirements are critical aspects of avionics systems governed by standards. We have shown how our approach to periodic messages is applicable to them as well.

References

1. ETSI ES 201 873-1 (2013-04). The Testing and Test Control Notation version 3, Part 1: TTCN-3 Core notation, V4.5.1 (April 2013)
2. Testing Technologies, TTworkbench - an Eclipse based TTCN-3 IDE (2011), http://www.testingtech.com/products/ttworkbench.php
3. Hartman, A., Katara, M., Olvovsky, S.: Choosing a Test Modeling Language: A Survey. In: Bin, E., Ziv, A., Ur, S. (eds.) HVC 2006. LNCS, vol. 4383, pp. 204–218. Springer, Heidelberg (2007)

4. Schieferdecker, I., Bringmann, E., Großmann, G.: Continuous TTCN-3: Testing of Embedded Control Systems. In: Proceeding of SEAS 2006, pp. 29–36 (2006)
5. Efkemann, C., Peleska, J.: Model-Based Testing for the second generation of Integrated Modular Avionics. In: Proceedings of ICSTW 2011, pp. 55–62 (2011)
6. Laurent, O.: Using Formal Methods and Testability Concepts in the Avionics Systems Validation and Verification. In: proceedings of ICST 2010, pp. 1–10 (2010)
7. Makedonski, P., Grabowski, J., Neukirchen, H.: Validating the Behavioral Equivalence of TTCN-3 Test Cases. In: Proceeding of VALID 2009, pp. 117–122 (2009)
8. Audsley, N.C., Grigg, A.: Timing Analysis of the ARINC 629 Databus for real-time applications. Microprocessors and Microsystems 21(1-7), 55–61 (1997)
9. Gabillon, A., Gallon, L.: Availability of ARINC 629 Avionic Data Bus. Journal of Networks, Vol 1(6), 1–9 (2006)
10. Moy, Y., Ledinot, E., Delseny, H., Wiels, V., Monate, B.: Testing or Formal Verification: DO-178C Alternatives and Industrial Experience. IEEE Software (May/June 2013) (issue)
11. Easwaran, A., Lee, I., Sokolsky, O., Vestal, S.: A Compositional Scheduling Framework for Digital Avionics. In: University of Pennsylvania Scholarly Commons, Departmental Paper (August 24, 2009)
12. DOC-178C, Software Considerations in Airborne Systems and Equipment Certification, RTCA Inc., http://www.rtca.org/store_product.asp?prodid=803 (last accessed August 2013)
13. ETSI ES 201 873-5 (2013-04). The Testing and Test Control Notation version 3, Part 5: TTCN-3 Runtime Interface, V 4.5.1 (April 2013)
14. ETSI ES 202 781 TTCN-3: Extension: Configuration and Deployment Support, V 1.2.1 (June 2013)
15. ETSI ES 202 782 TTCN-3: Extension: Performance and Real-Time Testing, V 1.1.1 (July 2010)
16. ETSI ES 202 783 TTCN-3: Extension: Testing of Real-Time Systems, V 1.1.1, draft
17. ETSI ES 202 784 TTCN-3: Extension: Advanced parameterization, V 1.3.1 (April 2013)
18. ETSI ES 202 785 TTCN-3: Extension:Behavior Types, V 1.3.1 (April 2013)
19. ETSI ES 202 786 TTCN-3: Extension:Support of Interfaces with Continous Signals, V 1.1.1 (April 2012)
20. ETSI ES 202 789 TTCN-3: Extension: Extended TRI, V 1.2.1 (April 2013)
21. Wireshark software, http://www.wireshark.org/
22. Levine, D., Gill, C.D., Schmidt, D.C.: Dynamic Scheduling Strategies for Avionics Mission Computing. In: Proceedings of Digital Avionics Systems Conference, vol. 1, pp. C141–C158 (1998)
23. Hua, Y., Liu, X.: Scheduling Design and Analysis for End-to-End Heterogeneous Flows in an Avionics Network. In: University of Nebraska, Digital Commons, CSE Conference and Workshop Papers (2011)

Guided Algebraic Specification Mining for Failure Simplification

Alexander Elyasov, I.S. Wishnu B. Prasetya, and Jurriaan Hage

Dep. of Inf. and Computing Sciences, Utrecht University, Utrecht, The Netherlands
{A.Elyasov,S.W.B.Prasetya,J.Hage}@uu.nl

Abstract. Software systems often produce logs that capture information about their execution behaviour. When an error occurs, the log file with the error is reported for subsequent analysis. The longer the log file, the harder to identify the cause of the observed error. This problem can be considerably simplified if we reduce the log length, e.g., by removing events which do not contribute towards finding the error. This paper addresses the problem of log reduction by rewriting the reported log in such a way that it preserves the ability to reproduce the same error. The approach exploits rewrite rules inferred from a set of predefined algebraic rewrite rule patterns, exhibiting such properties as commutativity and identity. The paper presents an algorithm for rewrite rules inference, and a terminating reduction strategy based on these rules. Being log-based the inference algorithm is inherently imprecise. So the inferred rules need to be inspected by a human expert before actually being used for rewriting. The approach is language independent and highly flexible. The paper formally defines all used concepts and discusses a prototype implementation of a log reduction framework. The prototype was empirically validated on a web shop application.

Keywords: logging, fault localisation, log reduction, log rewriting, property mining.

1 Introduction

Application logs represent an important source of information about the real behavior of a system under test (SUT). A typical application log consists of an alternation of the events emitted by the application and application internal states before or after such events. By means of dynamic inference, often complemented with static analysis, the logs can be transformed into application models, commonly expressed as finite state machines (FSM) [15]. These FSM models are supposed to capture the complex interplay between data and control flow, have a moderate number of states, and at the same time precisely reflect the application semantics. As a recent empirical assessment [14] has shown this task is highly challenging, and in many respects depends on the type of logging abstraction as well as the quality of log data itself.

H. Yenigün, C. Yilmaz, and A. Ulrich (Eds.): ICTSS 2013, LNCS 8254, pp. 223–238, 2013.
© IFIP International Federation for Information Processing 2013

On the other hand, when a failure occurs logs, also become valuable for the failure context that helps to track down the root cause of the failure, or at least to reproduce the failure [13,11]. Such a failure context consists of the application states and events preceding the failure. In case of failure reproduction, the length of the failure context might directly impede the debugging process. To address this problem several techniques can be employed such as delta-debugging (DD) [27] and FSM model inference [18,15]. DD searches for a minimal failing sub-sequence that preserves the failure. It runs until no one event can be removed without breaking the ability to produce the failure. In practice, however, DD requires multiple online execution attempts which can be expensive or even not feasible at all. In contrast, once the FSM model of an application is inferred from logs, it can be used for minimisation of the failing sequence. The drawback of dynamically inferred FSM models is that the minimised sequence might lose the possibility to reproduce the failure due to of over-approximation.

To address the restrictions imposed by both DD and FSM inference, we propose a novel approach to failure simplification based on *guided mining of algebraic rules* and *failure revealing test case reduction by rewriting*. In comparison with DD, this approach does not require us to replay the failing sequence repeatedly. At the same time, it is less expensive than FSM inference, and it also more strongly resembles the failure related circumstances.

Our approach consists of two phases: 1) inference of rewrite rules from already collected logs based on a set of predefined *rewrite rule patterns*; and 2) turning the rewrite rules into event rewriting system, which is used for the reduction of the original failing test case to a smaller one that still preserves the failure. The predefined patterns represent common *algebraic properties* between the application events, such as commutativity and identity. Despite their apparent simplicity, these properties can be successfully used for log reduction, which has been verified on a model web store application example.

The main contributions of this paper are:

- It formally states the log reduction problem.
- A solution is proposed, which exploits the equivalence of event traces with respect to the final states in which these traces can result.
- A terminating and non-increasing reduction strategy is presented.
- Empirical validation is carried out on a web shop application example.

The paper has the following structure. Section 2 introduces a motivating example, the GCD application, and shows how the reduction approach works. In Section 3.1 the formal definitions of execution equivalence and event reduction system are given. The algebraic rewrite rule patterns and the reduction strategy are provided in Section 3.2 and 3.3 respectively. We discuss the implementation of the Log Reduction Framework in Section 4. Results of the empirical validation of inference and reduction parts are presented in Section 5. Related work is considered in Section 6. Section 7 concludes the paper and discusses future work.

2   Motivating Example

In this section, we introduce an example to illustrate the log reduction approach. The example is a GUI application for calculating the greatest common divisor (GCD) of two natural numbers. The application has three text fields X (the first number), Y (the second number), and R (the result), and two buttons *calc* and *clear*. When the application is initialised, all fields are empty by default.

An essential part of our approach is to use an *event-state logging model*. This model is discussed in detail in Section 3. For now, we only need to know that a log is composed of the alternation of events and states, where the events are the application events and the states are the abstract states of the application. That is, when an event is triggered, we log (serialise) the abstract application state at the end of the event, as well as a description of the event itself, which includes the event name (possibly the type) and the values of the event parameters. An event starts its execution in the state where the previous one has finished (except for the first event, which starts in some initial state).

We distinguish the following application events in our GCD example:

Event	Description
$setX(x)$	the user assigns the value x to the field X
$setY(y)$	the user assigns the value y to the field Y
calc	the user clicks the button *calc*, which changes the value of R
clear	the user clicks the button *clear*, which erases all fields

As an abstract state of the GCD application, let's take the triple $\{x, y, r\}$, where x, y and r are the values of the corresponding fields X, Y and R. At the beginning of an execution all fields are empty, consequently the variables associated with them are undefined. If the event *calc* is called when one of the fields is undefined, then nothing happens. Assume that the application has a fault in the implementation of the event $setX$, namely, $setX(x)$ always results in assigning zero to the field X. The corresponding error will be exposed as a failure in case the *calc* event is executed from the state where one of the variables x or y is equal to zero.

Now, let us consider the following execution sequence:

$$\tau = \quad \{?,?,?\} \xrightarrow{setX(3)} \{0,?,?\} \xrightarrow{setY(5)} \{0,5,?\} \xrightarrow{clear} \{?,?,?\} \xrightarrow{setX(9)} \{0,?,?\}$$
$$\xrightarrow{setY(4)} \{0,4,?\} \xrightarrow{setX(0)} \{0,4,?\} \xrightarrow{setY(3)} \{0,3,?\} \xrightarrow{setY(6)} \{0,6,?\} \xrightarrow{calc} \quad \textbf{error}$$

This sequence leads to an error due to an attempt to compute the GCD when x is equal to zero.

For the application model described above, two event sequences are equivalent if they result in the same final state starting from the same initial state. For instance, the following equivalences hold for the GCD application:

$$\forall e \in Event \; [e \qquad ; clear \qquad] = [clear \qquad \qquad]$$
$$[setX(x); setY(y)] = [setY(y); setX(x)]$$
$$[setX(x); setX(x')] = [setX(x') \qquad]$$
$$[setY(y); setY(y')] = [setY(y') \qquad]$$

The second rule, for instance, says that the order of assigning values to the fields X and Y does not matter with respect to the final state they produce. Applying these rules step by step to the original sequence τ, we can reduce it from nine entries to only four, such that the reduced sequence preserves the original error. Therefore, it gives less than half of the original test case exhibiting the same failure. With this reduced test case it should be easier to discover the error root cause, which consequently may decrease debugging time:

$$[setX(3); setY(5); clear; setX(9); setY(4); setX(0); setY(3); setY(6); calc]$$
$\equiv$ { apply [x;clear]=[clear] two times to setY and setX -}
$$[\qquad\qquad clear; setX(9); setY(4); setX(0); setY(3); setY(6); calc]$$
$\equiv$ { apply [setX(9);setY(4)]=[setY(4);setX(9)] -}
$$[\qquad\qquad clear; setY(4); setX(9); setX(0); setY(3); setY(6); calc]$$
$\equiv$ { apply [setX(9);setX(0)]=[setX(0)] -}
$$[\qquad\qquad clear; setY(4); \qquad setX(0); setY(3); setY(6); calc]$$
$\equiv$ { apply [setY(3);setY(6)]=[setY(6)] -}
$$[\qquad\qquad clear; setY(4); \qquad setX(0); setY(6); \qquad calc]$$
$\equiv$ { apply [setY(4);setX(0)]=[setX(0);setY(4)] -}
$$[\qquad\qquad clear; setX(0); \qquad setY(4); setY(6); \qquad calc]$$
$\equiv$ { apply [setY(4);setY(6)]=[setY(6)] -}
$$[\qquad\qquad clear; setX(0); \qquad setY(6); \qquad calc]$$

3   Formal Reduction Theory

In this section, we formally describe the reduction problem and present our solution. We start by defining an equivalence relation on logs and then describe the logging approach. This equivalence relation lies at the basis of the log reduction, the purpose of which is to decrease the length of a log by rewriting it to a smaller but equivalent one. We propose to learn special rewrite rules from logs that express simple and ubiquitous properties among the application events such as commutativity and idempotence. The learning is effective (Section 5.1), even if the logs are relatively small (hundreds of entries). Moreover, the application of the rules can result in a significant log reduction (Section 5.2).

3.1   Log and Event Trace Equivalence

Following the line of work Lorenzoli et al. [15], we assume that execution traces are produced by an *Extended Finite State Machine (EFSM)*, which implicitly underlines the application model. However, in our representation, the EFSM does not contain transition predicates, and the context variables are associated with the states instead of the transitions.

Definition 1 (EFSM). *An EFSM $\mathbb{E}$ is a 6-tuple (S, X, V, E, I, T), where*

- *S is a set of states,*
- *X is an n-dimensional space $X_1 \times \cdots \times X_n$,*
- *V is a state valuation function on S such that $V : S \to X$ is injective,*
- *E is a set of events,*
- *P is a set of inputs (event parameters),*
- *T is a transition function such that $T : S \times E \times P \to S$.*

Transition $((s, e, p), s')$ is denoted as $(s, e, p) \to s'$. For a given s and e, if $(s, e, p) \to s'$ for all p, we leave out p and write $(s, e) \to s'$. The symbol ϵ is a special virtual event without parameters that defines the transition $(s, \epsilon) \to s$. By its definition, an EFSM is *deterministic*.

Definition 2 (Execution). *Given a state s and a sequence of events with parameters $\tau = [e_1(p_1), \ldots, e_n(p_n)]$, τ is an execution of $\mathbb{E}$ starting from the state s if there is a sequence of transitions $(s_1, e_1, p_1) \to s_2, (s_2, e_2, p_2) \to s_3, \ldots, (s_n, e_n, p_n) \to s_{n+1}$ in $\mathbb{E}$ such that $s_1 = s$.*

The execution of τ starting from s is denoted as $s \mapsto \tau$, and we say that τ is executable from s. The function $\mathtt{finalState}$ returns the final state of the execution $s \mapsto \tau$, that is $\mathtt{finalState}(s \mapsto \tau) = s_{n+1}$.

Definition 3 (Execution Equivalence). *Two sequences of events with parameters τ_1 and τ_2 are equivalent ($\tau_1 \equiv \tau_2$) if for all $s \in S$: 1) τ_1 is executable from s ($s \mapsto \tau_1$) if and only if τ_2 is executable from s ($s \mapsto \tau_2$); and 2) $\mathtt{finalState}(s \mapsto \tau_1) = \mathtt{finalState}(s \mapsto \tau_2)$.*

Execution equivalence defines an *equivalence relation* on executions of EFSM. Indeed, it is reflexive, symmetric and transitive by definition. We say that two equivalent executions $\tau_1 \equiv \tau_2$ define a *rewrite rule*.

Definition 4 (Execution Trace or Log). *An execution trace or log Σ produced by an execution $s \mapsto \tau$ is the sequence:*

$$\Sigma = [(\epsilon, x_1), (e_1(p_1), x_2), \ldots, (e_l(p_n), x_{n+1})],$$

where all states are mapped into their associated values in the domain X, that is $x_i = V(s_i)$ and s_i is an intermediate state of $s \mapsto \tau$.

The function $\mathtt{final}$ returns the value corresponding to the final state of the log Σ, that is $\mathtt{final}(\Sigma) = x_{n+1}$.

When a user interacts with an application it generates logs in the sense of the definition above. Every state has a uniquely defined element from X associated with it, which is essentially what we see recorded in the log. We call that value the *application abstract state*. Two executions are considered to be equivalent based on those logged values instead of the states. This gives us the following *execution equivalence criterion* derived from a set of collected logs.

Criterion 1 (Execution Equivalence on Logs). *Let $\mathcal{L}$ be a set of logs produced by an application according to the Definition 4. Two event sequences τ_1 and τ_2 are considered to be equivalent on $\mathcal{L}$ if for all $\Sigma_1, \Sigma_2 \in \mathcal{L}$ resulted from the executions $s \mapsto \tau_1$ and $s \mapsto \tau_2$ respectively, it implies that $final(\Sigma_1) = final(\Sigma_2)$.*

Definition 5 (Event Reduction System). *Given a set of events E, an event reduction system $\mathfrak{R}$ defined by the set of rewrite rules R is a pair $(E^*, \to_R)$, where E^* is the set of execution sequences and $\to_R$ is a reduction relation on it.*

A reduction step $\tau_1 \to_R \tau_2$ entails the replacement of an occurrence π_1 in τ_1 ($\tau_1 = \phi\pi_1\psi$) by an equivalent execution π_2, i.e. $(\pi_1 \equiv \pi_2) \in R$. The result of this reduction is a new execution $\tau_2 = \phi\pi_2\psi$ that is equivalent to τ_1 with respect to Definition 3.

3.2   Rewriting Patterns

As we have already seen in the GCD example, some of the executions are equivalent and can form the bases of the reduction procedure. In general, executions turn out to be equivalent due to the nature of algorithmic languages that contain constructions such as loops, branches and recursions. Some equivalences are application specific, but some others commonly occur in many applications. Below we propose three patterns of the execution equivalences that we call *algebraic rewrite rule patterns*. They will form the basis for the event reduction in the following. The patterns are quite small (the executions consist of at most two events) and they express common algebraic relations such as commutativity. We believe that algebraic patterns represent commonly occurring equivalences and as a result can often be observed in the logs. That fact increases our confidence of their dynamic inference.

Skip: $[e(p)] \equiv \epsilon$
> Obviously, not all events have an effect on the application. Those events that do not interfere with the abstract state at all fall into the category of this pattern, which we call *skip-like*. The GCD application does not have any skip-like events. However, if the GCD abstract state only consisted of the variables x and y, then the *calc* event would become skip-like with respect to the chosen abstraction.

Zero: $[e(p); d(q)] \equiv [d(q)]$
> Some events may completely overwrite the effect of some preceding events. We call such events *zero-like* with respect to those preceding events. In the GCD application, the event *clear* annuls the effect of *setX*, *setY* and *calc*. A particular case of this pattern is when $e = d$, that is, whatever the application state is, an execution of $e(q)$ always overwrites the effect $e(p)$. The *setX* and *setY* events are examples of this particular case.

Com: $[e(p); d(q)] \equiv [d(q); e(p)]$

The last pattern asserts the property of two events being commutative. For example, the fields X and Y can be updated in any order, and therefore the corresponding events $setX$ and $setY$ are commutative, in other words they do not interact with each other.

In the sequel, we only consider event reduction systems formed by rules from these three categories $Skip$, $Zero$ and Com.

Definition 6 (Algebraic Event Reduction System). *We call the event reduction system $\Re_A = (E^*, \rightarrow_{R_A})$ algebraic if R_A is a disjoint union of R_s, R_z and R_c (denoted by $R_A = R_s \sqcup R_z \sqcup R_c$), where R_s, R_z and R_c are respective instances of $Skip$, $Zero$ and Com patterns.*

3.3   Reduction Strategy

Algorithm 1 presents a reduction procedure for an algebraic event trace reduction system that we later prove to be terminating and non-increasing. It terminates in polynomial time, but does not necessarily produce the maximal possible reduction that is reachable with a given set of rewrite rules. As an input the reduction procedure takes an execution τ and a set of algebraic rules R_A and returns a new execution τ' that is equivalent to τ but smaller. The procedure consists of the following key steps:

1. The initial set of rules R_A is enriched by the procedure `EnrichRules`. The enrichment consists in overlapping certain categories of rules from R_A (this resembles a step of the Knuth-Bendix algorithm [2]). It overlaps $Skip$ and $Zero$ rules (`OverlapSkip`), $Zero$ and $Zero$ rules (`OverlapZero`), and $Zero$ and Com rules (`OverlapMZero`). For example, taking the overlap of the rules $ab \rightarrow b$ and $bc \rightarrow c$ and applying them in a different order to the sequence abc, we get $ac \rightarrow c$ as a new possible reduction rule. Crossing $Zero$ and Com rules gives us the *mirror zero rules* (line 4), which are like zero with respect to reversed event sequence ($ba \equiv b$). These rules are used later at line 2 to get reduction by means of the `ZeroReduce` procedure in application to the reversed sequence.

2. The functions `GroupZeroCls` (`GroupMZeroCls`) groups $Zero$ ($MZero$) rules with equal right hand sides in the same equivalence class.

3. Next step is to remove all skip-like events by the procedure `ReduceSkip`.

4. The last reduction step recursively applies the `ZeroReduce` procedure to the event trace in both directions (from left to right (line 1) and right to left (line 2)) until a fixed point is reached. The procedure `ReduceZero` looks for the first occurrence of x in u. Then it exhaustively applies all rules from r_x to the part of u left from x (`ReduceImmediateZero` at line 5), and it also tries to combine zero with commutative rules (`ReduceZeroWithCom` at line 7). The latter combination allows us to discover zero reductions that are not enabled by default.

Algorithm 1. A reduction procedure for an execution trace

---

begin

 Data: An intial execution trace τ and a set of algebraic rewrite rules
 $$R_A = R_s \sqcup R_z \sqcup R_c$$
 Result: A reduced execution trace τ' such that $|\tau| \leqslant |\tau'|$ and $\tau \equiv \tau'$

 $R'_A \longleftarrow EnrichRules(R_A)$
 `// group zero (mzero) rules with equal RHS into classes`
 $\{R_z\} \longleftarrow GroupZeroCls(R'_A)$
 $\{R_{mz}\} \longleftarrow GroupMZeroCls(R'_A)$
 $\tau \longleftarrow ReduceSkip(R'_A, \tau)$ `// remove all skip-like events`
 repeat

1 | $\tau \longleftarrow ReduceZero(\{R_z\}, R_c, \tau, \epsilon)$
2 | $\tau \longleftarrow Reverse(ReduceZero(\{R_{mz}\}, R_c, Reverse(\tau), \epsilon))$
3 **until** τ *is unchanged*
 return τ

Function $EnrichRules(R_A = R_s \sqcup R_z \sqcup R_c)$
 $R'_s \longleftarrow OverlapSkip(R_s, R_z)$ $//\ ab \equiv b \wedge b \equiv \epsilon \Rightarrow a \equiv \epsilon$
 $R'_z \longleftarrow OverlapZero(R_z)$ $//\ ab \equiv b \wedge ca \equiv a \Rightarrow cb \equiv b$
4 $R_{mz} \longleftarrow OverlapMZero(R_z \cup R'_z, R_c)$ $//\ ab \equiv ba \wedge ab \equiv b \Rightarrow ba \equiv b$
 return $R_A \cup R'_s \cup R'_z \cup R_{mz}$

Function $ReduceZero(\{R_z\}, R_c, u, v)$
 $(r_x, (u', x, v')) \longleftarrow$ find first class $r_x \in \{R_z\}$ such that $u = u'xv'$
 if *search for* r_x *is succeeded* **then**
   repeat
     repeat
5 | $u' \longleftarrow ReduceImmediateZero(u', r_x)$
 | $//\ u' = u''y \wedge \exists(yx \equiv x \in r_x) \Rightarrow u' = u''$
6 | **until** u' *is unchanged*
7 | $u' \longleftarrow ReduceZeroWithCom(u, r_x, R_c)$
 | $//\ u' = wyu'' \wedge (yx \equiv x \in r_x) \wedge (\forall e \in u'' : com(e, y)) \Rightarrow u' = wu''$
8 | **until** u' *is unchanged*
 | $ReduceZero(\{R_z\}, R_c, u'x, v')$ `// recursive call`
   else return uv

Theorem 1 (Termination). *For the algebraic event reduction system* $\Re_A = (E^*, \rightarrow_{R_A})$, *the reduction relation* $\rightarrow_{R_A}$ *implemented by Algorithm 1 is terminating.*

Note, that reduction Algorithm 1 essentially applies only *Skip* and *Zero* rules, which form a non-cyclic reduction system. In order to prove termination, we need to show that the fix points are guaranteed to be reachable in all three cases (lines 3, 8 and 6). But this fact obviously follows from the invariant that each time the sequence is either reduced or not, the number of rules is finite, and they are acyclic. If the event sequence can not be reduced anymore, we have reached the corresponding fixed point.

Theorem 2 (Length Reduction). *For an algebraic event reduction system* $\Re_A = (E^*, \rightarrow_{R_A})$, *the reduction relation* $\rightarrow_{R_A}$ *implemented by Algorithm 1 is non-increasing.*

This property obviously follows the shape of reduction being applied. The algorithm only uses non-increasing reduction rules.

4   Implementation

In this section, we describe the architecture of our semi-automated Log Reduction Framework. The framework, including the inference and reduction part, has been implemented in Haskell. The complete structure of the framework is depicted in Figure 1. Given a reliable version *App* of the application, during the first phase (*1. executions*) *App* is subjected to user interaction in order to produce logs. The concrete rewrite rules are inferred (*3. concrete rewrite rules*) from the set of collected logs (*2. collect logs*) based on the predefined rewrite rule patterns. After that, they are automatically filtered according to a confidence level (*4. check rules*) and then passed to the expert (*5. report rules to the expert*). The rules at this stage might still contain false positives so the human inspection is needed to prevent possible mistakes (*6. accept rewrite rules*).

At some point a new version *App'* of the same application will be realised. It will replace *App* or will be employed simultaneously with *App*. We assume that rewrite rules accepted by the expert (phase 6) still hold for *App'*, otherwise the violation is immediately reported. If the user happens to produce a failure (*1'. failure*), the log containing the error message (*2'. error log*) should be passed on subsequent analysis with the purpose to localize the fault and suggest a bug fix. At this point, the second component of our framework goes into action. The failed log is reduced (*7. log rewriting*) with the help of the inferred rewrite rules. This log still reproduce the original failure found in *App'* but requires less steps. Finally, the reduced log is inspected (*8. reduced log*) by the tester or developer during the debugging instead of the original one.

5   Empirical Validation

The aim of this section is to provide a preliminary evaluation of the Log Reduction Framework. All experiments presented in this section were carried out on an Intel i5 (2.4 GHz) machine with 6GB of RAM under control of Ubuntu 12.04 OS. Reflecting the structure of the framework we provide a separate evaluation of its two main components, *Inference* and *Rewriting*. The framework has been deployed for the web shop application flexstore [1]. It is an application example for buying of mobile phones, provided by Adobe to demonstrate some features of the Flex SDK. The flexstore has all standard components of a web shop, such as a catalog, product filters and a shopping cart.

---

[1] http://examples.adobe.com/flex2/inproduct/sdk/flexstore/flexstore.html

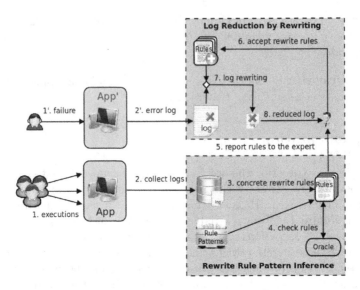

Fig. 1. Log Reduction Framework

We instrumented flexstore GUI events with the help of the FITTEST Automation Framework (AF) [20]. AF allows us to log GUI events and the application abstract states associated with them in the FITTEST Logging Format [20]. The user of AF provides an application abstraction function, which specifies the set of objects and fields to be logged. The resulting log fully conforms to the definition of log given in Section 3.1.

5.1   Inference Results

We generated a log of length 11000 entries, randomly invoking different flexstore events out of the 23 possible events. We considered two different state projections: high abstraction (2 variables, **Abs** = $high$) and low abstraction (7 variables, **Abs** = low). False positives were filtered by the use of a confidence level (**Conf** = yes), i.e., all rules with a confidence level lower than 0.99 were not accepted. Without the confidence level (**Conf** = no) it was sufficient for a rule to have at least one positive witness and zero negatives to be accepted as a rewrite rule. As we mentioned already, the inference algorithm can both report false positives and reject false negative rules. Therefore, an expert assessment is required to at least sift out the false positive ones, otherwise, we might end up with a nonequivalent sequence after reduction. We applied the inference algorithm to the log of length 11000, manually verified the results, and then took them as a *template* to count the number of erroneously accepted and rejected rules in all other measurements during the experiment. The aggregated data of the inference part are shown in Table 1. We used the logs of different sizes (initial segments of length from 100 up to 5000 entries taken from the original log) to infer the rules, and then

Table 1. Results of pattern inference for flexstore. The events recognised as skip-like are excluded from the subsequent inference of *Zero* or *Com* rules.

Patterns	Abs	Conf	11000			5000			2500			1000			500			100		
			m	p	n	m	p	n	m	p	n	m	p	n	m	p	n	m	p	n
Skip	low	yes	7	0	0	7	0	0	7	0	0	7	0	0	6	0	1	2	0	5
	low	no	7	0	0	7	0	0	7	0	0	7	0	0	7	0	0	7	4	0
	high	yes	9	0	0	9	0	0	9	0	0	9	0	0	8	0	1	2	0	7
	high	no	9	0	0	9	0	0	9	0	0	9	0	0	9	0	0	9	5	0
Zero	low	yes	26	0	0	15	6	11	13	13	13	11	22	15	4	5	22	0	0	26
	low	no	26	2	0	25	39	1	23	42	3	17	42	9	12	37	14	0	4	26
	high	yes	9	0	0	1	9	8	1	17	8	0	31	9	0	7	9	0	0	9
	high	no	26	0	0	8	15	1	6	30	3	3	46	6	2	42	7	0	4	9
Com	low	yes	10	0	0	8	3	2	2	0	8	0	0	10	0	1	10	0	0	10
	low	no	10	0	0	10	5	0	6	8	4	2	3	8	1	1	9	0	0	10
	high	yes	7	0	0	6	4	1	1	1	6	0	0	7	0	1	7	0	0	7
	high	no	7	0	0	7	9	0	4	11	3	1	5	6	0	2	7	0	0	7

we compared the inference outcome with the template. As a result, we calculated the number of correctly identified rules (m column) as well as the number of false positives (p column) and negatives (n column). Applying abstraction, we might obtain some new rules as well as lose some old ones. It is clear from Table 1 that to correctly identify all skip rules, it was already sufficient to have 1000 entries in the log. But for *Zero* or *Com* rules we missed or wrongly accepted some rules even for the log of 5000 entries. The choice of an appropriate confidence level is always a trade-off between the number of false positive rules we want to avoid and the number of potential false negatives we might lose because of being too exact. As we can see, in case of the *Zero* and *Com* rules, there are dozens of candidates, so it is wise to rely on the confidence level to decrease the number of false positives, especially if the amount of data in the logs is limited. For instance, we got rid of 33 false positive rules (reported 6 instead of 39 rules) of the type *Zero*, learnt from the log of 5000 entries.

5.2   Reduction Results

The purpose of the experiments in this subsection is to make an assessment of the failed executions reduction that can be achieved by the framework. We injected faults in the model application flexstore (one fault for each state variable out of seven) and have randomly driven the execution until a failure occurred. For every fault we ran this procedure 100 times in order to deal with randomness of executions. We used the set of concrete rewrite rules inferred from the log of 11000 events in Section 5.1 to form the algebraic event reduction system. The summarized data are presented in Table 2.

Let us choose a fault and closely consider its characteristics — for example, *grand_total* fault, which shows the strongest reduction result. The fault here

Table 2. Failure revealing test case simplification by reduction

max.red.ord, avg.red.ord, min.red.ord are maximum, average and minimum reduction orders respectively; *avg.org.len* is the average length of the original log, and *avg.red.len* is the average length of the reduced log.

Failure Type	max.red.ord	avg.red.ord	min.red.ord	avg.org.len	avg.red.len
cart_contents	23	5.62	1.5	35.19	6.35
ctlg_contents	20	4.55	1.67	45.43	12.4
comp_contents	21.2	6.07	1.33	40.42	6.44
filter_count	18	4.45	1.66	45.27	12.02
grand_total	104	9.68	1.5	19.61	2.25
#compare_cart	34	6.82	2.72	69.11	15.75
#products	31.6	6.83	1.99	42.82	6.59

consist in the restriction imposed on the total price of (variable *grand_total*) items in the shopping cart. In order to trigger this fault, it is sufficient to open the product catalog, purchase an arbitrary phone and submit the order. The corresponding row in Table 2 indicates that the maximal reduction that is achieved in one out 100 random executions is a factor of 104, although, on average the order of reduction is a factor of 10. It also says that on average the log is reduced from 20 to just over 2 events.

6   Related Work

Since our approach essentially consists of two parts: (1) learning specific rules from logs, and (2) then applying the reduction procedure based on these rules, we accordingly split the related work section.

6.1   Mining Properties from Logs

There are various categories of properties that can be learnt from logs. But these properties come under different names: invariants [6], specifications [10] and oracles [21].

The Daikon tool [6] discovers *assertions* (invariants) that hold at certain program points, e.g., method entry and exit. The assertions are templated predicates over program variables. They express invariants such as constant equality and ordering. Polynomial and array invariants, which Daikon is unable to discover, are presented in [19]. DySy obtains invariants that are specific for the observed program executions by using symbolic analysis [3]. The Daikon approach can be extended by the inference of behavioural models of an application [15], which are EFSMs that describe the interplay between data values and component interactions.

Temporal properties have also been thoroughly investigated. Therefore, several tools for learning them have been developed in recent years [7,1,24].

In contrast to Daikon's properties, which represent data-flow dependencies, the temporal properties describe control-flow relations, for instance, the precedence of function calls. The Perracotta tool [24] infers all pairs of events satisfying the property that p must be followed by s. A more general class of temporal properties can be inferred by the Ocd tool [7] — a tool for learning and enforcing temporal properties over function and method call sequences. These properties are predefined by templates, which are two-letter regular expressions (ab, ab^+, etc.). Synoptic [1] mines temporal properties, such as a always followed by b, and a always precedes by b, from partially ordered logs, and then uses these properties to visualise the application model.

The properties proposed in this paper belong to the category of *algebraic properties* (specifications) [9]. Hankel et al. [10] suggest discovering algebraic specifications by exercising the terms (dynamic part) generated from the algebraic signatures of program classes (static part). Adiheu [8] improves this approach by using Adabu's sequences of legal operations [4] expressed as non-deterministic FSA .

6.2   Log Reduction

Reduction always leads to the loss of information, in particular, we sacrifice the completeness of logged data. But there should exist an invariant that continues to hold during the reduction. For instance, someone might be interested in the presence of certain events in the reduced log. The invariant discussed in this paper has the ability to reproduce the same failure as the one contained in the original log.

Wang and Parnas [23] suggest to use trace specifications of software modules as a basis for trace rewriting to simulate module behaviour. The trace specifications completely describe the effect of an event trace execution on the application. In [23] the authors present smart trace rewriting, which is proved to be terminating and confluent. But a formal trace specification is often absent, and its inference brings us back to the questions raised in Section 6.1, namely how to get the specification in the first place.

Clustering techniques are found to be quite useful to reduce the length of logs, in particular, if logs are unstructured. So several clustering algorithms and tools have been introduced, e.g. [16]. Clustering assists the reduction in the following ways: 1) similar events can be grouped in clusters so that one event can represent the entire cluster; 2) event correlations can be learnt from logs [28]; and 3) outliers (events out the clusters) are potential candidates for anomalies.

Zawawy et al. [26] propose to filter logs with respect to a set of analysis goals and diagnostic hypotheses in order to assist root cause analysis. They suggest two reduction strategies: 1) filter events that are irrelevant to the failure by executing SQL queries generated from annotated goal models [25] capturing application requirements; and 2) apply Latent Semantic Indexing [5] to identify log entries connected with the query representing a particular aspect of the model. Kontogiannis et al. [12] suggest to reduce logs according to the chosen upfront sequence of *beacon* events. This approach exploits the collection of event dependency relations to construct the *Event Dependency Graph*. The graph is used later on to find all events correlating with the beacon sequence.

Delta Debugging [27] is able to reveal the *cause-effect chain* of a failure, isolating the relevant variables and values. This chain is essentially the reduced log we are looking for. The method compares the states obtained from a passing and failing run. This requires the ability to replay the failing execution multiple times, which is not required by our approach.

Lee et al. in [13] consider the reduction of log replaying, retaining the ability to reproduce the failure. The reduction is reached by reducing the amount of information that needs to be logged in order to replay the execution. The reduction is carried out at the unit level (loop iterations) by the offline analysis of the *enhanced log* — a log resulting from the execution of an instrumented program to collect some axillary runtime information.

BugRedux [11] synthesises and reduces in-house executions that could reproduce the failures observed in the field. BugRedux exploits additional information, for instance call sequences or complete traces, to produce an input that mimics the execution by means of symbolic analysis. Our reduction technique is purely based on the information presented in the log files, and it does not require the application source code to be available.

An FSA is a common way to represent an application model. Such a model can be learnt from logs as in [18] and used for root cause analysis. A failure is then recognised by observing that an execution trace is inconsistent with the FSA. The point of divergence indicates where the abnormal behaviour has started, and the application model can be used to find the shortest path to this point. This gives us a reduced failing execution trace. But, of course, building the precise application model from logs is an expensive task, and a lightweight approach to reduction might be preferable.

7 Conclusion and Future Work

In order to discriminate failures that might happen during the execution of an application, programmers try to provide as informative logs as possible. But if a failure occurs, we are not interested in all this excessive information to carry out the root cause analysis of that particular failure.

This paper addresses the issue of failed execution trace simplification that arises if we consider in-house or in the field debugging. We propose to infer algebraic properties among application events, and use them as the basis for our reduction system. We built a prototype of the log reduction framework based on these rules and validated it against the flexstore web application.

Future Work. There are several questions that were left beyond of the scope of this paper and which we consider to be a future work. The reduction algorithm for algebraic log reduction systems presented in this paper, does not guarantee reaching the maximal reduction. We have not yet investigated the desidability of this question. If the answer is positive, it will be interesting to provide an efficient algorithm for maximal reduction.

Apart from the three rewrite rule patterns discussed in Section 3.2, there exist some other patterns that we did not consider, for instance, $[e(p); d(p)] \equiv \epsilon$. This pattern states that d is an inverse of e. In general, some practical issues appear if we want to extend our reduction framework with new rewrite rule patterns, namely:

- How to infer the concrete instances of the rewrite rules for this pattern? The inference might be very expensive, require a huge amount of logging data, or generate too many false positives.
- How to incorporate a new pattern into the existing reduction algorithm and to build a new one that is as effective and powerful as the former one?

The answers to these questions require a trade-off between the pattern complexity, inference efficiency and reduction strength. These problems are beyond the scope of this paper and we consider them future work.

In this paper, we do not address the problem of the construction of abstract application state, although the strength of our approach very much relies on the having a good state abstraction. We assume that such abstraction has been already obtained by the use of known techniques [17,4,22].

Reduction performed with respect to some abstraction might lead to non-executable event sequences. Although, it is guaranteed by the approach that they still preserve the failure relevant data, some part of the execution relevant information might be abstracted over. In order to alleviate this issue, reduction can be combined with delta debugging [27], so that it produced both the executable and simplified test case.

Acknowledgements. This work is funded by the EU FITTEST project No. 257574.

References

1. Beschastnikh, I., Brun, Y., Schneider, S., Sloan, M., Ernst, M.D.: Leveraging existing instrumentation to automatically infer invariant-constrained models. In: ESEC/FSE, pp. 267–277 (2011)
2. Book, R.V., Otto, F.: String-rewriting systems (1993)
3. Csallner, C., Tillmann, N., Smaragdakis, Y.: DySy: dynamic symbolic execution for invariant inference. In: ICSE, pp. 281–290 (2008)
4. Dallmeier, V., Lindig, C., Wasylkowski, A., Zeller, A.: Mining object behavior with ADABU. In: WODA, pp. 17–24 (2006)
5. Deerwester, S., Dumais, S.T., Furnas, G.W., Landauer, T.K., Harshman, R.: Indexing by latent semantic analysis. Journal of the American Society for Information Science 41 (1990)
6. Ernst, M.D., Perkins, J.H., Guo, P.J., McCamant, S., Pacheco, C., Tschantz, M.S., Xiao, C.: The daikon system for dynamic detection of likely invariants. Sci. Comput. Program., 35–45 (2007)
7. Gabel, M., Su, Z.: Online inference and enforcement of temporal properties. In: ICSE, pp. 15–24 (2010)

8. Ghezzi, C., Mocci, A., Monga, M.: Efficient recovery of algebraic specifications for stateful components. In: IWPSE, pp. 98–105 (2007)
9. Guttag, J.V., Horning, J.J.: The algebraic specification of abstract data types. Acta Informatica 10, 27–52 (1978)
10. Henkel, J., Diwan, A.: Discovering algebraic specifications from java classes. In: Cardelli, L. (ed.) ECOOP 2003. LNCS, vol. 2743, pp. 431–456. Springer, Heidelberg (2003)
11. Jin, W., Orso, A.: BugRedux: Reproducing Field Failures for In-house Debugging. In: ICSE (2012)
12. Kontogiannis, K., Wasfy, A., Mankovskii, S.: Event clustering for log reduction and run time system understanding. In: SAC, pp. 191–192 (2011)
13. Lee, K.H., Zheng, Y., Sumner, N., Zhang, X.: Toward generating reducible replay logs. In: PLDI, pp. 246–257 (2011)
14. Lo, D., Mariani, L., Santoro, M.: Learning extended FSA from software: An empirical assessment. Journal of Systems and Software 85(9), 2063–2076 (2012)
15. Lorenzoli, D., Mariani, L., Pezzè, M.: Automatic generation of software behavioral models. In: ICSE, pp. 501–510 (2008)
16. Makanju, A., Brooks, S., Zincir-Heywood, A., Milios, E.: LogView: Visualizing event log clusters. In: PST, pp. 99–108 (2008)
17. Marchetto, A., Tonella, P., Ricca, F.: State-based testing of ajax web applications. In: 2008 1st International Conference on Software Testing, Verification, and Validation, pp. 121–130 (2008)
18. Mariani, L., Pastore, F.: Automated identification of failure causes in system logs. In: ISSRE, pp. 117–126 (2008)
19. Nguyen, T., Kapur, D., Weimer, W., Forrest, S.: Using dynamic analysis to discover polynomial and array invariants. In: ICSE, pp. 683–693 (2012)
20. Prasetya, I.S.W.B., Middelkoop, A., Elyasov, A., Hage, J.: D6.1: Fittest logging approach (2011)
21. Shahamiri, S.R., Wan-Kadir, W.M.N., Ibrahim, S., MohdHashim, S.: An automated framework for software test oracle. Information and Software Technology (2011)
22. Tonella, P., Nguyen, C.D., Marchetto, A., Kessler, F.B., Lakhotia, K., Harman, M.: Automated generation of state abstraction functions using data invariant inference (2013)
23. Wang, Y., Parnas, D.L.: Simulating the behavior of software modules by trace rewriting. IEEE Transactions on Software Engineering, 750–759 (1994)
24. Yang, J., Evans, D.: Dynamically inferring temporal properties. In: PASTE, pp. 23–28 (2004)
25. Yu, Y., Wang, Y., Mylopoulos, J., Liaskos, S., Lapouchnian, A., do Prado Leite, J.C.S.: Reverse engineering goal models from legacy code. In: RE, pp. 363–372 (2005)
26. Zawawy, H., Kontogiannis, K., Mylopoulos, J.: Log filtering and interpretation for root cause analysis. In: ICSM, pp. 1–5 (2010)
27. Zeller, A.: Isolating cause-effect chains from computer programs. In: FSE, pp. 1–10 (2002)
28. Zhou, W., Zhan, J., Meng, D., Xu, D., Zhang, Z.: LogMaster: Mining event correlations in logs of large scale cluster systems. CoRR (2010)

Spectrum-Based Fault Localization for Diagnosing Concurrency Faults

Feyzullah Koca[1,2], Hasan Sözer[2], and Rui Abreu[3]

[1] TUBITAK BILGEM, Information Technologies Institute, Kocaeli, Turkey
[2] Department of Computer Science, Özyeğin University, İstanbul, Turkey
{feyzullah.koca,hasan.sozer}@ozyegin.edu.tr
[3] Faculty of Engineering, University of Porto, Portugal
rui@computer.org

Abstract. Concurrency faults are activated by specific thread inter-leavings at runtime. Traditional fault localization techniques and static analysis fall short to diagnose these faults efficiently. Existing dynamic fault-localization techniques focus on pinpointing data-access patterns that are subject to concurrency faults. In this paper, we propose a spectrum-based fault localization technique for localizing faulty code blocks instead. We systematically instrument the program to create versions that run in particular combinations of thread interleavings. We run tests on all these versions and utilize spectrum-based fault localization to correlate detected errors with concurrently executing code blocks. We have implemented a tool and applied our approach on several industrial case studies. Case studies show that our approach can effectively and efficiently localize concurrency faults.

Keywords: Debugging, multithreading, concurrency faults, thread safety, dynamic analysis, spectrum-based fault localization.

1 Introduction

Concurrency faults are activated by specific thread interleavings at runtime, which makes them hard to detect by testing since they do not deterministically lead to an error. Traditional fault localization techniques and static analysis fall short to detect these faults efficiently. Existing dynamic fault-localization techniques focus on pinpointing data-access patterns that are subject to concurrency faults [9,12,19,20,25]. Although these techniques are effective in capturing faulty data-access patterns, the corresponding code blocks should still be identified by the programmer to locate and fix the defect. More importantly, not all concurrency faults are related to data access and shared memory. There exist various type of shared resources other than memory. Concurrent access to these shared resources (e.g., file access) can also lead to errors.

We have applied spectrum-based fault localization [1, 3, 10, 11] for directly pinpointing code blocks, of which multi-threaded execution leads to concurrency errors. In our approach, we systematically instrument a multi-threaded subject

H. Yenigün, C. Yilmaz, and A. Ulrich (Eds.): ICTSS 2013, LNCS 8254, pp. 239–254, 2013.

program to force context switch within different code blocks. As such, each version turns out to be actually the same program that is executed with a different combination of thread interleavings. We run tests on all the generated versions and utilize spectrum-based fault localization to correlate detected errors with concurrently executing code blocks. The result is a ranking of code blocks with respect to the probability that their re-entrance causes the detected errors. These code blocks should be analyzed by the programmer to introduce thread-safety.

We have implemented a tool, dubbed SCURF, and applied our approach on several industrial case studies. Case studies show that our approach can effectively and efficiently localize concurrency faults. The contributions of this paper are threefold

- We introduce a novel approach for localizing concurrency faults by means of spectrum-based fault localization techniques;
- We developed a toolset, *SCURF* that provides automation for our approach;
- We discuss our experiences in applying our approach in several industrial software projects.

The remainder of this paper is organized as follows. Section 2 provides background on spectrum-based fault localization. Section 3 introduces a motivating example. We introduce our approach in Section 4. Industrial case studies and the evaluation of the approach are presented in Section 5. Related studies are summarized in Section 6. Finally, conclusions are provided in Section 7.

2   Background: Spectrum-Based Fault Localization

The process of pinpointing the fault(s) that led to the observed symptoms (failures/errors) is called fault localization. Depending on the amount of knowledge that is required about the system's internal component structure and behavior, the most predominant approaches can be classified as *i)* statistical approaches or *ii)* reasoning approaches (for an overview of approaches, see [2]). The former approach uses an abstraction of program traces, dynamically collected at run-time (also known as program spectra [8]), to produce a list of likely candidates to be at fault [3, 10, 11], whereas the latter combines a static *model* of the expected behavior with a set of observations to compute the diagnostic report [14]. In this paper, we use a statistical technique, in particular spectrum-based fault localization [3,10] due its effectiveness in locating faults, while entailing low time and space complexity [2].

Spectrum-based fault localization (SFL) is a dynamic program analysis technique. The basic idea of SFL is that comparing the program behavior over multiple test runs can indicate which program components may be likely to contribute to an observed program failure. In the following, we assume that a program P comprises a set of components C and is executed using a set of test cases T that either pass or fail, with $M = |C|$ and $N = |T|$, respectively. Program (component) activity is recorded in terms of program spectra [3, 10, 11]. These data are collected at run-time and typically consist of a number of counters or flags for the different components of a program. Usually, the so-called *hit spectra* is used, indicating whether a component was involved in a (test) run or not.

$$
\begin{array}{c}
M \text{ components} \quad \text{error} \\
\text{vector} \\
N \text{ spectra} \left[
\begin{array}{cccc|c}
a_{11} & a_{12} & \dots & a_{1N} & e_1 \\
a_{21} & a_{22} & \dots & a_{2N} & e_2 \\
\vdots & \vdots & \ddots & \vdots & \vdots \\
a_{M1} & a_{M2} & \dots & a_{MN} & e_N
\end{array}
\right] \\
s_1 \quad s_2 \quad \dots \quad s_N
\end{array}
$$

Fig. 1. The ingredients of fault diagnosis

Both spectra and pass/fail information is input to SFL. The combined information is expressed in terms of the $N \times (M + 1)$ *activity matrix* A. An element a_{ij} is equal to 1 if component j took part in the execution of test run i, and 0 otherwise. The rightmost column of A, the error vector e, represents the test outcome. The element $e_i = a_{i,m+1}$ is equal to 1 if run i *failed*, and 0 if run i *passed*. For $j \leq M$ and $i \leq N$, the row A_{i*} indicates whether a component was executed in run i, whereas the column O_{*j} indicates in which runs component j was involved.

In SFL one measures the similarity between the error vector e and the activity profile vector A_{*j} for each component j (see Figure 1). This similarity is quantified by a *similarity coefficient*, s_j. In this work, we employ the Ochiai similarity coefficient, which was previously identified as the best coefficient to be used for SFL [3].

$$
s_j = \frac{n_{11}(j)}{\sqrt{(n_{11}(j) + n_{01}(j)) \cdot (n_{11}(j) + n_{10}(j))}}
\tag{1}
$$

where $n_{11}(j)$ is the number of failed runs in which part j is involved, $n_{10}(j)$ is the number of passed runs in which part j is involved, and $n_{01}(j)$ is the number of failed runs in which part j is not involved, i.e., formally and referring to Figure 1,

$$
n_{01}(j) = |\{i \mid a_{ij} = 0 \wedge e_i = 1\}|
$$
$$
n_{10}(j) = |\{i \mid a_{ij} = 1 \wedge e_i = 0\}|
$$
$$
n_{11}(j) = |\{i \mid a_{ij} = 1 \wedge e_i = 1\}|
$$

The Ochiai coefficient s_j associated with each component $C_j \in \mathcal{C}$ indicates the correlation between the executions of C_j and the observed incorrect program behavior. Applying the hypothesis that closely correlated components are more likely to be relevant to an observed misbehavior, s_j can be reinterpreted as "fault probability" and components can be listed (i.e., ranked) in order of likelihood to be at fault. Note that $n_{11}(j) + n_{10}(j)$ equals the number of runs in which part

j is involved, whereas $n_{11}(j) + n_{01}(j)$ equals the number of failed runs, which is the same for all j.

We adapted SFL for localizing concurrency faults. For this purpose, we modified the collected hit spectra and the analysis process. In the following, we present a motivating example, followed by our approach illustrated on this example.

3   Motivating Example

In this section, we present a running example for illustrating the problem and our solution. A C function, *addNumberToPhoneList*, is shown in Listing 1.1, which adds a name to a phone book. If the phone book already exists, the function just opens it (Line 12) and adds the name that is provided as an argument (Line 16). Otherwise, the function first creates the phone book (Line 6) and then adds the name into this newly created phone book.

Listing 1.1. The motivating example

```
1 int addNumberToPhoneList(char *name, char *number) {
2   FILE* fp;
3   int retVal = -1;
4
5   if(FALSE == doesPhoneListExist) { /* Component 1 */
6     fp = createPhoneBook();
7     if(NULL != fp) { /* Component 2 */
8       doesPhoneListExist = TRUE;
9     }
10  }
11  else { /* Component 3 */
12    fp = openPhoneBook();
13  }
14
15  if(NULL != fp ) { /* Component 4 */
16    retVal = addPhoneBook(fp, name, number);
17    (void) closePhoneBook(fp);
18  }
19  return retVal;
20 }
```

In a single-threaded environment, *addNumberToPhoneList* function works as expected. However, the function is subject to a concurrency fault when it is executed concurrently by multiple threads. To illustrate this problem, we have executed the function using three threads calling the *addNumberToPhoneList* function to add different entries. As a result, we would expect the phone book to contain three names. Most of the times, this was indeed the case. However, there were executions where the phone book had less than three entries. The reason is the concurrent execution of the function: a context switch can occur when a thread is in *component 1* (lines 5-10)[1]. This component creates a phone book and sets the global variable *doesPhoneListExist* to *true* to eliminate the need for creating a phone book again. Concurrent execution of *component 1* leads to an error because every newly created phone book deletes (overrides) the old one.

In a multi-threaded program, context switches may take place at any time depending on interrupts, operating devices, and the operating system scheduler. Although a program is not subject to an error in a single-threaded execution, multi-threaded execution can, in fact, lead to concurrency errors by enabling (uncontrolled) multiple entries to a component. This is a common issue we have observed in the industry when single-threaded legacy software is adopted within the context of multi-threaded software systems. The legacy software has not been developed with multi-threaded execution in mind, and testing does not always reveal the impact of re-entrance to the employed functions.

We propose and evaluate an approach to automatically detect errors and localize faults in multi-threaded execution of a program. We assume that the program itself is fault-free. As such, any detected error is due to a concurrency fault, caused by the multi-threaded execution of the program. Our approach is explained in the following section.

4   The Approach

Our approach is based on systematically instrumenting the program to trigger a context switch in different components. This enables us to test the same program in different thread interleavings, potentially triggering an error. We apply spectrum-based fault localization to reveal the particular thread interleavings of faulty components that lead to the detected errors. We have developed a toolset called *SCURF* to automate our approach[2], which is realized in three steps as described in the following.

In the first step, the program under test is instrumented to generate different versions each of which execute in different thread interleavings. At this step, the program code is instrumented also to collect spectra information at runtime. Second, each version is tested being subject to the same test suite. Program-spectra are collected for the number of re-entries to each component within a function. Third, the collected spectra are analyzed and correlated with the detected errors. All the components are ranked with respect to the probability that they are subject to a concurrency fault as the cause of the detected errors. These components should be further analyzed by the programmer and possibly considered for introducing thread-safety. In the following subsections, we explain the three steps of the approach in more detail.

---

[1] We refer to code blocks (encapsulated in while, for, if, else statement etc.) as *components* throughout the paper.

[2] SCURF currently supports C make file projects that are deployed on Linux-based operating systems only.

4.1   Step I. Code Instrumentation

In this step, the source code of the program is instrumented to collect program spectra at runtime and to control the scheduling of threads. The collected program spectra record the number of entries made to each component. To control the scheduling of threads, extra code is inserted at the beginning of each component that optionally[3] yields the current thread and forces a context switch. The instrumented code does not change the behavior of the program other than the thread interleavings.

SCURF inserts *sched yield* statements to force context switch at a component. This does not guarantee, in all cases, the scheduler to switch to another thread. We have utilized *usleep* statements in some Linux distributions instead. The code insertion for context switch is performed for each combination of components. That means that the instrumentation step generates $O(2^n)$ versions for a function with n components. However, in practice we have seen that the execution of $O(n)$ versions (context switch at one of the components each time) is usually enough to activate a concurrency fault.

4.2   Step II. Test Case Execution

In this step, the generated versions are executed being subject to the same test suite. We assume that a test oracle and test case(s) exist. For each test, a different thread interleaving occurs and program spectra are collected regarding the number of entries made to each component.

An example result, regarding the *addNumberToPhoneList* running example, for this step is presented in Table 1. Hereby, each row of this table represents a test run. The table is separated into three parts. The first part shows for each component, if a context switch is enforced or not. For example, for the first line, we know that context switch will be forced only in the first component which corresponds to the first *if* statement in the original code. The second part of the table shows the number of entries made to each component during the test run. For example, from the first row we can see that in test run 1, the first, the second and the fourth components were executed three times, whereas the third component was not executed at all. The third, and the final part/column shows the error vector, i.e., whether an error was detected during the corresponding test run or not.

The table is generated incrementally. First, only one component is influenced at a time (test runs 1 through 4 in the example). Similarity calculation is applied for only these set of runs to check if there are significant differences in rankings. We name this step as *level-1*. Depending on the available resources and significance of the results, SCURF can move forward with *level-2*, in which context switch is forced in two of the components at each test run (test runs 5 through 10 in the example). As such, SCURF can incrementally refine the rankings as much as necessary and as long as resources are available [26].

---

[3] The option to activate the inserted code block can be set *ON* or *OFF* differently for each version.

Table 1. Spectra Collected During Test Runs of the Versions of the *addNumberTo-PhoneList* function

	Context Switch				Number of Entries				Error
	C1	C2	C3	C4	C1	C2	C3	C4	Vector
Run1	1	0	0	0	3	3	0	3	1
Run2	0	1	0	0	3	3	0	3	1
Run3	0	0	1	0	1	1	3	3	0
Run4	0	0	0	1	1	1	3	3	0
Run5	1	1	0	0	3	3	0	3	1
Run6	1	0	1	0	3	3	0	3	1
Run7	1	0	0	1	3	3	0	3	1
Run8	0	1	1	0	3	3	0	3	1
Run9	0	1	0	1	3	3	0	3	1
Run10	0	0	1	1	1	1	3	3	0
Run11	1	1	1	0	3	3	0	3	1
Run12	1	1	0	1	3	3	0	3	1
Run13	1	0	1	1	3	3	0	3	1
Run14	0	1	1	1	3	3	0	3	1
Run15	1	1	1	1	3	3	0	3	1

In the following subsection, we illustrate the third step of our approach at *level-1* for the running example.

4.3   Step III. Spectra Analysis

In this step, the collected spectra during test runs are analyzed to rank components with respect to the probability that they cause an error. Analysis is performed iteratively to refine the rankings incrementally until a significant result is achieved or as long as resources permit.

We use the Ochiai similarity metric [3] to correlate the detected errors with component entries at runtime. We have slightly modified this similarity metric to correlate errors with concurrent execution of components. The original metric considers whether a component is executed during a test run or not. In our case, we are interested for each test run, whether a component was executed multiple times by different threads or not. Therefore, we modified the metric such that $n_{11}(j)$ is the number of failed runs in which part j is executed multiple times concurrently, $n_{10}(j)$ is the number of passed runs in which part j is executed multiple times concurrently, and $n_{01}(j)$ is the number of failed runs in which part j is executed only once or not at all, i.e., formally,

$$n_{01}(j) = |\{i \mid a_{ij} \leq 1 \wedge e_i = 1\}|$$
$$n_{10}(j) = |\{i \mid a_{ij} > 1 \wedge e_i = 0\}|$$
$$n_{11}(j) = |\{i \mid a_{ij} > 1 \wedge e_i = 1\}|$$

For the example case, the component rankings are formed as shown in Table 2. Note that the calculations are based on the first group of test runs (*level-1*) only. As we can see from the output in Table 2, $s_0(j)$ is the highest for component 1 and component 2. That means, these components are most probably subject to a concurrency fault that leads to the detected errors. Either of these components or both of them needs to be thread-safe. Not only for this example, but also in our industrial case studies, we have seen that usually rankings at *level-1* already provide accurate diagnosis. In the following section, we present examples from such industrial case studies.

Table 2. Analysis Results for the First Group of Test Runs (*level-1*) of Versions of the *addNumberToPhoneList* function

	C1	C2	C3	C4	Error Vector
Run1	M	M	N	M	1
Run2	M	M	N	M	1
Run3	S	S	M	M	0
Run4	S	S	M	M	0
$n_{11}(j)$	2	2	0	2	
$n_{10}(j)$	0	0	2	2	
$n_{01}(j)$	0	0	2	0	
$s_0(j)$	1.0	1.0	0.0	0.707	

M: Multiple Exec. $(a_{ij} > 1)$, **S**: Single Exec. $(a_{ij} = 1)$ **N**: No Exec. $(a_{ij} = 0)$

After testing a function, SCURF continues to test other functions that are called by that function. For instance, the function *createPhoneBook* is called by the *addNumberToPhoneList* function (Line 6). Hence, after testing the *addNumberToPhoneList* function, if the user asks, SCURF proceeds with testing the *createPhoneBook* function. Similarly, the functions *openPhoneBook*, *addPhoneBook* and *closePhoneBook* will be tested as well. SCURF continues to follow the call hierarchy until the tested function does not call any other function or it makes calls to POSIX functions only, e.g., *strcpy*, *strcat* and *sprintf*.

5   Industrial Case Studies and Evaluation

SCURF has been applied in the context of different industrial software projects that have been developed within TUBITAK. TUBITAK[4] is a government institution, which was formed in 1964. Since then, it has been responsible for many large-scale software development projects for the Turkish government. At TUBITAK, we have observed that one of the common root causes of concurrency faults was the adoption of legacy software within the context of multi-threaded software systems. Usually, the previously implemented functions have been designed to be single-threaded, without multi-threaded execution in consideration.

---

[4] The Scientific and Technological Research Council of Turkey.

Due to indeterministic behavior, testing does not always reveal the impact of concurrent execution and re-entrance to these previously implemented functions. Moreover, the lack of knowledge/documentation regarding the legacy software makes it even harder to locate a fault manually.

Several functions from different code bases were tested to *i)* check if their multi-threaded execution leads to an error, and if so, *ii)* locate the components that are subject to a concurrency fault as the root cause of the error. In the following subsections, we report three such faults that are detected/diagnosed by SCURF and discuss our experiences with SCURF. Due to confidentiality of the projects (and also for brevity), we present modified and simplified code examples. Nevertheless, they are representative examples to illustrate relevant cases and discuss our experiences.

Example 1. One of the concurrency faults was detected in a function called *pipe*; see its implementation in Listing 1.2. This function also calls other functions. The first lines of the *pipe* function is used for initialization. Then, a name (label) is obtained for the pipe to be created (line 8). Two file descriptors are opened with different access modes (lines 10 and 12). These descriptors are used as the read and write end of the pipe.

Listing 1.2. The implementation of the *pipe* function

```
1 int pipe(int fds[2]) {
2   int retVal = -1;
3   //...
4   if(FALSE == isPipeInitialized) {
5     funcRet = init();
6   }
7   if(0 == funcRet) {
8     funcRet = generateNewName(pipeName);
9     if(0 == funcRet) {
10      fds[0] = open(pipeName, O_CREAT | O_RDONLY, S_IRWXU);
11      if(0 <= fds[0]) {
12        fds[1] = open(pipeName, O_CREAT | O_WRONLY, S_IRWXU)↩
           ;
13        if(0 <= fds[1]) {
14          retVal = 0;
15        }
16        else {
17          close(fds[0]);
18          remove(pipeName);
19        }
20      }
21    }
22  }
23  return retVal;
24 }
```

Table 3. Spectra collected for level-1 of the versions of the *pipe* function

	Context Switch						Number of Entries						Error
	C1	C2	C3	C4	C5	C6	C1	C2	C3	C4	C5	C6	Vector
Run1	1	0	0	0	0	0	2	1	1	1	1	0	1
Run2	0	1	0	0	0	0	1	2	2	2	2	0	0
Run3	0	0	1	0	0	0	1	2	2	2	2	0	0
Run4	0	0	0	1	0	0	1	2	2	2	2	0	0
Run5	0	0	0	0	1	0	1	2	2	2	2	0	0
Run6	0	0	0	0	0	1	1	2	2	2	2	0	0

During the testing phase of the *pipe* function at *level 1*, SCURF collected the spectra shown in Table 3. In this table, we can see that an error was detected during the first test run. Note that we assume the *pipe* function to be fault-free in a single-threaded environment. Therefore, the detected error must have been caused by a concurrency fault. SCURF stopped execution after *level-1*. As such, there are 6 test runs in total and in each test run, only one component is influenced to force a context switch. SCURF runs two threads concurrently to test the function. Therefore the number of entries for each component are either 0, 1, or 2. Multiple execution of looping components are still treated as a single execution if being iterated within the same thread. Based on the results listed in Table 3, SCURF calculated fault probabilities for each component as shown in Table 4.

Table 4. Analysis results for level-1 of versions for the *pipe* function

	C1	C2	C3	C4	C5	C6	Error Vector
Run1	M	S	S	S	S	N	1
Run2	S	M	M	M	M	N	0
Run3	S	M	M	M	M	N	0
Run4	S	M	M	M	M	N	0
Run5	S	M	M	M	M	N	0
Run6	S	M	M	M	M	N	0
$n_{11}(j)$	1	0	0	0	0	0	
$n_{10}(j)$	0	5	5	5	5	0	
$n_{01}(j)$	0	1	1	1	1	1	
$s_0(j)$	1.0	0.0	0.0	0.0	0.0	0.0	

According to the results in Table 4, it can be seen that the reason for concurrency violation is multiple execution of *component 1*, before any thread leaves that component. In this case, the cause of the concurrency fault is a call to another function, *init*. This function is supposed to run only once even though the *pipe* function can be called multiple times. Therefore, its multiple execution was intended to be prevented by a global variable named as *isPipeInitialized*. However, the access to this variable should be protected for thread-safe execution.

To remove the fault, *component 1* was protected by a lock mechanism. Although the solution is easy to implement, it is not always easy to locate such a concurrency fault manually. Automated error detection and fault diagnosis facilitated by SCURF helped to perform this task with almost no effort.

Example 2. It turns out that the function *generateNewName*, which is called by the *pipe* function (Line 8), is also subject to a concurrency fault as detected by SCURF. There are no issues regarding the sequential execution of the function, which is shown in Listing 1.3. The function serves as a name generator until it reaches a limit that is imposed by the system. Every call to this function is supposed to return a new name.

Listing 1.3. The implementation of the *generateNewName* function

```
1 int generateNewName(char *fileName) {
2 //...
3 while((0 != fileNameList[index])
4      && (index < MAX_NUM_OF_FILES)) { /* Component 1 */
5   index++;
6 }
7 if(MAX_NUM_OF_FILES != index) { /* Component 2 */
8   fileNameList[index] = index + 1;
9 //...
10   retVal = 0;
11 }
12 else { /* Component 3 */
13   retVal = ERANGE;
14 }
15 return retVal;
16 }
```

SCURF detected a concurrency error for this function during the *level-1* tests. *Component 2* was associated with the detected error. When we check the code in Listing 1.3, we can figure out that concurrent access to the global variable named as *fileNameList* leads to an error because of uncontrolled access both in *component 1* and *component 2*. As such, both of these components must be protected together. SCURF was of valuable help to detect the error and locate the fault for this function. Nevertheless, manual analysis was necessary to successfully remove the concurrency fault concerning both *component 1* and *component 2*.

Example 3. The third case we present is regarding a concurrency fault in a function called *syncResources*. This function also makes calls to other functions but all these functions are thread-safe. However, there is a concurrency fault due to the implementation of the *syncResources* function itself. The function reads from a buffer of a device and transfers the data to another stream to be synchronized with the file system. Every call of this function synchronizes the buffers and flushes them to a permanent storage space. The function has 4 components. This case is particularly interesting because SCURF was able to diagnose the fault only after the test runs at *level-2*. The collected spectra can be seen in Table 5. A concurrency error was not triggered when only one component is influenced at a time to trigger a context switch. At *level-2*, two components were influenced at each test run to trigger an error. For instance, to trigger the error detected in test run 7, the execution of both components 1 and 4 were influenced. To trigger the error detected in test run 9, on the other hand, the execution of both components 2 and 4 were influenced. SCURF blamed three components for the detected errors. We figured out that an uncontrolled access to a global variable in these components caused the errors.

Table 5. Spectra collected during the first and second group of test runs (level-2) of the versions of the *syncResources* function

	Context Switch				Number of Entries				Error
	C1	C2	C3	C4	C1	C2	C3	C4	Vector
Run1	1	0	0	0	2	2	2	2	0
Run2	0	1	0	0	2	2	2	2	0
Run3	0	0	1	0	1	1	1	1	0
Run4	0	0	0	1	1	1	1	1	0
Run5	1	1	0	0	2	2	2	2	0
Run6	1	0	1	0	2	2	2	2	0
Run7	1	0	0	1	2	2	2	1	1
Run8	0	1	1	0	2	2	2	2	0
Run9	0	1	0	1	2	2	2	1	1
Run10	0	0	1	1	1	1	1	1	0

5.1   Performance and Scalability

One might claim that it could be impractical to instrument the code for all possible thread interleavings. This leads to 2^n versions for a function with n components. However, in practice we have seen that test runs at *level-1* are usually enough to diagnose a concurrency fault. At this level, only one component is influenced to trigger a context switch at each test run. As a result, n versions are enough for a function with n components. Only in the third case, SCURF needed to make use of test runs at *level-2*. Based on these observations we have implemented an incremental approach, inspired by approximation algorithms [26]. As such, SCURF can proceed until an error is detected or refine the rankings as much as necessary and as long as resources are available [26]. Tests on different versions can also be performed in parallel to improve scalability.

We performed tests on a Pentium 4 - 3.0 GHz HT Single core 32-bit desktop computer running openSUSE 12.1. In our first study, we executed functions of different size (with respect to the number of components) in 2 threads concurrently. For each of these tests, we measured the time it takes to localize a concurrency fault. For functions that have 6, 16 and 26 components, an error was triggered in 494 ms., 645 ms. and 720 ms., respectively.

In our second study, we performed measurements for different number of threads. The functions that have 6, 16 and 26 components are executed with 6, 12 and 24 threads, respectively. SCURF detected and diagnosed an error within 499 ms., 509 ms. and 547 ms., listed in the order of the corresponding tests.

Our approach is incomparable with respect to stress testing. We have applied stress testing on the *generateNewName* function (Listing 1.3). Even if the function was concurrently being executed in 24 different threads, the concurrency error was still not triggered after 100,000 tests. The error was triggered by SCURF within milliseconds.

5.2 Assumptions and Threats to Validity

SCURF requires that a test oracle and test case(s) are available for testing the functions of the subject system. Also, the original program should not be subject to an error when executed in a single-threaded manner. Otherwise, not all the detected errors can be associated with concurrency issues.

We instrument the program code to force context switches at different components. Inevitably, the effects of our instrumentation are dependent on the platform and the operating system. We perform our tests by assigning the same priority to all the child threads used for test runs, and a higher priority to the parent thread where these threads are created and joined. As such, all the child threads are created before any other terminates. Also, we use FIFO scheduling to eliminate the context switch because of time quantum.

The running time is dependent on the test cases and the algorithmic complexity of the function being tested. Hence, our performance measures can not be interpreted as absolute measures. They only reflect relative measures for a particular case/function.

6 Related Work

There is a large body of related work on analysis and detection of concurrency problems. The first attempt to address this problem focused on detecting race conditions[5]. Static analysis techniques addressing this issue include those based on type systems [6], model checking [16], and general program analysis [17]. There were also dynamic analysis techniques proposed like RecPlay [23] and Eraser [24] However, these techniques were subject to a significant number of false positives. In our approach, we cope with this issue by exploiting a probability score to rank the components instead of providing a binary decision.

More recent dynamic analysis techniques such as CCI [9] and Bugaboo [13] rely on predicate-based fault localization of concurrent programs. In particular, CCI samples shared-memory accesses during program executions and computes

---

[5] A race condition occurs when multiple threads perform unsynchronized access (with at least one of the threads writing) to a shared memory location.

likelihood scores for those memory accesses. Similarly, DefUse [25] samples def-use pairs between two threads. It finds the def-use pairs that are in failed executions and not in passed executions. Recon [12] compares memory accesses with the five previous memory accesses to compute the likelihood scores regarding the faulty memory accesses. CTrigger [18] profiles the program execution to identify thread interleavings correlated to atomicity violation bugs. Aspect oriented techniques have been used [5] for weaving assert statements that verify sequential access. The main distinction of our approach from these studies is that we do not employ passive monitoring. We instrument the code to force the application to run in different combinations of thread interleavings. This improves the diagnostic accuracy. As a complementary approach for improving the diagnostic accuracy, one can utilize test frameworks such as MultithreadedTC [22] to generate test cases that deterministically exercise specific interleavings of threads in an application.

PCT [4] is proposed as a randomized scheduler for finding concurrency bugs. This scheduler quantifies the probability of missing bugs. The quantification is based on so-called *depth* of the bug, which is defined as the minimum number of scheduling constraints that are sufficient to find the bug. Bugs that have higher depths are revealed in fewer schedules, making them harder to detect and diagnose. Experimental results show that in practice, many bugs (e.g., ordering errors, atomicity violations, and deadlocks) have small depths [4]. This result is also consistent with our observations. SCURF is able to diagnose most of the concurrency bugs at *level-1* already, by just influencing the execution of one component at a time.

Yet another approach for detecting concurrency errors is by detecting violations of the atomic property. It has been suggested that atomicity is a property that could be checked to detect concurrent errors at a more abstract, higher-level. The main limitation of atomicity violation detectors is the need for the user to annotate the source code, incurring a considerable overhead during the development phase of the software [7].

Similar to our approach, Falcon [19] and recently introduced UNICORN [21] also utilize spectrum-based fault localization for localizing concurrency faults. Conversely to our approach, both Falcon and UNICORN rank data access patterns (e.g., Read1, Write2, Read1) instead of statements/code blocks. However, not all concurrency problems are about data access. This was also the case for our motivating example.

Chess [15] is a concurrent unit testing tool that can provide fine-grained diagnosis regarding concurrency bugs. In our approach, we can detect such bugs at the component level. As an advantage over Chess, SCURF does not require additional scaffolding or test code to facilitate concurrency testing. An existing test suite prepared for functional unit testing can be used as is. Moreover, tests can be run in different processes in parallel.

7 Conclusion and Future Work

Concurrency faults are hard to diagnose. We have observed that adoption of legacy software in the context of multi-threaded software systems is one of the common root causes of these faults. It becomes even harder to manually locate concurrency faults when legacy software is involved. Therefore, we proposed a 3-step automated approach to diagnose these faults. We first instrument the code to force the program to run in different combinations of thread interleavings. At runtime, we collect information regarding the number of entries to each code block for each test. Then, we employ spectrum-based fault localization to correlate the detected errors with code blocks. Our tool, called SCURF, has been applied in the context of several industrial software systems. We have seen that our approach can accurately localize concurrency faults. We also obtained promising results with respect to performance and scalability.

As future work, we plan to experiment with various diagnostic algorithms that exploit the information regarding the number of times components get executed. Another interesting work is to use static analysis to determine where to enforce context switches, as such reducing the number of tests needed.

Acknowledgement. We thank the anonymous reviewers for their feedback to improve this paper. We also thank software developers and managers at TUBITAK BILGEM for sharing their code base with us and supporting our analysis.

References

1. Abreu, R., Zoeteweij, P., Golsteijn, R., van Gemund, A.: A practical evaluation of spectrum-based fault localization. Journal of Systems and Software 82(11), 1780–1792 (2009)
2. Abreu, R.: Spectrum-based Fault Localization in Embedded Software. Ph.D. thesis, Delft University of Technology (2009)
3. Abreu, R., Zoeteweij, P., van Gemund, A.J.C.: On the accuracy of spectrum-based fault localization. In: Proceedings of Testing: Academic and Industrial Conference Practice and Research Techniques, Windsor, UK, pp. 89–98 (2007)
4. Burckhardt, S., Kothari, P., Musuvathi, M., Nagarakatte, S.: A randomized scheduler with probabilistic guarantees of finding bugs. ACM SIGPLAN Notices 45(3), 167–178 (2010)
5. Dobbelsteen, J., Golsteijn, R., van de Laar, P.: An infrastructure for traceability to increase insight in complex embedded systems. Tech. Rep. PR-TN 2006/00506, Philips Electronics (2006)
6. Flanagan, C., Freund, S.N.: Type-based race detection for java. ACM SIGPLAN Notices 35(5), 219–232 (2000)
7. Flanagan, C., Qadeer, S.: A type and effect system for atomicity. ACM SIGPLAN Notices 38(5), 338–349 (2003)
8. Harrold, M., Rothermel, G., Wu, R., Yi, L.: An empirical investigation of program spectra. ACM SIGPLAN Notices 33(7) (1998)

9. Jin, G., Thakur, A., Liblit, B., Lu, S.: Instrumentation and sampling strategies for cooperative concurrency bug isolation. ACM SIGPLAN Notices 45(10), 241–255 (2010)

10. Jones, J.A., Harrold, M.J.: Empirical evaluation of the tarantula automatic fault-localization technique. In: Proceedings of the International Conference on Automated Software Engineering, Long Beach, California, USA, pp. 273–282 (2005)

11. Liblit, B., Naik, M., Zheng, A.X., Aiken, A., Jordan, M.I.: Scalable statistical bug isolation. In: Proceedings of the Conference on Programming Language Design and Implementation, Chicago, Illinois, USA, pp. 15–26 (2005)

12. Lucia, B., Wood, B., Ceze, L.: Isolating and understanding concurrency errors using reconstructed execution fragments. ACM SIGPLAN Notices 47(6), 378–388 (2011)

13. Lucia, B., Ceze, L.: Finding concurrency bugs with context-aware communication graphs. In: Proceedings of the International Symposium on Microarchitecture, New York, NY, USA, pp. 553–563 (2009)

14. Mayer, W., Stumptner, M.: Evaluating models for model-based debugging. In: Proceedings of the International Conference on Automated Software Engineering, L'Aquila, Italy, pp. 128–137 (2008)

15. Musuvathi, M., Qadeer, S., Ball, T., Basler, G., Nainar, P., Neamtiu, I.: Finding and reproducing heisenbugs in concurrent programs. In: Proceedings of the USENIX Conference on Operating Systems Design and Implementation, pp. 267–280 (2008)

16. Musuvathi, M., Qadeer, S.: Iterative context bounding for systematic testing of multithreaded programs. In: Proceedings of the Conference on Programming Language Design and Implementation, New York, NY, USA, pp. 446–455 (2007)

17. Naik, M., Aiken, A.: Conditional must not aliasing for static race detection. In: Proceedings of the Symposium on Principles of Programming Languages, New York, NY, USA, pp. 327–338 (2007)

18. Park, S., Lu, S., Zhou, Y.: CTrigger: exposing atomicity violation bugs from their hiding places. ACM SIGPLAN Notices 44(3), 25–36 (2009)

19. Park, S., Vuduc, R., Harrold, M.: Falcon: fault localization in concurrent programs. In: Proceedings of the International Conference on Software Engineering, pp. 245–254 (2010)

20. Park, S., Harrold, M.J., Vuduc, R.: Griffin: grouping suspicious memory-access patterns to improve understanding of concurrency bugs. In: Proceedings of the 2013 International Symposium on Software Testing and Analysis. ACM (2013)

21. Park, S., Vuduc, R., Harrold, M.J.: A unified approach for localizing non-deadlock concurrency bugs. In: International Conference on Software Testing, Verification and Validation, Montreal, QC, pp. 51–60 (2012)

22. Pugh, W., Ayewah, N.: Unit testing concurrent software. In: Proceedings of the International Conference on Automated Software Engineering, pp. 513–516 (2007)

23. Ronsse, M., De Bosschere, K.: Recplay: a fully integrated practical record/replay system. ACM Transactions on Computer Systems 17(2), 133–152 (1999)

24. Savage, S., Burrows, M., Nelson, G., Sobalvarro, P., Anderson, T.: Eraser: a dynamic data race detector for multithreaded programs. ACM Transactions on Computer Systems 15(4), 391–411 (1997)

25. Shi, Y., Park, S., Yin, Z., Lu, S., Zhou, Y., Chen, W., Zheng, W.: Do I use the wrong definition?: Defuse: definition-use invariants for detecting concurrency and sequential bugs. ACM SIGPLAN Notices 45(10), 160–174 (2010)

26. Vazirani, V.: Approximation Algorithms. Springer (2003)

A Dynamic Approach
to Locating Memory Leaks

Kostyantyn Vorobyov[1], Padmanabhan Krishnan[2], and Phil Stocks[1]

[1] Centre for Software Assurance, Bond University, Gold Coast, Australia
{kvorobyo,pstocks}@bond.edu.au
[2] Oracle Labs, Brisbane, Australia
paddy.krishnan@oracle.com

Abstract. We present a dynamic approach to memory leak detection and reporting to aid the debugging process. We track memory allocations and aliases during execution, which allows us not only to detect leaks, but also locate the point of the leak in the source code. The level of tracking can be customised by the user. This analysis is safe in the presence of pointer aliasing – a benefit of the dynamic approach, as such problems are hard to solve using static analysis (or lead to many false positives). Our technique works by instrumenting programs with statements that track memory allocations, capture alias information, and monitor potential leaks. By tracking only location and size of memory allocation, rather than monitoring every bit, as is common in other approaches, we keep memory overhead very low. We demonstrate the applicability of our approach on a number of open-source programs and a few SPEC CPU benchmarks. Our experiments show that the overheads compare favourably with current analysis tools such as Valgrind.

Keywords: Memory leak, Program instrumentation, Monitoring.

1 Introduction

Memory monitoring through program instrumentation has been extensively researched for the past two decades, resulting in a number of proprietary and open source tools, such as Purify [1], Valgrind [2], Insure++ [3], Intel Parallel Inspector [4] and others. These tools are often used during test phase, as dynamic analysis is reliable and safe in the presence of pointer aliasing – a problem, for which static techniques do not scale or lead to many false positives. For example, it has become a common practice to monitor test-suite execution, which allows to automatically enable additional oracles for the cost of extra overhead.

The state-of-the-art monitoring techniques for memory leak detection use binary instrumentation, which injects code that observes execution and detects memory defects at the assembly level. This allows the monitoring of each operation, including operations that occur in third party libraries. Even though proven to be useful, binary instrumentation techniques have a number of limitations. Firstly, as it observes every operation and tracks each bit of allocated memory, binary instrumentation is known to produce massive memory and run-time

H. Yenigün, C. Yilmaz, and A. Ulrich (Eds.): ICTSS 2013, LNCS 8254, pp. 255–270, 2013.

overheads. While this may have little impact during the development process, it makes it hard to deploy these tools in performance testing, where runs of unmodified programs may take a long time to execute. Additionally, these tools default to reporting memory leaks using locations of allocation, which does not always provide enough information to eliminate detected defects. Finally, as instrumentation is performed at the assembly level, binary instrumentation techniques are inevitably platform and architecture dependent.

In this paper we present a monitoring approach to memory leak detection that reports where the leakage occurs. This information can facilitate the debugging process. In contrast to binary instrumentation we modify source code of programs by inserting statements to record and update memory state, observe execution and detect memory leaks. In our approach we track memory at the block level, recording only locations and sizes of allocated blocks, which avoids monitoring of every bit and minimises memory overheads. We associate each tracked block with two types of locations: allocation and access. The allocation locations are assigned only once when blocks are created on the heap. The locations of access are updated based on the execution of the program. Every time a block containing references is updated, the access locations are also updated to reflect reachability of the block via some program variable. This is achieved by dynamically computing the dereference of a block's address space. The dereference computation is *tunable* by abstractly specifying memory areas that do not contain pointers and therefore can not leak. This yields a technique where run-time overheads can be reduced for the cost of reporting less debugging information without losing precision. At the end of execution we report unreachable blocks that have not been de-allocated along with the information where it was allocated and where the leakage occurred.

We have a prototype implementation (called Skiff) for monitoring C programs. We demonstrate the applicability of our approach by analysing real UNIX programs and SPEC benchmarks and report the results of our experimentation.

The overall contributions made by this paper are as follows:

- A tunable monitoring approach to memory leak detection that uses source code instrumentation and identifies locations of leakage.
- A proof-of-concept implementation of our technique.
- An empirical evaluation of our approach by comparing the results produced by our tool to the results produced by a state-of-the-art memory profiler. This evaluation demonstrates that in observing test suites of applications the overheads introduced by our technique are much lower.

The rest of the paper is organised as follows. In Section 2 we discuss syntax and semantics of a simple imperative language we use to describe our technique at the abstract level. Section 3 presents a technical description of our approach and shows how to apply it on C programs. Section 4 discusses empirical results of a prototype implementation and Section 5 gives an overview of related work. We give our concluding remarks and discuss future directions in Section 6.

2   Syntax and Memory Semantics

We present our approach at the abstract level using a simple imperative language. We now describe the syntax and semantics of this language.

Figure 1 shows an abstract imperative language similar to the *WHILE* [5] programming language extended with memory allocation and operations for manipulating pointers.

t	::=	$\mathbb{N}$
v	::=	*Vars*
e	::=	$t \mid v \mid e \oplus e \mid \mathbf{deref}(e)$
c	::=	$\mathtt{skip} \mid \mathbf{def}(v) \mid c; c \mid \mathtt{if}\ e\ \mathtt{then}\ c_1\ \mathtt{else}\ c_2 \mid \mathtt{while}\ e\ \mathtt{do}\ c \mid \mathtt{begin}\ c\ \mathtt{end} \mid$
		$\langle l\colon \mathbf{deref}(v) := e \rangle \mid \langle l\colon v := e \rangle \mid \langle l\colon v := \mathtt{malloc}(e) \rangle \mid \mathtt{free}(e)$
P	::=	$\mathtt{begin}\ c\ \mathtt{end}$

Fig. 1. Abstract Language

Expressions e consist of constants $t \in \mathbb{N}$, variables $v \in$ *Vars* (where set *Vars* denotes the set of variables), composite expressions $e \oplus e$, where $\oplus$ is a binary operator and dereference operator $\mathbf{deref}(e)$. Command c consists of atomic commands ($\mathtt{skip}$), variable definitions ($\mathbf{def}(v)$), conditional expressions ($\mathtt{if}\ e\ \mathtt{then}$ $c_1\ \mathtt{else}\ c_2$), loops ($\mathtt{while}\ e\ \mathtt{do}\ c$), scopes ($\mathtt{begin}\ c\ \mathtt{end}$), sequential composition ($c; c$), labelled assignments $\langle l\colon v := e \rangle$ and $\langle l\colon \mathbf{deref}(v) := e \rangle$, where label l identifies source location of the command (e.g., a source code line number) and built-in memory allocation and de-allocation commands $\langle l\colon v = \mathtt{malloc}(e) \rangle$ and $\mathtt{free}(e)$ respectively. The command $\mathtt{malloc}$ allocates a new memory block (e.g., a sequence of contiguous memory cells) of size specified by expression e and binds the address of the first cell in the allocated segment to a variable v. $\mathtt{free}(e)$ de-allocates a memory block, whose first address is given by expression e. If no such block exists the statement is equivalent to $\mathtt{skip}$. Program P is a sequence of commands within a scope.

We now introduce our semantics of the memory model to formally define memory leaks. We let *Scope* denote the set of scope identifiers and set $\mathbb{N}$ to represent a memory address. A particular memory block is denoted by a pair over $\mathbb{N}$ representing start and end addresses of the block. Let $\mathcal{B} = \mathbb{N} \times \mathbb{N}$ be the set of all blocks. Then, memory allocation is a subset of such pairs. Formally, the set of all possible allocations $\mathcal{A}$ is $\mathcal{P}(\mathcal{B})$, where $\mathcal{P}$ is the powerset operator. Typical elements are denoted by σ and we require that allocated blocks are disjoint, and that the start address is not greater than the end address (and assume blocks represent allocation of contiguous chunks of memory).

Memory mapping m_σ is the set of pairs $\mathbb{N} \times \mathbb{N}$, where each pair $(i, t) \in m_\sigma$ represents a valid memory block. The set of all possible memory mappings is denoted by the set $\mathcal{M} = \mathcal{P}(\mathbb{N} \times \mathbb{N})$, that is m_σ is an element of $\mathcal{M}$. A memory mapping is valid only if each address mapped to a value lies within the allocated block.

Store usage by program (denoted μ) is the set of triples $Vars \times Scope \times \mathbb{N}$, where a triple $(v, s, t) \in \mu, v \in Vars, s \in Scope, t \in \mathbb{N}$ in a particular state represents a variable v defined at scope s and bound to a numeric constant t. Formally, the set of all possible store usages $\mathcal{S}$ is $\mathcal{P}(Vars \times Scope \times \mathbb{N})$, where store usage in a particular state μ is an element of $\mathcal{S}$.

Finally, we let the set Lab denote the set of all program labels. An element $l \in Lab$ denotes either a defined source location (such as a line number) or an undefined one (denoted by $\perp$). We use labels to track usage of blocks during memory allocation and assignments. We let function $loc : \mathbb{N} \times \mathbb{N} \to Lab$ denote usage tracking in a particular state. For example, a label associated with a block $(a, b) \in \sigma$, where σ is a valid allocation, is retrieved using $loc(a, b)$. The set of all such functions is denoted Lt (for label tracking).

2.1 Operational Semantics

Malloc: $\dfrac{}{\langle l: v = \mathtt{malloc}(e) : \sigma, m_\sigma, \mu, loc, \langle s_1, ..., s_n \rangle \rangle \to \langle \mathtt{skip} : \sigma^*, m_\sigma, \mu^*, loc^*, \langle s_1, ..., s_n \rangle \rangle}$

$\sigma^* = \sigma \cup \{(eval(v, \sigma, m_\sigma, \mu, s_1), eval(v + e, \sigma, m_\sigma, \mu, s_1)\}$
$\mu^* = \mu \setminus \{(w, s, t) \mid (w, s, t) \in \mu \wedge w = v\} \cup \{(w, s, eval(v, \sigma, m_\sigma, \mu, s_1)) \mid (w, s, t') \in \mu \wedge w = v \wedge s = s_1\}$
$loc^*(a, b) = \begin{cases} l & \text{if } (a, b) = (eval(v, \sigma, m_\sigma, \mu, s_1), eval(v + e, \sigma, m_\sigma, \mu, s_1)) \\ loc(a, b) & \text{otherwise} \end{cases}$

Free1: $\dfrac{}{\langle \mathtt{free}(e) : \sigma, m_\sigma, \mu, loc, \langle s_1, ..., s_n \rangle \rangle \to \langle \mathtt{skip} : \sigma \setminus \{(a, b)\}, m_\sigma \setminus \{(i, t) \mid a \leq i \leq b\}, \mu, loc^*, \langle s_1, ..., s_n \rangle \rangle}$ $(\exists (a, b) \in \sigma : a = eval(e, \sigma, m_\sigma, \mu, s_1))$
$loc^*(e, f) = \begin{cases} loc(e, f) \text{ if } (e, f) \neq (a, b) \\ \perp \qquad \text{otherwise} \end{cases}$

Free2: $\dfrac{}{\langle \mathtt{free}(e) : \sigma, m_\sigma, \mu, loc, \langle s_1, ..., s_n \rangle \rangle \to \langle \mathtt{skip} : \sigma, m_\sigma, \mu, loc, \langle s_1, ..., s_n \rangle \rangle}$ $(\nexists (a, b) \in \sigma : a = eval(e, \sigma, m_\sigma, \mu, s_1))$

VariableAssignment: $\dfrac{}{\langle l: v = e : \sigma, m_\sigma, \mu, loc, \langle s_1, ..., s_n \rangle \rangle \to \langle \mathtt{skip} : \sigma, m_\sigma, \mu^*, loc^*, \langle s_1, ..., s_n \rangle \rangle}$
$\mu^* = \mu \setminus \{(w, s, t) \mid (w, s, t) \in \mu \wedge w = v\} \cup \{(w, s, eval(v, \sigma, m_\sigma, \mu, s_1)) \mid (w, s, t') \in \mu \wedge w = v \wedge s = s_1\}$
$loc^*(a, b) = \begin{cases} l & \text{if } (a, b) \in R_v^+(\sigma, m_\sigma, \mu, s, v) \\ loc(a, b) & \textit{otherwise} \end{cases}$

MemoryAssignment: $\dfrac{}{\langle l: \mathbf{deref}(v) = e : \sigma, m_\sigma, \mu, loc, \langle s_1, ..., s_n \rangle \rangle \to \langle \mathtt{skip} : \sigma, m_\sigma^*, \mu, loc^*, \langle s_1, ..., s_n \rangle \rangle}$
$m_\sigma^* = m_\sigma \setminus \{(a, b) \mid (a, b) \in m_\sigma \wedge a = eval(\mathbf{deref}(v), \sigma, m_\sigma, \mu, s_1)\}$
$\cup \{eval(v, \sigma, m_\sigma, \mu, s_1), eval(e, \sigma, m_\sigma, \mu, s_1)\}$
$loc^*(a, b) = \begin{cases} l & \text{if } (a, b) \in R_v^+(\sigma, m_\sigma, \mu, s, v) \\ loc(a, b) & \textit{otherwise} \end{cases}$

Fig. 2. Operational Semantics

The operational semantics of commands (with key rules shown in Figure 2) is defined as a relation $\to$ on *configurations*, where a configuration is a tuple $\langle c : \sigma, m_\sigma, \mu, loc, Scope^* \rangle$, such that c is a program command, σ is a memory allocation, m_σ is a memory mapping, μ is a store usage, loc is a function that identifies command labels associated with allocated memory blocks, and $Scope^*$ is a sequence of scope identifiers (e.g., sequence $\langle s_1, ..., s_n \rangle$, where $s_1, ..., s_n \in Scope$ are distinct identifiers of executed scopes).

The rule for $\langle l\colon v := \mathtt{malloc}(e)\rangle$ adds a new block to σ and updates the block pointed to by v to the new block (indicated by the change to μ). The rule for $\mathtt{free}(e)$ removes the block identified by e from σ. Rule $\langle l\colon v := e\rangle$ for variable assignments update store usage, while rule $\langle l\colon \mathbf{deref}(v) := e\rangle$ for memory assignments modifies memory mapping, i.e., allows to write to a memory location through a variable dereference. Additionally, each of the above rules modify label function loc, which associates labels with allocated blocks and thus is the key to label tracking. We discuss this behaviour in detail in Section 3. The rules for the other commands are standard and are not presented.

In the next few paragraphs we summarise the key concepts underlying our technique. We elaborate only on concepts that are relevant for memory leaks. The behaviour of expressions is standard in that the result of their evaluation is defined by function $eval(e, \sigma, m_\sigma, \mu, s)$ that evaluates to a constant $t \in \mathbb{N}$, where e is an expression, σ is a memory allocation, m_σ is a memory mapping, μ is a store usage and $s \in Scope$ is an executed scope. I.e., $eval(e, \sigma, m_\sigma, \mu, s) = t$ denotes expression e that evaluates to a constant t in scope s, where $\sigma \in \mathcal{A}$ is a valid allocation, $m_\sigma \in \mathcal{M}$ is a valid memory mapping and $\mu \in \mathcal{S}$ is a store usage.

A variable v in scope s points to a memory block if the value in the variable lies within that block. This is formally given using Definition 1.

Definition 1 (Points to via variable). *Given a valid memory allocation $\sigma \in \mathcal{A}$, valid memory mapping $m_\sigma \in \mathcal{M}$, store usage by program $\mu \in \mathcal{S}$, scope $s \in Scope$ and variable $v \in Vars$, v is said to **point** to an allocated memory block $(a, b) \in \sigma$ in scope s if and only if $a \leq eval(v, \sigma, m_\sigma, \mu, s) \leq b$.*

Given a valid memory allocation σ, valid memory mapping m_σ, store usage μ and scope s, a given block $(a, b) \in \sigma$ can point to another block $(c, d) \in \sigma$ in scope s, if and only if a memory address within (a, b) is mapped to an address that lies within (c, d). The relation R_b in Definition 2 defines this formally.

Definition 2 (Points to via block). *Given a valid memory allocation $\sigma \in \mathcal{A}$, valid memory mapping $m_\sigma \in \mathcal{M}$, store usage by program $\mu \in \mathcal{S}$, scope $s \in Scope$ and allocated memory block $(a, b) \in \sigma$, binary relation:*

$$R_b(\sigma, m_\sigma, \mu, s, (a, b)) = \{(e, f) \mid (e, f) \in \sigma \wedge$$
$$\exists i \in \mathbb{N}: a \leq i \leq b \wedge e \leq eval(\mathbf{deref}(i), \sigma, m_\sigma, \mu, s) \leq f\}$$

*defines the set of memory blocks in σ, block (a, b) **points to**.*

Thus, in allocation σ, memory mapping m_σ, store usage μ and scope s, block (a, b) points to block (c, d) if and only if $(c, d) \in R_b(\sigma, m_\sigma, \mu, s, (a, b))$.

In a memory allocation σ, memory mapping m_σ, store usage μ and scope s, a given block (say b_n) is accessible from another block (say b_0) if there is a sequence of blocks $b_1, \cdots, b_{n-1}$ such that for all i between 0 and $n-1$, b_i points to b_{i+1}. This is formally defined by the relation R_b^+ in Definition 3.

Definition 3 (Accessibility). *Given a valid memory allocation $\sigma \in \mathcal{A}$, valid memory mapping $m_\sigma \in \mathcal{M}$, store usage by program $\mu \in \mathcal{S}$, scope $s \in Scope$ and allocated memory block $(a, b) \in \sigma$, binary relation:*

$$R_b^+(\sigma, m_\sigma, \mu, s, (a,b)) = \{(e,f) \mid (e,f) \in R_b(\sigma, m_\sigma, \mu, s, (a,b)) \vee$$
$$(\exists (c,d) \in R_b(\sigma, m_\sigma, \mu, s, (a,b)) : (e,f) \in R_b^+(\sigma, m_\sigma, \mu, s, (c,d))\}$$

*defines the set of blocks **accessible** from (a, b).*

Thus, for a memory allocation σ, memory mapping m_σ, store usage μ and scope s, memory block $(c, d) \in \sigma$ is accessible from block $(a, b) \in \sigma$ if and only if $(c, d) \in R_b^+(\sigma, m_\sigma, \mu, s, (a, b))$.

Given a memory allocation σ, block $(a, b) \in \sigma$, memory mapping m_σ, store usage μ and scope s, variable $v \in Vars$ references (a, b) if v points to (a, b) or there exists some block $(c, d) \in \sigma$, such that v points to (c, d) and (a, b) is accessible via (c, d). This is formally defined by the relation R_v^+ in Definition 4.

Definition 4 (Reference). *Given a valid memory allocation $\sigma \in \mathcal{A}$, block $(a, b) \in \sigma$, valid memory mapping $m_\sigma \in \mathcal{M}$, store usage $\mu \in \mathcal{S}$, scope $s \in Scope$ and variable $v \in Vars$, binary relation*

$$R_v^+(\sigma, m_\sigma, \mu, s, v) = \{(a,b) \mid (a,b) \in \sigma : a \leq eval(v, \sigma, m_\sigma, \mu, s) \leq b \vee$$
$$(\exists (c,d) \in \sigma : c \leq eval(v, \sigma, m_\sigma, \mu, s) \leq d \wedge (a,b) \in R_b^+(\sigma, m_\sigma, \mu, s, (c,d)))\}$$

*defines the set of blocks **referenced** by variable v.*

Thus, given a memory allocation $\sigma \in \mathcal{A}$, memory mapping $m_\sigma \in \mathcal{M}$, store usage by program $\mu \in \mathcal{S}$ and scope $s \in Scope$, variable $v \in Vars$ references allocated memory block $(a, b) \in \sigma$, if $(a, b) \in R_v^+(\sigma, m_\sigma, \mu, s, v)$.

Given the above we can define **memory leak** as follows:

Definition 5 (Memory leak). *Given a valid memory allocation $\sigma \in \mathcal{A}$, valid memory mapping $m_\sigma \in \mathcal{M}$, store usage $\mu \in \mathcal{S}$ and scope s, a memory block $(a, b) \in \sigma$, is a **memory leak** with respect to store usage by program μ, if there exists no triple $(v, s, t) \in \mu$, $v \in Vars$, $s \in Scope$, $t \in \mathbb{N}$, such that $(a, b) \in R_v^+(\sigma, m_\sigma, \mu, s, v)$. That is, block (a, b) is not referenced by program variables from the given store usage.*

3   Memory Leak Detection

We now present technical details of the memory leak detection technique. Our approach consists of two stages: static and dynamic. At the static stage we instrument an input program (say P to obtain P') with statements that monitor the execution of P to detect memory leaks. At the dynamic stage we run P', which reports occurred memory leaks (if any) at the end of its execution.

To keep track of the memory state during the execution of P we use an explicit data-structure T_σ. A particular state of T_σ describes the state of memory that has been tracked during the execution of the transformed program P'. T_σ is the set of 4-tuples of values (i.e., $T_\sigma \in \mathcal{P}(\mathbb{N} \times \mathbb{N} \times \mathbb{N} \times \mathbb{N})$). An element (a, b, l_a, l_u) of T_σ

represents a memory block (a, b) (where a and b are its start and end addresses), such that at program location l_a block (a, b) was allocated and referenced via a variable at label l_u. We further refer to labels l_a and l_u as to allocation and usage labels respectively.

We now describe functions that operate on T_σ. The function **insert**(T_σ, a, b, l) adds the element $(a, b, l, 0)$ (where 0 represents an undefined label) to T_σ. The function **delete**(T_σ, a) removes elements whose start address is a. Given a memory address c the function **lookup**(T_σ, c) searches through the elements of T_σ and returns a memory block (a, b), if there exists an element (a, b, l_a, l_u) of T_σ, such that c lies within (a, b), or a pair $(0, 0)$ (where $(0, 0)$ represents an invalid block) otherwise. The function **update**(T_σ, a, l) modifies a usage label of a particular element of T_σ identified by a start address of the tracked memory block it represents.

The function **updateLabel** is the main memory tracking function. Its task is to update usage labels of memory blocks that participated in assignments. Informally, a usage label associated with a block of memory identifies a source location at which that memory block was accessible. For example, given an assignment statement $\langle l : v = e \rangle$, where v is a variable and e is an expression, **updateLabel** sets usage labels of all memory blocks referenced by v to l.

The semantics of **updateLabel** is as follows. Given an input value val (such that val is a value to which some variable v at label l evaluates), **updateLabel** identifies the set of memory blocks (say R) referenced by v (i.e., memory blocks that can be accessed through v). R is populated by recursively dereferencing values stored in blocks pointed to by v and then calling **lookup** on the values obtained by dereferencing. Valid memory blocks returned by **lookup** are then added to R. For example, given that v points to a memory block (a, b), which in turn points to some block (c, d), **updateLabel** first dereferences the value of v, identifies (a, b) as being pointed to by v and adds it to R. Further, it dereferences each value in the range $[a, b]$ and adds (c, d) to R (since (a, b) points to (c, d)). It then searches through the range $[c, d]$ and finalises the search (since block (c, d) does not point to any other blocks). The fourth argument, *mode*, may be used to constrain the generation of the set R and reduce the amount of reported information for the benefit of speed of execution. We further discuss the application of *mode* and describe different modes of operation of our technique in Subsection 3.1. For each element $(a, b) \in R$ the function **update**(T_σ, a, l) (where l is the input label) is executed which updates the usage labels associated with blocks v references to l. The function **report**(T_σ) reports memory leaks based on the state of T_σ, such that for each element (a, b, l_a, l_u) that belongs to T_σ, a memory block (a, b) is reported as a memory leak, such that (a, b) was allocated at location l_a and last referenced by a variable at location l_u.

3.1   Syntactic Transformations

We now present the set of syntactic transformations, i.e., instrumenting the source code, in Figure 3. The first step of our transformation instruments an input program with a data structure T_σ to keep track of the memory state (Figure 3, Rule *Program*).

Malloc: $\overline{\langle l: v := \mathtt{malloc}(w)\rangle} \rightarrow \langle l: v := \mathtt{malloc}(w)\rangle;$ *Free:* $\overline{\mathtt{free}(v)} \rightarrow \mathbf{delete}(T_\sigma, v);$
                                  $\mathbf{insert}(T_\sigma, v, v + w, l);$ $\mathtt{free}(v);$

MemAssign: $\overline{\langle l: \mathbf{deref}(v) := e\rangle} \rightarrow \langle l: \mathbf{deref}(v) := e\rangle;$
                             $\mathbf{updateLabel}(T_\sigma, v, l, mode);$

                                                   $c \rightarrow c'$

VarAssign: $\overline{\langle l: v := e\rangle} \rightarrow \langle l: v := e\rangle;$ *Prog:* $\begin{array}{ll} \mathtt{begin} \rightarrow & \mathtt{begin} \\ \quad c; & \quad \mathbf{def}(T_\sigma); \mathbf{def}(mode); \ c'; \\ \mathtt{end} & \quad \mathbf{report}(T_\sigma); \\ & \mathtt{end} \end{array}$
                             $\mathbf{updateLabel}(T_\sigma, v, l, mode);$

Fig. 3. Syntactic Transformations

Calls to **insert** and **delete**, which track allocated and de-allocated memory blocks, are injected into P via rules *Malloc* and *Free* (Figure 3). That is, each statement that allocates memory (i.e., $\langle l: v := \mathtt{malloc}(w)\rangle$) is followed by a call to $\mathbf{insert}(T_\sigma, v, v + w, l)$, where v evaluates to the start address of the allocated block, expression $v + w$ evaluates to its end address and l is a block's allocation label. Similarly, before each statement that de-allocates memory (i.e., a call to $\mathtt{free}(\mathtt{v})$), a call to $\mathbf{delete}(T_\sigma, v)$, that removes an element of T_σ that refers to a de-allocated block, is made.

Each assignment statement is appended with a call to **updateLabel**, which tracks assignments of memory blocks referenced by variables. That is, calls to **updateLabel** update usage labels, which allows us to collect information on the propagation of data blocks. At any given state, a usage label associated with a block indicates a source location at which that block was last known to be referenced by a variable.

Since **updateLabel** is the main cause of the run-time overhead, its behaviour can be controlled externally by constraining the search for memory blocks referenced by a variable via limiting the search to the traversal of blocks of particular sizes only, where the maximal size of a traversed block is given by parameter *mode*. Currently, our approach supports *Minimal*, *Partial* and *Full* modes. In the *Minimal* mode **updateLabel** does not track usage labels. Hence, the reported information is limited to the existence of memory leaks and the locations of their allocation. In the *Full* mode, each block is traversed. In the *Partial* mode only the blocks of size less than *mode* are traversed. This avoids traversal of large blocks that may not contain pointers.

Finally, we insert a call to $\mathbf{report}(T_\sigma)$, before P terminates.

At the dynamic stage of our approach we execute an instrumented program P', which reports memory leaks at the end of execution. A program run, for which T_σ is empty, does not leak any memory. Otherwise, each element of T_σ (say (a, b, l_a, l_u)) is reported as the memory leak of size $(b - a)$ allocated at program location l_a and last known to be referenced by a variable at l_u.

3.2   Application on C Programs

The technical details of the approach presented above are at the abstract level and need to be mapped to a concrete level to be able to apply them on a realistic programming language. We now discuss the extensions required to use our approach with C programs.

Due to the semantics of the C programming language, where stack-allocated memory blocks are automatically freed, additionally to a block's start and end addresses we record its type of allocation (i.e., stack, heap, global). This is to be able to distinguish between memory that is de-allocated explicitly or implicitly. Stack memory blocks are recorded to T_σ explicitly, via inserting calls to **insert** immediately after definitions of local variables. The sizes of stack blocks are determined via the `sizeof` operator. Further, each stack block added to T_σ is assigned an identifier of a scope it was allocated in.

Unlike in the abstract language, C statements are not labelled. To be able to generate all the required information we instrument the program with a stack that keeps track of entered functions and program locations associated with them. Thus the top element of the stack holds the location of the executed line, while other elements indicate locations of entered functions that lead to current function.

To be able to track all allocated heap memory we redefine memory allocation and de-allocation functions, which, apart from the normal functionality, insert or remove elements of T_σ. This is possible as the GNU C library defines `malloc` and similar functions as weak aliases. The original definitions of functions such as `malloc` are replaced with our instrumented ones. Such an approach allows for recording all heap memory, including blocks allocated by library functions for which no source code is available, e.g., `strdup`. Thus in practice we can report leaks for a larger class of programs than described formally.

Since in C programs values of pointers may be affected by function calls, function arguments are processed similarly to assignment statements.

4   Results

We have implemented our technique in a prototype tool called Skiff for programs written in the C programming language. Skiff is built on top of the *Clang* [6] compiler architecture (LLVM project, version 2.9 [7]). The platform for all results reported here was an Intel Core i5-2400 3.1 GHz machine with 4GB of RAM, running Gentoo Linux.

To evaluate the efficiency of our approach we have performed a number of experiments that involved instrumentation and dynamic analysis of well-known UNIX utilities, such as `find`, `grep`, `gzip`, `diff`, `patch`, `rcs`, `locate` and `rm`, and C benchmarks from the CPU2000 and CPU2006 sets developed by the Standard Performance Evaluation Corporation (SPEC). In this section we also report the results produced by Valgrind [8] (a state-of-the-art system for debugging and profiling programs) on the same test subjects and compare them to the results collected using our approach.

During experimentation with UNIX utilities we monitored execution of their test suites and calculated overheads per test suite. Runs of CPU benchmarks were performed using the test data set provided by SPEC.

Note, that this evaluation focusses on the value of extended memory leak reports of the *Full* mode of Skiff and performance overheads, rather that on the number of discovered defects. This is because both techniques are sound and do not report false alarms. The reliability of Valgrind has been established by various experiments over the years. We manually checked that the output from Skiff is consistent with Valgrind's output.

We now report the results of our experimentation. We first outline differences in reporting of *Full* mode of Skiff and Valgrind and point out the benefits of locating sources of memory leaks. We then compare and discuss performance overheads incurred by different modes of Skiff and Valgrind.

Figure 4 demonstrates the difference in reporting schemes of Valgrind and Skiff in the *Full* mode. This uses a memory leak found in GNU locate (Findutils 4.4.2). The Valgrind report (on the left) shows the allocation site of this leak using a stack trace. Skiff (on the right) also uses stack traces to report leaks and shows the allocation site of the leak (a stack trace above the line of asterisks) and the source of leaked memory (a stack trace of below the line). Additionally, our tool reports variable names (e.g., procdata, highlighted in gray), that referenced the leaked memory block prior to the leakage. This removes ambiguity, as a single line of code in C may contain multiple statements.

```
128 bytes in 1 blocks are definitely lost    * 128 bytes
==11936== at 0x402B7B8:                       Allocation: xmalloc.c:49
        malloc (vg_replace_malloc.c:270)        [35]:xmalloc [locate.c:1106]
==11936== by 0x80515F9:                         [33]:search_one_database [locate.c:1884]
        xmalloc (xmalloc.c:49)                  [8]:dolocate [locate.c:1940]
==11936== by 0x804AAE0:                       *****************************************
        search_one_database (locate.c:1106)   Leak: locate.c:879 [ alias: procdata ]
==11936== by 0x804BDC3:                         [349]:visit_count [locate.c:375]
        dolocate (locate.c:1884)                [191]:visit [locate.c:385]
==11936== by 0x804BF43:                         [33]:search_one_database [locate.c:1884]
        main (locate.c:1940)                    [8]:dolocate [locate.c:1940]
```

Fig. 4. Valgrind vs. *Full* Mode Memory Leak Report

We now discuss performance overheads of Skiff and Valgrind.

Figures 5 and 6 outline the difference in memory and run-time overheads produced by Valgrind and Skiff run in the *Minimal* mode. That is, the reports produced by both tools are similar and include detected memory leaks and their allocation sites as call traces. The Y-axis measures overhead ratio (comparing to the run-time or memory consumption of unmodified programs) and each point on the X-axis stands for a series of runs of a program.

It can be seen that the run-time and memory overheads produced by our tool are lower than Valgrind's. The memory overhead produced by Skiff averages to 15% with the highest spike of approximately 3 times in equake only. Memory overheads of Valgrind are much higher, ranging from 1.6 to 34 times with the

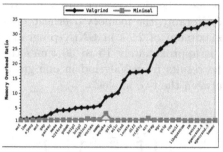

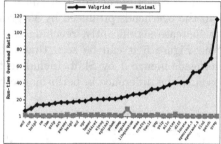

Fig. 5. Valgrind vs. *Minimal* Mode. Memory Overhead.

Fig. 6. Valgrind vs. *Minimal* Mode. Run-time Overhead.

average of 15 times. The run-time overhead exhibited by both tools compares similarly. The overhead produced by Skiff is on average approximately 80%, while the average run-time overhead of Valgrind is 30.8 times, ranging from 6.8 to 116 times. Note, that spikes, such as 116 times in `grep` can be partially attributed to a high number of invocations of programs during test suite execution (e.g., over 1250 runs in `grep` test suite), where each invocation causes Valgrind to dynamically instrument a binary monitor memory. This is different to our approach, where we eliminate such overhead by instrumenting source code and compile monitoring capabilities in. Additionally, we track memory at the block level and store only the delta of information, such as block addresses, sizes etc., whereas Valgrind monitors each byte individually. That is, our overhead is proportional to the number of memory blocks allocated by a program, whereas Valgrind's is proportional to the overall amount of allocated memory. Note, that while on average block-level tracking proves to yield low overhead, it may increase if many small blocks are allocated. This is exhibited, by the `equake` benchmark where overheads can be 3 times for memory and 9 times for run-time. Finally, it should be noted that in the *Minimal* mode we monitor only allocation and de-allocation operations, which is computationally light. Of course, this does not produce useful debugging information.

The run-time overhead in the *Full* mode varies and may increase significantly based on sizes of memory blocks a program manipulates. This is because our main run-time overhead is due to computation, i.e., iteration through address ranges of memory blocks and identifying pointers in assignments. Thus, the main factor that influences overhead is the size of memory blocks traversed (i.e., size of manipulated data structures) and the frequency of their use (i.e., the number of statements that trigger `updateLabel`). Thus, we may expect larger overheads for SPEC benchmarks, as these programs are crafted to routinely perform computationally intensive tasks (such as archiving, compilation etc.) on large data chunks. We now discuss the results of our experimentation.

Figure 7 depicts the run-time overheads of our prototype run in the *Full* and *Minimal* modes and Valgrind on the set of UNIX utilities. It can be seen that in the *Full* mode our overhead increases, spanning from 1.3 times (in `gzip`) to almost 11 times in the `rcs` test suite. These overheads, however, are still lower than the overheads produced by Valgrind. Notably, the memory overhead does not increase significantly, reaching the maximum of 21% in UNIX programs. From Figure 5 it can be seen that this is approximately 15 to 30 times the overheads incurred by Skiff. Including the results from Valgrind in one graph obscures the difference in performance between the two modes.

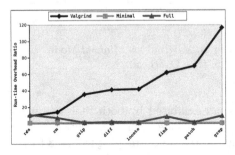
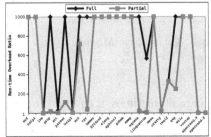

Fig. 7. UNIX: Run-time Overhead   **Fig. 8.** SPEC CPU: Run-time Overhead

It is important to note that Skiff in *Full* mode does not always outperform Valgrind – especially on the SPEC CPU benchmarks. Sometimes our run-time overhead is extremely high (over 1000 times). The main factor that contributes to such overhead is the size of memory blocks allocated. The larger the size of the memory allocated, the longer it takes to run **updateLabel**. This behaviour is confirmed via experimentation in *Partial* mode. When we limit traversal of memory blocks by the size of the largest data structure, i.e., assuming that larger blocks are *data only* blocks and do not contain any pointers, the overheads are significantly reduced as depicted in Figure 8 which for the sake of clarity does not show the data associated with Valgrind. One can compare the performance of Valgrind and Skiff in *Full* mode by combining the data from Figures 6 and 8. The raw data is available from the authors on request.

For example, the overhead for the `lbm` benchmark is reduced from 566 to only 5 times. The excessive overhead of benchmarks, which continue to perform similarly to the *Full* mode, is due to the structure of some SPEC benchmarks, where a large amount of memory is allocated statically, irrelevant of the input size. Note, that while developing programs such allocations are rarely used.

The relation between increased run-time overhead and the amount of memory allocated by programs is illustrated in Figure 9. The presentation of these data is split because of the difference in the run-time overhead ratios and thus the scale of the figures is different. In the set of UNIX utilities (Figure 9, leftmost plot) the main purpose of the associated test suites is to evaluate functional correctness of programs, where memory consumption does not exceed 5 megabytes and thus Skiff, even in *Full* mode, outperforms Valgrind. In the SPEC CPU benchmarks (Figure 9, center and rightmost plots) memory consumption is much higher. The center plot of Figure 9 shows that Skiff in *Minimal* mode always outperforms

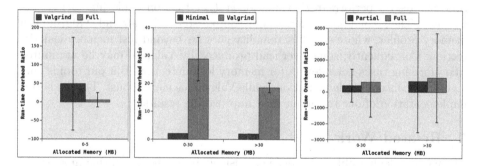

Fig. 9. Overhead Relative to Memory Usage. Left to right: UNIX Programs (Full vs. Valgrind), SPEC CPU (Minimal vs. Valgrind), SPEC CPU (Partial vs. Full).

Valgrind with negligible overheads and low variance. The rightmost plot of Figure 9 compares the overheads incurred by Skiff in *Partial* and *Full* modes. Note, memory size alone does not affect the overheads. If each allocated block contains pointers, then these pointers need to be tracked, adding to overheads, while if the allocated blocks contain only data they need not be tracked, reducing the overheads. This is shown by the variance in the overheads. What this means is that the overhead is not consistently high. Note that abnormal cases with extreme overhead in SPEC CPU should be attributed to the design pattern of SPEC benchmarks which are aimed at performance evaluation. The memory consumption, however, affects only *Full* or *Partial* modes.

Our approach is mainly useful in the domain of functional testing, where program correctness is established through runs with small inputs. In addition to memory leak detection, our technique can provide useful information that facilitates debugging. Note, that our experimentation with UNIX utilities indicates that with small inputs Skiff overheads may be lower than the overheads of conventional monitoring using Valgrind. Our approach can also be used in performance testing, where program runs are significantly heavier, in both memory consumption and run-time. Our experimentation suggests that for memory leak detection our technique uses considerably less resources than DBI, while still producing the same level of output, especially in *Minimal* or *Partial* mode.

4.1 Threats to Validity

We now discuss factors that may have affected the validity of our results. The first factor is the choice of programs and the input data used in our experimentation. Even though, during experimentation with UNIX utilities we used realistic programs and representative inputs (i.e., test suites that are associated with the utilities), which should account for exercising most of the paths, there is no evidence that applying our technique on different programs or using different input values will yield similar results. Similarly, during our second experiment with SPEC CPU benchmarks, the input values provided may not be representative for the development process. This is because SPEC concentrates on performance evaluation, rather that on exploring various behaviours. The second issue refers to our comparison with Valgrind. Valgrind is a memory profiler, whose core functionality goes far beyond just memory leak detection. Consequently, some overhead produced by Valgrind may be attributed to performing tasks not relevant for memory leak detection. But our tool is only a proof-of-concept implementation, while Valgrind is more robust. Thus, a better implementation of our technique may improve the results.

5   Related Work

The memory leak problem has been extensively researched, resulting in a variety of memory leak detection techniques that use static and dynamic analyses. We now summarise papers that are directly relevant to our approach.

One of the most common approaches in memory profiling is to track memory usage at the byte level via binary instrumentation. One of the earliest attempts is *Purify* [1]. *Purify* statically inserts additional instructions directly into object files monitoring memory allocation and every read or write performed by a program under test. More recent approaches, such as Dr. Memory [9], use dynamic binary instrumentation (DBI). In DBI, an executable is analysed using extra code added to it at run-time. Despite the strengths of DBI, such as soundness and the ability to monitor any memory operation, DBI may produce high overhead in both execution time and memory consumption, while still reporting only allocation sites of leaked blocks. In our approach we have the benefit of locating the source of leakage without incurring the overheads associated with DBI.

Insure++ [3] is a memory profiler for C and C++. Unlike profilers that exclusively instrument binaries, Insure++ can operate at the source code level. Unfortunately, implementation details of this tools is not publicly available.

Determining precise locations of memory leakage has also been investigated. Maebe et al. [10] have presented a technique that tracks all pointers to the allocated memory using reference count. In their approach authors keep track of pointers by monitoring load and store operations that may change pointer structure of a program, detecting locations of memory leakage. The downside of this technique is that it can report both false positive and false negative results. Clause and Orso [11] developed a similar technique that detects sources of memory leaks, called LEAKPOINT. LEAKPOINT tracks memory using dynamic taint analysis. A tainted pointer identifies an access alias to that memory block. LEAKPOINT updates the taint as execution proceeds by observing operations on pointers. This uses a *propagation policy* which models each such operation. At run-time LEAKPOINT keeps track of pointer count per allocated memory block (i.e., taint marks associated with pointers) and identifies leakage locations as the locations where pointer count dropped to zero. The main weakness of LEAKPOINT is that its propagation policy is neither sound nor complete. That is, while LEAKPOINT may soundly identify memory leak existence, the reported sources of leaked memory are not guaranteed to be correct. Finally, LEAKPOINT is a DBI approach (built on top of Valgrind) and thus also suffers from very high overheads (e.g., the authors report overheads that are 300 times) Our technique addresses a similar question by using on-the-fly computation rather than reference count. This makes our technique both sound and complete which we have formally proven. Also note, that our technique correctly handles cases such as p1 = p2 + 1; and p++; where p is moved past the end of a block.

Another approach that can potentially detect location of leakage, is Boehm GC [12] – a garbage collector for C and C++ languages that uses a variation of the mark-and-sweep algorithm. If used as a leak detector, Boehm GC reports memory blocks that are no longer accessible as memory leaks. This, however, relies on a periodic scanning of program address space to determine *lost* memory and thus can not determine precise locations of leakage.

6   Conclusions

We have presented a tunable monitoring approach to locating memory leaks. Our technique uses source-to-source transformations to instrument an input program with statements to monitor its memory state of and report leaks before the modified program terminates. Our approach has the benefit of locating program points at which leaked memory was lost. This aids the debugging process, providing developers with extra information that can be then used to eliminate detected defects. Additionally, our approach provides tuned monitoring via different modes of execution enabled at run-time. In the *Full* mode extra information of leakage locations is produced for the cost of larger overheads. *Minimal* mode minimises overheads using a conventional reporting scheme that outputs only allocation sites. *Partial* mode reduces overheads by tracking leakage locations of memory blocks of particular sizes only.

We have implemented our approach in a prototype tool called Skiff for C programs. During our experimentation we monitored execution of a number of well-known UNIX applications and SPEC CPU benchmarks. Further, the results of our tool were compared to the results produced by Valgrind. Our experimentation shows that in conventional reporting, where only allocation sites of leaked blocks are determined, our approach significantly outperforms Valgrind. Such results indicate that for memory leak detection Skiff may be used as a replacement for binary instrumentation tools, producing similar results with considerably less system resources. Experimentation with *Full* mode shows that our overheads directly depend on the amount of memory allocated by programs and increase as memory consumption grows. Analysis of UNIX utilities showed Skiff performed better than Valgrind mainly due to relatively small allocated blocks. However, Skiff performed considerably worse on SPEC benchmarks, which focus on performance evaluation and thus use large inputs. We demonstrated the applicability of overhead tuning using *Partial* mode, where in some cases we reduced large overheads of SPEC benchmarks by not tracking large data blocks for leakage. Overall we can conclude that leakage detection at the current stage is mainly useful in the domain of functional testing, where program correctness is established with runs with relatively small inputs.

In the future we are looking to improving the performance of our technique for large allocations. Our preliminary experimentation shows that the high overheads incurred are due to tracking blocks that do not leak or are accessible globally. Thus, rather than instrumenting each statement, we could use lightweight but sound static program analysis to filter out statements that cannot leak. We would also like to consider alternate or extended instrumentations that detect other memory faults, such as, for example, use after free errors.

Acknowledgement. The first author is supported by a grant from Oracle Labs. The second author was affiliated with Bond University when most of this work was done.

References

1. Hastings, R., Joyce, B.: Purify: Fast detection of memory leaks and access errors. In: Proceedings of the Winter USENIX Conference, pp. 125–136 (January 1992)
2. Seward, J., Nethercote, N.: Using valgrind to detect undefined value errors with bit-precision. In: Proceedings of the USENIX Annual Technical Conference, USENIX, pp. 17–30 (2005)
3. Parasoft (Insure++), http://www.parasoft.com/jsp/products/insure.jsp
4. Intel: (Parallel inspector),
   http://software.intel.com/en-us/intel-parallel-inspector
5. Nielson, H.R., Nielson, F.: Semantics with applications - a formal introduction. Wiley Professional Computing. Wiley (1992)
6. clang: a C language family frontend for LLVM (March 2012),
   http://clang.llvm.org
7. Lattner, C., Adve, V.: LLVM: A Compilation Framework for Lifelong Program Analysis & Transformation. In: Proceedings of the International Symposium on Code Generation and Optimization, CGO 2004. IEEE Computer Society, Washington, DC (2004)
8. Nethercote, N., Seward, J.: Valgrind: A framework for heavyweight dynamic binary instrumentation. In: Proceedings of the ACM SIGPLAN Conference on Programming Language Design and Implementation, PLDI 2007, vol. 42, pp. 89–100. ACM, New York (2007)
9. Bruening, D., Zhao, Q.: Practical memory checking with Dr. Memory. In: Proceedings of the Annual IEEE/ACM International Symposium on Code Generation and Optimization, CGO 2011, pp. 213–223. IEEE Computer Society, Washington, DC (2011)
10. Maebe, J., Ronsse, M., Bosschere, K.D.: Precise detection of memory leaks. In: Proceedings of the International Workshop on Dynamic Analysis, pp. 25–31 (May 2004)
11. Clause, J.A., Orso, A.: LEAKPOINT: Pinpointing the causes of memory leaks. In: Proceedings of the ACM/IEEE International Conference on Software Engineering, ICSE 2010, vol. 1, pp. 515–524. ACM (May 2010)
12. Boehm, H.: Dynamic memory allocation and garbage collection. Computers in Physics 9, 297–303 (1995)

Towards a GUI Test Model
Using State Charts and Programming Code

Daniel Mauser[1], Alexander Klaus[2], and Konstantin Holl[2]

[1] Daimler AG, Ulm, Germany
[2] Fraunhofer IESE, Kaiserslautern, Germany
daniel.mauser@daimler.com,
{alexander.klaus,konstantin.holl}@iese.fraunhofer.de

Abstract. Modern human machine interfaces provide a sophisticated structure and logic to ease their use. As they are the only mean to control the system behind, extensive testing and highest quality is required in the automotive domain. A common testing approach in literature is to derive the necessary test cases from a formal model. However, redundancy and data dependency still hinder manual modeling in the industrial context. In this paper, we present preliminary work to address these obstacles. As a first step, we combined depictive state charts with reusable programming code. We modeled parts of the graphical user interface of a state-of-the-art infotainment system and successfully generated a test suite that covers our testing goal to reach each button at least once.

Keywords: automotive, human machine interface, model based testing.

1 Introduction

An automotive human machine interface (HMI) provides system functionality to the user. The main interface is usually represented by a graphical user interface (GUI). Figure 1 shows an example for such a GUI including a possible screen structure. According to [1], a GUI "is essential to customers, who must use it whenever they need to interact with the system". However, testing automotive HMIs leads to more challenges than testing standard PC applications, caused by the special characteristics of automotive HMIs, e.g., the dynamic menu behavior and the large set of variants [2]. Effective usage of an automotive HMI by the user requires an effective quality assurance process. Failures during the usage while driving may lead to a distraction of the driver.

The complexity of the specification in the automotive domain is typically handled by the definition of conditions that represent the states of connected applications and devices. They consist of internal conditions, such as the selection of an option (e.g., "ESP on/off"), and of external conditions, such as the availability of a functionality (e.g., "ESP available/unavailable"). The state of the conditions influences, e.g., the availability or visibility of menu entries. As modern automotive infotainment systems comprise hundreds of specified conditions, managing the complexity manually is not feasible. Every condition can

H. Yenigün, C. Yilmaz, and A. Ulrich (Eds.): ICTSS 2013, LNCS 8254, pp. 271–276, 2013.

Fig. 1. The SUT is structured in four vertical menus that hold the clickable elements

be set to various values; this results in an extremely large number of possible combinations. Handling the amount of conditions can be done by modeling the set of conditions and its effects within a test model. It describes the conditions and its dependencies and leads to a simplification for the test engineer. Defining rules for test case derivation enables the possibility to cover the complexity of the conditions. Hence, a test generator can automatically generate test cases with the intended test coverage. This increases the controllability for reaching every menu entry which is desired to be tested. The testing goal, to ensure that all menu entries are reachable, is important for all types of integration tests.

While developing these kinds of test models, we experienced the following two major issues: The first issue is that widget behavior often depends on data such as system conditions or inserted data. One example is the entry behavior of a menu: in the system under test, menu widgets have a property "entryStrategy" that influences, which of the the containing button elements is focused the first time the menu is entered, which again depends on what buttons are actually visible at this particular moment. Test models should support efficient means to describe this data dependency. The second major issue is redundancy of behavior. Due to the modular nature of most user interfaces, atomic elements, so called widgets (buttons, menus, ...), are reused in order to ease the specification (consistent interaction concepts) and implementation (reuse of software modules). Explicitly modeling each instance of all widget types occurring in an entire system is time consuming and error prone in development and maintenance. To reduce the probability of errors, mechanisms to facilitate consistent modeling have to be applied. In software engineering, these challenges are faced by code that is structured hierarchically and modularly. Logic is encapsulated in classes that are instantiated every time this particular logic is needed. In the context of an ongoing industrial research project we currently adopt this concept for modeling HMI behavior accordingly, for test case generation purposes.

This paper is structured as follows: after discussing related work regarding applicability in our context, we present excerpts of our ongoing work to develop a modularly structured test model. The paper concludes with a first appraisal of the approach and an outlook on the intended next steps.

2   Related Work

A good overview on model based testing (MBT) in general can be obtained in [3], whereas [4] focuses on MBT of GUIs in particular. As a testing approach should easily integrate in a software development lifecycle, one crucial point is the model as basis for test generation. In the automotive domain, UML state charts are "widely established in HMI specification and development" [2, P. 24]. Various approaches for MBT of GUIs use state based modeling ([5–9]). A widely used technique for model based GUI testing is reverse engineering, i.e., executing the application and analyzing the GUI ([5–7]). However, as these approaches rely on the availability of source code, reverse engineering is not applicable in our domain. An OEM, such as Daimler, usually assigns the task of creating an HMI to suppliers and receives a package containing both hard- and software. In such cases, it is not feasible for OEMs to extract the software or to use reverse engineering, since there is no operating system supporting these techniques and the input mechanisms are different.

An approach that presumes manual modeling has been presented in [8]. The authors use domain specific state machines and model transformations to obtain product line and variant specific test models. Their solution is "to integrate domain knowledge into the state machine metamodel" [8], working with a combination of EMF[1] and Xtext[2]. Although the presented approach appears to be promising, no test case generator is available to make use of the results. Therefore, we decided to adapt the method bearing in mind available tools for generation. Established solutions are, e.g., Microsoft Spec Explorer[3] or Conformiq Qtronic[4]. Qtronic relies on hierarchical UML state machines as models, which can be enriched with a custom modeling language, which is a superset of Java [10]. Test cases are generated using symbolic execution [10]. Spec Explorer uses models created with Spec#, a variant of C# [11]. The model is then explored to create test cases and capture the intended behavior [11]. The tool distinguishes between controllable and observable actions [11]. A comparison of different characteristics of both Spec Explorer and Qtronic can be found in [10].

3   Model Structure

Similar to the basic structure introduced by [8], we combine programming code and state charts to make use of the strengths of both approaches: state charts provide a clear structure of screens and their relationships and therefore ease retracing the generated test cases. Object oriented programming code is easy to reuse and provides efficient means to specify behavior. The established product "Conformiq Designer" supports these kinds of models.

---

[1] www.eclipse.org/emf/

[2] www.eclipse.org/Xtext/

[3] http://research.microsoft.com/en-us/projects/specexplorer/

[4] http://www.conformiq.com/

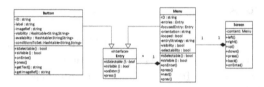

Fig. 2. The Screen and the Entry elements Menu and Button are the essential classes

We developed a "widget toolbox" containing the basic elements the user interface consists of: classes for buttons, menus and screens (see Figure 2). The **Entry** is the basic widget type that summarizes all methods that are necessary for the interaction concepts. Deriving classes have to implement methods that state on demand whether they are visible (displayed on screen) or available (visible and selectable). Entries further have to implement methods that are triggered once they are focused and once they are pressed. The **Button** represents entries that are clickable and contain content. This content can be textual (attribute: *label*) and/or a reference to an icon or symbol (attribute: *imageRef*). The attributes *visibility* and *availability* describe references to the system conditions the visibility/availability of the button object depends on. **Menus** are container elements for entries (attribute: *entries*). As menus can again contain menu objects, this class also implements the "Entry" interface and provides the respective methods. *isSelectable()* and *isVisible()* return the respective attributes that are set via constructor. Further, menus determine what containing Entry element is focused on next() and prev(). The **Screen** class is called from within the state machine. Therefore, methods for all user interactions that directly affect the content on the screen are provided. In this setup, this includes left, right, up, down, press, and back. Screen objects are the root element for all objects in the respective state space. E.g., for each application, such as Audio or Navi, a separate screen object is instantiated. As illustrated in Figure 1, the standard screen class provides three menu lines with horizontal orientation (Application Line, Playfield, Subfunction Line), which again are contained in the menu object *content*. The screen passes the user events through to the respective menus.

The **state chart** functions as main application. It consists of programming code that constructs the state machine object and a hierarchical graphical chart. Within the constructor, all necessary button, menu and screen objects are instantiated. These objects can then be used within the graphical part. An excerpt of the chart is shown in Figure 3. For modeling, the basic state chart elements are available. In our approach, we additionally distinguish between view states that refer to screen objects, and condition states that are used to evaluate system conditions. On the lowest level of the charts there are solely view states.

With the presented approach, we modeled parts of the audio application of the latest Mercedes Benz infotainment system (NTG4.5 High Edition) that provides the functionality to play music that is stored on connected media as well as to listen to radio. We assumed a fully equipped setup, including all available media types (HDD, audio and video DVD, AUX, etc.) and radio wavebands

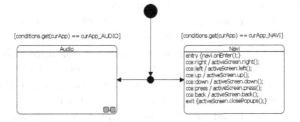

Fig. 3. The "Action" keyword of State Chart elements might refer to coded objects

(FM, LW, MW, DAB, etc.). We instantiated 15 screen, 57 menu and 138 button objects. As stated in Section 1, the testing goal is to set the system conditions to focus each button object at least once. To guide the **test case generation**, we use checkpoints in code and in the state charts. Hence, we added a checkpoint to the onEnter() method of the Button class to ensure that this method will be executed in every Button instance. The generator provided functionality to determine the necessary user interactions. To cover this state space, we had to declare 38 conditions. 26 test cases with a total of 616 test steps have been generated to fulfill the testing goal.

4   Discussion and Conclusion

In this paper, we present ongoing work on model-based black-box testing of graphical user interfaces in the domain of in-vehicle infotainment systems. We discussed basic challenges of manual model development and maintenance and pointed out that model complexity is originated in (a) the dependency of behavior on data and (b) the redundancy of logic. To address those complexity drivers we stress the need for modularly structured test models. Due to the context, manual model development is required. We developed a model structure that combines the strength of state charts to depict macro behavior with object oriented programming to allow complex data processing and modular reusability.

We developed a model to cover the audio application of a state-of-the-art infotainment system at Mercedes Benz. The disadvantageous redundancy could be handled successfully: general interaction concepts, such as the focus based navigation or list based screen structures, are described and maintained centrally; manual modeling was easy and allowed a satisfiable progress. The approach was stable regarding changes and allowed model-wide adaption of selective behavior. Due to the inheritance of object-oriented structures, several abstraction levels could be utilized: general Entries had been specialized to clickable Buttons, which again, if necessary for testing purposes, could be basis for more complex structures, such as Radio Buttons or Checkboxes. By doing so, details could be reduced to a level that could be handled manually. We successfully generated test cases using the proprietary generator "Conformiq Designer". As testing goal, we chose to focus every Button object at least once. The state charts were useful to retrace the generated test cases.

According to our experiences, the mixed approach appears to be appropriate: describing the entire behavior graphically would not have been feasible. An exclusively coded model would have been confusing and thus as error-prone as the real implementation. In future, we plan to advance the approach to automate the testing process. Next step will be to use the generated test suite as input for automatic test execution. Special attention will be drawn to the verification aspect. Due to the model structure, a data based description of all content to be displayed on screen could be exported at any time. We plan to embed this information in the test case description to provide an extensive basis to assess the system reaction, i.e., as test oracle.

References

1. Brooks, P.A., Robinson, B.P., Memon, A.M.: An initial characterization of industrial graphical user interface systems. In: Proceedings of International Conference on Software Testing Verification and Validation, ICST 2009, pp. 11–20. IEEE Computer Society (2009)
2. Duan, L.: Model-based testing of automotive hmis with consideration for product variability. Ph.D. dissertation, Ludwig-Maximilians-Universität München (2012)
3. Utting, M., Legeard, B.: Practical Model-Based Testing: A Tools Approach. Morgan Kaufmann Publishers Inc., San Francisco (2007)
4. Banerjee, I., Nguyen, B., Garousi, V., Memon, A.: Graphical user interface (gui) testing: Systematic mapping and repository. Information and Software Technology (2013)
5. Morgado, I.C., Paiva, A., Faria, J.P.: Reverse engineering of graphical user interfaces. In: The Sixth International Conference on Software Engineering Advances, ICSEA 2011, pp. 293–298 (2011)
6. Arlt, S., Podelski, A., Bertolini, C., Schäf, M., Banerjee, I., Memon, A.M.: Lightweight static analysis for gui testing. In: The 23rd IEEE International Symposium on Software Reliability Engineering, ISSRE 2012, pp. 301–310. IEEE (2012)
7. Hackner, D.R., Memon, A.M.: Test case generator for guitar. In: Schäfer, W., Dwyer, M.B., Gruhn, V. (eds.) ICSE Companion, pp. 959–960. ACM (2008)
8. Grandy, H., Benz, S.: Specification based testing of automotive human machine interfaces. In: Fischer, S., Maehle, E., Reischuk, R. (eds.) GI Jahrestagung. LNI, vol. 154, pp. 2720–2727. GI (2009)
9. Paiva, A.C., Tillmann, N., Faria, J.C., Vidal, R.F.: Modeling and testing hierarchical guis. In: Proceedings of the 12th International Workshop on Abstract State Machines (2005)
10. Sarma, M., Murthy, P.V.R., Jell, S., Ulrich, A.: Model-based testing in industry: a case study with two mbt tools. In: Proceedings of the 5th Workshop on Automation of Software Test, AST 2010, pp. 87–90. ACM, New York (2010)
11. Veanes, M., Campbell, C., Grieskamp, W., Schulte, W., Tillmann, N., Nachmanson, L.: Model-based testing of object-oriented reactive systems with spec explorer. In: Hierons, R.M., Bowen, J.P., Harman, M. (eds.) FORTEST. LNCS, vol. 4949, pp. 39–76. Springer, Heidelberg (2008)

A Tool for Supporting Developers in Analyzing the Security of Web-Based Security Protocols*

Giancarlo Pellegrino[1,2], Luca Compagna[2], and Thomas Morreggia[2]

[1] Eurecom, Sophia-Antipolis
giancarlo.pellegrino@eurecom.fr
[2] SAP AG
{giancarlo.pellegrino,luca.compagna}@sap.com,
thomas@morreggia.fr

Abstract. Security protocols are specified in natural language, are highly-configurable, and may not match the internal requirements of the development company. As a result, developers may misunderstand the specifications, may not grasp the security implications of configurations, and may deviate from the specifications introducing flaws. However, none of the existing security testing techniques provides the features, scalability, and usability to support developers in assessing the security of protocol configurations and deviations. This paper presents a tool that leverages on existing design verification and security testing techniques, and extends them to support developers in analyzing security protocols. We used the tool for the analysis of prominent security protocols (i.e., SAML SSO, OpenID, OAuth2), and of six industrial-size implementations.

1 Introduction

Security protocols are communication protocols that aim at providing security guarantees through the application of cryptographic primitives. Security protocols are at the core of modern business scenarios and enable partners to set up business environments. However, their specifications and implementations can be flawed as witnessed by the many vulnerabilities discovered in the past years [3,4,9,13]. Security protocols are specified in natural language and, as a consequence, can be misinterpreted by the developers. Moreover, the design of modern protocols considers the different deployment landscapes (e.g., mobile, or cloud scenarios). As a result, protocols feature different flows and a wide range of options. The number of options combinations makes it difficult for developers to understand the security implications. In addition, the protocol security recommendations delivered by the standardization bodies may not match the internal requirements of the software development company. As a result, implementations may deviate from the specifications and endanger the overall security. E.g., the SAML-based SSO for Google Apps until 2008 neglected few, yet important, message fields that allowed an attacker to impersonate a user and

---

* This work has been partially supported by the FP7-ICT Project SPaCIoS (no. 257876).

H. Yenigün, C. Yilmaz, and A. Ulrich (Eds.): ICTSS 2013, LNCS 8254, pp. 277–282, 2013.
© IFIP International Federation for Information Processing 2013

steal her confidential data [3]. To detect vulnerabilities, researchers have proposed several techniques at the different phases of the software life-cycle. Source code analysis looks for patterns into the source code or analyzes the data flow of the user-controlled inputs [10]. Black-box input fuzzers probe implementations with special values and analyze the output for detecting vulnerabilities [8]. Model checking checks whether the protocol design satisfies a given security property [4,13] and if not, the returned counterexample is used as a test case for the testing implementations [6,7,9]. However, none of these techniques provides the features, scalability, and usability to support developers in assessing the security of protocol options and deviations.

This paper presents a tool that leverages on existing design verification and security testing techniques, and extends them to support developers in analyzing the security of security protocols. The tool helps developers, software engineers, and security experts making decisions during the development process and detecting flaws both during the design and the deployment phases. It integrates existing verification and testing techniques that are described in other works [1,6,5] and it does not introduce new testing or verification techniques. The tool is not a product of SAP and it is not our intention to promote any other SAP product. The focus of this paper is to present a tool that is the result of three years of experience in applying cutting-edge security analysis techniques to industrial-size scenarios. We used the tool for the security analysis of prominent standard security protocols (i.e., SAML SSO, OpenID, and OAuth2) and of six industrial-size implementations.

Case Study

The SAML [12] SSO is a security protocol that enables business partner to authenticate users once and then let them access their services. The objective of a client C is to access to a resource at a service provider SP. An identity provider IdP authenticates C and issues authentication assertions (a signed authentication token). The protocol ends when SP consumes the assertions and grants or denies C the access to the resource. SAML SSO has two basic flows depending on whether the user requests the resource

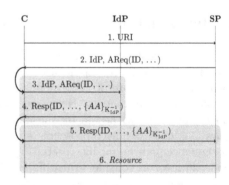

Fig. 1. SAML SSO SP-initiated flow without ARP

to SP (SP-initiated SSO), or to IdP (IdP-initiated SSO). Both flows can be used in combination with the *Artifact Resolution Protocol* (ARP) that allows SAML messages to be transported by reference rather than by value. In total, SAML SSO has six protocol flows (ARP can be used at most twice in each basic flow).

Figure 1 shows the SAML SSO SP-initiated without ARP. In step 1, C asks SP the resource at URI. In step 2, SP redirects C to IdP with the authentication request AReq(ID,...) where ID is uniquely identifying the request. Then SP stores ID in a table. In step 3, IdP authenticates C, builds the authentication assertion AA, and signs it with its private key. Then, IdP adds $\{AA\}_{K^{-1}_{IdP}}$ to Resp and forwards it to SP via C. SP first verifies the signature and then checks if its table contains ID. Finally, SP delivers the resource to C. At the end of the protocol run, C and SP are mutually authenticated (goal G1) and the resource is kept confidential for C (goal G2). The messages 3-4 and 5-6 in Figure 1 are exchanged over SSL/TLS communication channels.

In this paper we consider only few protocol options[1]: SP signs AReq, IdP signs Resp, and use of SSL/TLS in steps 1-2. In addition, developers would like to assess the security of design decisions. In this paper we consider the following decisions: SP does not store the ID in steps 1-2, and SP sets an HTTP cookie at step 2 and check it at step 5.

2   A Security Testing Tool

Our tool is a set of Eclipse plugins implementing existing testing and verification techniques [1,5,6]. The tool supports the specification of protocol options and implementation decisions, implements the design verification and model-based security testing workflows, and supports verification and test campaigns.[2]

(a) **Design verification:** The design verification workflow implements the formal analysis of security protocols via model checking. The process consists of three steps. First, the user writes the formal model and specify the security property. Then, the model checker explores the model for violation of the property. If a violation is discovered, the model checker returns a counterexample. Finally, the user inspects the counterexample using graphical viewers.

Our tool implements text editors to write formal models and properties (currently, it supports ASLan and ASLan++ languages[1]; both languages support macros for security properties) with features such as syntax highlighting, and problems highlighting (for syntax and semantic errors). It integrates the SAT-based Model Checker [2] for the formal verification, and UI components for displaying counterexamples as message sequence charts.

(b) **Configuration and Implementation decisions:** Our tool enables the specification of configuration options and implementation decisions. This is done through the *SPaCIoS navigator*. The navigator implements three main functionalities. First, it allows the specification of single protocol option (or decision) by means of labels. (A label is a text description and an arbitrary color.) Second, it allows for the creation of a new model (capturing the option) starting from an existing one and for marking it with labels. Finally, the navigator keeps track of all the model generated in a derivation tree in which the roots are the reference models. The tree and the labels are used later on for the preparation of the test/verification campaign so to create reports in the form of Figure 4.

---

[1] The other options of the same flow as well as the options of the other five protocol flows were considered in our analysis, but not shown in this paper.

[2] Plugins for the features (a) and (c) are available in the SPaCIoS Tool (http://www.spacios.eu/platform.php). The remaining features (b) and (d) are available upon request.

Figure 2 shows the navigator. The upper part displays the derivation tree in which each model (i.e., node tree) is associated to labels. A model can have more than one label. The lower part of the navigator shows the list of labels created during the analysis. They capture the configuration options of the SAML SSO standard that we used for supporting the developers at SAP.

(c) Model-based security testing:
The model-based security testing work-flow is used for testing implementations for detecting security flaws. It consists of five steps. First, the user writes the model and properties by using the text editor as explained in the design verification workflow. Second, the tool generates test cases using an external model checker (a test case is a counterexample). Third, the user defines the implementation under test adapter (IUTA). The IUTA is a data structure containing the mapping between model symbols and real values, the protocol participants under test, and a list of message adapters.

Fig. 2. The Navigator

IUTAs are created by using the IUTA editor. Fourth, the test cases are executed against the IUTA and, finally, the user inspects the results. Our tool supports HTTP conversation and message inspection. Moreover, the tool has a built-in web browser to visualize the content of HTTP responses.

This workflow implements the technique devised by Armando et al. [6] in which the formal model is compiled into a set of Java program fragments that are executed in the order of the abstract test case.

(d) Verification and Test Campaign: A verification campaign is the verification of several models. Similarly, the test campaign consists of the executions of several test cases.

Fig. 3. The Test Campaign Manager

Figure 3 shows the editor for the test campaign manager. It displays the list of test cases generated, and the IUTAs available. The user selects the test cases and the IUTAs, and she runs the campaign. At the end of the execution, the tool displays the HTTP conversations for off-line analysis. The result of a campaign is organized into tables. In addition, the tool logs the results and HTTP messages of all the test for future inspections.

3   Application to the Case Study

We modeled the flow of Figure 1 in ASLan++. For each option and decision, we created a label with the UI of Figure 2 and derived a model. We adjusted each new model for reflecting the option (resp. decision). Afterwards, we created and launched a verification campaign. Figure 4 shows an excerpt of the result of the campaign. The table is structured as follows. Each row is a model with unique identifier *MID*. The column *from* is a pointer to the model from which *MID* has been derived. The remaining columns are grouped by *Opt*, *Dec*, and *Res* respectively for options, decisions and results. We use y when the option (resp. decision) is used or when the model checker found a violation; we use n otherwise. For example, the model 2fc derives from 0fc (depicted in Figure 1) by adding the SSL/TLS channel in steps 1-2.

MID	from	Opt. SSL C-SP:AReq	Opt. Sign AReq	Opt. Sign AResp	Dec. SP set cookie	Dec. SP stores ID	Res. G1	Res. G2
0fc	-	n	n	n	n	y	y	n
2fc	0fc	y	n	n	n	y	y	n
4fc	2fc	y	y	n	n	y	y	n
5fc	4fc	y	y	y	n	y	y	n
...								
6fc	0fc	y	n	n	y	y	n	n
...								
7fc	5fc	y	y	y	y	n	n	n
...								

Fig. 4. Results for the SP-initiated protocol

Figure 4 shows the following results. First, the protocol suffers from a flaw in which G1 is not satisfied. Second, the protocol options are not sufficient for fixing the flaw. Third, the use of cookies solves the vulnerability. Fourth, the two implementation decisions do not endanger the security with respect to the properties G1 and G2. Finally, the security goal G2 is always reached.

Developers can use the results of Figure 4 to make decisions about the design and the implementations. For example, in security-sensitive scenarios, they may enforce the use of cookie and avoid storing the ID as a Denial-of-Service countermeasure.

The counterexamples returned by the model checker are used as test cases for probing the implementations. For example, we used the counterexample of 0fc to test SAML-based SSO for Google Apps and SimpleSAMLphp as reported by Armando et al. [4]. The former implements the configuration of 0fc while the latter 6fc. The test against SAML-based SSO for Google Apps succeeded proving that also the implementation suffers from the flaw [4]. The test against SimpleSAMLphp failed due to the use of the cookie [4]. We applied the same approach on the OpenID protocol and its implementations. The tests detected a flaw in both the specifications and implementations (Zoho Invoice with Google OpenID or Yahoo OpenID). In addition, we used the tool at SAP to assist developers during the development of the NGSSO and OAuth2. In the former, we analyzed all the six SAML SSO flows considering in total 15 protocol options,

and seven implementation decisions. In total we verified 85 formal models. In
the latter, we considered so far one protocol flow and seven protocol options.

4   Future Work and Conclusion

We plan to support other modeling languages more suitable for developers, e.g.,
the Alice-and-Bob notation [11] or UML sequence diagrams. In addition, we
plan to integrate inference techniques for creating models from traces [9] and to
integrate other test case generation techniques [7]. In conclusion, we presented a
model-driven security analysis and testing tool. It supports the evaluation of the
impact of implementation decisions and protocol configurations. The tool was
used for the security analysis of SAML SSO, OpenID, and OAuth2, and of six
industrial-size protocol implementations.

References

1. Armando, A., et al.: The AVANTSSAR Platform for the Automated Validation
   of Trust and Security of SOA. In: Flanagan, C., König, B. (eds.) TACAS 2012.
   LNCS, vol. 7214, pp. 267–282. Springer, Heidelberg (2012)
2. Armando, A., Carbone, R., Compagna, L.: Ltl model checking for security protocols. In: 20th IEEE CSF 2007 (July 2007)
3. Armando, A., Carbone, R., Compagna, L., Cuellar, J., Abad, L.T.: Formal Analysis
   of SAML 2.0 Web Browser Single Sign-On: Breaking the SAML-based Single Sign-
   On for Google Apps. In: Proc. of ACM FMSE 2008 (2008)
4. Armando, A., Carbone, R., Compagna, L., Cuéllar, J., Pellegrino, G., Sorniotti,
   A.: An authentication flaw in browser-based single sign-on protocols: Impact and
   remediations. Computers and Security 33 (2013)
5. Armando, A., Carbone, R., Compagna, L., Pellegrino, G.: Automatic security analysis of SAML-based single sign-on protocols. In: Digital Identity and Access Management: Technologies and Framework, ch. 10 (2011)
6. Armando, A., Pellegrino, G., Carbone, R., Merlo, A., Balzarotti, D.: From model-
   checking to automated testing of security protocols: Bridging the gap. In: Brucker,
   A.D., Julliand, J. (eds.) TAP 2012. LNCS, vol. 7305, pp. 3–18. Springer, Heidelberg
   (2012)
7. Büchler, M., Oudinet, J., Pretschner, A.: Semi-automatic security testing of web
   applications from a secure model. In: SERE 2012 (2012)
8. Doupé, A., Cova, M., Vigna, G.: Why johnny can't pentest: An analysis of black-
   box web vulnerability scanners. In: Kreibich, C., Jahnke, M. (eds.) DIMVA 2010.
   LNCS, vol. 6201, pp. 111–131. Springer, Heidelberg (2010)
9. Guangdong, B., Guozhu, M., Jike, L., Sai, S.V., Prateek, S., Jun, S., Yang, L.,
   Jinsong, D.: Authscan: Automatic extraction of web authentication protocols from
   implementations
10. Jovanovic, N., Krügel, C., Kirda, E.: Pixy: A static analysis tool for detecting web
    application vulnerabilities (short paper). In: IEEE Symposium on Security and
    Privacy, pp. 258–263. IEEE Computer Society (2006)
11. Mödersheim, S., Viganò, L.: The open-source fixed-point model checker for sym-
    bolic analysis of security protocols. In: Aldini, A., Barthe, G., Gorrieri, R. (eds.)
    FOSAD 2009. LNCS, vol. 5705, pp. 166–194. Springer, Heidelberg (2009)
12. OASIS Consortium. Security Assertion Markup Language V2.0 Tech. Overview
    (March 2008), http://wiki.oasis-open.org/security/Saml2TechOverview
13. Shmatikov, V., Mitchell, J.C.: Finite-state analysis of two contract signing proto-
    cols. Theoretical Computer Science 283(2), 419–450 (2002)

Finding Errors in Python Programs
Using Dynamic Symbolic Execution

Samir Sapra[1], Marius Minea[2], Sagar Chaki[1], Arie Gurfinkel[1],
and Edmund M. Clarke[1]

[1] Carnegie Mellon University, Pittsburgh, PA, USA[*]
[2] Politehnica University of Timișoara, Romania

Abstract. For statically typed languages, dynamic symbolic execution (also called concolic testing) is a mature approach to automated test generation. However, extending it to dynamic languages presents several challenges. Complex semantics, fragmented and incomplete type information, and calls to foreign functions lacking precise models make symbolic execution difficult. We propose a symbolic execution approach that mixes concrete and symbolic values and incrementally solves path constraints in search for alternate executions by lazily instantiating axiomatizations for called functions as needed. We present the symbolic execution model underlying this approach and illustrate the workings of our prototype concolic testing tool on an actual Python software package.

1 Introduction

Dynamic symbolic execution (DSE) has been very successful for generating tests and finding errors. It accumulates path constraints over symbolic inputs rather than executing with concrete values. Java Pathfinder [5], Pex [7], or KLEE [2] try all possible program paths, using full symbolic models also for environment interactions. Concolic testing, a variant used in DART [3], CUTE [6] and CREST [1], generates symbolic constraints guided by concrete executions, and then modifies them to explore alternate paths. Approximating some execution fragments through concretization proves useful even in the absence of complete models.

[*] This material is based upon work funded and supported by the Department of Defense under Contract No. FA8721-05-C-0003 with Carnegie Mellon University for the operation of the Software Engineering Institute, a federally funded research and development center. NO WARRANTY. THIS CARNEGIE MELLON UNIVERSITY AND SOFTWARE ENGINEERING INSTITUTE MATERIAL IS FURNISHED ON AN "AS-IS" BASIS. CARNEGIE MELLON UNIVERSITY MAKES NO WARRANTIES OF ANY KIND, EITHER EXPRESSED OR IMPLIED, AS TO ANY MATTER INCLUDING, BUT NOT LIMITED TO, WARRANTY OF FITNESS FOR PURPOSE OR MERCHANTABILITY, EXCLUSIVITY, OR RESULTS OBTAINED FROM USE OF THE MATERIAL. CARNEGIE MELLON UNIVERSITY DOES NOT MAKE ANY WARRANTY OF ANY KIND WITH RESPECT TO FREEDOM FROM PATENT, TRADEMARK, OR COPYRIGHT INFRINGEMENT. This material has been approved for public release and unlimited distribution. DM-0000479.

H. Yenigün, C. Yilmaz, and A. Ulrich (Eds.): ICTSS 2013, LNCS 8254, pp. 283–289, 2013.
© IFIP International Federation for Information Processing 2013

Compared to existing work in the context of static typing, symbolic execution for Python as dynamically typed language raises a series of new challenges:

i) The language complexity makes symbolic execution difficult: First, a more complex theory is needed to express path conditions precisely. Python objects have dictionaries of attributes and hence one needs to handle strings and maps. Dictionary keys can be added dynamically and can be arbitrary hashables, not just integers or strings. A variety of runtime errors and exceptions related to dynamic features are handled in different ways.

Moreover, Python is often used to glue together components in other languages, for which we may not have models. Library functions are often in native code, thus values become concretized during execution and can no longer be tracked symbolically. This work avoids the cost and complexity of eager full symbolic execution by using path constraints that mix concrete and symbolic values. These constraints are solved incrementally in a search for satisfying program inputs, lazily instantiating axiomatized models of executed functions as they are needed.

ii) Type information for objects is incomplete and fragmented. Type constraints are implicitly accumulated from successful runtime checks (objects must have the accessed attributes, be iterable, callable, etc.). An object's type may not be completely known: x[1] could be indexing a list, tuple, string, dictionary, or user-defined type. This complicates formalizing and tracking type constraints and also means a program can hide many more bugs. Since many conditions can be flipped to explore alternate types and program paths, it is crucial to steer this search efficiently and avoid exploring uninteresting execution paths. This work selects relevant conditions based on data dependencies, and uses the solver output (unsatisfiable core) to direct the choice of alternate paths.

A Motivating Example. Version 0.93 of dnuos (https://bitheap.org/dnuos/) – which creates collections of audio files – crashes on an empty directory. The bug is in function uniq (line 2 in Fig. 1) – accessing a list without a non-emptiness check. A faulty run has uniq called from types (l. 7) on a list created with map (l. 6) from method streams, which filters (l. 10) a list returned by children. The latter iterates (l. 13) over a list produced by os.listdir for the input pathname.

The challenges are: (i) to detect such errors automatically, i.e., finding a buggy path starting from a successful run (here, on a non-empty directory); and (ii) applying DSE in coverage mode to detect as many errors as possible.

We first describe in Sec. 2 the architecture of our concolic testing engine and the systematic search for alternate execution paths by lazily instantiating the needed constraints. Sec. 3 then briefly illustrates key aspects of i) the formalism used to represent Python path conditions, ii) the symbolic bytecode semantics, and iii) the axiomatization of library functions. Finally in Sec. 4, we show how these are tied together in our prototype CutiePy by revisiting the above example.

2   An Architecture for Concolic Testing

Dynamic symbolic execution is driven by a concrete execution with some initial inputs. A symbolic execution engine is run in lockstep, working with symbolic

```
1    def uniq(list):
2        list[0] = [ list[0] ]
3        return reduce(lambda A,x: x in A and A or A+[x], list)
4    def types(self):
5        if self._types != None: return self._types
6        types = map(lambda x: x.type(), self.streams())
7        self._types = uniq(types)
8    def streams(self):
9        ...
10       list = filter(_is_audio_file, self.children())
11   def children(self):
12       if self._children: return self._children
13       self._children = map(lambda x: os.path.join(self.path,x),
14                            os.listdir(self.path))
15       return self._children
```

Fig. 1. Code fragments from **dnuos** for processing a list of audio files

constraints over program variables, rather than concrete values. Given formal semantics for every instruction, these constraints can be accumulated in a *path condition*, which includes all branch conditions taken on the path, and characterizes all inputs for which the program will take the same path. To explore a new path, a branch condition is flipped and, together with the path condition leading to it, is passed to a solver which returns inputs to exercise the new path.

Our symbolic execution framework is distinguished by *how constraints are expressed and collected* for each instruction, and *how branches are flipped*. We describe the former in Sec. 3, including what to do when fully symbolic execution is not feasible. Here we outline how to find new executions (Algorithm 1).

A path condition is a list of clauses that are either *definitions* or *conditions*. Definitions have the form $v = f(s_1, \ldots, s_k)$ with v a variable and s_i constants or variables. Conditions can be explicit (program branch or loop conditions) or implicit, denoting statement execution without error (e.g., predicates hasattr, iscallable, isiterable). Program and library functions can be interpreted (fully formalized, cf. Sec. 3) or uninterpreted, if there is no complete model for them.

Given a path condition, the dependence set $Dep(C)$ of a clause is defined as:
– for a condition, $Dep(C)$ is the set of clauses that share variables with C.
– for a definition $v = f(s_1, \ldots, s_k)$, $Dep(C)$ is the set of all conditions that contain variables from C, plus any definitions of variables in the right-hand side of C.

Algorithm 1. Selection of alternate execution paths

1: **function** FLIP($[r_1, r_2, \ldots, r_k]$, *flipped*)
2:     $\Phi \leftarrow flipped \cup Dep^+(flipped)$
3:     **while** sat(Φ) **do**
4:         **if** $FV(\Phi) \subseteq \mathcal{I}$ **then return** sat_assignment
5:         **else** strengthen Φ with lemmas for $FV(\Phi) \setminus \mathcal{I}$
6:     $u \leftarrow \max\{i \mid i \leq k \wedge r_i \in unsat\_core(\Phi)\}$
7:     **for** r_j is explicit condition, $j = u$ downto 1 **do**
8:         **if** ($Inputs =$ FLIP($[r_1, r_2, \ldots r_{j-1}], \neg r_j$)) $\neq \emptyset$ **then return** *Inputs*
9:     **return** $\emptyset$ (* failed *)

Define $Dep^+(C)$ transitively as the smallest set such that $Dep(C) \subseteq Dep^+(C)$ and if $C' \in Dep^+(C)$ is an interpreted clause, then $Dep(C') \subseteq Dep^+(C)$.

Let $\mathcal{I}$ be the set of program inputs and $FV(\mathcal{C})$ be the set of variables in the set of clauses $\mathcal{C}$ that do not appear on the left-hand side of a definition.

Starting from a condition to be flipped, the algorithm propagates relevant constraints (obtained in l. 2) to program inputs. A key point is that uninterpreted functions are instantiated with lemmas (l. 5) lazily and incrementally. Thus we do not need an eager fully symbolic execution and can accommodate concretization, e.g., due to library functions, when collecting the path condition. Symbolic constraints for these functions are re-introduced to the extent needed. If no inputs are found for the chosen path, we flip the last condition affecting the unsatisfiable core, attempting to preserve the longest possible prefix of the given execution, and the process is repeated. To generate maximal test coverage rather than force a specific path, conditions are simply flipped one by one. In particular, flipping implicit conditions (hasattr, iterable) can find type errors.

3 A Symbolic Execution Model for Python

We briefly present the key points of a theory for expressing symbolic constraints from Python program executions. We describe the sorts and functions used, and give examples of bytecode semantics and axioms for Python library functions.

Sorts: We use the standard sorts Bool and Int, and an uninterpreted ObjectSort for Python objects. Since Python types are also objects, we define a sub-sort PyType of ObjectSort and constants for Python predefined types (PyBool, PyInt, PyNoneType, PyTuple, PyList, PyListiterator, PyDict) etc. For this prototype we do not distinguish plain from long integers, and do not handle floating point.

Functions and predicates that model properties of Python objects include:

- id : ObjectSort → Int   provides each object with a unique identity
- typeof : ObjectSort → PyType   gives the type of an object
- hasattr$_{name}$: ObjectSort → Bool   if an object has an attribute called *name*
- iscallable : ObjectSort → Bool   to check for a function or method
- iterable : ObjectSort → Bool   if object is array, dictionary, list, string, tuple

We also introduce several partial functions; they are used together with the corresponding conditions for the functions being defined:

- intof : ObjectSort → Int   maps an integer object (type PyInt) to its value
- iterof : ObjectSort → ObjectSort   makes an iterator from an isiterable object

The theory should be decidable and allow reasoning about objects whose types are being lazily discovered. We translate formulae expressed in this theory into linear integer arithmetic with uninterpreted functions and arrays (AUFLIA) over uninterpreted sorts and algebraic datatypes.

Axioms are encoded as universal sentences in an SMT solver (Z3 [4]). They are similar but distinct from the axiomatizations we introduce as partial interpretations of libraries or non-core language features. As example, we show an axiom for `list.append`, which returns `None` and mutates its first argument, as expressed using the function $Store$ from the AUFLIA theory.

$$\forall r, newL, oldL, v : \text{ObjectSort . typeof } oldL = \text{PyList} \Rightarrow$$
$$(newL, r) = \text{LIST\_APPEND}(oldL, v) \Rightarrow r = \text{PyNone} \wedge \text{typeof } newL = \text{PyList}$$
$$\wedge \text{ lenof } newL = \text{lenof } oldL + 1 \wedge \text{seqof } newL = Store(\text{seqof } oldL, \text{lenof } oldL, v)$$

Concolic execution semantics: Our implementation uses the `sys.settrace()` API and a custom build of the CPython interpreter. Symbolic execution is done in lockstep with the concrete Python interpreter, which at the bytecode level operates as a stack machine. A (single-threaded) running program corresponds to a stack of *frames*, each representing some executing function called by the parent frame. Let S denote a frame's associated *valuestack* of object references o. Name binding and variable lookup in a frame is done using its `locals`, `globals`, and `__builtins__` dictionaries; here we assume only a locals context called C.

Symbolic semantics are defined for each bytecode instruction, reflecting decisions such as whether to symbolically model or concretize various operations. The symbolic valuestack Σ of an execution frame may contain both symbolic expressions e and concrete object references o (in case of concretization); any concrete entries agree with the concrete valuestack. The symbolic context Γ is a mapping from strings (variable names) to symbolic expressions.

We present as example two rules for the symbolic semantics of `BINARY_SUBSCR`:

$$\frac{C, o :: o' :: S \rightarrow C, o'' :: S \quad e' \text{ symbolic}}{\Gamma, e :: e' :: \Sigma \Rightarrow \Gamma, Select(e', e) :: \Sigma}$$

typeof$(o') ==$ PyList $\quad o$ non-negative

$assert$ typeof $e =$ PyInt $\wedge$ typeof $e' =$ PyList
$\wedge$ hasattr$_{\_\_getitem\_\_} e' \wedge$ lenof $e' \geq e + 1$

$$\frac{C, o :: o' :: S \rightarrow C, o'' :: S \quad e' \text{ symbolic}}{\Gamma, e :: e' :: \Sigma \Rightarrow \Gamma, o'' :: \Sigma}$$

$assert$ hasattr$_{\_\_getitem\_\_} e'$

Both rules track the indexed collection e' symbolically. In rule 1, o' has the actual type `PyList`, and successful execution implies that o is an integer, which allows us to derive size constraints and track the result of subscripting symbolically. In rule 2, we assert (append to the path condition) the only constraint we learn, hasattr$_{\_\_getitem\_\_} e'$, and we push the concrete result $o'' = o'[o]$, onto Σ.

Concretization when calling functions that lack models (e.g., native code) is one of the main obstacles to building symbolic path conditions. On return from such a function, we re-introduce a symbolic variable for the result. This helps track data flow in spite of concretization. Treating the function as uninterpreted also allows us to lazily ignore conditions which are irrelevant for the testing goal.

For mutable objects, we exploit the Python bytecode interpreter to introduce the additional indirection needed to update referrers. For dictionaries, we model only fields that are updated with symbolic values. In both cases, we limit symbolic modeling to items that are strictly needed.

4 Case Study and Conclusions

We explain a run of our tool CutiePy on the example of Fig. 1. The unit test executes the call `audiodir.Dir(i_filename).types()` on input `i_filename="./dummy"`, in an environment where the directory ./dummy contains a single, valid music file. CutiePy produces a path condition with ~ 400 constraints (after instantiating partial interpretations). Of particular interest is generating a test that exercises the unchecked list access on line 2, which is compiled to bytecode BINARY_SUBSCR.

Since that list is produced by the built-in function map (Fig. 1, l. 6) written in C, we need a partial interpretation to reason about it. To achieve this, CutiePy replaces the standard map with a workable model given by the Python function: audiodir.__builtins__["map"] = lambda f,L: [f(x) for x in L]. Such models are inserted up-front and are present at what we designate as the 'first' call to FLIP. Thus, the path condition fragment Φ sent to Z3 by FLIP at line 3 is:

```
p385 == Not(lenof(v148) >= 1)                    flipped constraint
p384 == (typeof(v148) == PyList)
p377 == (v141, v148) == LIST_APPEND(v143, v147)  call to APPEND
p364 == (lenof(v143) == 0)                       execution of map model
p363 == (typeof(v143) == PyList)                 v143 empty initial list
```

Combined with the APPEND axiom of Sec. 3, Z3 finds these clauses inconsistent (unsatisfiable core: [p385,p377,p364,p363]). To break the unsat core, keeping a maximal execution prefix, lines 6–7 identify the condition Not(exhausted(v144)) as candidate for *flipped*. Intuitively, we want to flip the branch just prior to list.append (which contradicts our goal of a zero-length list). CutiePy has reasoned about l. 6 in Fig. 1 at bytecode level, concluding that map must return a list whose iterator (v144) will be immediately exhausted, i.e., an empty list.

In two more recursive calls, FLIP propagates constraints to primary inputs, but not with the intended bug-revealing trace. In the first call, line 7 of FLIP identifies $r_j = $ (exhausted (nexted_once v29)) as the next candidate for *flipped*. CutiePy has determined through bytecode-level reasoning that list should have ≥ 2 elements. In the next recursive call to FLIP, Dep^+ finally reaches constraints on the primary input i_filename, pending models for os.path.join and os.listdir. Here Φ is found unsat, and in line 7 $r_j = r_u = $ Not(exhausted(v29)); however, by this point execution has already diverged from our intended one.

When the right r_j is picked in line 7, CutiePy will discover the bug in uniq: exhausted(v144) requires filter returning an empty list (again an immediately exhausted iterator), which in turn necessitates map returning an empty list in l. 13, which via a partial axiomatization of os.path.listdir and appropriately set up environment leads to the new primary input i_filename="./emptydirectory".

When forcing execution to a particular point, flipping the right conditions impacts efficiency. A promising heuristic is to focus on loop conditions.

Our initial experiments have shown that for the dynamic features of Python a key challenge is tracking the right amount of symbolic information during execution. We show how to do this by lazily constructing and solving constraints, and using complete or partial axiomatizations of library functions as needed. Further evaluation will provide insight into the amount and types of bugs that can be automatically found, and how to tune the framework to effectively and efficiently zoom in on the most representative and relevant errors.

References

1. Burnim, J., Sen, K.: Heuristics for scalable dynamic test generation. In: 23rd International Conference on Automated Software Engineering, pp. 443–446. ACM (2008)
2. Cadar, C., Dunbar, D., Engler, D.: KLEE: Unassisted and automatic generation of high-coverage tests for complex systems programs. In: 8th OSDI. USENIX (2008)
3. Godefroid, P., Klarlund, N., Sen, K.: DART: directed automated random testing. In: Programming Language Design and Implementation, pp. 213–223. ACM (2005)
4. de Moura, L., Bjørner, N.S.: Z3: An efficient SMT solver. In: Ramakrishnan, C.R., Rehof, J. (eds.) TACAS 2008. LNCS, vol. 4963, pp. 337–340. Springer, Heidelberg (2008)
5. Păsăreanu, C.S., Rungta, N., Visser, W.: Symbolic execution with mixed concrete-symbolic solving. In: 20th ISSTA, pp. 34–44. ACM (2011)
6. Sen, K., Marinov, D., Agha, G.: CUTE: a concolic unit testing engine for C. In: 10th ESEC/13th SIGSOFT FSE, pp. 263–272. ACM (2005)
7. Tillmann, N., de Halleux, J.: Pex–white box test generation for.NET. In: Beckert, B., Hähnle, R. (eds.) TAP 2008. LNCS, vol. 4966, pp. 134–153. Springer, Heidelberg (2008)

Author Index

Abreu, Rui   239

Badri, Linda   114
Badri, Mourad   114

Castro, Mário Ventura de   180
Chaki, Sagar   283
Clarke, Edmund M.   283
Compagna, Luca   277

David, Alexandre   65

El-Fakih, Khaled   33
Elyasov, Alexander   223
Enoiu, Eduard Paul   1

Faria, João Pascoal   180
Feng, Lei   164
Flageol, William   114

Gaston, Christophe   82
Guo, Hai-Feng   17
Gurfinkel, Arie   283
Güttinger, Dennis   149

Haar, Stefan   98
Hage, Jurriaan   223
Hierons, Robert M.   82
Holl, Konstantin   271
Huang, Wen-ling   49

Ibing, Andreas   196

Klaus, Alexander   271
Koca, Feyzullah   239
Kozyura, Vitaly   149
Kremer, Dominik   149
Krishnan, Padmanabhan   255
Kroening, Daniel   133
Kushik, Natalia   33

Larsen, Kim G.   65
Le Gall, Pascale   82
Longuet, Delphine   98
Lundmark, Simon   164

Mauser, Daniel   271
Meinke, Karl   164
Melham, Tom   133
Mikučionis, Marius   65
Minea, Marius   283
Morreggia, Thomas   277

Nguena Timo, Omer L.   65
Niu, Fei   164

Paiva, Ana C.R.   180
Peleska, Jan   49
Pellegrino, Giancarlo   277
Pettersson, Paul   1
Peyton, Liam   207
Ponce de León, Hernán   98
Prasetya, I.S. Wishnu B.   223

Qiu, Zongyan   17

Rollet, Antoine   65

Sapra, Samir   283
Schrammel, Peter   133
Sindhu, Muddassar A.   164
Sözer, Hasan   239
Stepien, Bernard   207
Stocks, Phil   255
Sundmark, Daniel   1

Vorobyov, Kostyantyn   255

Wieczorek, Sebastian   149
Wong, Peter Y.H.   164

Yevtushenko, Nina   33